Murat Halstead

The story of the Philippines:

Natural riches, industrial resources, statistics of productions

Murat Halstead

The story of the Philippines:
Natural riches, industrial resources, statistics of productions

ISBN/EAN: 9783337732455

Printed in Europe, USA, Canada, Australia, Japan

Cover: Foto ©ninafisch / pixelio.de

More available books at **www.hansebooks.com**

THE STORY OF THE
PHILIPPINES.

NATURAL RICHES, INDUSTRIAL RESOURCES, STATISTICS OF PRODUCTIONS, COMMERCE
AND POPULATION; THE LAWS, HABITS, CUSTOMS, SCENERY AND CONDITIONS
OF THE CUBA OF THE EAST INDIES AND THE THOUSAND ISLANDS
OF THE ARCHIPELAGOES OF INDIA AND HAWAII, WITH
EPISODES OF THEIR EARLY HISTORY

THE ELDORADO OF THE ORIENT

Personal Character Sketches of and Interviews with Admiral Dewey, General Merritt,
General Aguinaldo and the Archbishop of Manila.

HISTORY AND ROMANCE, TRAGEDIES AND
TRADITIONS OF OUR PACIFIC POSSESSIONS.

EVENTS OF THE WAR IN THE WEST WITH SPAIN, AND THE CONQUEST OF CUBA AND PORTO RICO.

BY MURAT HALSTEAD,

War Correspondent in America and Europe, Historian of the Philippine Expedition.

Splendidly and Picturesquely Illustrated with Half-Tone Engravings from Photographs, Etchings
from Special Drawings, and the Military Maps of the Philippines, Prepared
by the War Department of the United States.

OUR POSSESSIONS PUBLISHING CO.

INSCRIBED

TO THE SOLDIERS AND SAILORS

OF

THE ARMY AND NAVY OF THE UNITED STATES,

With Admiration for Their Achievements

In the War With Spain;

Gratitude for the Glory They Have Gained for the American Nation,

And Congratulations That All the People of All the

Country Rejoice in the Cloudless Splendor of Their Fame

That is the Common and Everlasting

Inheritance of Americans.

AUTHOR'S PREFACE.

The purpose of the writer of the pages herewith presented has been to offer, in popular form, the truth touching the Philippine Islands. I made the journey from New York to Manila, to have the benefit of personal observations in preparing a history for the people. Detention at Honolulu shortened my stay in Manila, but there was much in studies at the former place that was a help at the latter. The original programme was for me to accompany General Merritt, Commander-in-Chief of the Philippine Expedition, but illness prevented its full realization, and when I arrived in Manila Bay the city had already been "occupied and possessed" by the American army; and the declaration of peace between the United States and Spain was made, the terms fully agreed upon with the exception of the settlement of the affairs of the Philippines. While thus prevented from witnessing stirring military movements other than those attending the transfer of our troops across the Pacific Ocean, an event in itself of the profoundest significance, the reference of the determination of the fate of the Philippine Islands to the Paris Conference, and thereby to the public opinion of our country, in extraordinary measure increased the general sensibility as to the situation of the southern Oriental seas affecting ourselves, and enhanced the value of the testimony taken on the spot of observers of experience, with the training of journalism in distinguishing the relative pertinence and potency of facts noted. Work for more than forty years, in the discussion from day to day of current history, has qualified me for the efficient exercise of my faculties in the labor undertaken. It has been my undertaking to state that which appeared to me, so that the reader may find pictures of the scenes that tell the Story that concerns the country, that the public may with enlightenment solve the naval, military, political, commercial and religious problems we are called upon by the peremptory pressure of the conditions local, and international, to solve immediately. This we have to do, facing the highest obligations of citizenship in the great American Republic, and conscious of the incomparably influential character of the principles that shall prevail through the far-reaching sweep of the policies that will be evolved. I have had such advantages in the assurance of the authenticity of the information set forth in the chapters following, that I may be permitted to name those it was my good fortune to consult with instructive results; and in making the acknowledgments due. I may be privileged to support the claim of diligence and success in the investigations made, and that I am warranted in the issue of this Story of the Philippines by the assiduous improvement of an uncommon opportunity to fit myself to serve the country.

Indebtedness for kind consideration in this work is gratefully acknowledged to Major-General Merritt, commanding the Philippine Expedition; Major-General Otis, who succeeds to the duties of military and civil administration in the conquered capital of the islands; Admiral George Dewey, who improved, with statesmanship, his unparalleled victory in the first week of the war with Spain, and raised the immense questions before us; General F. V. Greene, the historian of the Russo-Turkish war, called by the President to Washington, and for whose contributions to the public intelligence he receives the hearty approval and confidence of the people; Major Bell, the vigilant and efficient head of the Bureau of Information at the headquarters of the American occupation in the Philippines; General Aguinaldo, the leader of the insurgents of his race in Luzon, and His Grace the Archbishop of Manila, who gave me a message for the United States, expressing his appreciation of the excellence of the behavior of the American army in the enforcement of order, giving peace of mind to the residents in the distracted city of all persuasions and conditions, and of the service that was done civilization in the prevention, by our arms, of threatened barbarities that had caused sore apprehension; and, I may add, the Commissioner of the Organized People of the Philippines, dispatched to Washington accompanying General Greene; and of the citizens of Manila of high character, and conductors of business enterprises with plants in the community whose destiny is in the hands of strangers.

These gentlemen I may not name, for there are uncertainties that demand of them and command me to respect the prudence of their inconspicuity. This volume seems to me to be justified, and I have no further claim to offer that it is meritorious than that it is faithful to facts and true to the country in advocacy of the continued expansion of the Republic, whose field is the world.

Steamship China, Pacific Ocean, September 20, 1898.

THE ORIGIN OF THIS STORY OF THE PHILIPPINES.

The letter following is the full expression by the author of this volume of his purposes and principles in making the journey to the East Indies.

GOING TO THE PHILIPPINES.

Washington City, D. C., July 18.

With the authorization of the Military Authorities, I shall go to the Philippine Islands with General Merritt, the Military Governor, and propose to make the American people better acquainted with that remarkable and most important and interesting country. The presence of an American army in the Philippines is an event that will change broad and mighty currents in the world's history. It has far more significance than anything transpiring in the process of the conquest of the West India possessions of Spain, for the only question there, ever since the Continental colonies of the Spanish crown won their independence, has been the extent of the sacrifices the Spaniards, in their haughty and vindictive pride, would make in fighting for a lost Empire and an impossible cause with an irresistible adversary. That the time was approaching when, with the irretrievable steps of the growth of a living Nation of free people, we would reach the point where it should be our duty to accept the responsibility of the dominant American power, and accomplish manifest Destiny by adding Cuba and Porto Rico to our dominion, has for half a century been the familiar understanding of American citizens. Spain, by her abhorrent system, personified in Weyler, and illustrated in the murderous blowing up of the Maine with a mine, has forced this duty upon us; and though we made war unprepared, the good work is going on, and the finish of the fight will be the relegation of Spain, whose colonial governments have been, without exception, disgraceful and disastrous to herself, and curses to the colonists, to her own peninsula. This will be for her own good, as well as the redemption of mankind from her unwholesome foreign influences, typified as they are in the beautiful city of Havana, which has become the

THE ORIGIN OF THIS STORY.

center of political plagues and pestilential fevers, whose contagion has at frequent intervals reached our own shores.

In the Philippine Islands the situation is for us absolutely novel. It cannot be said to be out of the scope of reasonable American expansion and is in the right line of enlarging the area of enlightenment and stimulating the progress of civilization. The unexpected has happened, but it is not illogical. It must have been written long ago on the scroll of the boundless blue and the stars. The incident of war was the "rush" order of the President of the United States to Admiral Dewey to destroy the Spanish fleet at Manila, for the protection of our commerce. The deed was done with a flash of lightning, and lo! we hold the golden key of a splendid Asiatic archipelago of a thousand beautiful and richly endowed islands in our grip. This is the most brilliant and startling achievement in the annals of navies. Never before had the sweep of sea power, ordered through the wires that make the world's continents, oceans and islands one huge whispering gallery, such striking exemplification. There was glory and fame in it, and immeasurable material for the making of history. We may paraphrase Dr. Johnson's celebrated advertisement of the widow's brewery by saying: Admiral Dewey's victory was not merely the capture of a harbor commanding a great city, one of the superb places of the earth, and the security of a base of operations to wait for reinforcements commensurate with the resources of the United States of America—the victorious hero fixed his iron hand upon a wonderful opportunity it was the privilege of our Government to secure at large, according to the rights of a victorious Nation for the people thereof—a chance for the youth of America, like that of the youth of Great Britain, to realize upon the magnificence of India; and this is as Dr. Johnson said of the vats and barrels of the Thrale estate—"the potentiality of wealth beyond the dreams of avarice." It is a new departure, but not a matter for the panic or apprehension of conservatism, that the Stars and Stripes float as the symbol of sovereignty over a group of islands in the waters of Asia, that are equal to all the West Indies. If we are strangers there now we shall not be so long. We have a front on the Pacific Ocean, of three great States—Washington, equal to England; Oregon, whose grandeur rolls in the sound of her famous name, and incomparable California, whose title will be the synonym of golden good times forever. The Philippines are southwest from our western front doors. They have been the islands of our sunsets in the winter. Now they look to us for the rosy dawn out of which will come the clear brightness of the white light of mornings and the fullness of the ripening noons, all the year around. With our bulk of the North American continent bulging into both the great oceans, it was foreordained since the beginning when God created the earth, that we, the possessors of this imperial American zone, should be a great Asiatic Power. We have it now in evidence, written in islands among the most gorgeous of those that shine in the Southern seas—islands that are east from the Atlantic and west from the Pacific shores of the One Great Republic—that we may personify hereafter, sitting at the head of the table when the empires of the earth consult themselves as to the courses of empire. Our Course of Empire is both east and west.

The contact of American and Asiatic civilization in the Philippines, with the American army there, superseding the Spaniards, will be memorable as one of the matters of chief moment in the closing days of the nineteenth century, and remembered to date from for a thousand years. It is my purpose to write of this current history while it is a fresh, sparkling stream, and attempt something more than the recitation of the news of the day, as it is condensed and restrained in telegrams; to give it according to the extent of my ability and the advantages of my opportunity, the local coloring, the characteristic scenery; the pen pictures of the people and their pursuits; sketches of the men who are doers of deeds that make history; studies of the ways and means of the islanders; essays to indicate the features of the picturesque of the strange mixture of races; the revolutionary evolutions of politics; the forces that pertain to the mingling of the religions of the Occident and the Orient, in a chemistry untried through the recorded ages. It is a tremendous canvas upon which I am to labor, and I know full well how inadequate the production must be, and beg that this index may not be remembered against me. It is meant in all modesty, and I promise only that there will be put into the task the expertness of experience and the endeavor of industry.

CONTENTS.

Pages.
AUTHOR'S PREFACE...13-14
THE ORIGIN OF THIS STORY OF THE PHILIPPINES..............15-17

CHAPTER I.
ADMIRAL DEWEY ON HIS FLAGSHIP.

A Stormy Day on Manila Bay—Call on Admiral Dewey—The Man in White—He Sticks to His Ship—How He Surprised the Spaniards—Every Man Did His Duty on May-Day—How Dewey Looks and Talks—What He Said About War With Germany in Five Minutes—Feeds His Men on "Delicious" Fresh Meat from Australia—Photography Unjust to Him.......................................29-37

CHAPTER II.
LIFE IN MANILA.

Character of the Filipinos—Drivers Lashing Laboring Men in the Streets—What Americans Get in Their Native Air—The Logic of Destiny —Manila as She Fell Into Our Hands—The Beds in the Tropics—A Spanish Hotel—Profane Yells for Ice—Sad Scenes in the Dining Room—Major-General Calls for "Francisco"—A Broken-Hearted Pantry Woman...38-44

CHAPTER III.
FROM LONG ISLAND TO LUZON.

Across the Continent—An American Governor-General Steams Through the Golden Gate—He is a Minute-Man—Honolulu as a Health Resort—The Lonesome Pacific—The Skies of Asia—Dreaming Under the Stars of the Scorpion—The Southern Cross............45-51

CHAPTER IV.
INTERVIEW WITH GENERAL AGUINALDO.

The Insurgent Leader's Surroundings and Personal Appearance—His Reserves and Ways of Talking—The Fierce Animosity of the Filipinos Toward Spanish Priests—A Probability of Many Martyrs in the Isle of Luzon..52-60

CONTENTS.

CHAPTER V.
THE PHILIPPINE MISSION.
Correspondence with Aguinaldo About It—Notes by Senor Felipe Agoncillo—Relations Between Admiral Dewey and Senor Aguinaldo—Terms of Peace Made by Spanish Governor-General with Insurgents, December, 1897—Law Suit Between Aguinaldo and Arlacho—Aguinaldo's Proclamation of May 24, 1898.....................61-68

CHAPTER VI.
THE PROCLAMATIONS OF GENERAL AGUINALDO.
June 16th, 1898, Establishing Dictatorial Government—June 20th, 1898, Instructions for Elections—June 23d, 1898, Establishing Revolutionary Government—June 23d, 1898, Message to Foreign Powers—June 27th, 1898, Instructions Concerning Details—July 23d, 1898, Letter from Senor Aguinaldo to General Anderson—August 1st, 1898, Resolution of Revolutionary Chiefs Asking Recognition—August 6th, 1898, Message to Foreign Powers Asking Recognition....69-85

CHAPTER VII.
INTERVIEW WITH ARCHBISHOP OF MANILA.
Insurgents' Deadly Hostility to Spanish Priests—The Position of the Archbishop as He Defined It—His Expression of Gratitude to the American Army—His Characterization of the Insurgents—A Work of Philippine Art—The Sincerity of the Archbishop's Good Words....86-90

CHAPTER VIII.
WHY WE HOLD THE PHILIPPINES.
The Responsibility of Admiral Dewey—We Owe It to Ourselves to Hold the Philippines—Prosperity Assured by Our Permanent Possession—The Aguinaldo Question—Character Study of the Insurgent Leader—How Affairs Would Adjust Themselves for Us—Congress Must Be Trusted to Represent the People and Firmly Establish International Policy..91-98

CHAPTER IX.
THE PHILIPPINE ISLANDS AS THEY ARE.
Area and Population—Climate—Mineral Wealth—Agriculture—Commerce and Transportation—Revenue and Expenses—Spanish Troops—Spanish Navy—Spanish Civil Administration—Insurgent Troops—Insurgent Civil Administration—United States Troops—United States Navy—United States Civil Administration—The Future of the Islands...99-136

CONTENTS.

CHAPTER X.
OFFICIAL HISTORY OF THE CONQUEST OF MANILA.

The Pith of the Official Reports of the Capture of Manila, by Major-General Wesley Merritt, Commanding the Philippine Expedition; General Frank V. Greene, General Arthur McArthur, and General Thomas Anderson, with the Articles of Capitulation, Showing How 8,000 Americans Carried an Intrenched City with a Garrison of 13,000 Spaniards, and Kept Out 14,000 Insurgents—The Difficulties of American Generals with Philippine Troops......................137-159

CHAPTER XI.
THE ADMINISTRATION OF GENERAL MERRITT.

The Official Gazette Issued at Manila—Orders and Proclamation of Major-General Wesley Merritt, Who, as Commander of the Philippine Expedition, Became, Under the Circumstances of the Capture of Manila, the Governor of That City............................160-172

CHAPTER XII.
THE AMERICAN ARMY IN MANILA.

Why the Boys Had a Spell of Homesickness—Disadvantages of the Tropics—Admiral Dewey and His Happy Men—How Our Soldiers Passed the Time on the Ships—General Merritt's Headquarters—What Is Public Property—The Manila Water Supply—England Our Friend—Major-General Otis, General Meritt's Successor.................173-183

CHAPTER XIII.
THE WHITE UNIFORMS OF OUR HEROES IN THE TROPICS.

The Mother Hubbard Street Fashion in Honolulu, and That of Riding Astride—Spoiling Summer Clothes in Manila Mud—The White Raiment of High Officers—Drawing the Line on Nightshirts—Ashamed of Big Toes—Dewey and Merritt as Figures of Show—The Boys in White...184-187

CHAPTER XIV.
A MARTYR TO THE LIBERTY OF SPEECH.

Dr. Jose Rizal, the Most Distinguished Literary Man of the Philippines, Writer of History, Poetry, Political Pamphlets, and Novels, Shot on the Luneta of Manila—A Likeness of the Martyr—The Scene of His Execution, from a Photograph—His Wife Married the Day Before His Death—Poem Giving His Farewell Thoughts, Written in His Last Hours—The Works That Cost Him His Life—The Vision of Friar Rodriguez........................... 188-201

CONTENTS.

CHAPTER XV.
EVENTS OF THE SPANISH-AMERICAN WAR.

No Mystery About the Cause of the War—The Expected and the Inevitable Has Happened—The Tragedy of the Maine—Vigilant Wisdom of President McKinley—Dewey's Prompt Triumph—The Battles at Manila and Santiago Compared—General Shafter Tells of the Battle of Santiago—Report of Wainwright Board on Movements of Sampson's Fleet in the Destruction of Cervera's Squadron—Stars and Stripes Raised Over Porto Rico—American and Spanish Fleets at Manila Compared—Text of Peace Protocol......................202-240

CHAPTER XVI.
THE PEACE JUBILEE.

The Lessons of War in the Joy Over Peace in the Celebrations at Chicago and Philadelphia—Orations by Archbishop Ireland and Judge Emory Speer—The President's Few Words of Thrilling Significance—The Parade of the Loyal League, and the Clover Club Banquet at Philadelphia—Address by the President—The Hero Hobson Makes a Speech—Fighting Bob Evans' Startling Battle Picture—The Destruction of Cervera's Fleet—The Proclamation of Thanksgiving...241-259

CHAPTER XVII.
EARLY HISTORY OF THE PHILIPPINES.

The Abolishment of the 31st of December, 1844, in Manila—The Mystery of the Meridian 180 Degrees West—What Is East and West?—Gaining and Losing Days—The Tribes of Native Filipinos—They Had an Alphabet and Songs of Their Own—The Massacre of Magellan—His Fate Like That of Captain Cook—Stories of Long-Ago Wars—An Account by a Devoted Spanish Writer of the Beneficent Rule of Spain in the Philippines—Aguinaldo a Man Not of a Nation, But of a Tribe—Typhoons and Earthquakes—The Degeneracy of the Government of the Philippines After It Was Taken from Mexico—"New Spain"—The Perquisites of Captain-Generals—The Splendor of Manila a Century Ago..................260-275

CHAPTER XVIII.
THE SOUTHERN PHILIPPINES.

Important Facts About the Lesser Islands of the Philippine Archipelago—Location, Size and Population—Capitals and Principal Cities—Rivers and Harbors—Surface and Soil—People and Products—Leading Industries—Their Commerce and Business Affairs—The Monsoons and Typhoons—The Terrors of the Tempests and How to Avoid Them...276-293

CONTENTS.

CHAPTER XIX.
SPECIFICATIONS OF GRIEVANCES OF THE FILIPINOS.

An Official Copy of the Manifesto of the Junta Showing the Bad Faith of Spain in the Making and Evasion of a Treaty—The Declaration of the Renewal of the War of Rebellion—Complaints Against the Priests Defined—The Most Important Document the Filipinos Have Issued—Official Reports of Cases of Persecution of Men and Women in Manila by the Spanish Authorities—Memoranda of the Proceedings in Several Cases in the Court of Inquiry of the United States Officers..294-307

CHAPTER XX.
HAWAII AS ANNEXED.

The Star Spangled Banner Up Again in Hawaii, and to Stay—Dimensions of the Islands—What the Missionaries Have Done—Religious Belief by Nationality—Trade Statistics—Latest Census—Sugar Plantation Laborers—Coinage of Silver—Schools—Coffee Growing...........308-318

CHAPTER XXI.
EARLY HISTORY OF THE SANDWICH ISLANDS.

Captain James Cook's Great Discoveries and His Martyrdom—Character and Traditions of the Hawaiian Islands—Charges Against the Famous Navigator and Effort to Array the Christian World Against Him—The True Story of His Life and Death—How Charges Against Cook Came to Be Made—Testimony of Vancouver, King and Dixon, and Last Words of Cook's Journal—Light Turned on History That Has Become Obscure—Savagery of the Natives—Their Written Language Took Up Their High Colored Traditions and Preserved Phantoms—Scenes in Aboriginal Theatricals—Problem of Government in an Archipelago Where Race Questions Are Predominant—Now Americans Should Remember Captain Cook as an Illustrious Pioneer..319-344

CHAPTER XXII.
THE START FOR THE LAND OF CORN STALKS.

Spain Clings to the Ghost of Her Colonies—The Scene of War Interest Shifts from Manila—The Typhoon Season—General Merritt on the Way to Paris—German Target Practice by Permission of Dewey—Poultney Bigalow with Canoe, Typewriter and Kodak—Hongkong as a Bigger and Brighter Gibraltar..................................345-349

CONTENTS.

CHAPTER XXIII.
KODAK SNAPPED AT JAPAN.

Glimpses of China and Japan on the Way Home from the Philippines—Hongkong a Greater Gibraltar—Coaling the China—Gangs of Women Coaling the China—How the Japanese Make Gardens of the Mountains—Transition from the Tropics to the Northern Seas—A Breeze from Siberia—A Thousand Miles Nothing on the Pacific —Talk of Swimming Ashore..................................350-359

CHAPTER XXIV.
OUR PICTURE GALLERY.

Annotations and Illustrations—Portraits of Heroes of the War in the Army and Navy, and of the Highest Public Responsibilities—Admirals and Generals, the President and Cabinet—Photographs of Scenes and Incidents—The Characteristics of the Filipinos—Their Homes, Dresses and Peculiarities in Sun Pictures—The Picturesque People of Our New Possessions................................360-365

CHAPTER XXV.
CUBA AND PORTO RICO.

Conditions In and Around Havana—Fortifications and Water Supply of the Capital City—Other Sections of the Pearl of the Antilles—Porto Rico, Our New Possession, Described—Size and Population—Natural Resources and Products—Climatic Conditions—Towns and Cities—Railroad and Other Improvements—Future Possibilities..366-398

CHAPTER XXVI.
THE LADRONES.

The Island of Guam a Coaling Station of the United States—Discovery, Size and Products of the Islands............................399-400

ILLUSTRATIONS.

Frontispiece.........Major-General Merritt, Governor-General of the Philippines.
1. The Principal Gate to the Walled City.
2. The Cathedral at Manila.
3. Public Buildings in Manila.
4. The Monument of Magellinos in the Walled City.
5. Southern Islanders—Showing Cocoanut Palms and the Monkey Tree.
6. A Railroad Station North of Manila—Spaniards Airing Themselves.
7. United States Peace Commissioners.
8. Senator Frye.
9. Senator Gray.
10. Ex-Secretary of State Day.
11. Senator Davis.
12. Whitelaw Reid.
13. The Luneta—Favorite Outing Grounds of Manila, and a Place for Executing Insurgents.
14. A Group of the Unconquerable Mohamedans.
15. Savage Native Hunters.
16. Girl's Costume to Show One Shoulder.
17. Parade of Spanish Troops on One of Their Three Annual Expeditions to the Southern Islands.
18. An Insurgent Outlook Near Manila.
19. Philippine Author-Martyr, His Wife and His Execution.
20. Dr. Rizal.
21. Dr. Rizal's Execution.
22. Dr. Rizal's Wife.
23. Dining Room in General Merritt's Palace at Manila.
24. A Native House.
25. Riding Buffaloes Through Groves of Date Palms.
26. A Native in Regimentals.
27. A Country Pair.
28. Peasant Costumes.
29. Woodman in Working Garb.
30. Oriental Hotel, Manila.
31. San Juan del Monte, Where Revolution Started.
32. Brigadier-General E. S. Otis.
33. Brigadier-General Thomas M. Anderson.
34. General Greene's Headquarters at Manila.
35. Manila and Its Outskirts, Showing Malate.
36. Principal Gate to the City.
37. Attack on Manila, Showing Position of Our Ships and Troops.
38. Fortifications of Manila.

26   ILLUSTRATIONS.
39. Interior of the Fortifications of Manila.
40. Fort Santiago at Manila, Where the American Flag Was Raised.
41. Official Map of the Hawaiian Islands.
42. Ex-Consul General Fitzhugh Lee, Now Major-General Commanding.
43. Official Map by the War Department of the Seat of War in the Philippines.
44. The Destruction of Cervera's Spanish Squadron at Santiago.
45. Display in Manila Photograph Gallery, Insurgent Leaders.
46. A Bit of Scenery in Mindanao, Showing Tropical Vegetation.
47. Admiral Dewey's Fleet That Won the Battle of Manila Bay.
48. The Flagship Olympia.
49. The Baltimore.
50. The Concord.
51. The Raleigh.
52. The Boston.
53. The Petrel.
54. An Execution Entertainment on the Luneta.
55. Victims Reported Dead After the Execution.
56. Fort Weyler, Built by General Weyler When Governor of the Philippines.
57. A Public Square in Manila.
58. Scene after an Execution, Showing Prostrate Figures of the Dead.
59. A Review of Spanish Filipino Volunteers.
60. Spanish Troops Repelling an Insurgent Attack on a Convent.
61. A Spanish Festival in Manila.
62. Flowers of the Philippines.
63. The Battle of Manila Bay—In the Heat of the Raging Fight.
64. Group of Filipinos Who Want Independence.
65. Loading Buffaloes with Produce in Luzon.
66. Natives Fishing from a Canal Boat.
67. Scene Before an Execution.
68. Great Bridge at Manila.
69. Business Corner in Manila.
70. A Suburb of Manila, Showing a Buffalo Market Cart.
71. Aguinaldo and His Compatriots.
72. Senor Aguinaldo.
73. Senor Montsusgro.
74. Senor Natividah.
75. Senor Ninisgra.
76. Senor Rins.
77. Senor Belavinino.
78. Senor Covinbing.
79. Senor Mascordo.
80. Senor Arbacho.
81. Senor Pilar.

ILLUSTRATIONS. 27

82. Senor Viola.
83. Senor Francisco.
84. Senor Llansoo.
85. Filipina Preparing for a Siesta.
86. Cathedral of Manila After Earthquake.
87. Spanish Reinforcements Crossing Bridge Over Pasig River.
88. A Beheaded Spaniard—Sign of the Order of Katipunan.
89. Archbishop of Manila. His Protograph and Autograph Presented to Mr. Halsted, the Author.
90. The Sultan of Jolo in Mindanao.
91. Photograph and Autograph of Aguinaldo, as Presented by Him to Mr. Halsted, the Author.
92. A Spanish Dude—An Officer at Manila.
93. Government Building in Pampanga.
94. Church at Cavite.
95. Masacue—Town in Cavite.
96. Natives Taking Refreshments.
97. Spanish Soldiers Crossing Bridge Over Pasig River.
98. Official Map of the Isle of Luzon, Prepared by War Department.
99. The President and His Cabinet.
100. President McKinley.
101. Secretary of State Hay.
102. Secretary of the Treasury Gage.
103. Secretary of War Alger.
104. Secretary of the Navy Long.
105. Attorney General Griggs.
106. Postmaster General Smith.
107. Secretary of the Interior Bliss.
108. Secretary of Agriculture Wilson.
109. Naval Heroes of Santiago.
110. Admiral Sampson.
111. Admiral Schley.
112. Captain Chadwick, of the New York.
113. Captain Cooke, of the Brooklyn.
114. Captain Clarke, of the Oregon.
115. Captain Evans, of the Iowa.
116. Captain Higginson, of the Massachusetts.
117. Captain Philip, of the Texas.
118. Commander Wainwright, of the Gloucester.
119. Lieutenant R. P. Hobson.
120. Military Heroes of Santiago and Porto Rico.
121. Major-General Miles.
122. Major-General Shafter.

ILLUSTRATIONS.

123. Major-General Wheeler.
124. Major-General Brooke.
125. Brigadier-General Wood.
126. Colonel Roosevelt.
127. Brigadier-General F. V. Greene.
128. Admiral Dewey, the Hero of Manila.
129. Captain Sigsbee, Commander of the Ill-fated Maine.
130. Shipping in Manila Harbor.

THE PRESIDENT AND HIS CABINET.
(Photo of Long Copyrighted 1897 by Purdy of Boston.)
(Photo of McKinley Copyrighted by Elmer Chickering.)
(Photo of Smith Copyrighted by Rockwood.)

THE HERO OF MANILA.

CHAPTER I.

ADMIRAL DEWEY ON HIS FLAGSHIP.

A Stormy Day on Manila Bay—Call on Admiral Dewey—The Man in White—He Sticks to His Ship—How He Surprised Spaniards—Every Man Did His Duty on May-Day—How Dewey Looks and Talks—What He Said About War with Germany in Five Minutes—Feeds His Men on "Delicious" Fresh Meat from Australia—Photography Unjust to Him.

Steaming across Manila Bay from Cavite to the city on an energetic ferry-boat, scanning the wrecks of the Spanish fleet still visible where the fated ships went down, one of them bearing on a strip of canvas the legible words "Remember the 'Maine,'" the talk being of Dewey's great May-day, we were passing the famous flag-ship of the squadron that was ordered to destroy another squadron, and did it, incidentally gathering in hand the keys of an empire in the Indies for America, because the American victor was an extraordinary man, who saw the immensity of the opportunity and improved it to the utmost, some one said: "There is the Admiral now, on the quarter-deck under the awning—the man in white, sitting alone!" The American Consul at Manila was aboard the ferry-boat, and said to the captain he would like to speak to the Admiral. The course was changed a point, and then a pause, when the Consul called, "Admiral!" And the man in white stepped to the rail and responded pleasantly to the greeting—the Consul saying:

"Shall we not see you ashore now?"

"No," said the man in white, in a clear voice; "I shall not go ashore unless I have to."

Some one said: "This would be a good chance to go. Come with us."

The man in white shook his head, and the ferryman ordered full speed, the passengers all looking steadily at the white figure until it became a speck, and the fresh arrivals were shown the objects of the greatest interest, until the wrecks of the Oriental fleet of the Spaniards were no longer visible, and there was only the white walls to see of Cavite's arsenal and the houses of the navy-yard, and the more stately structures of Manila loomed behind the lighthouse at the mouth of the Pasig, when the eyes of the curious were drawn to the mossback fort that decorates as an antiquity the most conspicuous angle of the walls of "the walled city."

There was a shade of significance in the few words of the Admiral that he would not go ashore until he must. He has from the first been persistent in staying at Manila. There has been nothing that could induce him to abandon in person the prize won May 1st. His order from the President was to destroy the Spanish fleet. It was given on the first day of the legal existence of the war, counting the day gained, in crossing the Pacific Ocean from the United States to the Philippines, when the 180th degree of longitude west from Greenwich is reached and reckoned. It was thus the President held back when the war was on; and the next day after Dewey got the order at Hongkong he was on the way. The Spaniards at Manila could not have been more astonished at Dewey's way of doing, if they had all been struck by lightning under a clear sky. They had no occasion to be "surprised," having the cable in daily communication with Madrid, and, more than that, a Manila paper of the last day of April contained an item of real news—the biggest news item ever published in that town! It was from a point on the western coast of the island of Luzon, and the substance of it that four vessels that seemed to be men-of-war, had been sighted going south, and supposed to be the American fleet.

What did the Spaniards suppose the American fleet they knew well had left Hongkong was going south for? If Admiral Dewey had been a commonplace man he would have paused and held a council of war nigh the huge rock Corregidor at the mouth of Manila Bay. There is a channel on either side of that island, and both were reputed to be guarded by torpedoes. The Spaniards had an enormous stock of munitions of war—modern German guns enough to have riddled the fleet of American cruisers—and why did they not have torpedoes? They had the Mauser rifle, which has wonderful range, and ten millions of smokeless powder cartridges. Marksmen could sweep the decks of a ship with Mausers at the distance of a mile, and with the smokeless cartridges it would have been mere conjecture where the sharpshooters were located. There are rows of armor-piercing steel projectiles from Germany still standing around rusting in the Spanish batteries, and they never did any more than they are doing. It is said—and there is every probability of the truth of the story—that some of these bolts would not fit any gun the Spaniards had mounted. The Admiral paid no attention to the big rock and the alleged torpedoes, but steamed up the bay near the city where the Spaniards were sleeping. He was hunting the fleet he was ordered to remove, and found it very early in the morning. Still the thunder of his guns seems to thrill and electrify the air over the bay, and shake the city; and the echoes to ring around the world, there is no question—not so much because the Americans won a naval victory without a parallel, as that Dewey improved the occasion, showing that he put brains into his business. They say—that is, some people seem to want to say it and so do—that Dewey is a strange sort of man; as was said of Wolfe and Nelson, who died when they won immortality. Dewey lives and is covered with glory. It has been held that there were not enough Americans hurt in the Manila fight to make the victory truly great. But the same objection applies to the destruction of Cervera's fleet when he ran away from Santiago. General Jackson's battle at New Orleans showed a marvelously small loss to Americans; but it was a good deal of a victory, and held good, though won after peace with England had been agreed upon. The capture of Manila is valid, too. Spain surrendered before the town did. If Dewey had been an every-day kind of man, he would have left Manila when he had fulfilled the letter of his orders, as he had no means of destroying the Spanish army, and did not want to desolate a city, even if the Spaniards held it. He remained and called for more ships and men, and got them.

"How is it?" "Why is it?" "How can it be?" are the questions Admiral Dewey asks when told that the American people, without exception, rejoice to celebrate him—that if one of the men known to have been with him May 1st should be found out in any American theater he would be taken on the stage by an irresistible call and a muscular committee of enthusiasts, and the play could not go on without "a few words" and the "Star Spangled Banner," "Hail Columbia," "Yankee Doodle," "Dixey" and "My Country, 'tis of Thee"; that the hallelujah note would be struck; that cars are chalked "for Deweyville"; that the board fences have his name written, or painted, or whittled on them; that there are Dewey cigars; that blacksmith-shops have the name Dewey scratched on them, also barn doors; and that if there are two dwelling-houses and a stable at a cross-roads it is Deweyville, or Deweyburg or Deweytown; that there is a flood of boy babies named Dewey, that the girls sing of him, and the ladies all admire him and the widows love him, and the school children adore him. The Admiral says: "I hear such things, and altogether they amaze me—the newspapers, the telegrams, the letters become almost unreal, for I do not comprehend what they say of my first day's work here. There was not a man in the fleet who did not do his duty."

The Admiral is told that he need not think to stay away until the people who have him on their minds and in their hearts are tired of their enthusiasm; that he cannot go home undiscovered and without demonstrations that will shake the earth and rend the skies; that the boys will drag the horses from his carriage, and parade the streets with him as a prisoner, and have it out with him, giving him a good time, until it will be a hard time, and he might as well submit to manifest destiny! His country wanted another hero, and he was at the right place at the right time, and did the right thing in the right way; and the fact answers all questions accounting for everything. Still he has a notion of staying away until the storm is over and he can get along without being a spectacle. Why, even the ladies of Washington are wild about him. If he should appear at the White House to call on the President, the scene would be like that when Grant first met Abraham Lincoln.

One rough day on the bay I took passage in a small steam-launch to visit the Olympia, where the Admiral's flag floated, to call on him. There was plenty of steam, and it was pleasant to get out a good way behind the breakwater, for the waves beyond were white with anger, and the boat, when departing from partial shelter, had proceeded but two or three hundred yards when it made a supreme effort in two motions—the first, to roll over; the second, to stand on its head. I was glad both struggles were unsuccessful, and pleased with the order: "Slow her up." The disadvantages of too much harbor were evident. The slow-ups were several, and well timed, and then came the rise and fall of the frisky launch beside the warship, the throwing of a rope, the pull with a hook, the stand off with an oar, the bounding boat clearing from four to ten feet at a jump; the clutch, the quick step, the deft avoidance of a crushed foot or sprained ankle, with a possible broken leg in sight, the triumphant ascent, the safe landing, the sudden sense that Desdemona was right in loving a man for the dangers he had passed, the thought that there should be harbors less fluctuating, a lively appreciation of the achievements of pilots in boarding Atlantic liners. The broad decks of the Olympia, built by the builders of the matchless Oregon, had a comforting solidity under my feet. The Admiral was believed to be having a nap; but he was wide awake, and invited the visitor to take a big chair, which, after having accompanied the launch in the dance with the whitecaps, was peculiarly luxurious. The Admiral didn't mind me, and had a moment's surprise about an observer of long ago strolling so far from home and going forth in a high sea to make a call. I confessed to being an ancient Wanderer, but not an Ancient Mariner, and expressed disapprobation of the deplorable roughness of the California Albatross, a brute of a bird—a feathered ruffian that ought to be shot.

The Admiral would be picked out by close attention as the origin of some millions of pictures; but he is unlike as well as like them. Even the best photographs do not do justice to his fine eyes, large, dark and luminous, or to the solid mass of his head with iron-brown hair tinged with gray. He is a larger man than the portraits indicate; and his figure, while that of a strong man in good health and form and well nourished, is not stout and, though full, is firm; and his step has elasticity in it. His clean-shaven cheek and chin are massive, and drawn on

ADMIRAL DEWEY ON HIS FLAGSHIP.

fine lines full of character—no fatty obscuration, no decline of power; a stern but sunny and cloudless face—a good one for a place in history; no show of indulgence, no wrinkles; not the pallor of marble, rather the glint of bronze—the unabated force good for other chapters of history. It would be extremely interesting to report the talk of the Admiral; but there were two things about him that reminded me of James G. Blaine, something of the vivid personality of the loved and lost leader; something in his eye and his manner, more in the startling candor with which he spoke of things it would be premature to give the world, and, above all, the absence of all alarm about being reported—the unconscious consciousness that one must know this was private and no caution needed. A verbatim report of the Admiral would, however, harm no one, signify high-toned candor and a certain breezy simplicity in the treatment of momentous matters. Evidently here was a man not posing, a hero because his character was heroic, a genuine personage—not artificial, proclamatory, a picker of phrases, but a doer of deeds that explain themselves; a man with imagination, not fantastic but realistic, who must have had a vision during the night after the May-day battle of what might be the great hereafter; beholding under the southern constellations the gigantic shadow of America, crowned with stars, with the archipelagoes of Asia under her feet and broad and mighty destinies at command.

It was the next day that he anchored precisely where his famous ship was swinging when I sat beside him; and his words to the representative of three centuries of Spanish misrule had in them an uncontemplated flash from the flint and steel of fixed purpose and imperial force. "Fire another gun at my ships and I will destroy your city."

We can hardly realize in America how flagrant Europeanism has been in the Manila Bay; how the big German guns bought by Spain looked from their embrasures; how a powerful German fleet persisted in asserting antagonism to Americanism, and tested in many ways the American Admiral's knowledge of his rights and his country's policy until Admiral Dewey told, not the German Admiral, as has been reported, but his flag lieutenant, "Can it be possible that your nation means war with mine? If so, we can begin it in five minutes." The limit had been reached, and the line was drawn; and Dewey's words will go down in our records with those of Charles Francis Adams to Lord John Russell about the ironclads built in England for the Confederacy: "My Lord, I need not point out to your lordship that this is war."

Perhaps the German Admiral had exceeded the instructions of his Imperial

Government, and the peremptory words of the American Admiral caused a better understanding, making for peace rather than for war.

Next to the Americans the English have taken a pride in Admiral Dewey, and they are in the Asiatic atmosphere our fast friends. They do not desire that we should give up the Philippines. On the contrary, they want us to keep the islands, and the more we become interested in those waters and along their shores, the better. They know that the world has practically grown smaller and, therefore, the British Empire more compact; and they find Russia their foe. They see that with the Pacific Coast our base of operations looking westward, we have first the Hawaiian Islands for producers and a coal station, naval arsenal, dockyards for the renovation and repair and replenishment of our fleets; and they see that we have reserved for ourselves one of the Ladrones, so that we will have an independent route to the Philippines. The Japanese have cultivated much feeling against our possession of Hawaii, the animus being that they wanted it for themselves; and likewise they are disturbed by our Pacific movement, anticipating the improvement of the most western of the Alutian Islands, an admirable station overlooking the North Pacific; all comprehending with Hawaii, the Alutian Island found most available, the Ladrone that we shall reserve and the Philippines, we shall have a Pacific quadrilateral; and this is not according to the present pleasure and the ambition for the coming days, of Japan. England would have approved our holding all the islands belonging to the Spanish, including the Canaries, and Majorca and Minorca and their neighboring isles in the Mediterranean, and take a pride in us. She has been of untold and inestimable service to us in the course of the Spanish War, and her ways have been good for us at Manila, while the Germans have been frankly against us, the Russians grimly reserved, and the French disposed to be fretful because they have invested in Spanish bonds upon which was raised the money to carry on the miserable false pretense of war with the Cubans. One day while I was on the fine transport Peru, in the harbor of Manila, the American Admiral's ship saluted an English ship-of-war coming in that had saluted his flag, and also displayed American colors in recognition that the harbor of Manila was an American port. That was the significance of the flashes and thundering of the Admiral's guns and the white cloud that gathered about his ship that has done enough for celebrity through centuries.

Admiral Dewey created the situation in the Philippines that the President wisely chose by way of the Paris Conference to receive the deliberate judgment of the Senate and people of the United States. Dewey has been unceasingly deeply concerned about it. His naval victory was but the beginning. He might have sailed away from Manila May 2d, having fulfilled his orders; but he had the high and

ADMIRAL DEWEY ON HIS FLAGSHIP.

keen American spirit in him, and clung. He needed a base of operations, a place upon which to rest and obtain supplies. He had not the marines to spare to garrison a fort save at Cavite, twelve miles from Manila; and he needed chickens, eggs, fresh meat and vegetables; and it was important that the Spanish Army should be occupied on shore. Hence, Aguinaldo, who was in Singapore, and the concentration of insurgents that had themselves to be restrained to make war on civilized lines. One of the points of the most considerable interest touching the Filipinos is that the smashing defeat of the fleet of Spain in Manila Bay heartened them. They have become strong for themselves. The superiority of the Americans over the Spaniards as fighting men is known throughout the islands Spain oppressed; and the bonds of the tyrants have been broken. It should not be out of mind that the first transports with our troops did not reach Manila for six weeks, and that the army was not in shape to take the offensive until after General Merritt's arrival, late in July. All this time the American Admiral had to hold on with the naval arm; and it was the obvious game of Spain, if she meant to fight and could not cope with the Americans in the West Indies, to send all her available ships and overwhelm us in the East Indies. At the same time the German, French, Russian and Japanese men-of-war represented the interest of the live nations of the earth in the Philippines. As fast as possible Admiral Dewey was re-enforced; but it was not until the two monitors, the Monterey and Monadnock, arrived, the latter after the arrival of General Merritt, that the Admiral felt that he was safely master of the harbor. He had no heavily armored ships to assail the shore batteries within their range, and might be crippled by the fire of the great Krupp guns. It was vital that the health of the crews of his ships should be maintained, and the fact that the men are and have been all summer well and happy is not accidental. Admiral Dewey took the point of danger, if there was one, into his personal keeping, by anchoring the Olympia on the Manila side of the bay, while others were further out and near Cavite; and throughout the fleet there was constant activity and the utmost vigilance. There was incessant solicitude about what the desperate Spaniards might contrive in the nature of aggressive enterprise. It seemed incredible to Americans that nothing should be attempted. How would a Spanish fleet have fared for three months of war with us in an American harbor? There would have been a new feature of destructiveness tried on the foe at least once a week.

The Spaniards ashore seemed to be drowsy; but the Americans were wide awake, ready for anything, and could not be surprised; so that we may commend as wisdom the Spanish discretion that let them alone. The ship that was the nearest neighbor of Admiral Dewey for months of his long vigil flew the flag of Belgium.

She is a large, rusty-looking vessel, without a sign of contraband of war, or of a chance of important usefulness about her; but she performed a valuable function. I asked half a dozen times what her occupation was before any one gave a satisfactory answer. Admiral Dewey told the story in few words. She was a cold-storage ship, with beef and mutton from Australia, compartments fixed for about forty degrees below zero. Each day the meat for the American fleet's consumption was taken out. There was a lot of it on the deck of the Olympia thawing when I was a visitor; and the beef was "delicious." I am at pains to give Dewey's word. While the Spaniards ashore were eating tough, lean buffalo—the beasts of burden in the streets, the Americans afloat rejoiced in "delicious" beef and mutton from Australia. It was explained that the use of cold-storage meat depended upon giving it time to thaw, for if it should be cooked in an icy state it would be black and unpalatable, losing wholly its flavor and greatly its nourishing quality. Australia is not many thousand miles from the Philippines—and one must count miles by the thousands out there. The Belgians have a smart Consul at Manila who is a friend of mankind.

One of the incidents in the battle of Manila—all are fresh in the public memory—is that Admiral Dewey did not make use of the conning-tower—a steel, bomb proof, for the security of the officer in command of the ship—the Captain, of course, and the commander of the fleet, if he will.

This retreat did not prove, in the battle of Yalu and the combats between the Chileans and Peruvians, a place of safety; but as a rule there is a considerable percentage of protection in its use. Admiral Dewey preferred to remain on the bridge—and there were four fragments of Spanish shells that passed close to him, striking within a radius of fifteen feet. The Admiral, when told there had been some remark because he had not occupied the conning-house in the action, walked with me to the tower, the entrance to which is so guarded that it resembles a small cavern of steel—with a heavy cap or lid, under which is a circular slit, through which observations are supposed to be made. "Try it," the Admiral said, "and you find it is hard to get a satisfactory view." He added, when I had attempted to look over the surroundings: "We will go to the bridge;" and standing on it he annotated the situation, saying: "Here you have the whole bay before you, and can see everything." I remarked: "The newspaper men are very proud of the correspondent of the Herald who was with you on the bridge;" and the Admiral said: "Yes; Stickney was right here with us."

There were many reasons for the officer commanding the American fleet that day to watch closely the developments. The Spaniards had, for their own purposes, even falsified the official charts of the bay. Where our vessels maneuvered and the flagship drew twenty-two feet of water and had nine feet under the keel, the chart called for fifteen feet only!

It is not a secret that the President wanted Admiral Dewey, if it was not in his opinion inconsistent with his sense of duty, to go to Washington. Naturally the President would have a profound respect for the Admiral's opinion as to the perplexing problem of the Philippines. The Admiral did not think he should leave his post. He could cover the points of chief interest in writing, and preferred very much to do so, and stay right where he was "until this thing is settled." The opinion of the Admiral as to what the United States should do with, or must do about, the political relations of the Philippines with ourselves and others, have not been given formal expression; but it is safe to say they are not in conflict with his feeling that the American fleet at Manila should be augmented with gunboats, cruisers and two or three battle-ships. It was, in the opinion of the illustrious Admiral, when the Peace Commission met in Paris, the time and place to make a demonstration of the sea power of the United States.

The personal appearance of Admiral Dewey is not presented with attractive accuracy in the very familiar portrait of him that has been wonderfully multiplied and replenished. The expression of the Admiral is not truly given in the prints and photos. The photographer is responsible for a faulty selection. The impression prevails that the hero is "a little fellow." There is much said to the effect that he is jaunty and has excess of amiability in his smile. He weighs about 180 pounds, and is of erect bearing, standing not less than five feet ten inches and a quarter. His hair is not as white as the pictures say. The artist who touched up the negative must have thought gray hair so becoming that he anticipated the feast of coming years. The figure of the Admiral is strong, well carried, firm, and his bearing that of gravity and determination, but no pose for the sake of show, no pomp and circumstance, just the Academy training showing in his attitude—the abiding, unconscious grace that is imparted in the schools of Annapolis and West Point—now rivaled by other schools in "setting up." The Admiral is of solidity and dignity, of good stature and proportions; has nothing of affectation in manners or insincerity in speech; is a hearty, stirring, serious man, whose intensity is softened by steady purposes and calm forces, and moderated by the play of a sense of humor, that is not drollery or levity, but has a pleasing greeting for a clever word, and yields return with a flash in it and an edge on it.

CHAPTER II.
LIFE IN MANILA.

Character of the Filipinos—Drivers Lashing Laboring Men in the Streets—What Americans Get in Their Native Air—The Logic of Destiny—Manila as She Fell into Our Hands—The Beds in the Tropics—A Spanish Hotel—Profane Yells for Ice—Sad Scenes in the Dining Room—Major-General Calls for "Francisco"—A Broken-Hearted Pantry Woman.

The same marvelous riches that distinguish Cuba are the inheritance of Luzon. The native people are more promising in the long run than if they were in larger percentage of the blood of Spain, for they have something of that indomitable industry that must finally work out an immense redemption for the eastern and southern Asiatics. When, I wonder, did the American people get the impression so extensive and obstinate that the Japanese and Chinese were idlers? We may add as having a place in this category the Hindoos, who toil forever, and, under British government, have increased by scores of millions. The southern Asiatics are, however, less emancipated from various indurated superstitions than those of the East; and the Polynesians, spread over the southern seas, are a softer people than those of the continent. However, idleness is not the leading feature of life of the Filipinos, and when they are mixed, especially crossed with Chinese, they are indefatigable. On the Philippine Islands there is far less servility than on the other side of the sea of China, and the people are the more respectable and hopeful for the flavor of manliness that compensates for a moderate but visible admixture of savagery. We of North America may be proud of it that the atmosphere of our continent, when it was wild, was a stimulant of freedom and independence. The red Indians of our forests were, with all their faults, never made for slaves. The natives of the West Indies, the fierce Caribs excepted, were enslaved by the Spaniards, and perished under the lash. Our continental tribes—the Seminoles and the Comanches, the Sioux and Mohawks, the Black Feet and the Miamis—from the St. Lawrence to Red River and the oceans, fought all comers—Spaniards, French and English— only the French having the talent of polite persuasion and the gift of kindness that won the mighty hunters, but never subjugated them. We may well encourage the idea that the quality of air of the wilderness has entered the soil. When, in Manila, I have seen the men bearing burdens on the streets spring out of the way of those riding in carriages, and lashed by drivers with a viciousness that no dumb animal should suffer, I have felt my blood warm to think that the men of common hard labor in my country would resent a blow as quickly as the man on horseback—that even the poor black—emancipated the other day from the subjugation of slavery by a masterful and potential race, stands up in conscious manhood, and that the teachings of the day are that consistently with the progress of the country—as one respects himself, he must be respected—and that the air and the earth have the inspiration and the stimulus of freedom. The Chinese and Japanese are famous as servants—so constant, handy, obedient, docile, so fitted to minister to luxury, to wait upon those favored by fortune and spurred to execute the schemes for elevation and dominance, and find employment in the enterprise that comprehends human advancement. It must be admitted that the Filipinos are not admirable in menial service. Many of them are untamed, and now, that the Americans have given object lessons of smiting the Spaniards, the people of the islands that Magellinos, the Portuguese, found for Spain, must be allowed a measure of self-government, or they will assert a broader freedom, and do it with sanguinary methods. As Americans have heretofore found personal liberty consistent with public order—that Republicanism was more stable than imperialism in peaceable administration, and not less formidable in war, it seems to be Divinely appointed that our paths of Empire may, with advantage to ourselves, and the world at large, be made more comprehensive than our fathers blazed them out. But one need not hesitate to go forward in this cause, for we have only gone farther than the fathers dreamed, because, among their labors of beneficence, was that of building wiser than they knew, and there is no more reason now why we should stop when we strike the salt water of the seas, and consent to it that where we find the white line of surf that borders a continent we shall say to the imperial popular Republic, thus far and no farther shalt thou go, and here shall thy proud march be stayed—than there was that George Washington, as the representative of the English-speaking people; should have assumed that England and Virginia had no business beyond the Allegheny Mountains, and, above all, no right to territory on the west of the Allegheny and Kanawha, and north of the Ohio river, a territory then remote, inhabited by barbarians and wanted by the French, who claimed the whole continent, except the strip along the Atlantic possessed by the English colonies. Washington was a believer in the acquisition of the Ohio country. He was a man who had faith in land—in ever more land. It is the same policy to go west now that it was then. Washington crossed the Allegheny and held the ground. Jefferson crossed the Mississippi, and sent Louis and Clark to the Pacific; and crossing the great western ocean now is but the logic of going beyond the great western rivers, prairies and mountains then. We walk in the ways of the fathers when we go conquering and to conquer along the Eastward shores of Asia.

One of the expanding and teeming questions before the world now, and the authority and ability to determine it, is in the hands of the Commander-in-Chief of the Army of the United States, is whether Manila shall become an American city, with all the broad and sweeping significance attaching thereto. Manila was not dressed for company when I saw her, for she had just emerged from a siege in which the people had suffered much inconvenience and privation. The water supply was cut off, and the streets were not cleaned. The hotels were disorganized and the restaurants in confusion. The trees that once cast a grateful shade along the boulevards, that extended into the country, rudely denuded of their boughs, had the appearance of the skeletons of strange monsters. The insurgent army was still in the neighborhood in a state of uneasiness, feeling wronged, deprived, as they were, of an opportunity to get even with the Spaniards, by picking out and slaying some of the more virulent offenders. There was an immense monastery, where hundreds of priests were said to be sheltered, and the insurgents desired to take them into their own hands and make examples of them. The Spaniards about the streets were becoming complacent. They had heard of peace, on the basis of Spain giving up everything but the Philippines, and there were expectations that the troops withdrawn from Cuba might be sent from Havana to Manila, and then, as soon as the Americans were gone, the islanders could be brought to submission by vastly superior forces. There were more rations issued to Spanish than to American soldiers, until the division of the Philippine Expedition with Major-General Otis arrived, but the Americans were exclusively responsible for the preservation of the peace between the implacable belligerents, and the sanitary work required could not at once be accomplished, but presently it was visible that something was done every day in the right direction. There was much gambling with dice, whose rattling could be heard far and near on the sidewalks, but this flagrant form of vice was summarily suppressed, we may say with strict truth, at the point of the bayonet. The most representative concentration of the ingredients of chaos was at the Hotel Oriental, that overlooked a small park with a dry fountain and a branch of the river flowing under a stone bridge, with a pretty stiff current, presently to become a crowded canal. It is of three lofty stories and an attic, a great deal of the space occupied with halls, high, wide and long. The front entrance is broad, and a tiled floor runs straight through the house. Two stairways, one on either side, lead to the second story, the first steps of stone. In the distance beyond, a court could be seen, a passable conservatory—but bottles on a table with a counter in front declared that this was a barroom, as it was. The next thing further was a place where washing was done, then came empty rooms that might be shops; after this a narrow and untidy street, and then a livery stable—a sort of monopolistic cab stand, where a few ponies and carriages were to be found—but no one understood or did anything as long as possible, except to say that all the rigs were engaged now and always. However, a little violent English language, mixed with Spanish, would arouse emotion and excite commotion eventuating in a pony in harness, and a gig or carriage, and a desperate driver, expert with a villainous whip used without occasion or remorse.

The cool place was at the front door, on the sidewalk, seated on a hard chair, for there was always a breeze. The Spanish guests knew where the wind blew, and gathered there discussing many questions that must have deeply interested them. But they had something to eat, no authority or ability to affect any sort of change, and unfailing tobacco, the burning of which was an occupation. The ground floor of the hotel, except the barroom, the washroom, the hall, the conservatory and the hollow square, had been devoted to shop keeping, but the shop keepers were gone, perhaps for days and perhaps forever! Stone is not used to any great extent in house interiors, except within a few feet of the surface of the earth. Of course, there is no elevator in a Spanish hotel. That which is wanted is room for the circulation of air. Above the first flight of stairs the steps have a deep dark red tinge, and are square and long, so that each extends solidly across the liberal space allotted to the stairway. The blocks might be some stone of delightful color, but they are hewn logs, solid and smooth, of a superb mahogany or some tree of harder wood and deeper luxuriance of coloring. The bedrooms are immensely high, and in every way ample, looking on great spaces devoted to wooing the air from the park and the river. The windows are enormous. Not satisfied with the giant sliding doors that open on the street, revealing windows—unencumbered with sash or glass, there are sliding doors under the window sills, that roll back right and left and offer the chance to introduce a current of air directly on the lower limbs. One of the lessons of the tropics is the value of the outer air, and architecture that gives it a chance in the house. It is a precious education. The artificial light within must be produced by candles, and each stupendous apartment is furnished with one tallowy and otherwise neglected candle stick, and you can get, with exertion, a candle four inches long. There is a wardrobe, a wash stand, with pitcher and basin, and a commode, fans, chairs, and round white marble table, all the pieces placed in solitude, so as to convey the notion of lonesomeness. The great feature is the bed. The bedstead is about the usual thing, save that there is no provision for a possible or impossible spring mattress, or anything of that nature. The bed space is covered with bamboo, platted. It is hard as iron, and I can testify of considerable strength, for I rested my two hundred pounds, and rising a few pounds, on this surface, with no protection for it or myself for several nights, and there were no fractures. There is spread on this surface a Manila mat, which is a shade tougher and less tractable than our old style oilcloth. Upon this is spread a single sheet, that is tucked in around the edges of the mat, and there are no bed clothes, absolutely none. There is a mosquito bar with only a few holes in it, but it is suspended and cannot under any circumstances be used as a blanket. There is a pillow, hard and round, and easy as a log for your cheek to rest upon, and it is beautifully covered with red silk. There is a small roll, say a foot long and four inches in diameter, softer than the pillow, to a slight extent, and covered with finer and redder silk, that is meant for the neck alone. The comparatively big red log is to extend across the bed for the elevation it gives the head, and the little and redder log, softer so that you may indent it with your thumb, saves the neck from being broken on this relic of the Spanish inquisition. But there is a comforter—not such' a blessed caressing domestic comforter as the Yankees have, light as a feather, but responsive to a tender touch. This Philippine comforter is another red roll that must be a quilt firmly rolled and swathed in more red silk; and it is to prop yourself withal when the contact with the sheet and the mat on the bamboo floor of the bedstead, a combination iniquitous as the naked floor—becomes wearisome. It rests the legs to pull on your back, and tuck under your knees. In the total absence of bed covering, beyond a thin night shirt, the three red rolls are not to be despised. The object of the bed is to keep cool, and if you do find the exertion of getting onto—not into—the bed produces a perspiration, and the mosquito bar threatens suffocation, reliance may be had that if you can compose yourself on top of the sheet (which feels like a hard wood floor, when the rug gives way on the icy surface and you fall) and if you use the three rolls of hard substance, covered with red silk, discreetly and considerately, in finding a position, and if you permit the windows—no glass—fifteen feet by twelve, broadcast, as it were, to catch the breath of the river and the park; if you can contrive with infinite quiet, patience and pains to go to sleep for a few hours, you will be cool enough; and when awakened shivering there is no blanket near, and if you must have cover, why get under the sheet, next the Manila mat, and there you are! Then put your troublesome and probably aching legs over the bigger red roll, and take your repose! Of course, when in the tropics you cannot expect to bury yourself in bedclothing, or to sleep in fur bags like an arctic explorer. The hall in front of your door is twelve feet wide and eighty long, lined with decorative chairs and sofas, and in the center of the hotel is a spacious dining room. The Spaniard doesn't want breakfast. He wants coffee and fruit—maybe a small banana—something sweet, and a crumb of bread. The necessity of the hour

LIFE IN MANILA. 43

is a few cigarettes. His refined system does not require food until later. At 12 o'clock he lunches, and eats an abundance of hot stuff—fish, flesh and fowl—fiery stews and other condolences for the stomach. This gives strength to consider the wrongs of Spain and the way, when restored to Madrid, the imbeciles, who allowed the United States to capture the last sad fragments of the colonies, sacred to Spanish honor, shall be crushed by the patriots who were out of the country when it was ruined. It will take a long time for the Spaniards to settle among factions the accounts of vengeance. One of the deeper troubles of the Spaniards is that they take upon themselves the administration of the prerogatives of him who said "Vengeance is mine." The American end of the dining room contains several young men who speak pigeon Spanish, and Captains Strong and Coudert are rapidly becoming experts, having studied the language in school, and also on the long voyage out. There are also a group of resident Englishmen and a pilgrim from Norway, but at several tables are Americans who know no Spanish and are mad at the Spaniards on that provocation among other things.

There is, however, a connecting link and last resort in the person of a young man—a cross between a Jap and Filipino. He is slender and pale, but not tall. His hair is roached, so that it stands up in confusion, and he is wearied all the time about the deplorable "help." It is believed he knows better than is done—always a source of unhappiness. His name is Francisco; his reputation is widespread. He is the man who "speaks English"—and is the only one—and it is not doubted that he knows at least a hundred words of our noble tongue. He says, "What do you want?" "Good morning, gentlemen"; "What can I do for you?" "Do you want dinner?" "No, there is no ice till 6 o'clock." He puts the Americans in mind of better days. Behind this linguist is a little woman, whose age might be twenty or sixty, for her face is so unutterably sad and immovable in expression that there is not a line in it that tells you anything but that there is to this little woman a bitterly sad, mean, beastly world. She must be grieving over mankind. It is her duty to see that no spoon is lost, and not an orange or banana wasted, and her mournful eyes are fixed with the intensity of despair upon the incompetent waiters, who, when hard pressed by wild shouts from American officers, frantic for lack of proper nourishment, fall into a panic and dance and squeal at each other; and then the woman of fixed sorrow, her left shoulder thin and copper-colored, thrust from her low-necked dress, her right shoulder protected, is in the midst of the pack, with a gliding bound and the ferocity of a cat, the sadness of her face taking on a tinge of long-suffering rage. She whirls the fools here and there as they are wanted. Having disentangled the snarl, she returns to the door from which her eyes command both the pantry and the dining-room to renew her solemn round of mournful vigilance. The Americans are outside her jurisdiction. She has no more idea what they are than Christopher Columbus, when he was discovering America, knew where he was going. When Francisco does not know what the language (English) hurled at him means he has a far-away look, and may be listening to the angels sing, for he is plaintive and inexpressive. He looks so sorry that Americans cannot speak their own language as he speaks English! But there are phrases delivered by Americans that he understands, such as, "Blankety, blank, blank—you all come here." Francisco does not go there, but with humble step elsewhere, affecting to find a pressing case for his intervention, but when he can no longer avoid your eye catching him he smiles a sweet but most superior smile, such as becomes one who speaks English and is the responsible man about the house.

There never was one who did more on a capital of one hundred words. His labors have been lightened slightly, for the Americans have picked up a few Spanish words, such as, "Ha mucher, mucher—don't you know? Hielo, hielo!" Hielo is ice, and after the "mucher" is duly digested the average waiter comes, by and by, with a lump as big as a hen's egg and is amazed by the shouts continuing "hielo, hielo!" pronounced much like another and wicked word.

"Oh, blanketination mucher mucher hielo!" The Filipinos cannot contemplate lightly the consumption of slabs of ice. The last words I heard in the dining-room of the Hotel Oriental were from a soldier with two stars on each shoulder: "Francisco, oh, Francisco," and the little woman with left shoulder exposed turned her despairing face to the wall, her sorrow too deep for words or for weeping.

CHAPTER III.

FROM LONG ISLAND TO LUZON.

Across the Continent—An American Governor-General Steams Through the Golden Gate—He Is a Minute-Man—Honolulu as a Health Resort—The Lonesome Pacific—The Skies of Asia—Dreaming Under the Stars of the Scorpion—The Southern Cross.

Spain, crowded between the Mediterranean and the Atlantic, was the world's "West" for many centuries, indeed until Columbus found a further West, but he did not go far enough to find the East Indies. The United States is now at work in both the East and West Indies.

Our Manila expeditions steamed into the sunsets, the boys pointing out to each other the southern cross. The first stage of a journey, to go half round the world on a visit to our new possession, was by the annex boat from Brooklyn, and a rush on the Pennsylvania train, that glimmers with gold and has exhausted art on wheels, to Washington, to get the political latitude and longitude by observation of the two domes, that of the Capitol, and the library, and the tremendous needle of snow that is the monument to Washington, and last, but not least, the superb old White House.

The next step was across the mountains on the Baltimore and Ohio, the short cut between the East and the West, traversed so often by George Washington to get good land for the extension of our national foundations. The space between Cincinnati and Chicago is cleared on the "Big Four" with a bound through the shadow of the earth, between two rare days in June, and the next midnight, the roaring train flew high over the Missouri River at Omaha, and by daylight far on the way to Ogden. The country was rich in corn and grass, and when one beholds the fat cattle, lamentations for the lost buffalo cease. It is a delight to see young orchards and farmhouses, and cribs and sheds fortified against tornadoes by groves, laid out with irritating precision to confront the whirling storms from west and south. The broad bad lands in which the tempests are raised devour the heart of the continent.

I made note of the 888-mile post beyond Omaha, but the 1,000-mile telegraph pole and tree glided away while I was catching the lights and shadows on a fearfully tumbled landscape. The alkali has poisoned enormous tracts, and the tufts of sagebrush have a huge and sinister monotony. Looking out early in the morning there was in our track a "gaunt grey wolf" with sharp ears, unabashed by the roar of the train. His species find occasional scraps along the track and do not fear the trains. Then I saw something glisten in the herbage, and it was a rattlesnake, if it were not a whisky bottle.

The gigantic lumps of tawny earth, with castellated crags of stone, ghostly ruins one would say of cities that perished thousands of years before the bricks were made for Babylon. Profound beds for vanished torrents yawned into a scrap of green valley, and the glitter of a thread of water. A town blossomed from a coal mine, and there was an array of driven wells with force pumps to quench the thirst of seething and raging locomotives. A turn in the line and a beautiful cloud formation like billows of white roses, massive, delicately outlined fantastic spires like marble mountains, carved—ah! the cloud comes out clear as if it were a wall of pearl, and there are the everlasting mighty hills with their brows of exquisite snow!

These are lofty reservoirs from which the long days glowing with sunshine send down streams of water at whose touch the deserts bloom. The eye is refreshed as we make a closer acquaintance of the mountains. Where water flows and trees "wag their high tops" there is hope of homes. There are canyons that cause one to smile at remembrances of what were considered the dizzy gorges of the Alleghenies. There is a glow as of molten lead in one corner of a misty valley far away. It is Salt Lake, the Dead Sea of America. Beyond this at an immense elevation is a lake with the tinge of the indigo sky of the tropics. If one could stir a portion of the Caribbean Sea into Lake Geneva, the correct tint could be obtained. Thirty miles of snow sheds announce progress in the journey to the Pacific. There is still heat and dust, but beside the road are villages; and there are even fountains.

Each stream is a treasure, and its banks are rich with verdure. There are sleek cows on bright grass. The mountains are no longer forbidding. They take on robes of loveliness. The valleys broaden and on the easy slopes there are orchards where the oranges glisten. There are clusters of grapes. We have come upon that magic land, California. There is golden music in the name. This is a conquest. The war in which it was won was not one of philanthropy. We gathered an empire.

General Merritt never minded the weather, whether the wind blew or not, and instead of holding his ship for several hours after the appointed time, wanted to know five minutes after 10 o'clock whether the time for starting was not 10 o'clock and by whom the boat was detained. At ten minutes after 10 the gangplank was swung free, with a desperate man on it who scrambled on with the help of long legs and a short rope As the ship swung from the dock and got a move on there were thousands of men and women exalted with emotion, and there were crowded steamers and tugs toppling with swarming enthusiasts resounding with brass bands and fluttering with streaming flags. The ladies were especially frantic. Spurts of white smoke jetted from forts and there were ringing salutes. Steam whistles pitched a tune beyond the fixed stars. The national airs with thrilling trumpet tones pierced the din, and a multitude of voices joined with the bands giving words and tone to the magnetic storm. How many miles the Newport was pursued I cannot conjecture. There were tall ladies standing on the high decks of tugs that were half buried in the foam of the bay, but as long as they could hold a "Star Spangled Banner" in one hand, and a few handkerchiefs in another, their skirts streaming in grace and defiance before the rising gale, they sang hosannas, and there were attitudes both of triumph and despair as the fair followers, dashed with spray, gave up the chase, passionately kissing their hands god-speed and good-by. This was going to the Indies through the Golden Gate!

A breakage of dishes, that sounded as though the ship were going to pieces, belied the prophesy that beyond the bar there was to be no moaning; and the Pacific would not be pacified. However, the reputation of the ocean was good enough to go to sleep on, but the berths squirmed in sympathy with the twisting and plunging ship. It was not a "sound of revelry by night," to which the wakeful listened through the dismal hours, and in the morning there was a high sea—grand rollers crowned with frothy lace, long black slopes rising and smiting like waves of liquid iron.

The Pacific was an average North Atlantic, and it was explained by the tale that the peaceful part of this ocean is away down South where the earth is most rotund, and the trade winds blow on so serenely that they lull the navigators into dreams of peace that induce a state of making haste slowly and a willingness to forget and be forgotten, whether—

>Of those who husbanded the golden grain
>Or those who flung it to the winds like rain.

The gulls are not our snowy birds of the Atlantic. We are lonesome out here, and the Albatross sweeps beside us, hooded like a cobra, an evil creature trying to hoodoo us, with owlish eyes set in a frame like ghastly spectacle glasses.

General Merritt's blue eyes shone like diamonds through the stormy experiences while the young staff officers curled up as the scientists did on the floor, and smiled a sort of sickly smile! The highest compliment that can be paid them is that the group of officers and gentlemen surrounding the commander of the expedition to the Philippines, express his own character.

It was funny to find that the private soldiers were better served with food than the General and his staff. There was reform, so as to even up the matter of rations, but the General was not anxious and solicitous for better food. His idea of the correct supper after a hard day's service is a goodly sized sliced onion with salt, meat broiled on two sticks, hard tack, a tin cup of coffee, for luxuries a baked potato, a pipe of tobacco, a nip of whisky, a roll in a blanket and a sleep until the next day's duties are announced by the bugle.

As the gentlemen of the staff got their sea legs, and flavored the narration of their experiences with humor, I found myself in a cloudy state and mentioned a small matter to the brigadier surgeon, who whipped out a thermometer and took my temperature, and that man of science gave me no peace night or day, and drove me from the ship into Paradise—that is to say I was ordered to stay at Honolulu. Through a window of the Queen's hospital I saw lumps of tawny gold that were pomegranates shaking in the breeze, another tree glowed with dates, and a broad, vividly green hedge was rich with scarlet colors. I was duly examined by physicians, who were thorough as German specialists. I had, in the course of a few hours, a nap, a dish of broth, a glass of milk, a glass of ice water and an egg nog. That broth flowed like balm to the right spot. It was chicken broth. When I guzzled the egg nog I would have bet ten to one on beating that fever in a week, and the next morning about 4:30, when there was competitive crowing by a hundred roosters, I was glad of the concert, for it gave assurance of a supply of chickens to keep up the broth and the eggs that disguised the whiskey.

Two days later I gave up the egg nog because it was too good for me. I knew I did not deserve anything so nice, and suspected it was a beneficence associated with a cloud on my brow. I had the approval of the hospital physician as to egg nog, and he cut off a lot of dainties sent by the Honolulu ladies, who must have imagined that I was one of the heroes of the war. Their mission is to make heroes happy. I was detained under the royal palms, and other palms that were planted by the missionaries, four weeks, and got away on the ship Peru with Major-General Otis, and when we had gone on for a fortnight, as far as from the Baltic to Lake Erie, we saw some rocks that once were Spanish property.

As we left Honolulu the air was already a-glitter with Star Spangled Banners. There are three great points to be remembered as to the annexation of Hawaii:

1. There is not to be a continuance of the slavery of Asiatics in the new possession.

2. "Manhood suffrage" is not to be extended to Asiatics, often actually as under strictly conventional constitutional construction.

3. The archipelago is to be a United States territory, but not a State of the United States. Ex-President Harrison says in his most interesting book: "This Country of Ours," which should be one of our national school books:

"Out of the habit of dealing with the public domain has come the common thought that all territory that we acquire must, when sufficiently populous, be erected into States. But why may we not take account of the quality of the people as well as of their numbers, if future acquisitions should make it proper to do so? A territorial form of government is not so inadequate that it might not serve for an indefinite time."

It is to be remarked of the Hawaiian Islands that they did not possess the original riches of timber that distinguished the West Indies, especially Cuba, where Columbus found four varieties of oranges. One of the features of Hawaiian forestry is the Royal Palm, but it was not indigenous to the islands. The oldest of the stately royalists is not of forty years' growth, and yet they add surprising grace to many scenes, and each year will increase their height and enhance their beauty.

Hawaiians will be saved from extinction by miscegenation. There will be no harm done these feeble people by the shelter of the flag of the great republic. The old superstitions prevail among them to an extent greater than is generally understood. I had the privilege of visiting an American home, the background of which was a rugged mountain that looked like a gigantic picture setting forth the features of a volcanic world. Far up the steep is a cave in which the bones of many of the old savages were deposited in the days of civil war and inhuman sacrifices. The entrance was long ago—in the days the Hawaii people describe as "Before the Missionaries." The hole going to the holy cavern was closed, but there is still pious watching over the place of bones, and if there are climbers of the mountain not to be trusted with the solemn secrets of ancient times, they are stalked by furtive watchmen of the consecrated bones, and no doubt the ever alert sentinels would resist violation of the sepulchre in the rocks; and the natives are careful to scatter their special knowledge that the spot is haunted by supernatural shapes and powers. The Americans living in the midst of these mysteries are rather proud of the ghosts they never see, but have to put up with the haunting guard still ministering to the gods that dwelt in the shrines where the shadows of extinct volcanoes fall, long before the masterful missionaries planted their first steps in the high places.

After twenty-two days' steaming from San Francisco—Queen's Hospital time not counted—we were directly south of China's Yellow Sea, and within a few hours of sighting the isle of Luzon.

Only at Honolulu, all the way from San Francisco, was there a sail or a smoke not of a vessel of the Philippine expedition. All the long days and nights the eye swept the horizon for companionship, finding only that of our associates in adventure, and very little of them. Even the birds seem to shrink from the heart of the watery world spread between America and Asia; and the monsters of the deep are absent. One day, about a thousand miles from California, a story spread of a porpoise at play, but the lonely creature passed astern like a bubble. Bryant sang of the water fowl that flew from zone to zone, guided in certain flight on the long way over which our steps are led aright, but the Pacific zones are too broad for even winged wanderers. The fish that swarm on our coast do not seem to find home life or sporting places in this enormous sea. Only the flying fish disturb the silky scene and flutter with silver wings over the sparkling laces that glisten where the winds blow gently, and woo the billows to cast aside the terrors of other climes and match the sky of blue and gold in beauty; but, unlike the stars, the waves do not differ in glory, and the spread of their splendor, when they seem to roll over a conquered universe, appeals to the imagination with the solemn suggestion not that order rules but that old chaos settles in solemn peace. The days terminate on this abyss in marvelous glories. The glowing spectacle is not in the west alone, but the gorgeous conflagration of the palaces we build in dreams spreads all around the sky. The scene one evening in the vicinity of the sun departing in Asia to light up the morning of the everlasting to-morrow touching America with magical riches, was that of Niagara Falls ten thousand times magnified and turned to molten gold, that burned with inconceivable luster, while the south and north and east were illuminated with strange fires and soft lights, fading and merged at last in the daffodil sky. Then the west became as a forest of amazing growth, and the ship entered its dusky recesses like a hunter for game such as the world never saw—and we looked upon the slow-fading purple islands that are the northern fringes of the greater one of the Philippines, and studied the rather faint and obscure Southern Cross and the stately sheen of the superb constellation of the Scorpion. It is a pity to have to say that the Cross of the South is a disappointment—has to be explained and made impressive by a diagram. It is more like a kite than a cross; has a superfluous star at one corner. and no support at all of the idea of being like a cross unless it is worked up and picked into the fancy. The North Star shines on the other side of the ship, and the Great Dipper dips its pointers after midnight, into the mass of darkness that is the sea when the sun and moon are gone.

The voyage from Honolulu to the farther Pacific was not so long that we forgot the American send-off we got in that Yankee city. The national airs sounded forth gloriously and grand. Flags and hankerchiefs fluttered from dense masses of spectators, and our colors were radiant above the roofs. There was, as usual, a mist on the mountains, and over Pearl Harbor glowed the arch of the most vivid rainbow ever seen; and Honolulu is almost every day dipped in rainbows. This was a wonder of splendor. The water changed from a sparkling green to a darkly luminous blue. From the moment the lofty lines of the coast—our mountains now—faded, till the birds came out of the west, the Pacific Ocean justified its name. The magnificent monotony of its stupendous placidity was not broken except by a few hours of ruffled rollers that tell of agitations that, if gigantic, are remote.

The two thousand and one hundred miles from California to Honolulu seemed at first to cover a vast space of the journey from our Pacific coast to the Philippines, but appeared to diminish in importance as we proceeded and were taught by the persistent trade winds that blew our way, as if forever to waft us over the awful ocean whose perpetual beauty and placidity were to allure us to an amazing abyss, from which it was but imaginative to presume that we, in the hands of infinite forces, should ever be of the travelers that return. Similar fancies beset, as all the boys remember—the crews of the caravels that carried Columbus and his fortunes. There were the splendors of tropical skies to beguile us; the sea as serene as the sky to enchant us! What mighty magic was this that put a spell upon an American army, seeking beyond the old outlines of our history and dreams, to guide us on unfamiliar paths? What was this awakening in the soft mornings, to the thrilling notes of the bugle? The clouds were not as those we knew in other climes and years. We saw no penciling of smoke on the edges of the crystal fields touched up with dainty ripples too exquisite to be waves—that which is a delight for a moment and passes but to come again, in forms too delicate to stay for a second, save in those pictures that in the universe fill the mind with memories that are like starlight. The glancing tribes of flying fish became events. We followed the twentieth parallel of longitude north of the equator, right on, straight as an arrow's flight is the long run of the ship—her vapor and the bubbles that break from the waters vanishing, so that we were as trackless when we had passed one breadth after another of the globe, as the lonesome canoes of the Indians on the Great Lakes.

CHAPTER IV.

INTERVIEW WITH GENERAL AGUINALDO.

The Insurgent Leader's Surroundings and Personal Appearance—His Reserves and Ways of Talking—The Fierce Animosity of the Filipinos Toward Spanish Priests—A Probability of Many Martyrs in the Isle of Luzon.

Practically all persons in the more civilized—and that is to say the easily accessible—portions of the Philippine Islands, with perhaps the exception of those leading insurgents who would like to enjoy the opportunities the Spaniards have had for the gratification of greed and the indulgence of a policy of revenge, would be glad to see the Americans remain in Manila, and also in as large a territory as they could command.

Spaniards of intelligence are aware that they have little that is desirable to anticipate in case the country is restored to them along with their Mausers and other firearms, great and small, according to the terms of capitulation. They get their guns whether we go and leave them or we stay and they go. It is obvious that the insurgents have become to the Spaniards a source of anxiety attended with terrors. The fact that they allowed themselves to be besieged in Manila by an equal number of Filipinos is conclusive that their reign is over, and they are not passionately in favor of their own restoration. Their era of cruel and corrupt government is at an end, even if we shall permit them to make the experiment. Their assumed anxiety to stay, is false pretense. They will be hurt if they do not go home.

The exasperation of the Filipinos toward the church is a phenomenon, and they usually state it with uncandid qualifications of the inadequate definition of the opinions and policy made by General Aguinaldo. Representations of my representative character as an American journalist, that gave me an importance I do not claim or assume to have, caused the appearance at my rooms, in Manila, of insurgents of high standing and comprehensive information, and of large fortunes in some cases. I was deeply impressed by their violent radicalism regarding the priests. At first they made no distinction, but said flatly the priests were the mischiefmakers, the true tyrants, and next to the half-breed Filipinos crossed with Chinese—who are phenomenal accumulators of pecuniary resources—the money-makers, who profited wrongfully by the earnings of others.

And so "the priests must go," they said, and have no choice except that of de-

GENERAL AGUINALDO, HIS PHOTOGRAPH AND AUTOGRAPH, AS PRESENTED TO MR. HALSTEAD.

ARCHBISHOP OF MANILA, HIS PHOTOGRAPH, AND AUTOGRAPH, AS PRESENTED TO MR. HALSTEAD.

portation or execution. In few words, if they did not go away they would be killed. When close and urgent inquiry was made, the native priests were not included in the application of this rule. The Spanish priests were particularly singled out for vengeance, and with them such others as had been "false to the people" and treacherous in their relations to political affairs.

The number to be exiled or executed was stated at 3,000. The priests are panicky about this feeling of the natives, as is in evidence in their solicitude to get away. They at least have no hope of security if the Spaniards should regain the mastery of the islands. Two hundred and fifty of them in vain sought to get passage to Hongkong in one boat. I was informed on authority that was unquestionable that the eviction or extermination of the Spanish priests was one of the inevitable results of Filipine independence—the first thing to be done.

It was with three objects in view that I had an interview with General Aguinaldo: (1) To ascertain exactly as possible his feeling and policy toward the United States and its assertion of military authority; (2) to inquire about his position touching the priests, (3) and to urge him to be at pains to be represented not only at Washington, but at Paris. As regards the latter point, it was clear that the people of the Philippines, whatever they might be, ought to be represented before the Paris conference. No matter what their case was, it should be personally presented, even if the representatives were witnesses against rather than for themselves. In the interest of fair play and the general truth the Philippine population should put in an appearance at the seat of the government of the United States for the information of the President, and at the scene of the conference to testify; and I was sure it would appear in all cases that they were at least better capable of governing themselves than the Spaniards to govern them. There could be no form of government quite so bad as that of the fatal colonial system of Spain, as illustrated in the Philippines and in the Americas.

General Aguinaldo was neither remote nor inaccessible. His headquarters were in an Indian village, just across the bay, named Bacoor, and in less than an hour a swift steam launch carried Major Bell, of the bureau of information, a gallant and most industrious and energetic officer, and myself, to water so shallow that we had to call canoes to land in front of a church that before the days of Dewey was riddled by the fire of Spanish warships because occupied by insurgents. The walls and roof showed many perforations. The houses of the village were of bamboo, and there were many stands along the hot and dusty street on which fruit was displayed for sale.

INTERVIEW WITH GEN. AGUINALDO.

The General's house was about as solid a structure as earthquakes permit, its roof of red tile instead of the usual straw. His rooms were in the second story, reached by a broad stairway, at the top of which was a landing of liberal dimensions and an ante-room. The General was announced at home and engaged in writing a letter to General Merritt—then his rather regular literary exercise. There were a dozen insurgent soldiers at the door, and as many more at the foot and head of the stairs, with several officers, all in military costume, the privates carrying Spanish Mausers and the officers wearing swords. We were admitted to an inner room, with a window opening on the street, and told the General would see us directly. Meanwhile well-dressed ladies of his family passed through the audience room from the General's office to the living rooms, giving a pleasant picture of domesticity.

The door from the study opened and a very slender and short young man entered with a preoccupied look that quickly became curious. An attendant said in a low voice, "General Aguinaldo." He was unexpectedly small—could weigh but little over 100 pounds—dressed in pure white, and his modesty of bearing would have become a maiden. The first feeling was a sort of faint compassion that one with such small physical resources should have to bear the weighty responsibilities resting upon him. Major Bell had often met him, and introduced me. The General was gratified that I had called, and waited for the declaration of my business. He had been informed of my occupation; the fact that I had recently been in Washington and expected soon to be there again; was from Ohio, the President's state, a friend of his, and had written a book on Cuba, a task which gave me, as I had visited the Island of Cuba during the war, an acquaintance with the Spanish system of governing colonies.

The interpreter was a man shorter than the General, but not quite so slight. His hair was intensely black and he wore glasses. He is an accomplished linguist, speaks English with facility and is acknowledged by the priests to be the equal of any of them in reading and speaking Latin. It is to be remarked that while Aguinaldo is not a man of high education he has as associates in his labors for Philippine independence a considerable number of scholarly men. It is related that in a recent discussion between a priest and an insurgent, the latter stated as a ground of rebellion that the Spaniards did nothing for the education of the people, and was asked, "Where did you get your education?" He had been taught by the Jesuits.

My first point in talking with Aguinaldo was that the people of the Philippines ought to be strongly represented in Paris, and of the reasons briefly presented, the foremost was that they sought independence, and should be heard before the com-

INTERVIEW WITH GEN. AGUINALDO. 55

mission by which their fate would be declared for the present, so far as it could be, by a tribunal whose work was subject to revision. The general's information was that the Paris conference would be opened September 15, an error of a fortnight, and his impression was that the terms regarding the Philippines would be speedily settled, so that there could not be time to send to Paris, but there had been a determination reached to have a man in Washington.

It is to be taken into account that this interview was before anything had been made known as to the mission which General Merritt undertook, and that in a few days he set forth to perform, and that the terms of the protocol had not been entirely published in Manila. I told the general it was not possible that the Philippine problem could speedily be solved, and made known to him that the transport China, which holds the record of quick passage on the Pacific, was to sail for San Francisco in three days, and he would do well to have his men for Washington and Paris go on her if permission could be obtained, as there was no doubt it could, and I mentioned the time required to reach Washington and Paris—that one could be on a trans-Atlantic steamer in New York six hours after leaving Washington, that the Philippine commissioners going to Paris should make it a point to see the President on the way, and the whole matter one of urgency, but it was certainly not too late to act.

The General said it had been thought a representative of the islands and of the cause of the people should go to Washington, but the man was in Hongkong. He could, however, be telegraphed, so that he could catch the China at Nagasaka, Japan, where she would have to stop two days to take coal. The Washington commissioner might go to Paris, but instructions could not reach him before he left Hongkong, as it would not be desirable to telegraph them. Upon this I stated if it suited his convenience and he would send instructions by me, I was going on the China, and would charge myself with the special confidential care of his dispatches and deliver them to the commissioner at the coaling station, when he should join the ship; and if it was the desire of the General to have it done I would telegraph the President that Philippine commissioners were on the way. These suggestions were received as if they were agreeable, and esteemed of value.

The conversation turned at this point to the main question of the future government of the Philippines, and I inquired what would be satisfactory to the General, and got, of course, the answer, "Philippine independence." But I said after the United States had sent a fleet and destroyed the Spanish fleet and an army in full possession of Manila she was a power that could not be ignored; and what would be thought of her assuming the prerogative of Protector? She could not escape responsibility. His views as to the exact line of demarkation or distinction between the rights of the United States and those of the people of the islands should be perfectly clear, for otherwise there would be confusion and possibly contention in greater matters than now caused friction.

I endeavored to indicate the idea that there might be an adjustment on the line that the people of the Philippines could manage their local matters in their own way, leaving to the United States imperial affairs, the things international and all that affected them, the Filipinos looking to the administration of localities. I had asked questions and stated propositions as if it were the universal consent that General Aguinaldo was the dictator for his people and had the executive word to say; but when it came to drawing the fine lines of his relations with the United States as the embodiment of a revolutionary movement, he became shy and referred to those who had to be consulted.

His words were equivalent to saying his counselors must, in all matters of moment, be introduced. It came to the same thing at last as to his commissioner or commissioners to Washington or Paris, one or both, and he also asserted the purpose of having the congress elected assemble at a railroad town—Moroles, about fifty miles north of Manila—a movement it is understood that is under the guidance of others than the General, the bottom fact being that if there should be a Philippine Republic Aguinaldo's place, in the judgment of many who are for it, would be not that of chief magistrate, but the head of the army. There are others and many of them of the opinion that he is not a qualified soldier. The congress assembled at Moroles, and has made slow progress.

It may as well be remembered, however, that the distinctions of civil and military power have been always hard to observe, in Central and South American states, whose early Spanish education has been outgrown gradually, and with halting and bloody steps. General Aguinaldo, then engaged in evolving a letter to General Merritt, has since issued proclamations that yield no share to the United States in the native government of the islands. But there are two things definitely known, as if decreed in official papers, and probably more so; that the Filipinos of influential intelligence would be satisfied with the direction of local affairs and gladly accept the protectorate of the United States on the terms which the people of the United States may desire and dictate.

The greater matter is that whenever it is the fixed policy of the United States to accept the full responsibility of ruling the Philippines, neither Aguinaldo nor any other man of the islands would have the ability to molest the steady, peaceable, beneficent development of the potentiality of our system of justice to the people, and the preservation by and through the popular will of the union of liberty under the law, and order maintained peaceably or forcibly according to needs.

In continuation of his explanation that he had to refer matters to others called his counselors, disclaiming the presumption in my questions of his personal responsibility for the conduct of the native insurrection, General Aguinaldo said with the greatest deliberation and the softest emphasis of any of his sayings, that the insurgents were already suspicious of him as one who was too close a friend of the Americans, and yielded too much to them, and that there was danger this feeling might grow and make way with his ability to do all that he would like in the way of keeping the peace. There were, he said, inquiries to the effect: What had the insurgents got for what they had done in the capture of Manila? Were they not treated by the Americans with indifference?

Major Bell interposed to say that the Americans were in the Philippines not as politicians, but as soldiers, and had the duty of preserving order by military occupation, and it was not possible there could be maintained a double military authority—two generals of equal powers in one city under martial law. There must be one master and no discussion. The United States could take no secondary attitude or position—would treat the insurgents with great consideration, but they of necessity were exclusively responsible for the carrying out of the provisions of the capitulation.

This was exactly to the point, and the interpreter cut his rendering of it, using but few words, and they did not cheer up the General and those about him. Evidently they want to know when and where they realize. It had been noticeable that the greater importance Aguinaldo attaches to what he is saying the lower his voice and the more certainly he speaks in a half whisper with parted lips, showin teeth and tongue; and he has a surprising faculty of talking with the tip of his tongue, extended a very little beyond his lips. There was something so reserved as to be furtive about his mouth, but his eyes were keen, straight and steady, showing decision, but guarding what he regarded the niceties of statement. However, his meaning that there were insurgents who were finding fault with him was not so much indicative of a rugged issue as a confession of impending inabilities.

He had nothing to say in response to Major Bell's explicit remark about the one-man and one-country military power, but the action of the insurgents in removing their headquarters—or their capital, as they call it—to a point forty miles from Manila, proves that they have come to an understanding that the soldiers of the United States are not in the Philippines for their health entirely, or purely in the interest of universal benevolence. The Filipinos must know, too, that they could never themselves have captured Manila. It is not inapt to say that the real center of the rebellion against Spain is, as it has been for years, at Hongkong.

I reserved what seemed the most interesting question of the interview with the Philippine leader to the last. It was whether a condition of pacification was the expulsion of the Catholic priests as a class. This was presented with reference to the threats that had been made in my hearing that the priests must go or die, for they were the breeders of all trouble. Must all of them be removed in some way or another? If not, where would the line be drawn? The lips of the General were parted and his voice quite low and gentle, the tongue to a remarkable degree doing the talking, as he replied, plainly picking words cautiously and measuring them. The able and acute interpreter dealt them out rapidly, and his rendering gave token that the Filipinos have already had lessons in diplomacy—even in the Spanish style of polite prevarication—or, if that may be a shade too strong, let us say elusive reservation—the use of language that is more shady than silence, the framing of phrases that may be interpreted so as not to close but to continue discussion and leave wide fields for controversy. The General did not refer to his counselors, or the congress that is in the background and advertised as if it were a new force.

The words of the interpreter for him were:

"The General says the priests to whom objection is made, and with whom we have a mortal quarrel, are not our own priests, but the Spaniards' and those of the orders. We respect the Catholic church. We respect our own priests, and, if they are friends of our country, will protect them. Our war is not upon the Catholic church, but upon the friars, who have been the most cruel enemies. We cannot have them here. They must go away. Let them go to Spain. We are willing that they may go to their own country. We do not want them. There is no peace until they go."

I said my information was that the objectionable Orders expressly proscribed by the insurgents were the Dominicans, Augustines, Franciscans and Recollects, but that the Jesuits were not included. This was fully recited to the General, and with his eyes closing and his mouth whispering close to the interpreter's cheek he gave his answer, and it was quickly rendered:

"The Jesuits, too, must go. They also are our enemies. We do not want them. They betray. They can go to Spain. They may be wanted there, not here; but not here, not here."

The question whether the friars must make choice between departure and death was not met directly, but with repetitions—that they might be at home in Spain, but

INTERVIEW WITH GEN. AGUINALDO. 59

could not be a part of the independent Philippines; and, significantly, they should be willing to go when wanted, and would be. Two Catholic priests—Americans, not Spaniards—were at this moment waiting in the ante room, to ask permission for the priests Aguinaldo has in prison to go back to Spain, and the General could not give an answer until he had consulted his council. Probably he would not dare to part with the priests, and an order from him would be disregarded. They have many chances of martyrdom, and some of them have already suffered mutilation.

Something had been said about my cabling the President as to the Filipinos' determination to send a representative to Paris, and I had tendered my good offices in bearing instructions to a commissioner from Hongkong to meet the China at Nagasaki, the Japanese railway station, where the American transports coal for their long voyage across the Pacific. But that matter had been left in the air. General Aguinaldo had said he would be obliged if I would telegraph the President, and I thought if the decision was that there was to be a Philippine representative hurried to Paris, it was something the President would be glad to know. I was aware there might be a difficulty in getting permission for a special messenger to go on the China to Japan to meet the commissioners going from Hongkong, and I would be willing to make the connection, as I had offered the suggestion. But it was necessary to be absolutely certain of General Aguinaldo's decision before I could cable the President; therefore, as I was, of course, in an official sense wholly irresponsible, I could communicate with him without an abrasion of military or other etiquette. It was the more needful, as it would be a personal proceeding, that I should be sure of the facts. Therefore I asked the General, whose time I had occupied more than an hour, whether he authorized me to telegraph the President that a commission was going to Paris, and desired me to render any aid in conveying information.

The General was troubled about the word "authorized," and instead of saying so concluded that I must have a deep and possibly dark design and so he could not give me the trouble to cable. The assurance that it would not be troublesome did not remove the disquiet. I could not be troubled, either, as a bearer of dispatches. The General could not authorize a telegram without consulting. In truth, the General had not made up his mind to be represented in Paris, holding that it would be sufficient to have an envoy extraordinary in Washington.

Others, without full consideration, in my opinion, concur in this view. I can imagine several situations at Paris in which a representative Filipino would be of service to the United States, simply by standing for the existence of a state of facts in the disputed islands. I dropped the matter of being a mediator, having planted the Paris idea in the mind of the Philippine leader, who is of the persuasion that he is the dictator of his countrymen, for the sake of his country, until he wishes to be evasive, and then he must consult others who share the burdens of authority, and told him when taking my leave I would like to possess a photograph with his autograph and the Philippine flag. In a few minutes the articles were in my hands, and passing out, there were the American priests in the ante-room, the next callers to enter the General's apartment. Their business was to urge him to permit the Catholic priests held as prisoners by the insurgents—more than 100, perhaps nearly 200 in number—to go home.

When the news came that General Merritt had been ordered to Paris, and would pass through the Red sea en route, taking the China to Hongkong to catch a peninsular and oriental steamer, I telegrahed the fact to General Aguinaldo over our military wires and his special wire, and his commissioner, duly advised, became, with General Merritt's aid, at Hongkong a passenger on the China.

He is well known to the world as Senor Filipe Agoncello, who visited Washington City, saw the President and proceeded to Paris.

CHAPTER V.

THE PHILIPPINE MISSION.

Correspondence With Aguinaldo About It—Notes by Senor Felipe Agoncillo—Relations Between Admiral Dewey and Senor Aguinaldo—Terms of Peace Made by Spanish Governor-General with Insurgents, December, 1897—Law Suit Between Aguinaldo and Artacho—Aguinaldo's Proclamation of May 24, 1898.

When General Merritt decided to hold the China for a day to take him to Hongkong on the way to Paris, I telegraphed Aguinaldo of the movements of the ship, and received this dispatch from the General:

"War Department, United States Volunteer Signal Corps, sent from Bakoor August 29, 1898.—To Mr. Murat Halstead, Hotel Oriente, Manila: Thankful for your announcing China's departure. We are to send a person by her if possible, whom I recommend to you. Being much obliged for the favor.

"A. G. ESCAMILLA,"
"Private Secretary to General Aguinaldo."

On the same day the General sent the following personal letter:

"Dear Sir: The bearer, Dr. G. Apacible, is the person whom was announced to you in the telegram.

"I am desirous of sending him to Hongkong, if possible, by the China, recommending him at the same time to your care and good will. Thanking you for the favor, I'm respectfully yours, EMILIO AGUINALDO Y FAMY.

"Mr. Murat Halstead, Manila.
"Bakoor, 29th August, 1898."

General Aguinaldo proceeded vigorously to make use of his knowledge that the China would go to Hongkong for General Merritt and sent his secretary and others to me at the Hotel Oriente, but they arrived after I had left the house. They came to the China and General Merritt had not arrived and did not appear until within a few minutes of the start. Then the deputation from the insurgent chieftain had an interview with him, asking that two of their number should go to Hongkong on the China to express fully the views of the insurgent government to to the commissioner, Don Felipe Agoncillo, chosen to represent the Filipinos at Washington and Paris and to ask that he be allowed to go to the United States on the China. When the committee saw General Merritt he was taking leave of Admiral

Dewey, and the General, who had not heard of this movement until that moment—the question being entirely new—invited the opinion of the Admiral, who said there was "certainly no objection," and on the contrary, it would be very well to permit the passage of the deputation to Hongkong and of the commissioner appointed from that city to Washington. General Merritt at once in half a dozen words gave the order, and the journey began.

General Greene, who reads and translates Spanish with facility and whose Spanish speech is plain, treated with marked courtesy the Filipino committee to Hongkong and thence the commissioner and his secretary from Hongkong to San Francisco, on the way to Washington and Paris. General Greene, while according distinction to the representatives of the insurgents, stated to them that his attentions were personal and he could not warrant them official recognition at Washington or anything more than such politeness as gentlemen receive from each other. The commissioner was Don Felipe Agoncillo, and his secretary, Sixto Lopez

Saturday, September 24, the Salt Lake newspapers contained stories to the effect that the Germans had entered into an alliance offensive and defensive with the Aguinaldo government and would furnish equipments for an army of 150,000 men. We were on the Union Pacific Railroad at the time, and I called the attention of Don Felipe Agoncillo to this remarkable intelligence and asked him what he thought of it. He said emphatically that it was "Nothing," "No true," "Nothing at all," and he laughed at the comic idea. There was also in the Salt Lake newspapers a statement that the Aguinaldo 'government' had sent to President McKinley a letter strongly expressing good-will and gratitude. There did not seem to be much news in this for Don Felipe, but it gave him much pleasure, and he, not perhaps diplomatically but enthusiastically, pronounced it good.

WHAT AGONCILLO APPROVED.

The dispatch marked with his approbation by the Philippine commissioner was the following from Washington, under date of September 23:

"The President doubtless would be glad to hear any views these Filipinos might care to set forth, being fresh from the islands and thoroughly acquainted with the wishes of the insurgents. But it would be plainly impolitic and inconsistent for the President, at this date and pending the conclusion of the peace conference at Paris, to allow it to be understood, by according a formal reception to the delegates, that he had thereby recognized the Philippine government as an independent nationality. His attitude toward the Filipinos would be similar to that assumed by him toward the Cubans. As the Filipinos have repeatedly, by public declaration, sought to convey the impression that the United States representatives in Manila have at some time during the progress of the war recognized Aguinaldo as an independent ally, and entered into formal co-operation with him, it may be stated that the government at Washington is unaware that any such thing has happened. Admiral Dewey, who was in command of all the United States forces during the most critical period, expressly cabled the Secretary of the Navy that he had entered into no formal agreement with Aguinaldo. If General Otis followed his instructions, and of that there can be no doubt, he also refrained from entering into any entangling agreements. As for Consul-General Wildman, any undertaking he may have assumed with Aguinaldo must have been upon his own personal and individual responsibility, and would be without formal standing, inasmuch as he has not the express authorization from the State Department absolutely requisite to negotiations in such cases. Therefore, as the case now stands, the peace commissioners are free to deal with the Philippine problem at Paris absolutely without restraint beyond that which might be supposed to rise from a sense of moral obligation to avoid committing the Filipinos again into the hands of their late rulers."

Senor Agoncillo, the commissioner of the Philippine insurgents at Paris, made, in conversations on the steamer China, when crossing the Pacific Ocean from Nagasaka to San Francisco, this statement in vindication of Aguinaldo, and it is the most complete, authoritative and careful that exists of the relations between Admiral Dewey and the insurgent leader:

BRIEF NOTES BY SENOR AGONCILLO.

"On the same day that Admiral Dewey arrived at Hongkong Senor Aguinaldo was in Singapore, whither he had gone from Hongkong, and Mr. Pratt, United States Consul-General, under instructions from the said Admiral, held a conference with him, in which it was agreed that Senor Aguinaldo and other revolutionary chiefs in co-operation with the American squadron should return to take up arms against the Spanish government of the Philippines, the sole and most laudable desire of the Washington government being to concede to the Philippine people absolute independence as soon as the victory against the Spanish arms should be obtained.

"By virtue of this argument Senor Aguinaldo proceeded by the first steamer to Hongkong for the express purpose of embarking on the Olympia and going to Manila; but this intention of his was not realized, because the American squadron left Hongkong the day previous to his arrival, Admiral Dewey having received from his government an order to proceed immediately to Manila. This is what Mr. Wildman, United States Consul-General in Hongkong, said to Senor Aguinaldo in the interview which took place between them. A few days after the Spanish squadron had been totally destroyed in the Bay of Manila by the American squadron, the latter obtaining a most glorious triumph, which deserved the fullest congratulations and praise of the Philippine public, the McCullough arrived at Hongkong and her commander said to Senor Aguinaldo that Admiral Dewey needed him (le necesitaba) in Manila and that he brought an order to take him on board said transport, as well as other revolutionary chiefs whose number should be determined by Senor Aguinaldo, and, in fact, he and seventeen chiefs went to Cavite on the McCullough.

"Senor Aguinaldo began his campaign against the Spaniards the very day that he received the 1,902 Mauser guns and 200,000 cartridgegs, which came from Hongkong. The first victory which he obtained from the Spaniards was the surrender or capitulation of the Spanish General, Senor Pena, who was the Military Governor of Cavite, had his headquarters in the town of San Francisco de Malabon, and his force was composed of 1,500 soldiers, including volunteers.

"The revolutionary army in six days' operations succeeded in getting possession of the Spanish detachments stationed in the villages of Bakoor, Imus, Benakayan, Noveleta, Santa Cruz de Malabon, Rosario and Cavite Viejo.

"On June 9 last the whole province of Cavite was under the control of the provisional revolutionary government, including many Spanish prisoners and friars, 7,000 guns, great quantities of ammunition and some cannon.

"At the same time that the province of Cavite was being conquered other revolutionary chiefs were carrying on campaigns in the Batangas, Laguna, Tayabas, Nueva Eciza, Bulcan, Batangas Pampanga and Morong, which were under control of the revolutionary army by June 12, and such progress was made by the Philippine revolution in the few days of campaign against the Spaniards that by August 3 last it held under conquest fifteen important provinces of the island of Luzon; these provinces are being governed by laws emanating from the provisional revolutionary government and in all of them perfect order and complete tranquility reign.

"It is to be noted that the Spanish government has sent to Senor Aguinaldo various emissaries, who invited him to make common cause with Spain against the United States, promising him that the government of the Spanish nation would concede to him anything he might ask for the Philippine people. But Senor Aguinaldo has invariably replied to those emissaries that it was too late and that he could not consider any proposition from the Spanish government, however beneficial it might be to the Philippines, because he had already pledged his word of honor in favor of certain representatives of the government at Washington.

"In view of this positive resolution of Senor Aguinaldo there began forthwith the intrigues of the Spanish enemy directed against the life of Senor Aguinaldo.

PEACE CONVENTION OF DECEMBER, 1896.

"Senor Aguinaldo, in his own name and in that of the other chiefs and subordinates, obligated himself to lay down their arms, which, according to an inventory, were to be turned over to the Spanish government, thus terminating the revolution. His Excellency the Governor and Captain-General, Don Fernando Primo de Rivera, as the representative of His Majesty's government in the Philippines, obligated himself on his side (1) to grant a general amnesty to all those under charges or sentenced for the crime of rebellion and sedition and other crimes of that category: (2) to introduce into the Philippines all reforms necessary for correcting in an effective and absolute manner the evils which for so many years had oppressed the country, in political and administrative affairs; and (3) an indemnity of $800,000, payable at the following dates: A letter of credit of the Spanish Filipine Bank for $400,000 against the Hongkong and Shanghai Bank in Hongkong was to be delivered to Senor Aguinaldo on the same day that he should leave Biak-va-Bato, where he had established his headquarters, and should embark on the steamer furnished by the Spanish government (this letter of credit was in point of fact delivered); $200,000 was to be paid to the said Senor Aguinaldo as soon as the revolutionary general, Senor Ricarte, should receive his telegram ordering him to give up his arms, with an inventory thereof, to the commissioner designated by his excellency the Governor and Captain-General, Don Fernando Primo de Rivera; and the remaining $200,000 should be due and payable when the peace should be a fact, and it should be understood that peace was a fact when the Te Deum should be sung by order of his excellency the Governor and Captain-General of the Philippines.

"Senor Aguinaldo complied in every respect, so far as he was concerned, with the peace agreement. But the Spanish government did not observe a similar conduct, and this has been deplored and still is deeply deplored by the Philippine people. The general amnesty which was promised has remained completely a dead letter. Many Filipinos are still to be found in Fernando Po and in various military prisons in Spain suffering the grievous consequences of the punishment inflicted upon them unjustly and the inclemencies of the climate to which they are not accustomed. Some of these unfortunates, who succeeded in getting out of those prisons and that exile, are living in beggary in Spain, without the government furnishing them the necessary means to enable them to return to the Philippines.

"In vain has the Philippine public waited for the reforms also promised. After the celebration of the compact of June, and the disposition of the arms of the revolutionists the Governor-General again began to inflict on the defenseless natives of the country arbitrary arrest and execution without judicial proceedings solely on the ground that they were merely suspected of being secessionists; proccedings which indisputably do not conform to the law and Christian sentiments.

"In the matter of reforms the religious orders again began to obtain from the Spanish government their former and absolute power. Thus Spain pays so dearly for her fatal errors in her own destiny!

"In exchange for the loftiness of mind with which Senor Aguinaldo has rigidly carried out the terms of the peace agreement, General Primo de Rivera had the cynicism to state in the congress of his nation that he had promised no reform to Senor Aguinaldo and his army, but that he had only given them a piece of bread in order that they might be able to maintain themselves abroad. This was re-echoed in the foreign press, and Senor Aguinaldo was accused in the Spanish press of having allowed himself to be bought with a handful of gold, selling out his country at the same time. There were published, moreover, in those Spanish periodicals caricatures of Senor Aguinaldo which profoundly wounded his honor and his patriotism.

"Senor Aguinaldo and the other revolutionists who reside in Hongkong agreed not to take out one cent of the $400,000 deposited in the chartered bank and the Hongkong and Shanghai Bank, the only amount which Senor Aguinaldo received from the Spanish government on account of the stipulated indemnity, but to use it for arms in order to carry on another revolution in the Philippines, in case the Spanish government should fail to carry out the peace agreement, at least in so far as it refers to general amnesty and reforms. All the above named revolutionists, Senor Aguinaldo setting the example, resolved to deny themselves every kind of comfort during their stay in Hongkong, living in the most modest style, for the purpose of preventing a reduction by one single cent of the above named sum of $400,000, which they set aside exclusively for the benefit of their country.

LAW SUIT BETWEEN DON J. ARTACHO AND DON E. AGUINALDO.

"Senor Artacho, induced by the father solicitor of the Dominicans and the Consul-General of Spain, filed in the courts of that colony a summons against Don E. Aguinaldo, asking for a division of the above-mentioned $400,000 between those revolutionary chiefs who resided in Hongkong. Artacho and three others, who joined the revolution in its last days and rendered little service to it, were the only ones who desired a division of this money; whereas forty-seven revolutionaries, many of whom were most distinguished chiefs, were opposed to it, supporting the resolution which Senor Aguinaldo had previously taken in regard to it. Senor Aguinaldo, in order to avoid all scandal, did everything possible to avoid appearing in court answering the summons of Artacho, who, realizing that his conduct had made himself hated by all Filipinos, agreed in a friendly arrangement to withdraw his suit, receiving in exchange $5,000; in this way were frustrated the intrigues of the solicitor of the Dominican order and of the Spanish Consul, who endeavored at any cost to destroy the $400,000 by dividing it up.

'Artacho is now on trial before a judicial court on charges preferred by various revolutionists for offenses which can be proved; he has no influence in the revolutionary party."

PROCLAMATION OF GENERAL AGUINALDO.
MAY 24TH, 1898.

Filipinos:

The Great Nation North America, cradle of true liberty and friendly on that account to the liberty of our people, oppressed and subjugated by the tyranny and despotism of those who have governed us, has come to manifest even here a protection which is decisive, as well as disinterested, towards us considering us endowed with sufficient civilization to govern by ourselves this our unhappy land. To maintain this so lofty idea, which we deserve from the now very powerful Nation North America, it is our duty to detest all those acts which belie such an idea, as pillage, robbery and every class of injury to persons as well as to things. With a view to avoiding international conflicts during the period of our campaign, I order as follows:

Article I. The lives and property of all foreigners, including Chinese and all Spaniards who either directly or indirectly have joined in taking arms against us are to be respected.

Article II. The lives and property of those who lay down their arms are also to be respected.

Article III. Also are to be respected all sanitary establishments and ambulances, and likewise the persons and things which may be found either in one or the other, including the assistants in this service, unless they show hostility.

Article IV. Those who disobey what is prescribed in the preceding articles will be tried by summary court and put to death, if such disobedience shall cause assassination, fire, robbery and violation.

Given at Cavite, the 24th of May, 1898.

EMILIO AGUINALDO.

It is to be remarked of this semi-official statement that Admiral Dewey did not make any promises he could not fulfill to Aguinaldo; did not assume to speak for the President or the army of the United States, but gave guns and ammunition to the insurgents, who aided him in maintaining a foothold on the shore. The insurgents did not win Dewey's victory, but aided to improve it. Without the aid of the American army Manila might have been destroyed, but could not have been captured intact. General Merritt settled the question of the status of the insurgent army with respect to the capture of Manila in a summary and sound way when he said there could be but one military authority in a military government, and as the commanding general of the Philippine expedition of the United States, he was that authority.

CHAPTER VI.

THE PROCLAMATIONS OF GENERAL AGUINALDO.

June 16th, 1898, Establishing Dictatorial Government—June 20th, 1898, Instructions for Elections—June 23d, 1898, Establishing Revolutionary Government—June 23d, 1898, Message to Foreign Powers—June 27th, 1898, Instructions Concerning Details—July 23d, 1898, Letter From Senor Aguinaldo to General Anderson—August 1st, 1898, Resolutions of Revolutionary Chiefs Asking for Recognition—August 6th, 1898, Message to Foreign Powers Asking Recognition.

One of the most critical questions in the situation of the Philippines is the precise position of the leader of the insurgents, General Aguinaldo. His utterances in his official character of leader of the natives who for years have been in rebellion against Spain, have been but fragmentary, as they have come before the people. We give for the public information the consecutive series of proclamations.

No. 1.

To the Philippine Public:

Circumstances have providentially placed me in a position for which I can not fail to recognize that I am not properly qualified, but since I can not violate the laws of Providence nor decline the obligations which honor and patriotism impose upon me, I now salute you, Oh, My Beloved People!

I have proclaimed in the face of the whole world that the aspiration of my whole life, the final object of all my efforts and strength is nothing else but your independence, for I am firmly convinced that that constitutes your constant desire and that independence signifies for us redemption from slavery and tyranny, regaining our liberty and entrance into the concert of civilized nations.

I understand on the other hand that the first duty of every government is to interpret faithfully popular aspirations. With this motive, although the abnormal circumstances of the war have compelled me to institute this Dictatorial Government which assumes full powers, both civil and military, my constant desire is to surround myself with the most distinguished persons of each Province, those who by their conduct, deserve the confidence of their province to the end that the true necessities of each being known by them, measures may be adopted to meet these necessities and apply the remedies in accordance with the desires of all.

I understand moreover the urgent necessity of establishing in each town a solid and robust organization, the strongest bulwark of public security and the sole means of securing that union and discipline which are indispensable for the establishment of the Republic, that is Government of the people for the people, and warding off the international conflicts which may arise.

Following out the foregoing considerations I decree as follows:

Article I. The inhabitants of every town where the forces of the Spanish government still remain, will decide upon the most efficacious measures to combat and destroy them, according to the resources and means at their disposal, according to prisoners of war the treatment most conformable to humanitarian sentiments and to the customs observed by civilized nations.

Article II. As soon as the town is freed from Spanish domination, the inhabitants most distinguished for high character, social position and honorable conduct both in the center of the community and in the suburbs, will come together in a large meeting in which they will proceed to elect by a majority of votes, the chief of the town and a head man for each suburb, considering as suburbs not only those hitherto known as such, but also the center of the community.

All those inhabitants who fulfill the conditions above named, will have the right to take part in this meeting and to be elected, provided always that they are friendly to Philippine independence and are twenty years of age.

Article III. In this meeting shall also be elected by a majority of votes, three delegates; one of police and internal order, another of justice and civil registry and another of taxes and property.

The delegate of police and internal order will assist the Chief in the organization of the armed force, which for its own security each town must maintain, according to the measure of its resources and in the preservation of order, government and hygiene of its population.

The delegate of justice and civil registry will aid the Chief in the formation of courts and in keeping books of registry of births, deaths and marriage contracts, and of the census.

The delegate of taxes and property will aid the chief in the collection of taxes, the administration of public funds, the opening of books of registry of cattle and real property, and in all work relating to encouragement of every class of industry.

Article IV. The Chief, as President, with the head men and the above mentioned delegates, will constitute the popular assemblies who will supervise the exact fulfillment of the laws in force and the particular interests of each town.

The head man of the center of the community will be the Vice President of the assembly, and the delegate of justice its secretary.

The head men will be delegates of the Chief within their respective boundaries.

Article V. The Chiefs of each town after consulting the opinion of their respective assemblies, will meet and elect by majority of votes the Chief of the Province and three councilors for the three branches above mentioned.

The Chief of the Province as President, the Chief of the town which is the capital of the Province, as Vice President, and the above named councilors will constitute the Provincial Council, which will supervise the carrying out of the instructions of this government in the territory of the Province, and for the general interest of the Province, and will propose to this government the measures which should be adopted for the general welfare.

Article VI. The above named chiefs will also elect by majority of votes three representatives for each one of the Provinces of Manila and Cavite, two for each one of the Provinces classified as terminal in Spanish legislation, and one for each one of the other Provinces and Politico-Military commands of the Philippine Archipelago.

The above named representatives will guard the general interests of the Archipelago and the particular interests of their respective Provinces, and will constitute the Revolutionary Congress, which will propose to this government the measures concerning the preservation of internal order, and external security of these islands, and will be heard by this government on all questions of grave importance. The decision of which will admit of delay or adjournment.

Article VII. Persons elected to any office whatsoever in the form prescribed in the preceding article can not perform the functions of the same without the previous confirmation by this government, which will give it in accordance with the certificates of election.

Representatives will establish their identity by exhibiting the above named certificates.

Article VIII. The Military Chiefs named by this government in each Province will not intervene in the government and administration of the Province, but will confine themselves to requesting of the Chiefs of Provinces and towns the aid which may be necessary both in men and resources, which are not to be refused in case of actual necessity.

Nevertheless, when the Province is threatened or occupied by the enemy in whole or in part, the military chief of highest rank therein may assume powers of the Chief of the Province, until the danger has disappeared.

Article IX. The government will name for each Province a commissioner, specially charged with establishing therein the organization prescribed in this decree, in accordance with instructions which this government will communicate to him.

Those military chiefs who liberate the towns from the Spanish domination are commissioners by virtue of their office.

The above named commissioners will preside over the first meetings held in each town and in each Province.

Article X. As soon as the organization provided in the decree has been established all previous appointments to any civil office, whatsoever, no matter what their origin or source, shall be null and void, and all instructions in conflict with the foregoing are hereby annulled.

Given at Cavite, the 18th of June, 1898.

EMILIO AGUINALDO.

No. 2.

For the execution and proper carrying out of what is prescribed in the decree of this government concerning the management of the Provinces and towns of the Philippine Archipelago, I decree as follows:

INSTRUCTIONS.

Concerning the Management of the Provinces and towns.

(Then follow 45 rules concerning the elections, formation of the police, the courts and the levying and collection of taxes.)

Given at Cavite, 20th of June, 1898.

EMILIO AGUINALDO.

No. 3.

DON EMILIO AGUINALDO Y FAMY,

President of the Revolutionary Government of the Philippines, and General in Chief of Its Army.

This government desiring to demonstrate to the Philippine people that one of its ends is to combat with a firm hand the inveterate vices of the Spanish administration, substituting for personal luxury and that pompous ostentation which have made it a mere matter of routine, cumbrous and slow in its movements, another administration more modest, simple and prompt in performing the public service: I decree as follows:

CHAPTER I.

OF THE REVOLUTIONARY GOVERNMENT.

Article I. The dictatorial government will be entitled hereafter the revolutionary government, whose object is to struggle for the independence of the Philippines until all nations, including the Spanish, shall expressly recognize it, and to prepare the country so that a true republic may be established.

The dictator will be entitled hereafter President of the Revolutionary Government.

Article II. Four secretaryships of government are created; one of foreign affairs, navy and commerce; another of war and public works; another of police and internal order, justice, education and hygiene; and another of finance, agriculture, and manufacturing industry.

The government may increase this number of secretaryships, when it shall find in practice that this distribution is not sufficient for the multiplied and complicated necessities of the public service.

Article III. Each secretaryship shall aid the President in the administration of questions concerning the different branches which it comprises.

At the head of each one shall be a secretary who shall not be responsible for the decrees of the Presidency, but shall sign them with the President, to give them authority.

But if it shall appear that the decree has been promulgated on the proposition of the secretary of the department, the latter shall be responsible conjointly with the President.

Article IV. The secretaryship of foreign affairs will be divided into three bureaus, one of diplomacy, another of navy and another of commerce.

The first bureau will study and dispose of all questions pertaining to the management of diplomatic negotiations with other powers and the correspondence of this government with them. The second will study all questions relating to the formation and organization of our navy and the fitting out of such expeditions as the necessities of the revolution may require; and the third will have charge of everything relating to internal and external commerce, and the preliminary work which may be necessary for making treaties of commerce with other nations.

Article V. The secretaryship of war will be divided into two bureaus; one of war, properly speaking, and the other of public works.

The first bureau will be subdivided into four sections: One of campaigns, another of military justice, another of military administration, and another of military health.

The section of campaigns will have charge of the appointment and formation of the certificates of enlistment and service of all who serve in the revolutionary militia; of the direction of campaigns; the preparation of plans, works of fortification, and preparing reports of battles; of the study of military tactics for the army and the organization of the general staff, artillery and cavalry; and finally, of the determination of all other questions concerning the business of campaigns and military operations.

The section of military justice will have charge of everything relating to courts of war and military tribunals; the appointment of judges and counsel and the determination of all questions of military justice; the section of military administration will be charged with the furnishing of food and other supplies necessary for the use of the army; and the section of military health will have charge of everything relating to the hygiene and healthfulness of the militia.

Article VI. The other secretaryships will be divided into such bureaus as their branches may require and each bureau will be subdivided into sections according to the nature and importance of the work it has to do.

Article VII. The secretary will inspect and supervise all the work of his secretaryship and will determine all questions with the President of the government.

At the head of each bureau will be a director and in each section an officer provided with such number of assistants as may be specified.

Article VIII. The President will appoint the secretaries of his own free choice and in concert with them will appoint all the subordinate officials of each secretaryship.

In order that in the choice of persons it may be possible to avoid favoritism, it must be fully understood that the good name of the country and the triumph of the revolution require the services of persons truly capable.

Article IX. The secretaries may be present at the revolutionary congress in order that they may make any motion in the name of the President or may be interpolated publicly by any one of the representatives; but when the question which is the object of the motion shall be put to vote or after the interpolation is ended they shall leave and shall not take part in the vote.

Article X. The President of the government is the personification of the Philippine people, and in accordance with this idea it shall not be possible to hold him responsible while he fills the office.

His term of office shall last until the revolution triumphs, unless, under extraordinary circumstances, he shall feel obliged to offer his resignation to congress, in which case congress will elect whomsoever it considers most fit.

CHAPTER II.

OF THE REVOLUTIONARY CONGRESS.

Article XI. The Revolutionary Congress is the body of representatives of the Provinces of the Philippine Archipelago elected in the manner prescribed in the decrees of the 18th, present month.

Nevertheless, if any Province shall not be able as yet to elect representatives because the greater part of its towns shall have not yet succeeded in liberating themselves from Spanish domination, the government shall have power to appoint as provisional representatives for this Province those persons who are most distinguished for high character and social position, in such numbers as are prescribed by the above named decree, provided always that they are natives of the Province which they represent or have resided therein for a long time.

Article XII. The representatives having met in the town which is the seat of the revolutionary government, and in the building which may be designated, will proceed to its preliminary labors, designating by plurality of votes a commission composed of five individuals charged with examining documents accrediting each representative, and another commission, composed of three individuals, who will examine the documents which the five of the former commission exhibit.

Article XIII. On the following day the above named representatives will meet again and the two commissions will read their respective reports concerning the legality of the said documents, deciding by an absolute majority of votes on the character of those which appear doubtful.

This business completed, it will proceed to designate, also by absolute majority, a President, a Vice President, and two secretaries, who shall be chosen from among the representatives, whereupon the congress shall be considered organized, and shall notify the government of the result of the election.

Article XIV. The place where congress deliberates is sacred and inviolable, and no armed force shall enter therein unless the President thereof shall ask therefor in order to establish internal order disturbed by those who can neither honor themselves nor its august functions.

Article XV. The powers of congress are: To watch over the general interest of the Philippine people, and the carrying out of the revolutionary laws; to discuss and vote upon said laws; to discuss and approve prior to their ratification treaties and loans; to examine and approve the accounts presented annually by the secretary of finance, as well as extraordinary and other taxes which may hereafter be imposed.

Article XVI. Congress shall also be consulted in all grave and important questions, the determination of which admits of delay or adjournment; but the President of the government shall have power to decide questions of urgent character, but in that case he shall give account by message to said body of the decision which he has adopted.

Article XVII. Every representative shall have power to present to congress any project of a law, and every secretary on the order of the President of the government shall have similar power.

Article XVIII. The sessions of congress shall be public, and only in cases which require reserve shall it have power to hold a secret session.

Article XIX. In the order of its deliberations, as well as in the internal government of the body the instructions which shall be formulated by the congress itself shall be observed. The President shall direct the deliberations and shall not vote except in case of a tie, when he shall have the casting vote.

Article XX. The President of the government shall not have power to interrupt in any manner the meeting of congress, nor embarrass its sessions.

Article XXI. The congress shall designate a permanent commission of justice which shall be presided over by the auxilliary vice president or each of the secretaries, and shall be composed of those persons and seven members elected by plurality of votes from among the representatives.

This commission shall judge on appeal the criminal cases tried by the Provincial courts; and shall take cognizance of and have original jurisdiction in all cases against the secretaries of the government, the chiefs of Provinces and towns, and the Provincial judges.

Article XXII. In the office of the secretary of congress shall be kept a book of honor, wherein shall be recorded special services rendered to the country, and considered as such by said body. Every Philippino, whether in the military or civil service, may petition congress for notation in said book, presenting duly accredited documents describing the service rendered by him on behalf of the country, since the beginning of the present revolution. For extraordinary services, which may be rendered hereafter, the government will propose said notation accompanying the proposal with the necessary documents justifying it.

Article XXIII. The congress will also grant, on the proposal of the government rewards in money, which can be given only once to the families of those who were victims of their duty and patriotism, as a result of extraordinary acts of heroism.

Article XXIV. The acts of congress shall not take effect until the President of the government orders their fulfillment and execution. Whenever the said

President shall be of the opinion that any act is unsuitable or against public policy, or pernicious, he shall explain to congress the reasons against its execution, and if the latter shall insist on its passage the President shall have power to oppose his veto under his most rigid responsibility.

CHAPTER III.

OF MILITARY COURTS AND JUSTICE.

Article XXV. When the chiefs of military detachments have notice that any soldier has committed or has perpetrated any act of those commonly considered as military crimes, he shall bring it to the knowledge of the commandant of the Zone, who shall appoint a judge and a secretary, who shall begin suit in the form prescribed in the instructions dated the 20th of the present month. If the accused shall be of the grade of lieutenant or higher, the said commandant shall himself be the judge, and if the latter shall be the accused, the senior commandant of the Province shall name as judge an officer who holds a higher grade, unless the same senior commandant shall himself have brought the suit. The judge shall always belong to the class of chiefs.

Article XXVI. On the conclusion of the preliminary hearing, the senior commandant shall designate three officers of equal or higher rank to the judge and the military court shall consist of the said officers, the judge, the councilor and the President. The latter shall be the commandant of the Zone, if the accused be of the grade of sergeant or less, and the senior commandant if he be of the grade of lieutenant or higher. This court shall conduct the trial in the form customary in the Provincial courts, but the judgment shall be appealable to the higher courts of war.

Article XXVII. The superior court shall be composed of six members, who shall hold rank not less than brigadier generals, and the judge advocate. If the number of generals present in the capitol of the revolutionary government shall not be sufficient the deficiency shall be supplied by representatives designated and commissioned by congress. The president of the court shall be the general having the highest rank of all, and should there be more than one having equal rank, the president shall be elected from among them by absolute majority of votes.

Article XXVIII. The superior court shall have jurisdiction in all cases affecting the higher commandants, the commandants of Zones and all officers of the rank of major or higher.

Article XXIX. Commit Military Crimes: 1st. Those who fail to grant the necessary protection to foreigners, both in their persons and property, and those who similarly fail to afford protection to hospitals and ambulances, including persons and effects which may be found in possession of one or the other, and those engaged in the service of the same, provided always they commit no hostile act. 2d. Those who fail in the respect due to the lives, money and jewels of enemies who lay down their arms, and of prisoners of war. 3d. Filipinos who place themselves in the service of the enemy acting as spies or disclosing to them secrets of war and the plans of revolutionary positions and fortifications, and those who present themselves under a flag of truce without justifying properly their office and their personality; and 4th, those who fail to recognize a flag of truce duly accredited in the forms prescribed by international law.

Will Commit also Military Crimes: 1st. Those who conspire against the unity of the revolutionists, provoking rivalry between chiefs and forming divisions and armed bands. 2d. Those who solicit contributions without authority of the government and misappropriate the public funds. 3d. Those who desert to the enemy, or are guilty of cowardice in the presence of the enemy, being armed; and, 4th, those who seize the property of any person who has done no wrong to the revolution, violate women and assassinate or inflict serious wounds on unarmed persons and commit robberies or arson.

Article XXX. Those who commit the crimes enumerated will be considered as declared enemies of the revolution, and will incur the penalties prescribed in the Spanish penal code, and in the highest grade.

If the crime shall not be found in the said code, the offender shall be imprisoned until the revolution triumphs unless the result of this shall be an irreparable damage, which in the judgment of the tribunal shall be a sufficient cause for imposing the penalty of death.

ADDITIONAL CLAUSES.

The government will establish abroad a revolutionary committee, composed of a number not yet determined of persons most competent in the Philippine Archipelago. This committee will be divided into three delegations; one of diplomacy, another of the navy and another of the army.

The delegation of diplomacy will manage and conduct negotiations with foreign cabinets with a view to the recognition of the belligerency and independence of the Philippines.

The delegation of the navy will be charged with studying and organizing the Philippine navy and preparing the expenditures which the necessities of the revolution may require.

The delegation of the army will study military tactics and the best form of organization for the general staff, artillery and engineers and whatever else may be necessary in order to fit out the Philippine Army under the conditions required by modern progress.

Article XXXII. The government will issue the necessary instructions for the proper execution of the present decree.

Article XXXIII. All decrees of the dictatorial government in conflict with the foregoing are hereby annulled.

Given at Cavite, the 23d of June, 1898.

EMILIO AGUINALDO.

INSTRUCTIONS.

Desiring to bring about a proper execution of the decree dated the 23d of the present month, and to provide that the administrative measures shall not result hereafter in the paralysis of public business, but that, on the contrary, it shall constitute the best guarantee of the regularity, promptitude and fitness in the transaction of public business, I give the following instructions and decree:

(Then follow ten rules concerning the details of installing the government.)

Cavite, the 27th of June, 1898.

EMILIO AGUINALDO.

MESSAGE OF THE PRESIDENT OF THE PHILIPPINE REVOLUTION.

If it is true, as it is true, that political revolutions properly understood, are the violent means which people employ to recover the sovereignty which naturally belongs to them, usurped and trampled upon by a tyrannical and arbitrary government. no revolution can be more righteous than that of the Philippines, because the people have had recourse to it after having exhausted all the pacific means which reason and experience could suggest.

The ancient Kings of Castile felt obliged to consider the Philippines as a brother people, united to the Spanish in a perfect participation of aims and interests, so much so that when the Constitution of 1812 was promulgated, at Cadiz, on account of the War of Spanish Independence, these islands were represented in the Spanish Cortez; but the interests of the Monastic corporations which have always found unconditional support in the Spanish Government, overcame this sacred duty and the Philippines remained excluded from the Spanish Constitution, and the people at the mercy of the discretionary or arbitrary powers of the Governor-General.

In this condition the people claimed justice, begged of the metropolis the recognition and restitution of their secular rights by means of reforms which should assimilate in a gradual and progressive manner, the Philippines to the Spaniards; but their voice was quickly throttled and their sons received as the reward of their self-denial, deportation, martyrdom and death. The religious corporations with whose interests, always opposed to those of the Philippine people, the Spanish Government has been identified, scoffed at these pretensions and answered with the knowledge of that Government that Spanish liberties have cost blood.

What other recourse then remained to the people for insisting as in duty bound on regaining its former rights? No alternative remained except force and, convinced of that, it has had recourse to revolution.

And now it is not limited to asking assimilation to the Spanish Political Constitution, but it asks a definite separation from it; it struggles for its independence in the firm belief that the time has arrived in which it can and ought to govern itself.

There has been established a Revolutionary Government, under wise and just laws, suited to the abnormal circumstances through which it is passing, and which, in proper time, will prepare it for a true Republic. Thus taking as a sole model for its acts, reason, for its sole end, justice, and, for its sole means, honorable labor, it calls all Philippinos its sons without distinction of class, and invites them to unite firmly with the object of forming a noble society, not based upon blood nor pompous titles, but upon the work and personal merit of each one; a free society, where exist neither egotism nor personal politics which annihilate and crush, neither envy nor favoritism which debase, neither fanfaronade nor charlatanism which are ridiculous.

And it could not be otherwise. A people which has given proofs of suffering and valor in tribulation and in danger, and of hard work and study in peace, is not destined to slavery; this people is called to be great, to be one of the strongest arms of Providence in ruling the destinies of mankind; this people has resources and energy sufficient to liberate itself from the ruin and extinction into which the Spanish Government has plunged it, and to claim a modest but worthy place in the concert of free nations.

Given at Cavite the 23d of June, 1898.

EMILIO AGUINALDO.

TO FOREIGN GOVERNMENTS.

The Revolutionary Government of the Philippines, on its establishment, explained, through the message dated the 23d of June last, the true causes of the Philippine Revolution, showing, according to the evidence, that this popular movement is the result of the laws which regulate the life of a people which aspires to progress and to perfection by the sole road of liberty.

The said Revolution now rules in the Provinces of Cavite, Batangas, Mindoro, Tayabas, Laguna, Morong, Bulacan, Bataan, Pampanga, Neuva-Ecija, Tarlac, Pangasinan, Union, Infanta, and Zambales, and it holds besieged the capital of Manila.

In these Provinces complete order and perfect tranquility reign, administered by the authorities elected by the Provinces in accordance with the organic decrees dated the 18th and 23d of June last.

The Revolution holds, moreover, about 9,000 prisoners of war, who are treated in accordance with the customs of war between civilized nations and humane sentiments, and at the end of the war it has more than 30,000 combatants organized in the form of a regular army.

In this situation the chiefs of the towns comprised in the above mentioned Provinces, interpreting the sentiments which animate those who have elected them, have proclaimed the Independence of the Philippines, petitioning the Revolutionary Government that will entreat and obtain from foreign Governments recognition of its belligerency and its independence, in the firm belief that the Philippine people have already arrived at that state in which they can and ought to govern themselves.

This is set forth in the accompanying documents, subscribed by the above named chiefs.

Wherefore, the undersigned, by virtue of the powers which belong to him as President of the Revolutionary Government of the Philippines and in the name and representation of the Philippine people, asks the support of all the powers of the civilized world, and earnestly entreats them to proceed to the formal recognition of the belligerency of the Revolution and the Independence of the Philippines; since they are the means designated by Providence to maintain the equilibrium between peoples, sustaining the weak and restraining the strong, to the end that by these means shall shine forth and be realized the most complete justice in the indefinite progress of humanity.

Given at Bacoor, in the Province of Cavite, the 6th day of August, 1898.

The President of the Revolutionary Government,

EMILIO AGUINALDO.

STATEMENT.

The undersigned chiefs of towns comprising the Provinces hereinafter named, elected as such in the manner prescribed by the decree of the 18th and the instructions dated the 20th of June last, after having been confirmed in their respective offices by the President of the Government and having taken the prescribed oath before him, have met in full assembly previously called for that purpose for the purpose of discussing the solemn proclamation of Philippine independence.

The discussion took place with the prudence and at the length which so important a question demands and, after suitable deliberation, the following declarations were unanimously adopted:

The Philippine Revolution records on the one hand brilliant feats of arms, realized with singular courage by an improvised army almost without arms, and on the other the no less notable fact that the people, after the combat, have not entered upon great excesses nor pursued the enemy further; but have treated him, on the contrary, with generosity and humanity, returning at once to their ordinary and tranquil life.

Such deeds demonstrate, in an indisputable manner, that the Philippine people was not created, as all believed, for the sole purpose of dragging the chains of servitude, but that it has a perfect idea of order and justice, shuns a savage life, and loves a civilized life.

But what is most surprising in this people is that it goes on giving proofs that it knows how to frame laws, commensurate with the progress of the age, to respect them and obey them, demonstrating that its national customs are not repugnant to this progress; that it is not ambitious for power nor honors nor riches aside from the rational and just aspirations for a free and independent life, and inspired by the most lofty idea of patriotism and national honor; and that in the service of this idea and for the realization of that aspiration it has not hesitated in the sacrifice of life and fortune.

These admirable—and more than admirable, these wonderful—deeds necessarily engender the most firm and ineradicable convictions of the necessity of leaving the Philippines free and independent, not only because they deserve it, but because they are prepared to defend, to the death, their future and their history.

Filipinos are fully convinced that if individuals have need of material, moral and intellectual perfection in order to contribute to the welfare of their fellows. peoples require to have fullness of life; they need liberty and independence in order to contribute to the indefinite progress of mankind. It has struggled and will struggle, with decision and constancy, without ever turning back or retrograding before the obstacles which may arise in its path, and with unshakable faith that it will obtain justice and fulfill the laws of Providence.

And neither will it be turned aside from the course it has hitherto followed by the unjustifiable imprisonment, tortures, assassinations, and the other vandal acts committed by the Spaniards against the persons of peaceful and defenseless Filipinos. The Spaniards believe themselves released from every legal obligation toward the Filipinos for the sole reason that the belligerency of the Revolution has not been recognized, taking no account of the fact that over and above every law, whether written or prescriptive, are placed with imprescriptible characters, culture, national honor and humanity. No; the Filipinos have no need ever to make use of reprisals because they seek independence with culture, liberty with unconditional respect for the law, as the organ of justice, and a name purified in the crucible of human sentiments.

In virtue of the foregoing considerations the undersigned, giving voice to the unanimous aspiration of the people whom they represent, and performing the offices received from them and the duties pertaining to the powers with which they are invested,

Proclaim solemnly in the face of the whole world the Independence of the Philippines;

Recognize and respect Senor Don Emilio Aguinaldo y Famy as President of the Revolutionary Government, organized in the manner prescribed by decree of the 23d and instructions of the 27th of June last, and beg the said President that he will ask and obtain from foreign Governments the recognition of its belligerency and independence, not only because this act constitutes a duty of justice, but also because to no one is it permitted to contravene natural laws nor stifle the legitimate aspiration of a people for its amelioration and dignification.

Given in the Province of Cavite the 1st day of August, of the year of our Lord 1898, and the first year of Philippine independence.

Follow the signatures of the local Presidents of the Provinces of Cavite and many others.

The undersigned, Secretary of the Interior, certifies, That the present document is a literal copy of the original, which is deposited in the Secretaryship under his charge; in proof of which he signs it, with the approval of the President of the Revolutionary Government in Bacoor, the 6th day of August, 1898.

El Presidente del G. R.,
EMILIO AGUINALDO.
El Secretano del Interior,
LEANDRO IBARRA.

LETTER FROM SEÑOR AGUINALDO TO GENERAL ANDERSON.

July 23d, 1898.

To Brigadier-General T. M. Anderson, U. S. A., etc., etc., Cavite.

In answer to the letter of your Excellency dated the 22nd of the present month, I have the honor to manifest to you the following:

That even supposing that the effects existing in the storehouse of Don Antonio Osorio were subject to capture, when I established myself in the plaza (town) of Cavite, Admiral Dewey authorized me to dispose of everything that I might find in the same, including the arms which the Spanish left in the arsenal. But as he was aware that said effects belonged to the personal property (ownership) of a Filipino, who traded with them by virtue of a contribution to the Spanish Government, I would not have touched them had not the owner placed them at my disposition for the purposes of the war.

I came from Hong Kong to prevent my countrymen from making common cause with the Spanish against the North Americans, pledging, before, my word to Admiral Dewey to not give place to (to allow) any internal discord because (being) a judge of their desires I had the strong conviction that I would succeed in both objects; establishing a government according to their desires.

Thus it is that at the beginning I proclaimed the dictatorship, and afterwards, when some of the Provinces had already liberated themselves from Spanish domination, I established a revolutionary government that to-day exists, giving it a democratic and popular character, as far as the abnormal circumstances of war permitted, in order that they (the Provinces) might be justly represented and administered to their satisfaction.

It is true that my government has not been acknowledged by any of the foreign powers; but we expect that the great North American nation, which struggled first for its independence and afterwards for the abolition of slavery, and is now actually struggling for the independence of Cuba, would look upon it with greater benevolence than any other nation. Because of this we have always acknowledged the right of preference as to our gratitude.

Debtor to the generosity of the North Americans, and to the favors which we have received through Admiral Dewey, and being more desirous than any other of preventing any conflict which would have as a result foreign intervention which must be extremely prejudicial not alone to my nation, but also to that of Your Excellency, I consider it my duty to advise you of the undesirability of disembarking North American troops in the places conquered by the Filipinos from the

Spanish, without previous notice to this government, because as no formal agreement yet exists between the two nations, the Philippine people might consider the occupation of its territories by North American troops as a violation of its rights.

I comprehend that without the destruction of the Spanish squadron the Philippine revolution would not have advanced so rapidly; because of this I take the liberty of indicating to Your Excellency the necessities that before disembarking troops you should communicate in writing to this government the places that are to be occupied, and also the object of the occupation, that the people may be advised in due form and (thus) prevent the commission of any transgression against friendship. I can answer for my people, because they have given me evident proofs of their absolute confidence in my government, but I cannot answer for that which another nation, whose friendship is not well guaranteed, might inspire in it (the people); and it is certain that I do this not as a menace, but as a further proof of the true and sincere friendship which I have always professed to the North American people in the complete security that it will find itself completely identified with our cause of liberty.

I am, with respect,   Your obedient servant,
                                                  EMILIO AGUINALDO.

CHAPTER VII.

INTERVIEW WITH THE ARCHBISHOP OF MANILA.

Insurgents' Deadly Hostility to Spanish Priests—The Position of the Archbishop as He Defined It—His Expression of Gratitude to the American Army—His Characterization of the Insurgents—A Work of Philippine Art—The Sincerity of the Archbishop's Good Words.

The intense feeling by the Philippine insurgents against the Spanish priests made it seem very desirable to see the Archbishop of Manila, and he informed two American priests that he would have pleasure in making an expression of his views to me to be placed before the people of the United States. He had been charged with extreme vindictiveness and the responsibility of demanding that the city should be defended to the last extremity, when actually, in the consultation of dignitaries that took place, and the surrender of the capital was demanded by Generall Merritt and Admiral Dewey, he declared the situation hopeless and that it was a plain duty to prevent the sacrifice of life. He was overruled by the peculiar folly that has caused Spain in the course of the war to inflict heavy and avoidable losses upon herself. Indeed, the war originated in the Spanish state of mind that it was necessary to open fire and shed blood for the honor of the arms of Spain. The Spanish officers knew they could not save Manila from the hands of the Americans while the command of the sea by our fleet was indisputable and we had unlimited reserves to draw upon to strengthen the land forces, irrespective of the swarms of insurgents pressing in the rear and eager to take vengeance for centuries of mismanagement and countless personal grievances. It was the acknowledgment of the Spanish Captain-General, when he received the peremptory summons from Merritt and Dewey to give up the city, that there was no place of refuge for the women and children, the sick and the wounded; and yet it was insisted that the honor of Spain required bloodshed—not much, perhaps, but enough to prove that the army of Spain was warlike. When the American army had been reinforced so as to have 8,000 men ready to take the field, General Merritt and Admiral Dewey had a conference and agreed to send the Spaniards in authority a formal notification that in forty-eight hours they would bombard and assail the defenses of the city of Manila if it were not surrendered. The Spanish reply was that the Americans could commence operations at once, but there was no place where the women and children, the wounded and the sick could go to find a place of security. This was tantamount to a declaration that the Spaniards were sliding into a surrender, but wanted to make a claim to the contrary.

The residence of the Archbishop is within the walled city and a very substantial edifice, the stone work confined to the lower story and hardwood timber freely used in massive form instead of stone. His grace was seated at a small table in a broad hall, with a lamp and writing material before him. He is imposing as a man of importance and his greeting was cordial to kindliness. He said his acknowledgments were personally due the American people for the peace of mind he had enjoyed during the occupation of the city by the army of the United States, for its establishment of order and the justice in administration that relieved good citizens from oppression and alarm. He was glad to have Americans know his sensibility on this subject, and wanted me to convey his sentiments to the President.

When asked what it was that caused the insurgents to be so ferocious against the priests and resolved on their expulsion or destruction he said the rebels were at once false, unjust and ungrateful. They had been lifted from savagery by Catholic teachers, who had not only been educators in the schools but teachers in the fields. The same Catholic Orders that were singled out for special punishment had planted in the islands the very industries that were sources of prosperity, and the leaders of the insurgents had been largely educated by the very men whom now they persecuted. Some of the persecutors had been in Europe and became revolutionists in the sense of promoting disorder as anarchists. It was the antagonism of the church to murderous anarchy that aroused the insurgents of the Philippines to become the deadly enemies of priests and church orders. It was true in Spain, as in the Philippines, that the anarchists were particularly inflamed against the church. His grace did not seem to have heard of the American anarchist, but the European revolutionist has received a large share of his attention.

He produced a box of cigars, also a bottle of sherry, and chatted comfortably and humorously. There was one thing then that he had in his heart—that his anxiety for peace and appreciation of order as enjoyed under the American military government should be recorded and responsibly reported to the people of the United States. The American priests had informed him that I was a friend of long standing of President McKinley, and he again enjoined that I should declare his sentiments to the President. A beautiful work of wood carving was shown on an easel, which had a frame of hard wood, the whole, easel and frame, with elaborately wrought ornamentation, cut out of one tree. It was at once strong and graceful, simple and decorative. The picture was a gold medallion, raised on a plate of silver, an excellent likeness of his grace. It was evident that the refinements of art were known to "these barbarians of the Philippines," for their works testified.

His grace announced that he would return my call, and his convenience being consulted, the time was fixed for him to appear at 11 o'clock the next day, Sunday, and he came accordingly, accompanied by three priests, the chaplain of the First California, Father Daugherty who sailed with General Merritt to Manila, and Father Boyle, the superintendent of the famous observatory founded by the Jesuits, who was a typical Irishman of a strong and humorously hearty type. Father Boyle had one of the most perfect methods of speaking English in the Irish way that I have ever heard, and admitted that he had resided in England long enough to be born there; and this was great fun. It is not too much to say that the institution he represented is illustrious.

The cathedral of Manila is within the walled city and of immense proportions. It was shattered by an earthquake, and in its reconstruction wood rather than marble was used for the supporting pillars within, but no one would find out that the stately clusters of columns were not from the quarries rather than the forests, unless personally conducted to the discovery. Here 2,000 Spanish soldiers, held under the articles of capitulation, were quartered, consumed their rations and slept, munching and dozing all around the altar and pervading the whole edifice. The other great churches, five in number, in the walled city, were occupied in the same way. The Archbishop was anxious to have the soldiers otherwise provided with shelter, and if not all of them could be restored to their ordinary uses it was most desirable, in his opinion, the cathedral should be.

It is estimated that 2,000 of the American soldiers in the expeditionary force are Catholics, and Father Daugherty was anxious to preach to them in English. During the call upon me by the Archbishop this subject was discussed, and the suggestion made that the Americans had tents in great number that they did not occupy and that would probably not be preserved by keeping them stored in that hot and trying climate. They might be pitched on the Luneta, which is beside the sea, and the town thus relieved of 13,000 men, who, herded in churches, produced unsanitary conditions. This seemed reasonable, and the policy of the change would have a tendency to develop an element of good-will not to be despised and rejected. It might be that the cathedral alone could be cleared without delay or prejudice with a pleasant effect, and if so why not? His grace was certainly diplomatic and persuasive in stating the case, and his attendants were animated with zeal that the Americans should have the credit of re-opening the cathedral for worship. It was true the Spanish garrison first occupied it, but if the necessity that its ample roof should protect soldiers from the torrential rains had existed perhaps it had ceased to be imperative. The matter was duly presented to the military authorities, and the objection found to immediate action that the Spanish prisoners of war should not for the time be located outside the walled city. They must be held where they could be handled.

Coincident with the call of the Archbishop came Captain Coudert, of the distinguished family of that name in New York, and his grace was deeply interested in that young man and warmly expressed his gratification in meeting an American officer of his own faith. The Archbishop is a man of a high order of capacity, and his influence has been great. His position is a trying one, for it would be quite impossible for him to remain in Manila if the insurgents should become the masters of the situation. The claim of hostile natives that the Spanish priests have an influence in matters of state that make them a ruling class is one that they urge when expressing their resolve that the Friars must go. The Spanish policy, especially in the municipal governments, has been to magnify the office of the priests in political functions. The proceedings of a meeting of the people in order to receive attention or to have legal standing must be certified by a priest. It is the Spanish priest that is wanted in matters of moment, and the laws make his presence indispensable. The Spanish priests are, therefore, identified in the public mind with all the details of misgovernment. The civilized Filipinos profess christianity and faith in the native priests, carefully asserting the distinction. In his conversation with me, General Aguinaldo repeatedly referred to the necessity of consulting his advisers, and said he had to be careful not to offend many of his followers, who thought he had gone very far in his friendship for the United States. He gave emphasis to the assertion that they were "suspicious" of him on that account. It was my judgment at first that the General, in stopping short when a question was difficult and referring to the Council he had to consult, was showing a capacity for finesse, that he really had the power to do or to undo, though he has not a personal appearance of possible leadership. Now this, even, has been modified. His Council seems to be the real center of power. When I was talking with Aguinaldo there were two American priests waiting to propose the deportation of his prisoners who were priests, and he had to refer that question. The Council has decided to keep the priests in confinement, and it is remarked that the General desired to give up his prisoners and was false in saying he favored sending them to Spain. There are misapprehensions in this association. He has no doubt thought well of holding fast his most important hostages. If he personally desired to release the priests, he probably would not venture to do it. He is not so silly as to believe in his own inviolability by bullets, and digestion of poisons; and those who are such savages as to confide in these superstitions are not unlikely to try experiments just to strengthen their faith. The potentiality of Aguinaldo as a personage is not so great as has been imagined, and if he attempts a rally against the American flag he will be found full of weakness.

The Archbishop, I was told, had much pleasure in meeting an American he was assured would attempt to be entirely just, and present him according to his own declarations to the people of the United States. He knew very well, unquestionably, the stories circulated in the American camps, that his voice had been loudest and last in urging hopeless war, in telling impossible tales of visionary Spanish reinforcements, and denouncing the Americans as "niggers" and "pigs." It is a fact that Spaniards have cultivated the notion among the rural Filipinos, that Americans are black men, and pigs is their favorite epithet for an American. The radical enemies of His Grace are, no doubt, responsible for unseemly stories about his animosities, for that he and those around him were sincere in their respect for, and gratitude toward the American army of occupation, for its admirable bearing and good conduct, was in itself too obviously true to be doubted.

CHAPTER VIII.

WHY WE HOLD THE PHILIPPINES.

The Responsibility of Admiral Dewey—We Owe It to Ourselves to Hold the Philippines—Prosperity Assured by Our Permanent Possession—The Aguinaldo Question—Character Study of the Insurgent Leader—How Affairs Would Adjust Themselves for Us—Congress Must Be Trusted to Represent the People and Firmly Establish International Policy.

If Admiral Dewey, after obeying the order of the President to destroy the Spanish fleet at Manila, had steamed away and sought a station to get coal to drive him somewhere else, there would have been no Philippine question on the other side of the world from Washington City. The Admiral desired to keep open telegraphic communication, and made a proposition to that effect, but the Spanish authorities curtly refused. Then the cable was cut by order of the Admiral, a section removed, and both ends marked by buoys. Reflection caused the Spaniards to regret that they had not consented to keep open the cable, that it might be used under restrictions by both belligerents. They mentioned their change of mind, and were told they were too late. The American Admiral may have been apprehensive, and he had reason to be, that the Spaniards, knowing they would be crushed in the West Indies if they risked a decisive naval engagement there, might send all their available ships of war to the Philippines, and secure a superiority of force, possibly to destroy their enemies at Manila. It is clear now that this is what the Spaniards ought to have tried to do. The Americans were committed to the blockade of Cuba, occupying all the vessels of war they had at hand, and the whole fleet of Spain could have been in the Suez Canal, on the way to Manila when the movement was known to our navy department. Then Admiral Dewey would, of course, have been warned by way of Hong Kong and a dispatch boat, that he should put to sea and take care of his men and ships. The result might have been the temporary restoration of the Philippines to Spain. Our Admiral, six hundred miles from Hongkong, the closest cable connection, could not afford to leave Manila in direct communication with Madrid. It was for this reason and not that he desired to keep out of way or orders, as some able publicists have kindly promulgated, that the Admiral cut the cable.

The gravest of his responsibilities came upon him after his victory freed the harbor of declared enemies, and placed the great city at his mercy. If the Spaniards used their big Krupp guns against his ships, he could bombard the city and burn it. He held the keys to the Philippines, with Manila under his guns, and the question before him then was the same before the country now. The question that incessantly presses is, whether the Dewey policy is to be confirmed, and the logic of the stay in the harbor, and the dispatch of troops to take the town made good. We hold the keys of the Philippines. Shall we continue to do so? This question transcends in immediate importance—inevitable consequence—remote as well as near, all the war with Spain has raised. So broad a matter should not be rested on narrow grounds, nor decided with haste. It ought to be scrutinized in all its bearings, and all susceptibilities and material affairs regarded, for it will affect all the people for all time.

What are the Philippines? They are the richest prize of soil and climate that has been at hazard in the world for many years—one that would be seized, if it could be done without war, by any of the great nations other than our own without hesitation. The only scruple we need entertain, the sole reason for deliberation, is because it is a duty of the government to be sure when there are imperial considerations to be weighed, that the people should be consulted. It was on this account distinctly, that the President knew the issue of the permanency of the possession of the Philippines was one of peculiar novelty and magnitude, that he permitted it to exist. Spain must have been as acquiescent in this as in yielding the independence of Cuba, and the concession to us without any intermediate formality of Porto Rico. It is not inconsistent with the policy of magnanimity that is generally anticipated after the victory of a great power over a lesser one, that we should hold the Philippines. We have only to keep the power we have in peace, and let it work as a wholesome medicine, and all the islands of the group of which Manila is the central point, will be ours without conflict. In our system there is healing for wounds, and attraction for the oppressed. The holding of the islands by Spain would signify the continued shedding of blood, and drainage of the vital resources of the peninsula. As against Spain the Philippines will be united and desperate unto death, while they would without coercion walk hand in hand with us, and become the greatest of our dependencies—not states, but territories.

It would be an act of mercy to Spain to send her soldiers and priests from the Philippines, home. Even if we consent that she may keep her South Sea possession, she will lose it as she has all the rest, for the story of the Philippines is that of Spanish South and Central America, and the modern story of Cuba is the old one of all countries South and West of the Gulf of Mexico and around by way of the Oceans to Argentina, Mexico, Venezuela, Peru, Chili, and the rest had the same bloody stream of history to trace, and sooner or later the tale must all be told. Since Spain has already surrendered Cuba and Porto Rico, the record of the Philippines is the last chapter of her colonial experiences, by which she has dazzled and disgusted the world, attaining from the plunder of dependencies wealth that she invested in oppressive warfare to sustain a depraved despotism and display a grandeur that was unsound, sapping her own strength in colonial enterprises that could not be other than without profit, because the colonies were the property of the crown, and the prey of caste.

The Spanish nation was forbidden by their government, not of the people or for the people, to profit by the colonies, and the viceroys, the captain-generals, and the whole official class were corrupted, and inefficient in all things, except methods of tyranny to procure a harvest of gold and silver not from the mines of the metals alone, but from the industries, whatever they were. The people at large were allowed no share in their own earnings, beyond a subsistence so scanty that deep humiliation and grievous hardship were the fateful rewards of labor.

It was because the colonial policy of Spain impoverished and degraded the Spaniards at home, through the injustice, greed and profligacy of those abroad, that the huge structure, once so great an imposition upon mankind, a rotten fabric so gilt that the inherent weakness was disguised, has finally fallen into universal and irretrievable ruin.

It is well Spain should retain the Canaries and the Balearic group, for they are as Spanish as any peninsular province, and legitimately belong therefore to the kingdom. The application of this principle excludes Spain from the Philippines, and their destiny have been committed by the failure of war to our hands. There is no nation that will dispute our peaceable possession of the Philippines. Any other nation's proprietorship will be challenged. Our authoritative presence in the islands will be a guarantee of peace. Any other assertion of supremacy will be the signal for war. Our assumption of sovereignty over the islands would quickly establish tranquility. Any other disposition of the burning questions now smoldering will cause an outburst of the flames of warfare. The Spaniards in Manila have been transient. They are not rooted in the soil. They all come and go like Captain-Generals, a mere official class, with the orders of the Church participating actively in secular concerns, more active as politicians than as teachers of religion. In the view of the native population it is as indispensable that the priests of Spain shall return to their native land as that the soldiers should go. The deportation of these people would remove classes of consumers and not affect unfavorably a productive industry, or the prosperity of a self-sustaining community, and there would be but rare instances of the severance of family ties.

It will be said of the affirmation that, the avowal of the possession of the Philippines as a responsibility without end would be a peace measure, and anything else make for war, does not take into account the attitude of the Philippine Dictator, by proclamation, General Aguinaldo, and his followers. We desire to speak with respect of the General, for he has shown in trying times, under strong temptations, the presence in his character of personal integrity in public matters, and reference is made to his refusal to consent to the division among insurgents alleged to be leaders, of the money paid by the Spaniards for the disarmament of the rebels, when two years ago there was an agreement upon the terms of a truce. This money transaction has been referred to as the sale of their cause by Aguinaldo and his associates, as if they, as individuals, had pocketed the usufruct of the bargain. The money was paid by Spain as an earnest of her sincerity, the Captain-General representing the force and good faith of the kingdom, in granting reforms to the Philippinos. On condition of insurgent disarmament the people of the island were to be allowed representation in the Spanish Cortes, the orders of the Church were to be removed from relations to the Government that were offensive to the people. There was a long list of articles of specification of the reforms that were to be granted, the usual liberality of words of promise always bestowed by Spain upon her colonists. The representatives of Spain denied nothing that was asked; and to give weight to the program of concessions, there was paid in hand to Aguinaldo, through a transaction between banks in Manila and Hongkong, four hundred thousand dollars, the first installment of eight hundred thousand dollars agreed upon.* The Spaniards probably understood that they were bribing the insurgents and paying a moderate sum to cheaply end the war; and it did not cost the authorities of Spain anything, for they exacted the money from the Manila Bank of Spain, and still owe the bank. Aguinaldo's understanding, acted upon, was different. He accepted the money as a war fund, and has held and defended it for the purchase of arms, and resumed hostilities when all promises of reform were broken, and nothing whatever done beyond the robbery of the bank to bribe the rebel chiefs, which was the Spanish translation. Of course, it was claimed by the enemies of Aguinaldo that he was bought and paid for, but he has maintained the fund, though there were those professors of rebellion, who made claims to a share of the money. The second installment of the money that the rebels were to have been paid is yet an obligation not lifted, and the hostilities were revived as soon as the craft of the Spanish negotiators in promising everything because

---

* In another chapter of this story of the Philippines will be found Senor Filipe Agoncello's personal account of this affair.

they meant to do nothing, became obvious. The actual proceedings in this case can be summed up in a sentence: The Spaniards took four hundred thousand dollars out of the Bank of Spain and gave it to the insurgents, for a temporary armistice. General Aguinaldo, though he appears very well in refusing to employ the money paid by Spain as a bribe for himself, has not the elements of enduring strength as the leader of the insurgents. As against the Spaniards he can keep the field, and carry on a destructive guerilla warfare, hopeless on both sides, like that going on in Cuba, when that island was invaded by the American army. But as against American rule the Philippinos would cease to be insurgents. The islanders will not be controlled by sentimentalism. Government by the United States would differ from that by Spain, as the two nations are different in character, in the nature of their political institutions, in their progressive movement. America is all active and free, and her freedom would be extended to the islanders. The transformation would be one from the paralysis of despotism to the life of liberty. The words despotism and freedom would instantly have a distinct business meaning. Make known in the city of Manila that the Americans will abandon it, and the reviving hopes of the men of affairs would be instantly clouded, and the depression deepen into despondency and despair. Let it be the news of the day that the Americans will stay, and the intelligence of the city would regard its redemption as assured, every drooping interest revive, and an era of prosperity unknown under the dismal incompetency of Spain, open at once. It is legitimate that there should be freedom of speech as to the details of the proceedings. If our Government should do what Admiral Dewey did when he was the master of Manila, because he had annihilated the Spanish fleet and had the power to destroy the city—cast anchor and stay where we are already in command—the task is neither so complex nor costly as its opponents claim. Our territorial system is one easy of application to colonies. We have had experience of it from the first days of our Government. There is no commandment that a Territory shall become a State in any given time, or ever. We can hold back a Territory, as we have Arizona and New Mexico, or hasten the change to Statehood according to the conditions, and the perfect movement of the machinery requires only the presence in Congress of dominant good sense. Congress is easily denounced, but no one has found a substitute for it, and it is fairly representative of the country. Congress will never gamble away the inheritance of the people. It will probably, in spite of all shortcomings, have its average of ability and utility kept up. Congress may go wrong, but will not betray. Our outlying possessions must be Territories until they are Americanized, and we take it Americans know what that word means. If a specification is wanted as a definition, we have to say the meaning is just what has happened in California since our flag was there. In the case of the Philippines, if we stick, and we do not see how we can help doing so, the President will, in regular course, appoint a Territorial Governor, and as a strong Government capable of quick and final decisions must be made, the Governor should be a military man, and have a liberal grant, by special Act of Congress, of military authority. He should be a prompt, and all around competent administrator. He will not have to carry on war offensive or defensive. He need not be in a hurry to go far from Manila. He will not be molested there. The country will gravitate to him. The opponents of the Republican form of Government, as it is in the United States and the Territories of the Nation will become insignificant in the Philippines. They will have no grievances, except some of them may not be called at once to put on the trappings of personal potentiality. General Aguinaldo would find all the reforms the Spanish promised when they paid him four hundred thousand dollars to prove their good intentions, free as the air. He could not make war against the benignancy of a Government, Republican in its form and its nature, which simply needs a little time, some years maybe, before erasing the wrongs that have had a growth of centuries. The American Governor-General need not send out troops to conquer districts,coercing the people. The people will soon be glad to see the soldiers of the United States, the representatives of the downfall and departure of the instruments of Spain. Aguinaldo and his party have a Congress. It might be an approved beginning of a Territorial Legislature, and the insurgent General might be the presiding officer. There would be abundant reason for the auspicious exercise of all his rights in the public service. As for the cost of the Philippines under our Government, that would fall upon the treasury of the United States. There can be no doubt that it would be for several years a considerable sum, but the public men who favored peace for the liberation of Cuba, did not make counting the cost the most prominent feature of the war they advocated, but accepted the fact that the national honor and fame, the glory of heroism and deeds of daring and sacrifice, are priceless, and their achievement beyond price. There is to be said under this head, that the Philippine Islands are of natural riches almost without parallel. The great isle of Luzon teems with productions that have markets the world over, and it is commonplace for the savages in the mountains to come out of their fastnesses with nuggets of gold to make purchases. Cotton, sugar, rice, hemp, coffee and tobacco, all tropical fruits and woods, are of the products. There is profusion of the riches that await the freedom of labor and the security of capital, and the happiness of the people. Under American government the Philippines would prosper, and it would be one of our tasks to frame legislation. The laws of Congress would be the higher code of law, and the Philippines would desire, and be invited, of course, to send their ablest men to be Territorial representatives in the Congress of the United States. In the name of peace, therefore, and in behalf of the dignity and authority of this Nation —in mercy to the Spaniards, in justice to the Filipinos, it is due ourselves, and should have the favor of all who would see our country expand with the ages, and walking in the footsteps of Washington and Jefferson, finding the path of empire that of freedom and taking our place as a great Power, accepting the logic of our history, and the discharge of the duties of destiny—we should hold on to the Philippines—and when the great distance of those islands from this continent is mentioned, remember that the Pacific may now be crossed in as few days as was the Atlantic forty years ago.

The labor questions and the silver questions even come into the Philippines problem to be scanned and weighed. In Eastern Asia, which we have invaded, and a part of which we have appropriated for a time, the people use silver for the measure of value, and in the islands that interest us, as they do not deal in the mysteries of rupees, but in dollars, the facts in the case are plainly within the common understanding. In Manila the Mexican dollar goes in ordinary small exchanges, payment of wages and settlement of bills, for fifty cents; but the banks sell the Mexicans twenty-one of them for ten gold dollars—an American eagle! So far as the native people go, labor and produce are counted in silver, and the purchaser, or employer gets as much for a silver dollar as for a gold dollar. The native will take ten dollars in gold for ten dollars only in all settlements of accounts, and would just as willingly —even more so, accept ten Mexican dollars as ten American dollars in gold coin. Salaries are paid and goods delivered according to the silver standard. Of course, in due time this state of things will pass away, if we hold to the gold standard, but as the case stands the soldiers and sailors of our army and fleet, paid under the home standard, receive double pay, and get double value received for clothing, tobacco and whatever they find they want—indeed, for the necessaries and luxuries of life. The double standard in this shape is not distasteful to the boys.

We have both theories and conditions confronting us in these aspects of the silver and labor questions. The Oriental people are obdurate in their partiality for silver. It is the cheaper labor that adheres to the silver standard, partially, it is held, because silver is the more convenient money for the payment of small sums. But labor cannot be expected, at its own expense, to sustain silver for the profit of capital, or rather of the middle man between labor and capital. Labor, so far as it is in politics in this country, should not, without most careful study and deliberation, conclude that its force in public affairs would be abated, and its policy of advancing wages antagonized by the absorption of the Philippines in our country. On the contrary, the statesmanship that is representative of labor may discover that it is a great fact, one of the greatest of facts, that the various countries and continents of the globe are being from year to year more and more closely associated, and that to those intelligently interested, without regard to the application of their views of justice or expediency, in the labor and silver questions—the convictions, the fanaticisms, of the vast silver nations—and enormous multitudes of the people of Asia, touching the silver standard —and the possible progress of labor, as a guiding as well as plodding ability increases incessantly in interest, and must grow in inheritance. As the conditions of progressive civilization are developed our interests cannot be wholly dissevered from those of the Asiatics. We would be unwise to contemplate the situation of to-day as one that can or should perpetuate itself. Suppose we accept the governing responsibility in the Philippines. It it not beyond the range of reasonable conjecture that American labor can educate the laborers of the Philippines out of their state of servitude as cheap laborers, and lead them to co-operate rather than compete with us, and not to go into the silver question further than to consent that it exists, and is in the simplest form of statement, whether the change in the market value of the two money metals is natural or artificial. It is necessary in common candor to state that the most complete solution of the money metal embarrassments would be through the co-operation of Asia and America. Europe is for gold, Asia for silver, and the Americas divided. Japan is an object lesson, her approximation to the gold standard has caused in the Empire an augmentation of the compensation of labor. This is not wholly due to the change in the standard. The war with China, the increase in the army and navy, and the absorption of laborers in Formosa, the new country of Japan, have combined with the higher standard of value, to elevate wages. All facts are of primary excellence in the formation of the policies of nations.

CHAPTER IX.

THE PHILIPPINE ISLANDS AS THEY ARE.

Area and Population—Climate—Mineral Wealth—Agriculture—Commerce and Transportation—Revenue and Expenses—Spanish Troops—Spanish Navy—Spanish Civil Administration—Insurgent Troops—Insurgent Civil Administration—United States Troops—United States Navy—United States Civil Administration—The Future of the Islands.

General Frank V. Greene made an exhaustive study of all reports of an official character regarding the area, population, climate, resources, commerce, revenue and expenses of the Philippines Islands, and prepared a memorandum for the general information that is the most thorough and complete ever made, and is the latest and highest authority on all the subjects to which it relates, and they include the solid information the business men of the United States want respecting our Asiatic associations. The memorandum is herewith submitted in substance, and all the particulars of public concern.

AREA AND POPULATION.

These islands, including the Ladrones, Carolinas and Palaos, which are all under the Government of Manila, are variously estimated at from 1,200 to 1,300 in number. The greater portion of these are small and of no more value than the islands off the coast of Alaska. The important islands are less than a dozen in number, and 90 per cent. of the Christian population live on Luzon and the five principal islands of the Visayas group.

The total population is somewhere between 7,000,000 and 9,000,000. This includes the wild tribes of the mountains of Luzon and of the islands in the extreme south. The last census taken by the Spanish Government was on December 31, 1887, and this stated the Christian population to be 6,000,000 (in round numbers). This is distributed as follows:

	Area.	Population.	Per Sq. Mile.
Luzon	44,400	3,426,000	79
Panay	4,700	735,000	155
Cebu	2,400	504,000	210
Leyte	3,300	279,000	71
Bohol	1,300	245,000	188
Negros	3,300	242,000	73
	59,800	5,422,000	91

THE PHILIPPINE ISLANDS AS THEY ARE.

The density of population in these six islands is nearly 50 per cent. greater than in Illinois and Indiana (census of 1890), greater than in Spain, about one-half as great as in France, and one-third as great as in Japan and China, the exact figures being as follows:

	Area.	Population.	Per Sq. Mile.
Illinois	56,000	3,826,351	68
Indiana	35,910	2,192,494	61
	91,910	6,018,755	64
Spain	197,670	17,565,632	88
France	204,092	38,517,975	189
Japan	147,655	42,270,620	286
China	1,312,328	383,253,029	292

The next most important islands, in the order of population, are:

	Area.	Population.	Per Sq. Mile.
Mindanao	34,000	209,000	6
Samar	4,800	186,000	38
Mindoro	4,000	67,000	17
Nomblon	600	35,000	58
Masbate	1,400	21,000	15
	44,800	518,000	11

Various smaller islands, including the Carolinas, Ladrones and Palaos, carry the total area and Christian population to—

140,000	6,000,000	43

This is considerably greater than the density of population in the States east of the Rocky Mountains. Owing to the existence of mountain ranges in all the islands, and lack of communication in the interior, only a small part of the surface is inhabited. In many provinces the density of population exceeds 200 per square mile, or greater than that of any of the United States, except Massachusetts and Rhode Island. The total area of the Philippines is about the same as that of Japan, but its civilized population is only one-seventh.

In addition to the Christian population, it is estimated (in the Official Guide) that the islands contain the following:

Chinese (principally in Manila)	75,000
Moors or Mohametans in Paragon and Jok	100,000
Moors or Mohametans in Mindanao and Basilan	209,000
Heathen in the Philippines	830,000
Heathen in the Carolinas and Palaos	50,000
	1,264,000

THE PHILIPPINE ISLANDS AS THEY ARE.

The Official Guide gives a list of more than thirty different races, each speaking a different dialect; but five-sixths of the Christian population are either Tagalos or Visayas. All the races are of the Malay type. Around Manila there has been some mixture of Chinese and Spanish blood with that of the natives, resulting in the Mestizos or Half-breeds, but the number of these is not very great.

As seen in the provinces of Cavite and Manila, the natives (Tagalos) are of small stature, averaging probably 5 feet 4 inches in height, and 120 pounds in weight for the men, and 5 feet in height, and 100 pounds in v eight for the women. Their skin is coppery brown, somewhat darker than that of the mulatto. They seem to be industrious and hard-working, although less so than the Chinese. By the Spaniards they are considered indolent, crafty, untruthful, cowardly and cruel, but the

ORIENTAL HOTEL, MANILA.

hatred between the Spaniards and the native races is so intense and bitter that the Spanish opinion of the natives is of little or no value. To us they seem industrious and docile, but there are occasional evidences of deceit and untruthfulness in their dealings with us. The bulk of the population is engaged in agriculture, and there were hardly any evidences of manufactures, arts or mining. The greater number seemed to be able to read and write, but I have been unable to obtain any exact figures on this subject. They are all devout Roman Catholics, although they hate the monastic orders.

In Manila (and doubtless also in Cebu and Iloilo) are many thousands of educated natives, who are merchants, lawyers, doctors and priests. They are well informed and have accumulated property. They have not traveled much, but there is said to be quite a numerous colony of rich Filipinos in Madrid, as well as in

Paris and London. The bibliography of the Philippines is said to number 4,500 volumes, the greater part of which have been written by Spanish priests and missionaries. The number of books on the subject in the English language is probably less than a dozen.

CLIMATE.

The climate is one of the best known in the tropics. The islands extend from 5 to 21 deg. north latitude, and Manila is in 14d. 35m. The thermometer during July and August rarely went below 79 or above 85. The extreme ranges in a year are said to be 61 and 97, and the annual mean, 81. There are three well-marked seasons, temperate and dry from November to February, hot and dry from March to May, and temperate and wet from June to October. The rainy season reaches its maximum in July and August, when the rains are constant and very heavy. The total rainfall has been as high as 114 inches in one year.

Yellow fever appears to be unknown. The diseases most fatal among the natives are cholera and smallpox, both of which are brought from China. Low malarial fever is brought on by sleeping on the ground or being chilled by remaining, without exercise, in wet clothes; and diarrhea is produced by drinking bad water or eating excessive quantities of fruit. Almost all of these diseases are preventable by proper precautions, even by troops in campaign. The sickness in our troops was very small, much less than in the cold fogs at camp in San Francisco.

MINERAL WEALTH.

Very little is known concerning the mineral wealth of the islands. It is stated that there are deposits of coal, petroleum, iron, lead, sulphur, copper and gold in the various islands, but little or nothing has been done to develop them. A few concessions have been granted for working mines, but the output is not large. The gold is reported on Luzon, coal and petroleum on Cebu and Iloilo, and sulphur on Leyte. The imports of coal in 1894 (the latest year for which the statistics have been printed) were 91,511 tons, and it came principally from Australia and Japan. In the same year the imports of iron of all kinds were 9,632 tons.

If the Cebu coal proves to be good quality there is a large market for it in competition with the coal from Japan and Australia.

AGRICULTURE.

Although agriculture is the chief occupation of the Philippines, yet only one-ninth of the surface is under cultivation. The soil is very fertile, and even after deducting the mountainous areas, it is probable that the area of cultivation can be very largely extended, and that the islands can support a population equal to that of Japan (42,000,000).

GENERAL FITZHUGH LEE, NOW MAJOR-GENERAL COMMANDING.

CAPTAIN SIGSBEE, COMMANDER OF THE ILL-FATED MAINE.

The chief products are rice, corn, hemp, sugar, tobacco, cocoanuts and cacao. Coffee and cotton were formerly produced in large quantities—the former for export and the latter for home consumption; but the coffee plant has been almost exterminated by insects, and the home made cotton clothes have been driven out by the competition of those imported from England. The rice and corn are principally produced in Luzon and Mindoro, and are consumed in the islands; the rice crop is about 765,000 tons; it is insufficient for the demand and 45,000 tons of rice were imported in 1894, the greater portion from Saigon, and the rest from Hongkong and Singapore; also 8,669 tons (say 60,000 barrels) of flour, of which more than two-thirds came from China and less than one-third from the United States.

The cacao is raised in the southern islands, the best quality of it in Mindanao. The production amounts to only 150 tons, and it is all made into chocolate and consumed in the islands.

The sugar cane is raised in the Visayas. The crop yielded, in 1894, about 235,000 tons of raw sugar, of which one-tenth was consumed in the islands and the balance, or 210,000 tons, valued at $11,000,000, was exported, the greater part to China, Great Britain and Australia.

The hemp is produced in southern Luzon, Mindoro, the Visayas and Mindanao. It is nearly all exported in bales. In the year 1894 the amount was 96,000 tons, valued at $12,000,000.

Tobacco is raised in all the islands, but the best quality and the greatest amount in Luzon. A large amount is consumed in the islands, smoking being universal among the women as well as the men, but the best quality is exported. The amount, in 1894, was 7,000 tons of leaf tobacco, valued at $1,400,000, and 1,400 tons of manufactured tobacco, valued at $1,750,000. Spain takes 30 per cent. and Egypt 10 per cent of the leaf tobacco. Of the manufactured tobacco, 70 per cent. goes to China and Singapore, 10 per cent. to England, and 5 per cent. to Spain.

Cocoanuts are grown in southern Luzon and are used in various ways. The products are largely used in the islands, but the exports, in 1894, were valued at $2,400,000.

Cattle, goats and sheep have been introduced from Spain, but they are not numerous. Domestic pigs and chickens are seen around every hut in the farming districts.

The principal beast of burden is the carabac or water buffalo, which is used for ploughing rice fields, as well as drawing heavy loads on sledges or on carts.

Large horses are almost unknown, but there are great numbers of native ponies, from nine to twelve hands high, but possessing strength and endurance far beyond their size.

COMMERCE AND TRANSPORTATION.

The internal commerce between Manila and the different islands is quite large, but I was unable to find any official records giving exact figures concerning it. It is carried on almost entirely by water, in steamers of 500 to 1,000 tons. There are regular mail steamers, once in two weeks, on four routes, viz.; Northern Luzon, Southern Luzon, Visayas and Mindanao; also a steamer every two months to the Carolinas and Ladrones, and daily steamers on Manila Bay. These lines are all subsidized. To facilitate this navigation extensive harbor works have been in progress at Manila for several years, and a plan for lighting the coasts has been made, calling for forty-three principal lights, of which seventeen have already been constructed in the most substantial manner, besides sixteen lights of secondary importance.

There is only one line of railway, built by English capital, running from Manila north to Dagupan, a distance of about 120 miles. The roads in the immediate vicinity of Manila are macadamized and in fairly good order; elsewhere they are narrow paths of soft, black soil, which becomes almost impassable in the rainy season. Transportation is then effected by sledges, drawn through the mud by carabaos. There are telegraph lines connecting most of the provinces of Luzon with Manila, and cables to the Visayas and southern islands, and thence to Borneo and Singapore, as well as a direct cable from Manila to Hongkong. The land telegraph lines are owned by the Government, and the cables all belong to an English company, which receives a large subsidy. In Manila there is a narrow gauge street railway, operated by horse power, about eleven miles in total length; also a telephone system, and electric lights.

Communications with Europe are maintained by the Spanish Trans-Atlantic Company (subsidized), which sends a steamer every four weeks from Manila and Barcelona, making the trip in about twenty-seven days. The same company also sends an intermediate steamer from Manila to Singapore, meeting the French Messagoric each way. There is also a non-subsidized line running from Manila to Hongkong every two weeks, and connecting there with the English, French and German mails for Europe, and with the Pacific mail and Canadian Pacific steamers for Japan and America.

There has been no considerable development of manufacturing industries in the Philippines. The only factories are those connected with the preparation of rice, tobacco and sugar. Of the manufactures and arts, in which Japan so excels, there is no evidence.

The foreign commerce amounted, in 1894, to $28,558,552 in imports, and

THE PHILIPPINE ISLANDS AS THEY ARE. 105

$33,149,984 in exports, 80 per cent. of which goes through Manila. About 60 per cent. of the trade is carried in British vessels, 20 per cent. in Spanish and 10 per cent. in German.

The value of the commerce with other countries in 1894 was as follows:

IN MILLIONS OF DOLLARS (SILVER).

	Imports.	Exports.
Spain	10.5	2.9
Great Britain	7.1	8.7
China	4.6	6.8
Germany	1.9	..
Saigon	.9	..
United States	.7	7.4
France	.7	1.2
Singapore	.4	1.7
Japan	.2	1.2
Australia	.1	2.6
Other Countries	1.5	.6
	25.6	33.1

It is interesting to note that next to Great Britain we are the largest customers of the Philippines, and that they export to us nearly three times as much as to Spain. On the other hand Spain sells to the Philippines fifteen times as much as we do.

The articles of import and their value in 1894 were as follows:

IN MILLIONS OF DOLLARS (SILVER).

	Spain.	Great Britain.	China.	Germany.	United States.	Other Countries.	Total.
Cotton Goods	3.9	4.0	.4	.3	..	.7	9.3
Cotton Yarns	1.2	.9	.2	.1	..	.1	2.5
Wines	1.8	..	..	..	..	.1	1.9
						Russia.	
Mineral Oils	..	..	.2	..	.4	.8	1.4
Iron	.2	.7	..	.2	..	.1	1.2
Rice	..	..	1.0	..	..	.1	1.1
Flour	..	..	.7	..	.2	..	.9
Sweet Meats	.5	..	..	..	..	.3	.8
Paper	.4	..	..	.1	..	.2	.7
Linen Goods	.1	.1	.1	..	..	.3	.6
Hats	.1	..	..	.3	..	.2	.6
Other Articles	2.3	1.4	2.0	.9	.1	.9	7.6
	10.5	7.1	4.6	1.9	.7	3.8	28.6

THE PHILIPPINE ISLANDS AS THEY ARE.

The articles of export and their value in 1894 were as follows:

IN MILLIONS OF DOLLARS (SILVER).

	Spain.	Great Britain.	China.	United States.	Australia.	Other Countries.	Total.
Hemp	..	5.3	.9	6.6	.6	1.1[a]	14.5
Sugar	.4	2.7	4.0	.7	1.9	1.3[b]	11.0
Man'f. Tobacco	.2	.1	.7	..	.1	.7[a]	1.3
Leaf Tobacco	1.1	..	..	..	..	.3	1.4
Coffee	.3	..	.1	..	..	..	.4
Cocoanuts	..	.6	.1	..	..	..	.7
Other Articles	.9	..	1.0	.1	..	1.3	3.3
	2.9	8.7	6.8	7.4	2.6	4.7	33.16

[a] Principally to Singapore.
[b] Principally to Japan.

With these islands in our possession and the construction of railroads in the interior of Luzon, it is probable that an enormous extension could be given to this commerce, nearly all of which would come to the United States. Manila cigars of the best quality are unknown in America. They are but little inferior to the best of Cuba, and cost only one-third as much. The coffee industry can be revived and the sugar industry extended, mainly for consumption in the far East. The mineral resources can be explored with American energy, and there is every reason to believe that when this is done the deposits of coal, iron, gold and lead will be found very valuable. On the other hand, we ought to be able to secure the greater part of the trade which now goes to Spain in textile fabrics, and a considerable portion of that with England in the same goods and in iron.

REVENUE AND EXPENSES.

The budget for the fiscal year ending June 30, 1897, was as follows:

INCOME.

1st. Direct Taxes	$8,496,170
2nd. Indirect Taxes (Customs)	6,200,550
3rd. Proceeds of Monopolies	1,222,000
4th. Lottery	1,000,000
5th. Income of Government Property	257,000
6th. Sundry Receipts	298,300
Total	$17,474,020

THE PHILIPPINE ISLANDS AS THEY ARE. 107

EXPENSES.

1st.	General Expenses, Pensions and Interest..........	$1,506,686
2nd.	Diplomatic and Consular Service...............	74,000
3rd.	Clergy and Courts.............................	1,876,740
4th.	War Department...............................	6,035,316
5th.	Treasury Department..........................	1,392,414
6th.	Navy Department..............................	3,562,716
7th.	Civil Administration...........................	2,195,378
8th.	Education.....................................	614,395

Total......................................$17,258,145

The Direct Taxes were as follows:
1st. Real Estate, 5 per cent. on income...............$ 140,280
2nd. Industry and Commerce........................ 1,400,700
3rd. Cedalas (Poll Tax)............................ 5,600,000
4th. Chinese Poll Tax..............................   510,190
5th. Tribute from Sultan of Jolo...................   20,000
6th. Railroads, 10 per cent. of Passenger Receipts.......   32,000
7th. Income Tax, 10 per cent. on Public Salaries........   730,000
8th. Sundry Taxes.................................   63,000

Total......................................$8,496,170

Indirect Taxes were as follows:
1st. Imports....................................... $3,600,000
2nd. Exports...................................... 1,292,350
3rd. Loading Tax..................................   410,000
4th. Unloading Tax................................   570,000
5th. Fines and Penalties..........................   27,000
6th. Special Tax on Liquors, Beer, Vegetables, Flour,
     Salt and Mineral Oils..........................   301,000

Total...................................... $6,200,350

Monopolies:
1st. Opium Contract...............................$ 576,000
2nd. Stamped Paper and Stamps.....................   646,000

Total...................................... $1,222,000

Lottery:
1st. Sale of Tickets, Less Cost of Prizes..............$ 964,000
2nd. Unclaimed Prizes.............................   30,000
3rd. Sundry Receipts..............................   6,000

Total...................................... $1,000,000

Income of Government Property:
1st. Forestry Privileges............................$ 170,000
2nd. Sale and Rent of Public Land and Buildings.......   85,000
3rd. Mineral Privileges............................   2,000

Total...................................... $257,000

THE PHILIPPINE ISLANDS AS THEY ARE.

Sundry Receipts:
   1st. Mint (Seignorage)..........................$200,000
   2nd. Sundries.................................... 98,300

      Total.................................$298,300

The largest source of income is th Cedala or Poll Tax. Every man and woman above 18 years of age, residing in the Philippines, whether Spanish subject or foreigner, is required to have in his or her possession a paper stating name, age, and occupation, and other facts of personal identity. Failure to produce and exhibit this when called upon renders anyone liable to arrest and imprisonment. This

SAN JUAN DEL MONTE, WHERE REVOLUTION STARTED

paper is obtained from the internal revenue office annually, on payment of a certain sum, varying, according to the occupation and income of the person from $0.75 to $20.00, and averaging about $3.00 for each adult. An extra sum of 2 per cent. is paid for expenses of collection. The tax is collected at the Tribunal in each pueblo, and 20 per cent. is retained for expenses of local administration, and 80 per cent. paid to the General Treasury. This tax falls heavily on the poor and lightly on the rich. The tax on industry and commerce is similarly graded according to the volume of business transacted by each merchant or mercantile corporation. The tax on real estate is absurdly low and levied only on municipal property and on the rent, not the value.

The tax on imports is specific and not ad valorum; it amounts to about 13 per cent. of estimated values. The free list is very small, nearly everything of commercial value which is imported being subject to duty. The revenue from imports has increased from $566,143 in 1865, to $3,695,446 in 1894. It was about the same in 1897. On the other hand the export tax, which was nothing in 1892, the loading tax, which was nothing in 1893, and the unloading tax, which was nothing in 1894, have all been increased in the last few years in order to meet the expenses of suppressing the insurrection. These three items yielded nearly $2,700,000 in 1897.

The monopoly of importing and selling opium is sold, by auction, to the highest bidder for a term of three years. The present contract runs until 1899, and yields $48,000 per month.

Every legal document must be drawn up on paper containing a revenue stamp, engraved and printed in Spain, and every note, check, draft, bill of exchange, receipt or similar document must bear a revenue stamp in order to be valid. These stamps and stamped paper yielded a revenue of $646,000 in 1897.

The lottery is conducted by the Government—the monthly drawings taking place in the Treasury (Hacienda) Department. The sale of tickets yielded $1,000,000 over and above prizes in 1897.

In a report to General Merritt, on August 29th, I recommended that the opium contract be cancelled and the lottery abandoned during our occupation of Manila; and as the poll tax and the tax on industry and commerce had been paid for the most part in the early part of the year, our chief sources of revenue were from the custom house, the sale of stamps and stamped paper, and the sale of such licenses as the law allowed (amusements, liquor saloons, etc.), for the benefit of the city of Manila as distinguished from the general revenue. I estimated the total at about $500,000 per month.

The expenses of administering the military government of occupation (apart from the expenses of the army) will consist of the current expenses of the office at the Provost Marshal General's office and its various bureaus—at the custom house, internal revenue office, and other offices—and the salaries of interpreters and minor employes who are anxious to resume work as soon as they dare do so. An estimate of these expenses was being prepared at the time I left, but was not completed. It can hardly exceed $200,000 per month and may be much less. This should leave $300,000 (silver) excess of income per month, to go towards the military expenses of occupation.

As soon as it is decided that we are to retain the islands it will be necessary to make a careful study of the sources of revenue and items of expenses for all the islands, with a view to thoroughly understanding the subject, before introducing the extensive changes which will be necessary.

CURRENCY.

The standard of value has always, until within a few years, been the Mexican milled dollar. The Spanish dollar contains a little less silver and, in order to introduce it and profit by the coinage, the Spaniards prohibited the importation of Mexican dollars a few years since. Large numbers of Mexican dollars remained

in that country, however, and others were smuggled in. The two dollars circulate at equal value.

All valuations of goods and labor are based on the silver dollar, and a change to the gold standard would result in great financial distress and many failures among the banks and mercantile houses in Manila. Their argument is that while an American ten-dollar gold piece will bring twenty-one silver dollars at any bank or house having foreign connections, yet it will not buy any more labor or any more hemp and sugar from the original producer than ten silver dollars. The products of the country are almost entirely agricultural, and the agricultural class, whether it sells its labor or its products, would refuse to accept any less than the accustomed wages or prices, on account of being paid in the more valuable coin. The result of the change would be that the merchant or employe would have to pay double for what he buys, and would receive no increase for what he sells. While trade would eventually adjust itself to the change, yet many merchants would be ruined in the process and would drag some banks down with them.

The Mexican dollar is the standard also in Hongkong and China, and the whole trade of the Far East has, for generations, been conducted on a silver basis. Japan has, within the last year, broken away from this and established the gold standard, but in doing so the relative value of silver and gold was fixed at 32½ to 1, or about the market rate.

PUBLIC DEBT.

I was unable to obtain any precise information in regard to the colonial debt. The last book on statistics of imports and exports was for the fiscal year 1894, and the last printed budget was for 1896-7, which was approved by the Queen Regent in August, 1896. Subsequent to this date, according to the statements made to me by foreign bankers, the Cortes authorized two colonial loans of $14,000,000 (silver) each, known as Series A and Series B. The proceeds were to be used in suppressing the insurrection. Both were to be secured by a first lien on the receipts of the Manila custom house.

Series A is said to have been sold in Spain and the proceeds to have been paid into the Colonial Office; but no part of them has ever reached the Philippines. Possibly a portion of it was used in sending out the 25,000 troops which came from Spain to the Philippines in the autumn of 1896.

Series B was offered for sale in Manila, but was not taken. An effort was then made to obtain subscribers in the Provinces, but with little or no success. The Government then notified the depositors in the Public Savings Bank (a branch of the Treasury Department similar to the postal savings bureaus in other countries) that their deposits would no longer be redeemed in cash, but only in Series B bonds. Some depositors were frightened and took bonds, others declined to do so. Then came the blockade of Manila and all business was practically suspended.

No printed report has been made concerning the debt, and I was unable to obtain any satisfactory statement of the matter from the treasury officials.

The exact in regard to the Series A bonds can be learned in Madrid; but it will be difficult to learn how many of Series B were issued and what consideration was received for them.

As already stated, both series of bonds rest for security on the receipts of the Manila custom house.

SPANISH TROOPS.

The Spanish prisoners of war number about 13,000, including about 400 officers. The infantry arms are about 32,000, the greater part Mauser model 1895, caliber 28, and the others Remingtons, model 1889, caliber 43. The ammunition is about 22,000,000 rounds. The field artillery consists of about twelve breech-loading steel guns, caliber 3 5-10 inches, and ten breech-loading mountain guns, caliber 3 2-10 inches. There are six horses (ponies) for each gun, but the harness is in bad order. Ammunition, about sixty rounds per gun, with possibly more in the arsenals. There are about 500 cavalry ponies, larger than the average of native horses, with saddles and equipments complete. There is also a battalion of engineers. The fortifications of the walled city are a fine sample of the Vauban type, on which military engineers expended so much ingenuity 150 years ago, and of which Spain possessed so many in her Flemish dominions. The first walls of Manila were built about 1590, but the present fortifications date from a short time after the capture and occupation of the place by the English, in 1762-64. They consist of bastions and curtains, deep, wet ditch, covered way, lunettes, demilunes, hornworks, and all the scientific accessories of that day. They are in a good state of preservation, and mount several hundred bronze guns, but they are chiefly of interest to the antiquarian. On the glaci- facing the bay, and also on the open space just south of the walls, are mounted 9-inch breech loaders, four in all, made at Hoatoria, Spain, in 1884. They are well mounted, between high traverses, in which are bomb-proof magazines.

These guns are practically uninjured, and Admiral Dewey has the breech blocks. While not as powerful as the guns of the present day of the same caliber, they are capable of effective service. Their location, however, is very faulty, as they are on the shore of the bay, with all the churches, public buildings and most valuable property immediately behind them. On the day after the naval battle Admiral Dewey sent word to the Governor-General that if these guns fired a shot at any of his vessels he would immediately reply with his whole squadron. Owing to their location, this meant a bombardment of the city. This threat was effective; these guns were never afterward fired, not even during the attack of August 13th, and in return the navy did not fire on them, but directed all their shells at the forts and trenches occupied by the troops outside of the suburbs of the city.

Within the walled city are the cathedral and numerous churches, convents and monasteries, the public offices, civil and military, military workshops and arsenals, barracks for artillery, cavalry and engineers, storehouses and a few dwellings and shops.

The infantry barracks are outside of the walls, four in number; viz.: Neysing, Fortin, Calzada and Fruita. They are modern and well constructed, and will accommodate about 4,000 men. They are now occupied by the United States troops.

Under the terms of the armistice the arms laid down by the Spanish troops on August 14th are to be returned to them whenever they evacuate the city. or the American army evacuates it. All other public property, including horses, artillery, public funds, munitions, etc., is surrendered to the United States unconditionally.

The question of sending back the troops to Spain is left absolutely to the decision of the authorities in Washington. They are all within the walled city, but as the public buildings are insufficient to accommodate them, they are quartered in the churches and convents. These buildings are not adapted for this purpose; they have no sinks, lavatories, kitchens or sleeping apartments, and there is great danger of an epidemic of sickness if the troops are not soon removed.

Pending their removal they are being fed with rations furnished by the United States Commissary Department, and the officers receive from the United States sufficient money for their support.

SPANISH NAVY.

At the outbreak of the war the naval force in the Philippines consisted of
  10 Cruisers.
  19 Gunboats.
  4 Armed Launches.
  3 Transports.
  1 Survey Boat.

Of these Admiral Dewey destroyed, on May 1st, ten cruisers and one transport, and he has since captured two gunboats. The Spaniards have sunk one transport and two or three gunboats in the Pasig River. There remain thirteen or fourteen gunboats, which are scattered among the islands. They are of iron, from 140 to 200 tons each, are armed with one breech-loading rifle, caliber 3 6-10 inches, and two to four machine guns, each caliber 44-100 to 1 inch. One of the captured boats, the Callao, under command of Lieutenant Tappan, United States Navy, and a crew of eighteen men, rendered very efficient service in the attack of August 13th. These boats would all be useful in the naval police of the islands. They will, however, probably be scuttled by the Spaniards before the islands are surrendered.

The Navy Yard at Cavite has barracks for about 1,500 men (now occupied by United States troops) and has shops and ways for light work and vessels of less than 1,000 tons. Many of the gunboats above mentioned were built there. The shallow depth of water in Canacoa or Cavite Bay would prevent the enlargement of this naval station to accommodate large vessels, and the plan of the Spaniards was to create a large naval station in Subig Bay, on which considerable money has already been spent.

SPANISH CIVIL ADMINISTRATION.

The Government of the Philippine Islands, including the Ladrones, Carolinas and Palaos, is vested in the Governor-General, who, in the language of the Spanish Official Guide, or Blue Book, "is the sole and legitimate representative in these islands of the supreme power of the Government of the King of Spain, and, as such, is th supreme head of all branches of the public service, and has authority to inspect and supervise the same, not excepting the courts of justice." The office is held by a Lieutenant-General in the Spanish army, and he is also Vice Royal Patron of the Indies, exercising in these islands the ecclesiastical functions conferred on the King of Spain by various Bulls of the Popes of Rome, Captain-General-in-Chief of the Army of the Philippines, Inspector-General of all branches of the service, Commander-in-Chief of the Naval Forces, and President of all corporations and societies which partake of an official character.

What corresponds to his Cabinet, or Ministry, consists of

(a) The Archbishop of Manila and four Bishops, who administer ecclesiastical affairs in the five dioceses into which the islands are divided for this purpose; the appointment of parish priests and curates, however, is vested in the Governor-General. The various religious orders which exercise so large an influence in the politics and business of the islands, viz.: Augustinians, Dominicans, Recollects,

Franciscans, Capuchins, Benedictines and Jesuits, are all under the management of the Bishops, subject to the supervision of the Pope, and the prerogatives of the King as Royal Patron, which prerogatives are exercised by the Governor-General as Viceroy.

(b) The High Court of Justice in Manila, which is the Court of Appeals in civil and governmental cases for all the islands. There are two principal criminal courts in Cebu and Vigan (northern Luzon) and appeal in criminal cases lies to these courts or to the High Court of Manila. In every Province there is a court of primary jurisdiction in both civil and criminal cases.

(c) The General, second in command, who is a General of Division in the Spanish army. He is the sub-inspector of all branches of the military service, is Military Governor of the Province and city of Manila and commands all the troops stationed therein, and in the absence or sickness of the Captain General he commands all the military forces in the islands.

(d) The General Commandant of Dock Yards and Squadron. This post is filled by a Vice Admiral in the Spanish navy, and he commands the naval forces, ships and establishments in the islands.

(e) The Minister of Finance, or Intendente General de Hacienda, who is charged with the collection of customs and internal taxes, the expenditures of public money, and the audit and control of public accounts.

(f) The Minister of the Interior, or Director General of Civil Administration, who is charged with all public business relating to public instruction, charities, health, public works, forests, mines, agriculture, industry and commerce, posts and telegraphs and meteorology.

For the purpose of local administration the islands are divided into Provinces and Districts, classified as follows:

        19 Civil Governments.
        24 Political-Military Governments.
        23 Political-Military Commands.
        15 Military Commands.

The most important of the Provinces are Manila, with a population of 400,238 (of which 10 per cent. are Chinese), and Cebu, with 504,076; and the least important districts are Balabas and Corregidor, with 420 and 320 respectively.

The governor or commandant has supreme control within his province or district of every branch of the public service, including the Courts of Justice, and each reports to the Governor General. The Guardia Civil or Gendarmerie, is subject only to his orders, and for arrests and imprisonment for political offenses, he is responsible, not to the law, but to the Governor General and the King.

The Civil Governments are governed by Civil Governors, of the rank in the Spanish Civil Service of Chiefs of Administration of the second class. The Political Military Governments and Commands are in charges of military and naval officers of various grades, according to their size and importance; ranging from General of Division at Mindanao, Brigadier-Generals at Cebu and Iloilo, Captain in the navy at Paragua, down to Lieutenant at Balabas and Corregidor.

The Civil or Military Governor is assisted by a secretary, a judge, an administrator of finances, a postmaster and a captain of police.

The affairs of cities are managed by a council (Ayuntamiento) consisting of a president, a recorder (Sindico), one or more mayors (Alcaldo), six to ten aldermen (Regidores) and a secretary.

Outside of the cities each province or district is divided into a number of villages or parishes (Pueblos); the total number of these is 1,055; in each there is a parish priest, a municipal captain, a justice of the peace, a school master and school mistress. The number of cities is very small, and the social life of the community depends almost wholly on the form of government of the Pueblos, or villages. In 1893 this was reorganized with the alleged intention of giving local self-government. The scheme is complicated and curious and only an outline of it can be given here. It is contained in full in the Royal Decree of May 19, 1893, a long document, supplemented by still longer regulations for carrying the same into effect.

In brief every Pueblo in which there are paid more than 1,000 Cedulas (poll tax) shall have a municipal tribunal consisting of five members, by whom its local affairs and funds shall be managed. The members are a

                Municipal Captain.
                Senior Lieutenant.
                Lieutenant of Police.
                Lieutenant of Agriculture.
                Lieutenant of Cattle.

And the Village Priest is required to attend all the important meetings.

The Captain holds office for four years, and is eligible for indefinite re-election; the Lieutenants hold office for four years also, one-half of them going out of office every two years, and they are ineligible for re-election until two years after the expiration of their term. Both Captains and Lieutenants are elected, on a day designated by the Governor, and in presence of the village priest, and outgoing Captain, by the Principalia, or body of principal men of the village. The village is subdivided into Barangayes, or group of about 100 families each, and for each Barangay there is a Chief or Headman (Cabeza), who is appointed by the Governor,

THE PHILIPPINE ISLANDS AS THEY ARE. 117

on the recommendation of the Municipal Tribunal. The Principalia is made up of

    Former Municipal Captains.
    Former Municipal Lieutenants.
    Former Gobernadorcilles.
    Chiefs of Barangayes.
    All inhabitants paying more than $50 annually in taxes.

The Principalia choose the 12 electors as follows:

    6 from the Chiefs of Barangayes.
    3 from Former Municipal Captains.
    3 from the largest taxpayers.

The electors hold office for six years, and one-third go out of office every two years.

The municipal Captain must be a resident of the village, more than 25 years of age, read and speak Spanish and be a Chief of Barangay. While the Municipal Tribunal nominally controls the local affairs, yet the Captain has the right to suspend all its acts which he considers against the public welfare, and report the matter to the Provincial Governor, who has power to rescind them; the Captain appoints all village employes, and removes them at will; he can also fine and punish them for petty offenses; he issues orders to the police and collects the taxes. He holds a commission as Delegate or Representative of the Governor General, and, in fact, he exercises within his little bailiwick the same supreme power that the governor exercises in the province, and the Governor General in the whole Archipelago.

In each province there is a Junta or Council, whose membership consists of

    The Administrator of Finance.
    Two Vicars.
    The Public Physician.

The latter Four Members must be residents of the Capital of the Province, and they are elected by the Municipal Captains, from a list of names submitted to them by the Junta with the approval of the Governor.

The functions of this Junta or Council are solely those of inspection and advice. It watches over affairs of the Municipal Tribunals, and reports to the Governor its advice and recommendations concerning them. The Municipal Captain is obliged to deposit the taxes in the Provincial Treasury, the keys of which are held by three members of the Council; he draws out the money in accordance with the municipal budget, and his accounts must be approved by his lieutenants, countersigned by the village priest, passed upon by the Provincial Council, and finally approved by the Governor.

The Governor has power to suspend the Municipal Captain or any of his colleagues for a period of three months, and the Governor General can remove one or all of them from office at will; and "in extraordinary cases or for reasons of public tranquility, the Governor shall have power to decree, without any legal process, the abolition of the Municipal Tribunals." (Article 45.)

In December, 1896, General Polavieja issued a decree, suspending the elections which were to take place that month for one-third of the municipal electors, and directed the Governors of Provinces to send in names of persons suitable for appointment, together with the recommendations of the village priest in each case.

An examination of this unique scheme of village government shows that one-half of the electors are to be chosen from persons holding a subordinate office and appointed by the Governor; that the village priest must be present at all elections and important meetings; that the Captain has all the responsibility, and he must also be of the class holding a subordinate office by appointment of the governor; that the acts of Municipal Tribunal can be suspended by the Captain and rescinded by the Governor; and, finally, if the Municipal Tribunal is offensive to the Governor General he can either remove its members and appoint others in their place or can abolish it altogether.

Such is the Spanish idea of self-government; the Minister of the Colonies, in submitting the decree to the Queen Regent, expatiated on its merits in giving the natives such full control of their local affairs, and expressed the confident belief that it would prove "most beneficent to these people whom Providence has confided to the generous sovereignty of the Spanish monarchs."

This scheme of government by Municipal Tribunals was highly approved by the natives, except that feature of it which placed so much power in the hands of the Governor and Governor General. This, however, was the essence of the matter, from the Spanish standpoint, and these portions of the Decree were the ones most fully carried out. The natives complained, on the one hand, of the delay in putting the Decree into operation, and on the other hand that so much of it as was established was practically nullified by the action of the Governors. Seeing that the Tribunals had really no power, the members soon turned their sessions (which the Decree required to be secret) into political meetings in favor of the insurrection. So the whole project is thus far a failure; and the local administration is in considerable disorder, apart from that caused by the insurgents. In point of fact self-government and representation are unknown in these islands. The Archbishop and the four Bishops are appointed by the Pope; the Governor General, military and naval officers and all officials with a salary exceeding about $2,000 (silver) are appointed by the King or the Minister of the Colonies. Yet all the expenses are paid from the Philippine Treasury; the salaries of all officials, military, naval, civil

BRIGADIER-GENERAL F. V. GREENE.

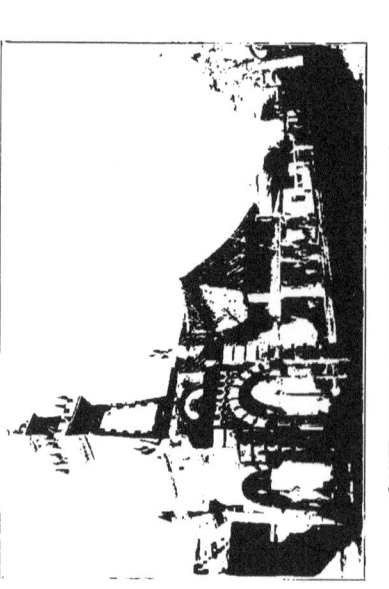

GOVERNMENT BUILDING IN PAMPANGA.

CHURCH AT CAVITE USED AS SPANISH FORT.

MASACUE, TOWN IN CAVITE BURNING.

NATIVES TAKING REFRESHMENTS.

and ecclesiastical, the expenses and pensions of the army, navy and church, the cost of the diplomatic and consular service in Japan, China and Singapore, even a portion of the expenses of the Colonial office, Madrid, and of pensions paid to the descendants of Columbus—all come out of the taxes raised in the islands. The natives have no place in the government, except clerks in the public offices at Manila and the petty positions in the villages and the Ayentamientos of cities, where their powers and responsibilities, as we have seen, are at all times limited and subject to revocation whenever disapproved by the Governor.

Though the population of the islands is 40 per cent. of that of Spain, they have no representation in the Cortes.

GEN. GREENE'S HEADQUARTERS AT MANILA.

There is a widespread report, almost universally believed by native Filipinos and by foreign merchants, and even acknowledged by many Spaniards, that pecuniary dishonesty and corruption exist throughout the whole body of Spanish office-holders, from the highest to the lowest. Forced contributions are said to be levied on the salaries of minor officials; the Regimental Paymasters and Commissaries are said to have sold part of the regimental stores for their own profit, the Collector of Customs and the Minister of Finance to have imposed or remitted fines at the Cus tom House and Internal Revenue Office, according to payment or non-payment of presents by merchants, the judges and court officials to have "borrowed" from attorneys large sums which are never paid, and even the Governor General is reported to have organized a regular system of smuggling in Mexican dollars, the importation of which was prohibited by law, on a fixed scale of payment to himself. The current report is that Weyler carried away over $1,000,000 as his savings during the three years from 1888 to 1891 that he held the office of Governor General, on a salary of $40,000 a year. Of the proof of these reports I have naturally no personal knowledge, but they are matters of common talk and belief, and they have been stated to me by responsible persons, who have long resided in the islands.

As above stated, the Governor General is supreme head of every branch of the public service, not excepting the Courts of Justice. How this power was exercised is shown in the hundreds of executions for alleged political offenses, which took place during the years 1895, 1896 and 1897, by the thousands deported to Mindanao and Fernando Po, and by the number of political prisoners in jail at the time of our entry into Manila. On the first examination which General McArthur, as Military Governor, made of the jail, about August 22nd, he released over 60 prisoners confined for alleged political offenses. One of them was a woman who had been imprisoned for eleven years, by order of the Governor General, but without any charges ever having been presented against her; another was a woman who had been in jail for three years on a vague charge, never formulated, of having carried a basket of cartridges to an insurgent.

The day of reckoning for three centuries of this sort of government came when Admiral Dewey destroyed the Spanish squadron on May 1st, 1898. An insurrection had been in progress from August, 1896, to December, 1897. Unable to suppress it the Government had made a written treaty with the insurgent leaders, paying them a large sum of money and promising to introduce various reforms on condition that they would leave the country. Hardly had the Spanish officials recovered from this when the appalling disaster of the destruction of their fleet occurred under their very eyes.

Then followed in rapid succession the naval blockade, the arrival of the insurgent leaders from Hongkong, the raising of the insurgent army, which blockaded Manila on the land side, and finally, the American troops. At the end of 104 days after the destruction of the Spanish fleet, the city surrendered to a combined land and naval attack of the American forces. On the day after the capitulation, the American Commander in Chief issued his proclamation establishing a military government, appointed a Military Governor, a Minister of Finance, a Collector of Customs, Collector of Internal Revenue, Postmaster and Judge of the Provost Court; took possession of all public funds (about $900,000), and all public offices, and as rapidly as possible put this government in operation.

The machinery of the Spanish Government was thoroughly disorganized when we entered Manila. The Courts of Justice, except the inferior criminal courts, had not been in session since early in May; the officials had been cut off from communication with the other islands and with Spain for over three months; there had been no customs to collect, and, owing to the entire suspension of business, but little internal revenue; a forced loan of $2,000,000 for military purpose had been extracted from the Spanish-Philippine Bank, and yet the troops were several months in arrears of pay; all government offices outside the walled city had been moved to temporary quarters within the walls and their records had been lost or thrown into confusion; the officials seeing the inevitable end in sight, were intent only on planning for their return to Spain.

This disorganization was completed when the American Military officers took charge of the Government, and every Spanish official, without exception, refused absolutely to continue in service. They were immediately dismissed and dispersed.

The situation thus created is without precedent in American history. When Scott captured the City of Mexico it was acknowledged on both sides that his occupation was only to be temporary, and there were no insurgents to deal with. When the Americans entered California they found only a scanty population, who were soon outnumbered by the American immigrants. But in the Philippine Islands there is a population of more than 7,000,000, governed by an alien race, whose representatives present in the Islands, including military and naval forces, clergy and civil employes do not exceed 30,000 in number. Against this Government an insurrection is in progress, which claims to have been successful in provinces containing a population of about 2,000,000. The city and province of Manila, with a population of 400,000 more, have been captured and occupied by a foreign army, but whether its occupation is to be temporary or permanent has not yet been decided.

Finally, the Government officials of all classes refuse to perform their functions; the desire of most of them is to escape to Spain. It was stipulated in the capitulation that they should have the right to do so at their own expense, and numbers of them, as well as friars, have already taken their departure. The Spanish officials have intense fear of the Insurgents; and the latter hate them, as well as the friars, with a virulence that can hardly be described. They have fought them with success, and almost without interruption for two years, and they will continue to fight them with increased vigor and still greated prospects of success, if any attempt is

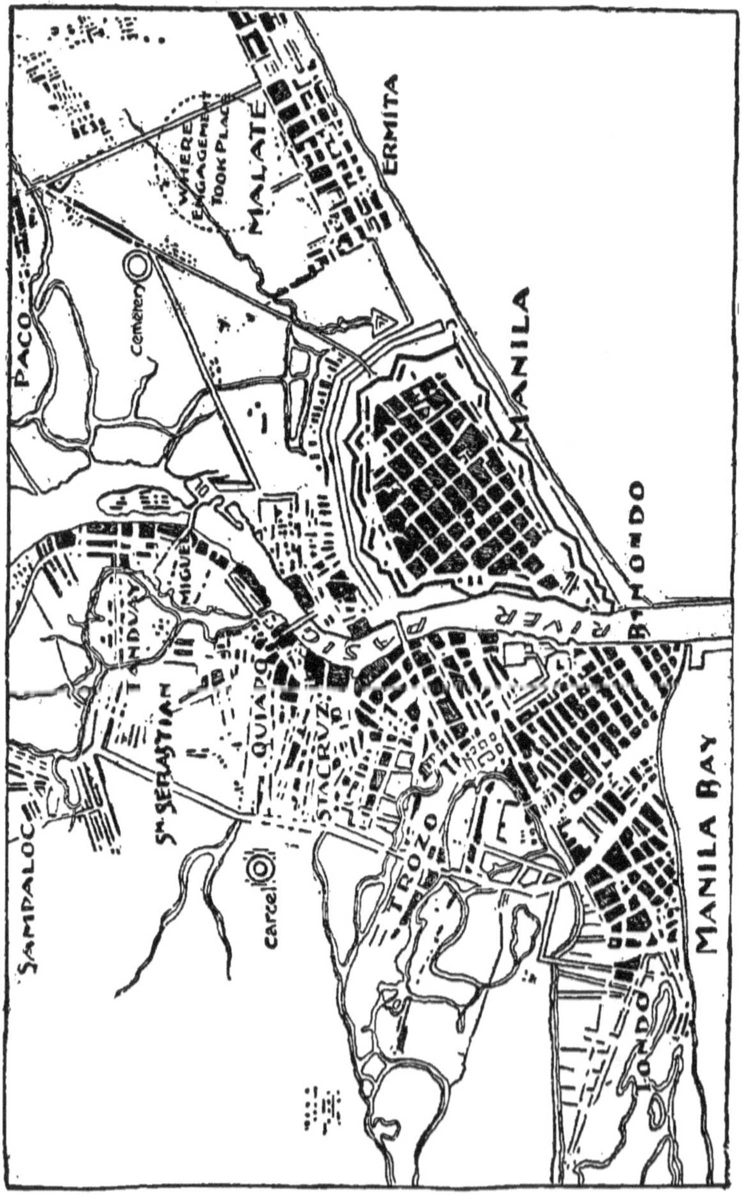

MANILLA AND ITS OUTSKIRTS, SHOWING MALATE.

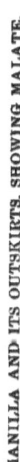

made to restore the Spanish Government. In its present disorganized condition the Spanish Government could not successfully cope with them; on the other hand, it would not surrender to them. The result, therefore, of an attempted restoration of Spanish power in any of the islands would simply be civil war and anarchy, leading inevitably and speedily to intervention by foreign nations whose subjects have property in the islands which they would not allow to be destroyed.

INSURGENT TROOPS.

It is very difficult to give figures for the exact numbers of insurgent troops. In his message to foreign governments of August 6th, asking for recognition of belligerency and independence, Aguinaldo claims to have a force of 30,000 men, organized into a regular army. This included the force in the provinces of Luzon outside of Manila. What was in evidence around Manila varied from 10,000 to 15,000. They were composed of young men and boys, some as young as fifteen years of age, recruited in the rural districts, having no property and nothing to lose in a civil war. They have received no pay and, although Aguinaldo speaks in his proclamation of his intention and ability to maintain order wherever his forces penetrate, yet the feeling is practically universal among the rank and file that they are to be compensated for their time and services and hardships by looting Manila.

Their equipment consists of a gun, bayonet and cartridge box; their uniform of a straw hat, gingham shirt and trousers and bare feet; their transportation of a few ponies and carts, impressed for a day or week at a time; for quarters they have taken the public building in each village or pueblo, locally known as the Tribunal, and the churches and convents; from these details are sent out to man the trenches. Their food while on duty consists of rice and banana leaves, cooked at the quarters and sent out to the trenches. After a few days or a week of active service they return to their homes to feed up or work on their farms, their places being taken by others to whom they turn over their guns and cartridges. Their arms have been obtained from various sources, from purchases in Hongkong, from the supply which Admiral Dewey found in the arsenal at Cavite, from capture made from the Spaniards. They are partly Mausers and partly Remingtons. Their ammunition was obtained in the same way. They have used it freely and the supply is now rather short. To replenish it they have established a cartridge factory at the village of Imus, about ten miles south of Cavite, where they have 400 people engaged in re-loading cartridges with powder and lead found at Cavite, or purchased abroad. They have no artillery, except a few antique Columbiads obtained from Cavite, and no cavalry. Their method of warfare is to dig a trench in front of the Spanish position, cover it with mats as a protection against the sun and rain, and during the night put their guns on top of the trench above their heads and fire in the general direction of the enemy. When their ammunition is exhausted they go off in a body to get a fresh supply in baskets and then return to the trenches.

The men are of small stature, from 5 feet to 5 feet 6 inches in height, and weigh from 110 to 130 pounds. Compared with them our men from Colorado and California seemed like a race of giants. One afternoon just after we entered Manila a battalion of the insurgents fired upon the outposts of the Colorado regiment, mistaking them, as they claimed, for Spaniards. The outpost retreated to their support, and the Filipinos followed; they easily fell into an ambush and the support, numbering about fifty men, surrounded the 250 Filipinos, wrenched the guns out of their hands and marched them off as unarmed prisoners—all in the space of a few minutes. Such a force can hardly be called an army, and yet the service which it has rendered should not be underestimated. Between 2,000 and 3,000 Spanish native troops surrendered to it during the months of June and July. It constantly annoyed and harrassed the Spaniards in the trenches, keeping them up at night and wearing them out with fatigue; and it invested Manila early in July so completely that all supplies were cut off and the inhabitants as well as the Spanish troops were forced to live on horse and buffalo meat, and the Chinese population on cats and dogs. It captured the water works of Manila and cut off the water supply, and, if it had been in the dry season, would have inflicted great suffering on the inhabitants for lack of water. These results, it is true, were obtained against a dispirited army, containing a considerable number of native troops of doubtful loyalty. Yet, from August, 1896, to April, 1897, they fought 25,000 of the best regular troops sent out from Spain, inflicting on them a loss of over 150 officers and 2,500 men, killed and wounded, and they suffered still greater losses themselves. Nevertheless, from daily contact with them for six weeks, I am very confident that no such results could have been obtained against an American army, which would have driven them back to the hills and reduced them to a petty guerilla warfare. If they attack the American army this will certainly be the result, and, while these guerilla bands might give some trouble so long as their ammunition lasted, yet, with our navy guarding the coasts and our army pursuing them on land, it would not be long before they were reduced to subjection.

INSURGENT CIVIL ADMINISTRATION.

In August, 1896, an insurrection broke out in Cavite, under the leadership of Emilio Aguinaldo, and soon spread to other provinces on both sides of Manila. It continued with varying successes on both sides, and the trial and execution of numerous insurgents, until December, 1897, when the Governor-General, Primo de

Rivera, entered into written agreement with Aguinaldo, the substance of the document, which is in possession of Senor Felipe Agoncillo, who accompanies me to Washington, being attached hereto and marked "A." In brief, it required that Aguinaldo and the other insurgent leaders should leave the country, the Government agreeing to pay them $800,000 in silver, and promising to introduce numerous reforms, including representation in the Spanish Cortes, freedom of the press, amnesty for all insurgents, and the expulsion of secularization of the monastic orders. Aguinaldo and his associates went to Hongkong and Singapore. A portion of the money, $400,000, was deposited in banks at Hongkong, and a lawsuit soon arose between Aguinaldo and one of his subordinate chiefs, named Artacho, which is interesting on account of the very honorable position taken by Aguinaldo. Artacho sued for a division of the money among the insurgents, according to rank. Aguinaldo claimed that the money was a trust fund and was to remain on deposit until it was seen whether the Spaniards would carry out their promised reforms, and if they failed to do so it was to be used to defray the expenses of a new insurrection. The suit was settled out of court by paying Artacho $5,000.

No steps have been taken to introduce the reforms, more than 2,000 insurgents who had been deported to Fernando Po and other places are still in confinement, and Aguinaldo is now using the money to carry on the operations of the present insurrection.

On the 24th day of April Aguinaldo met the United States Consul and others at Singapore and offered to begin a new insurrection in conjunction with the operations of the United States navy at Manila. This was telegraphed to Admiral Dewey and, by his consent, or, at his request, Aguinaldo left Singapore for Hongkong on April 26th, and, when the McCullough went to Hongkong early in May to carry the news of Admiral Dewey's victory, it took Aguinaldo and seventeen other revolutionary chiefs on board and brought them to Manila Bay. They soon after landed at Cavite, and the Admiral allowed them to take such guns, ammunition and stores as he did not require for himself. With these and some other arms which he had brought from Hongkong Aguinaldo armed his followers, who rapidly assembled at Cavite and, in a few weeks, he began moving against the Spaniards. Part of them surrendered, giving him more arms, and the others retreated to Manila.

Soon afterwards two ships, which were the private property of Senor Agoncillo and other insurgent sympathizers, were converted into cruisers and sent with insurgent troops to Subig Bay and other places, to capture provinces outside of Manila. They were very successful, the native militia in Spanish service capitulating with their arms in nearly every case without serious resistance. On the 18th of June

Aguinaldo issued a proclamation from Cavite establishing a Dictatorial Government, with himself as Dictator. In each village or pueblo a Chief (Jefe) was to be elected, and in each ward a Nendrum (Cabeza); also in each pueblo three delegates, one of Police, one of Justice, and one of Taxes. These were to constitute the Junta, or Assembly, and after consulting the Junta the Chiefs of pueblos were to elect a Chief of Province and three Counsellors, one of Police, one of Justice, and one of Taxes. They were also to elect one or more Representatives from each Province to form the Revolutionary Congress. This was followed on June 20th by a decree giving more detailed instructions in regard to the elections. On June 23d another decree followed, changing the title of the Government from Dictatorial to Revolutionary, and of the chief officer from Dictator to President; announcing a Cabinet with a Minister of Foreign Affairs, Marine and Commerce, another of War and Public Works, another of Police and Internal Order, Justice, Instruction and Hygiene, and another of Taxes, Agriculture and Manufactures; the powers of the President and Congress were defined, and a code of military justice was formulated. On the same date a manifesto was issued to the world explaining the reasons and purposes of the Revolution. On June 27th another decree was issued containing instructions in regard to elections. On August 6th an address was issued to Foreign Governments, stating that the Revolutionary Government was in operation and control in fifteen Provinces, and that in response to the petition of the duly elected Chiefs of these Provinces an appeal is made for recognition of belligerency and independence. Translations of these various documents are all apended, marked "B," "C," "D," "E," "F," "G" and "H."

The scheme of Government is set forth in the decree of June 23d, marked "D." An examination of this document shows that it provides a Dictatorship of the familiar South American type. All power is centered in the President, and he is not responsible to any one for his acts. He is declared to be "the personification of the Philippine public, and in this view cannot be held responsible while he holds office. His term will last until the Revolution triumphs." He appoints not only the heads of the departments, but all their subordinates, and without reference to Congress. This body is composed of a single Chamber of Representatives from each Province. The election is to be conducted by an agent of the President, and the qualifications of electors are "those inhabitants most distinguished for high character, social position and honorable conduct."

If any Province is still under Spanish rule its Representative is to be appointed by the President. Congress is to deliberate on "all grave and transcendental questions, whose decision admits of delay and adjournment, but the President may

THE PHILIPPINE ISLANDS AS THEY ARE.

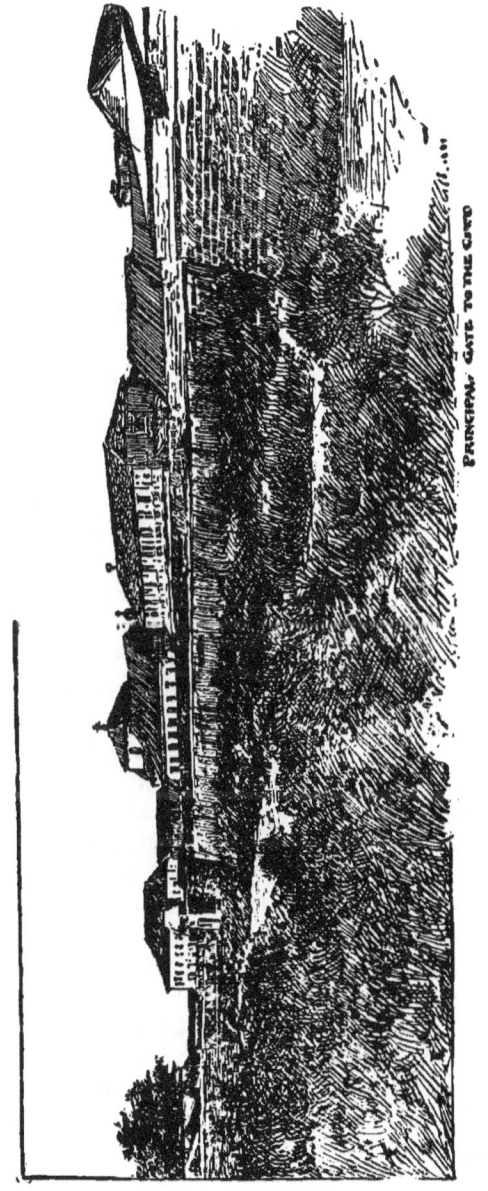

PRINCIPAL GATE TO THE CITY

decide questions of urgent character, giving the reasons for his decision in a message to Congress." The acts of Congress are not binding until approved by the President, and he has power of absolute veto.

Congress was to hold its first session at Saloles about September 28th.

While this scheme of Government is a pure despotism, yet it claims to be only temporary, and intended to "prepare the country so that a true Republic may be established." It also provides a rude form of governmental machinery for managing the affairs of the Provinces. To what extent it has actually gone into operation it is difficult to say. Aguinaldo claims, in his address of August 6th, that it is in force in fifteen Provinces, whose aggregate population is about 2,000,000. They include the island of Mindoro and about half of Luzon. None of those (except Cavíte) have yet been visited by Americans, and all communication with them by the Spanish Government at Manila has been cut off since May 1st.

In the province of Cavite and that portion of the Province of Manila outside of the city and of its suburbs, which was occupied by the insurgent troops as well as those of the United States, their military forces, military headquarters, etc., were very much in evidence, occupying the principal houses and churches in every village and hamlet, but there were no signs of Civil Government or administration. It was reported, however, that Aguinaldo's agents were levying taxes or forced contributions not only in the outside villages, but (after we entered Manila) by means of secret agents, in the market places of the city itself. At Aguinaldo's headquarters, in Bacoor, there were signs of activity and business, and it was reported that his Cabinet officers were in constant session there.

Aguinaldo never himself failed to claim all the prerogatives due to his alleged position as the de facto ruler of the country. The only general officer who saw him or had any direct communication with him was General Anderson. He did much to thwart this officer in organizing a native wagon train and otherwise providing for his troops, and he went so far, in a letter of July 23d (copy herewith marked "J"), as to warn General Anderson not to land American troops on Philippine soil without his consent—a notice which, it is hardly necessary to say, was ignored. The day before the attack on Manila he sent staff officers to the same General, asking for our plans of attack, so that their troops could enter Manila with us. The same request had previously been made to me by one of his Brigade Commanders, to which I replied that I was not authorized to give the information desired.

Aguinaldo did not call upon General Merritt on his arrival, and this enabled the latter to avoid any communication with him, either direct or indirect, until after Manila had been taken. General Merritt then received one of Aguinaldo's staff officers in his office as Military Governor. The interview lasted more than an hour. General Merritt referred to his proclamation as showing the conditions under which the American troops had come to Manila and the nature of the Military Government, which would be maintained until further orders from Washington. He agreed upon the lines outside of the city of Manila, up to which the insurgent troops could come, but no further with arms in their hands. He asked for possession of the water works, which was given, and, while expressing our friendship and sympathy for the Philippine people, he stated very positively that the United States Government had placed at his disposal an ample force for carrying out his instructions, and even if the services of Aguinaldo's forces had been needed as allies he should not have felt at liberty to accept them.

The problem of how to deal with Aguinaldo's Government and troops will necessarily be accompanied with embarrassment and difficulty, and will require much tact and skill in its solution. The United States Government, through its Naval Commander, has, to some extent, made use of them for a distinct military purpose, viz.: to harass and annoy the Spanish troops, to wear them out in the trenches, to blockade Manila on the land side, and to do as much damage as possible to the Spanish Government prior to the arrival of our troops, and for this purpose the Admiral allowed them to take the arms and munitions which he had captured at Cavite, and their ships to pass in and out of Manila Bay in their expeditions against other Provinces. But the Admiral has been very careful to give Aguinaldo no assurances of recognition and no pledges or promises of any description. The services which Aguinaldo and his adherents rendered in preparing the way for attack on Manila are certainly entitled to consideration, but, after all, they were small in comparison with what was done by our fleet and army.

There is no reason to believe that Aguinaldo's Government has any elements of stability. In the first place, Aguinaldo is a young man of twenty-three years. Prior to the insurrection of 1896 he had been a schoolmaster, and afterward Gobernadoreillo and Municipal Captain in one of the pueblos in the Province of Cavite. He is not devoid of ability, and he is surrounded by clever writers. But the educated and intelligent Filipinos of Manila say that not only is he lacking in ability to be at the head of affairs, but if an election for President was held he would not even be a candidate. He is a successful leader of insurgents, has the confidence of young men in the country districts, prides himself on his military ability, and if a Republic could be established the post he would probably choose for himself would be General-in-Chief of the Army.

In the next place, Aguinaldo's Government, or any entirely independent Government, does not command the hearty support of the large body of Filipinos, both in Manila and outside, who have property, education and intelligence. Their hatred of the Spanish rule is very keen and they will co-operate with Aguinaldo or any one else to destroy it. But after that is done they fully realize that they must have the support of some strong nation for many years before they will be in a position to manage their own affairs alone. The nation to which they all turn is America, and their ideal is a Philippine Republic, under American protection—such as they have heard is to be granted to Cuba. But when it comes to defining their ideas of protection and the respective rights and duties of each under it, what portion of the Government is to be administered by them and what portion by us; how the revenues are to be collected, and in what proportion the expenses are to be divided; they have no clear ideas at all; nor is it expected that they should have, after generations of Spanish rule without any experience in self government. The sentiment of this class, the educated native with property at stake, looks upon the prospect of Aguinaldo's Government and forces entering Manila with almost as much dread as the foreign merchants or the Spaniards themselves.

Finally, it must be remembered that this is purely a Tagalo insurrection. There are upwards of thirty races in the Philippines, each speaking a different dialect, but five-sixths of the entire Christian population is composed of the Tagalos and Visayas. The former live in Mindoro and the southern half of Luzon, and the latter in Cebu, Iloilo and other islands in the center of the group. The Tagalos are more numerous than the Visayas, but both races are about equal in civilization, intelligence and wealth. It is claimed by Aguinaldo's partisans that the Visayas are in sympathy with his insurrection and intend to send representatives to the congress. But it is a fact that the Visayas have taken no active part in the present insurrection nor in that of 1896, that the Spanish Government is still in full control at Cebu and Iloilo, and in the Viscayas islands, and that Aguinaldo has as yet made no effort to attack them. The Visayas number nearly 2,000,000, or about as many as the population of all the Tagalo Provinces, which Aguinaldo claims to have captured. There is no evidence to show that they will support his pretensions, and many reasons to believe that on account of racial prejudices and jealousies and other causes they will oppose him.

Upon one point all are agreed, except possibly Aguinaldo and his immediate adherents, and that is that no native government can maintain itself without the active support and protection of a strong foreign government. This being admitted it is difficult to see how any foreign government can give this protection without taking such an active part in the management of affairs as is practically equivalent to governing in its own name and for its own account.

UNITED STATES TROOPS AND NAVY.

I assume that the reports received at the War and Navy Departments give all the desired information in regard to the military forces of the United States.

At the time I left (August 30th) the Eighth Corps consisted of two divisions, numbering in all about 12,000 men, with 16 field guns and 6 mountain guns. No wagons or animals had then arrived.

One regiment was stationed within the walled city guarding its gates, and the captured guns and ammunition; a small force was at Cavite, and the bulk of the troops were in Manila, outside of the walled city. They were quartered in the Spanish barracks, which were all in good condition, and in convents and private houses. The health of the troops was excellent, notwithstanding the extraordinary hardships to which they had been subjected in the trenches before entering Manila.

Admiral Dewey had under his command the Charleston, Monterey and Monadnock, which arrived in July and August, the Callao and Leyte, which had been captured from the Spaniards, and the ships which were in the battle of May 1st, viz: Olympia, Boston, Baltimore, Raleigh, Concord, Petrel and McCullough. The health of the squadron was excellent. The Olympia and Concord were being docked and cleaned at Hongkong. Permission to use the docks at Nagasaki during the suspension of hostilities had been declined.

UNITED STATES CIVIL ADMINISTRATION.

We entered Manila on the afternoon of August 13th. On the 14th the capitulation was signed, and the same day General Merritt issued his proclamation establishing a Military Government. On the 15th General McArthur was appointed Military Commander of the walled city and Provost Marshal General of the City of Manila and its suburbs, and on the 17th I was appointed to take charge of the duties performed by the intendente General de Hacienda, or Minister of Finance, and all fiscal affairs. Representatives of the Postoffice Department had arrived on the Steamship China in July and they immediately took charge of the Manila Postoffice, which was opened for business on the 16th. The Custom House was opened on the 18th, with Lieutenant-Colonel Whittier as Collector, and the Internal Revenue office, with Major Bement as Collector on the 22nd. Captain Glass of the Navy was appointed Captain of the Port, or Naval Officer, and took charge of the office on August 19th. The collections of customs during the first ten days exceeded $100,000. The collection of internal revenue was small owing to the difficulty and delay in ascertaining what persons had or had not paid their taxes for the current year. The administration of Water Works was put in charge of Lieutenant Connor, of the Engineers, on August 25th, the Provost Court with Lieutenant-Colonel Jewett, Judge Advocate United States Volunteers, sitting as Judge, was appointed and held its first session on August 23rd.

The Provost Marshal General has charge of the Police, Fire, Health and Street Cleaning Departments, and the issuing of licenses. The Guardia Civil, or Gendarmerie of the City, proving indifferent and inefficient, they were disarmed and disbanded; the 13th Minnesota regiment was detailed for police duty, and one or more companies stationed in each Police Station, from which patrolmen were sent out on the streets to take the place of the sentries who had constantly patrolled them from the hour of entering the city.

The shops were all closed when we entered on Saturday afternoon, the 13th; on Monday some of them opened, and by Wednesday the Banks had resumed business, the newspapers were published, and the merchants were ready to declare goods at the Custom House, the tram cars were running and the retail shops were all open and doing a large business. There was no disorder or pillage of any kind in the city. The conduct of the troops was simply admirable, and left no ground for criticism. It was noted and commented upon by the foreign naval officers in the most favorable terms, and it so surprised the Spanish soldiers that a considerable number of them applied for permission to enlist in our service.

At the time I left General McArthur fully established his office as Provost Marshal General, and was organizing one by one the various bureaus connected with it, all with United States military officers in charge; the Provost Court was in daily session, sentencing gamblers and persons guilty of petty disturbances, and a military commission had just been ordered to try a Chinaman accused of burglary.

In various public offices I collected the following Spanish funds:

At the General Treasury..........................$795,517.71
At the Mint................................. 62,856.08
At the Internal Revenue Office..................... 24,077.60

$882,451.39

Of this amount there was in
Gold Coin...$ 4,200.00
Gold Bars,.. 3,806.08
Silver Coin....................................... 190,634.81
Copper Coin....................................... 297,300.00
Spanish Bank Notes................................ 216,305.00
Accepted Checks................................... 170,205.50

$882,451.39

The money was counted by a board of officers and turned over to Major C. H. Whipple, Paymaster U. S. A., as custodian of Spanish Public Funds. A few thousand dollars in other public offices were still to be collected.

The money received at the Custom House and other offices is turned in daily, at the close of business, to Major Whipple. Money for current expenses is furnished to heads of departments on their requisition, by warrant drawn by the Intendente General on the Custodian of Spanish Public Funds. The heads of the departments are to submit their vouchers and accounts monthly to an auditing department, which was being organized when I left.

All these public offices and funds were surrendered to me only on threat of using force and on granting permission to file a formal written protest. None of these had been received at the time I left, but the ground of verbal protest was that the officials recognized no authority in these islands but the Governor General appointed by the King of Spain, and without his order they were unwilling to surrender them. On the other hand, I recognized no authority of the Spanish Governor General who was merely a prisoner of war; I acted under the orders of General Merritt as the United States Military Governor, and in accordance with the terms of capitulation. The claim will probably be made by the Spanish officials that as we captured Manila a few hours after the peace protocol had been signed at Washington, this property still belongs to the Spaniards. But I believe that the law in such cases was clearly defined in decisions made by the United States Supreme Court in 1815. We captured Manila, and the capitulation (under which these funds became United States property) was signed by both parties, before either had received any notice of the protocol of suspension of hostilities.

On the opening of the Custom House several important questions arose for immediate decision. The first was in regard to Mexican dollars. The importation of these has for several years been prohibited, with a view of forcing the Spanish coinage (which contains less silver) into circulation. The large English banks represented that there was a scarcity of currency, owing to the amount which had been hoarded and sent away during the seige, and they agreed in consideration of being allowed to import Mexican dollars free of duty, to guarantee the notes and accepted checks of the Spanish bank, which should be received by us in payment of customs up to $200,000 at any one time. The Spanish bank was in difficulty, owing to the enormous amount which the Government had taken from it under the form of a forced loan, and any discrimination on our part against it would result in its failure, entailing widespread financial disturbance. As there seemed no reason against allowing the importation of Mexican dollars and many in favor of it, I recommended that the Custom House continue to receive the notes and checks of this bank in payment of customs (for which we were amply protected by the guarantee of the strong English banks) and with General Merritt's approval wrote to these banks authorizing them to import Mexican dollars free of duty until further notice.

The next question was in regard to the rate of duties on imports and exports. After a careful consideration of the matter, I recommended that the tariff be not changed until the question had been fully studied and ample notice given. General Merritt approved this and the customs are being collected on the Spanish tariff.

About a week after the Custom House was opened certain parties came to me representing that Consul General Wildman, of Hongkong, had informed them that United States goods would be admitted free of duty in Manila, that acting on this they had purchased a cargo of American illuminating oil in Hongkong, and that the payment of the heavy duty on it ($30 per ton, or about 8c per gallon) would ruin them. On consulting Lieutenant Colonel Crowder, Judge Advocate of the Eighth Army Corps, he pointed out the language of paragraph 5 of General Merritt's proclamation, which followed literally the instructions of the President, viz: "The Port of Manila will be open while our military occupation may continue, to the commerce of all neutral nations as well as our own, in articles not contraband of war, and upon payment of the prescribed rates of duty which may be in force at the time of the importation."

Under this there was clearly no authority for discriminating in favor of American goods, either coming direct from a United States Port or by transshipment at Hongkong.

The Collector of Customs was directed to act accordingly.

Another question was in regard to the importation of Chinamen into Manila. The Consul at Hongkong telegraphed to know if they would be admitted. As there had been no time for examining the treaties and laws in force on this subject, I replied with General Merritt's approval that for the present it was not practicable to admit Chinese laborers into Manila.

Another very important question which arose was in regard to trade with the other Philippine islands. Nearly all the hemp and the greater part of the sugar

OFFICIAL MAP OF THE ISLE OF LUZON, PREPARED BY THE WAR DEPARTMENT.

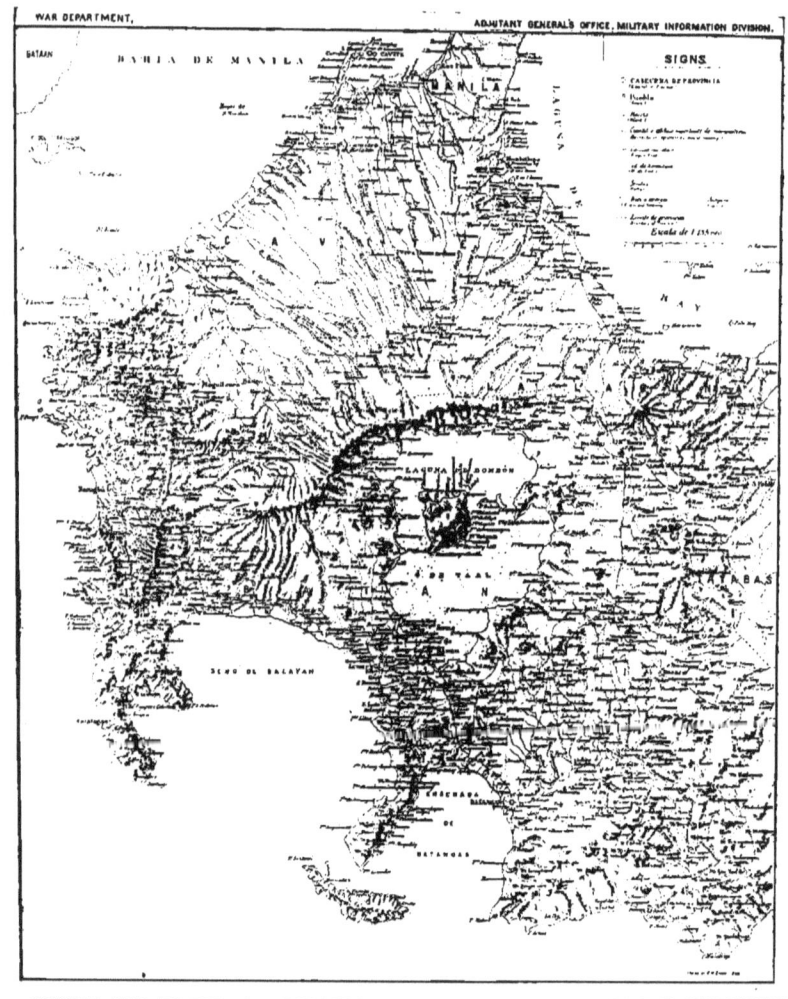

OFFICIAL MAP BY THE WAR DEPARTMENT OF THE SEAT OF WAR IN THE PHILIPPINES.

is grown in the Visayas. The hemp is bought by foreign merchants in Manila, who bring it there from the other islands, and export it, paying large duties to the Manila Custom House. These merchants were anxious to bring up their stock, of which a large amount had accumulated during the war, and ship it abroad. The ships engaged in this island trade were idle in the Pasig. They belonged to a Spanish corporation, owned entirely by Scotch capital, and had a Spanish Register. The owners were ready to transfer them to the American flag. Could these vessels be allowed to clear for the ports of Cebu and Iloio, which were in Spanish possession? The Judge Advocate advised me that they could not, without the express authority of the President. I so notified the owners of the ships and the hemp merchants. The day before I left Manila, however, Admiral Dewey received a cable from the Navy Department stating that Spanish ships had been granted the privilege of trading to American ports during the suspension of hostilities, and that American ships could be granted a similar privilege for Spanish ports. I understood that on the strength of this cable General Otis intended to allow the United States Consul at Manila to grant these vessels an American Register and then allow them to clear for the other islands. I do not know what the arrangement, if any was made, in regard to the payment of export duties at Iloilo. Clearly the hemp cannot pay export duties at both Iloilo and Manila, and the Spaniards are not likely to allow it to leave Iloilo free while we collect an export duty on it at Manila. Incidentally, this illustrates the complications and loss that will arise if the islands are subdivided. The principal merchants for all the islands are at Manila, and 90 per cent. of the duties in imports and exports are collected at its Custom House. A large part of the imports are redistributed through the islands; and all the hemp and sugar, which form the principal exports, come to Manila from other islands. If, then, we retain Luzon and give the other islands back to Spain or some other nation, that nation will impose import and export duties on everything coming from or to Manila. The foreign trade of that city as a distributing and collecting point for all the islands will be lost, and its prosperity will be destroyed; moreover, the Government revenue from that trade will be lost.

In view of the fact that Spanish officials declined to co-operate or assist in any way in the American government of Manila, the ease and rapidity with which order was maintained, the machinery of government put in operation and business reestablished, after our entry into Manila is very remarkable. For every position in the Government service, legal, administrative, financial, mechanical, clerical, men could be found in our volunteer ranks who were experienced in just that class of work at home, and they took charge of their Spanish positions with promptness and confidence.

Even in the matter of language no serious difficulty was encountered, for no less than 30 good interpreters were found in the California and Colorado regiments.

The Military Government as now organized and administered, fulfills all the requirements of preserving order and collecting the public revenue.

The civil courts, however, have yet to be organized, and their organization will present many difficulties.

CHAPTER X.

OFFICIAL HISTORY OF THE CONQUEST OF MANILA.

The Pith of the Official Reports of the Capture of Manila, by Major-General Wesley Merritt, Commanding the Philippine Expedition; General Frank V. Greene, General Arthur McArthur, and General Thomas Anderson, With the Articles of Capitulation, Showing How 8,000 Americans Carried an Intrenched City With a Garrison of 13,000 Spaniards, and Kept Out 14,000 Insurgents—The Difficulties of American Generals With Philippine Troops.

One of the most interesting events in the records of the fall of cities, that carried with them decisive factors affecting nations, is that of the conquest of Manila, by the army and navy of the United States in the memorable year of 1898. The victory of Admiral George Dewey May 1st, in the bay of Manila, nigh Cavite, has been celebrated in every clime and in all languages, and the great story is related in this book as one of universal fame, and given in outline and also in pen pictures meant to show the local coloring, and these are incidents most illustrative that are not familiar. The names of the ships and the officers of the victorious fleet, and the force of the contending squadrons in men and guns are herewith presented as an indisputable record.

Admiral Dewey held on to his command of the bay and city of Manila, braving all dangers—and they were many—and as fast as the army could be organized and equipped, reinforcements were forwarded. General Wesley Merritt was appointed the Commander in Chief of the expedition to the Philippines, and arrived at Cavite, July 25th. The official history of the operations that forced the surrender of the old Spanish capital in the East Indies has not received the public attention its unusual and instructive character demands, because the reports were not received in the States and given to the public until the Paris peace commission was assembling, and this singularly suggestive detail has been almost neglected. It is here for the first time consecutively arranged, annotated and adjusted, so as to tell the whole story. The part played by the insurgents is one that has not been stated by authority and with precision combining narrative form with the internal evidence of authenticity.

The first expeditionary force of the United States to arrive was that of General Thomas Anderson, on June 30, sixty days after Dewey's victory. The second expeditionary force, under General Frank V. Greene, arrived July 17, and the third, under General McArthur, July 30th, five days later than General Merritt, who found Rear Admiral George Dewey's war ships "anchored in line off Cavite, and just outside of the transports and supply vessels engaged in the military service." He was "in full control of the navigation of the bay, and his vessels passed and repassed within range of the water batteries of the town of Manila without drawing the fire of the enemy." This immunity of protected cruisers from the fire of nine-inch Krupp guns with an abundance of ammunition that was, and some that was

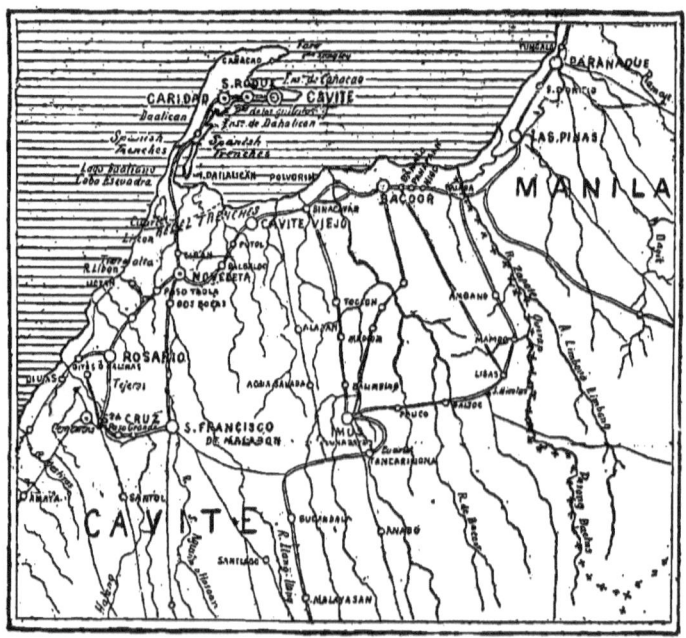

THE SEAT OF WAR IN CAVITE.

not serviceable, was due to the terrible prestige of the American Admiral and the consequent power of his word that if fired upon he would destroy the city. Anderson's Americans were, General Merritt reports, disposed as follows:

The Second Oregon, detachments of California Heavy Artillery, Twenty-third Infantry, and Fourteenth Infantry occupied the town of Cavite; while Brigadier General F. V. Greene, United States Volunteers, was encamped with his brigade, consisting of the Eighteenth Infantry, Third United States Artillery, Company A, Engineer Battalion, First Colorado, First California, First Nebraska, Tenth Pennsylvania, and Batteries A and B of the Utah Artillery, along the line of the bay shore near the village of Paranaque, about five miles by water and twenty-five miles by the roads from Cavite.

The Major General commanding visited General Greene's camp and made a reconnaissance of the position held by the Spanish, and also the opposing lines of the insurgent forces, finding General Greene's command encamped on a strip of sandy land running parallel to the shore of the bay and not far distant from the beach, but owing to the great difficulties of landing supplies "the greater portion of the force had shelter tents only, and were suffering many discomforts, the camp being in a low, flat place, without shelter from the heat of the tropical sun or adequate protection during the terrific downpours of rain so frequent at this season." The General commanding was at once struck "by the exemplary spirit of patient, even cheerful, endurance shown by the officers and men under such circumstances, and this feeling of admiration for the manner in which the American soldier, volunteer and regular alike, accept the necessary hardships of the work they have undertaken to do, has grown and increased with every phase of the difficult and trying campaign which the troops of the Philippine expedition have brought to such a brilliant and successful conclusion."

The left or north flanks of General Green's camp extended to a point on the "Calle Real," about 3,200 yards from the outer line of Spanish defenses of the city of Manila. This Spanish line began at the powder magazine, or old fort San Antonio, within a hundred yards of the beach and just south of the Malate suburb of Manila, and stretched away to the Spanish left in more or less detached works, eastward, through swamps and rice fields, covering all the avenues of approach to the town and encircling the city completely."

General Merritt defines with firmness and perspicuity his position regarding the Filipinos in these terms:

"The Filipinos, or insurgent forces at war with Spain, had, prior to the arrival of the American land forces, been waging desultory warfare with the Spaniards for several months, and were at the time of my arrival in considerable force, variously estimated and never accurately ascertained, but probably not far from 12,000 men. These troops, well supplied with small arms, with plenty of ammunition and several field guns, had obtained positions of investment opposite to the Spanish line of detached works throughout their entire extent; and on the particular road called the "Calle Real," passing along the front of General Greene's brigade camp and running through Malate to Manila, the insurgents had established an earthwork or trench within 800 yards of the powder-magazine fort. They also occupied as well the road to the right, leading from the village of Passay, and the approach by the beach was also in their possession. This anomalous state of affairs, namely, having a line of quasi-hostile native troops between our forces and the Spanish position, was, of course, very objectionable, but it was difficult to deal with, owing to the peculiar condition of our relations with the insurgents, which may be briefly stated as follows:

"Shortly after the naval battle of Manila Bay, the principal leader of the insurgents, General Emilio Aguinaldo, came to Cavite from Hongkong, and, with the consent of our naval authorities, began active work in raising troops and pushing the Spaniards in the direction of the city of Manila. Having met with some success, and the natives flocking to his assistance, he proclaimed an independent government of republican form, with himself as president, and at the time of my arrival in the islands the entire edifice of executive and legislative departments and subdivision of territory for administration purposes had been accomplished, at least on paper, and the Filipinos held military possession of many points in the islands other than those in the vicinity of Manila.

"As General Aguinaldo did not visit me on my arrival, nor offer his services as a subordinate military leader, and as my instructions from the President fully contemplated the occupation of the islands by the American land forces, and stated that "the powers of the military occupant are absolute and supreme and immediately operate upon the political condition of the inhabitants," I did not consider it wise to hold any direct communication with the insurgent leader until I should be in possession of the city of Manila, especially as I would not until then be in a position to issue a proclamation and enforce my authority, in the event that his pretensions should clash with my designs.

"For these reasons the preparations for the attack on the city were pressed, and military operations conducted without reference to the situation of the insurgent forces. The wisdom of this course was subsequently fully established by the fact that when the troops of my command carried the Spanish intrenchments, extending from the sea to the Pasay road on the extreme Spanish right, we were under no obligations, by prearranged plans of mutual attack, to turn to the right and clear the front still held against the insurgents, but were able to move forward at once and occupy the city and suburbs."

General Anderson was the first officer of the American army to arrive, and says Admiral Dewey gave him "every possible assistance," and favored him "with a clear statement of the situation." On the second day after he appeared at Cavite, which was one day after General Merritt's departure from San Francisco, he had "an interview with the insurgent chief, Aguinaldo, and learned from him that the

Spanish forces had withdrawn, driven back by his army as he claimed, to a line of defense immediately around the city and its suburbs. He estimated the Spanish forces at about 14,000 men, and his own at about the same number. He did not seem pleased at the incoming of our land forces, hoping, as I believe, that he could take the city with his own army, with the co-operation of the American fleet.

"Believing that however successful the insurgents may have been in guerilla warfare against the Spaniards, that they could not carry their lines by assault or reduce the city by siege, and suspecting, further, that a hearty and effective co-operation could not be expected, I had at once a series of reconnaissances made to exactly locate the enemy's lines of defense and to ascertain their strength."

The date of the impression made on General Anderson's mind as to the displeasure of Aguinaldo is important. The insurgent chief would have preferred the military distinctions to have been reserved for himself. General Anderson says of the Spanish attacks on General Greene's lines:

"These conflicts began on the night of July 31, as soon as the enemy had realized that we had taken the places of the Filipinos, and began a system of earthworks to the front of their old line. It may have been merely coincident, but these attacks and sorties began at the time the Captain General of Manila was relieved by his second in command. For more than six weeks the insurgents had kept up a bickering infantry fire on the Spanish trenches, firing occasionally some old siege pieces captured by Admiral Dewey at Cavite and given to Aguinaldo. These combats were never serious, and the Spaniards, so far as I know, made no sorties upon them. But there is no doubt of the fact that the Spaniards attacked our lines with force and vindictiveness, until they were informed that the bringing on of a general engagement would lead to a bombardment of the city. After this there was for several days a tacit suspension of hostilities."

As to the situation of General Greene, Brigadier General Merritt says:

"The difficulty in gaining an avenue of approach to the Spanish line lay in the fact of my disinclination to ask General Aguinaldo to withdraw from the beach and the 'Calle Real,' so that Greene could move forward. This was overcome by instructions to General Greene to arrange, if possible, with the insurgent brigade commander in his immediate vicinity to move to the right and allow the American forces unobstructed control of the roads in their immediate front. No objection was made, and accordingly General Greene's brigade threw forward a heavy outpost line on the "Calle Real" and the beach and constructed a trench, in which a portion of the guns of the Utah batteries was placed.

"The Spanish, observing this activity on our part, made a very sharp attack with

142 OFFICIAL HISTORY OF THE CONQUEST OF MANILA.

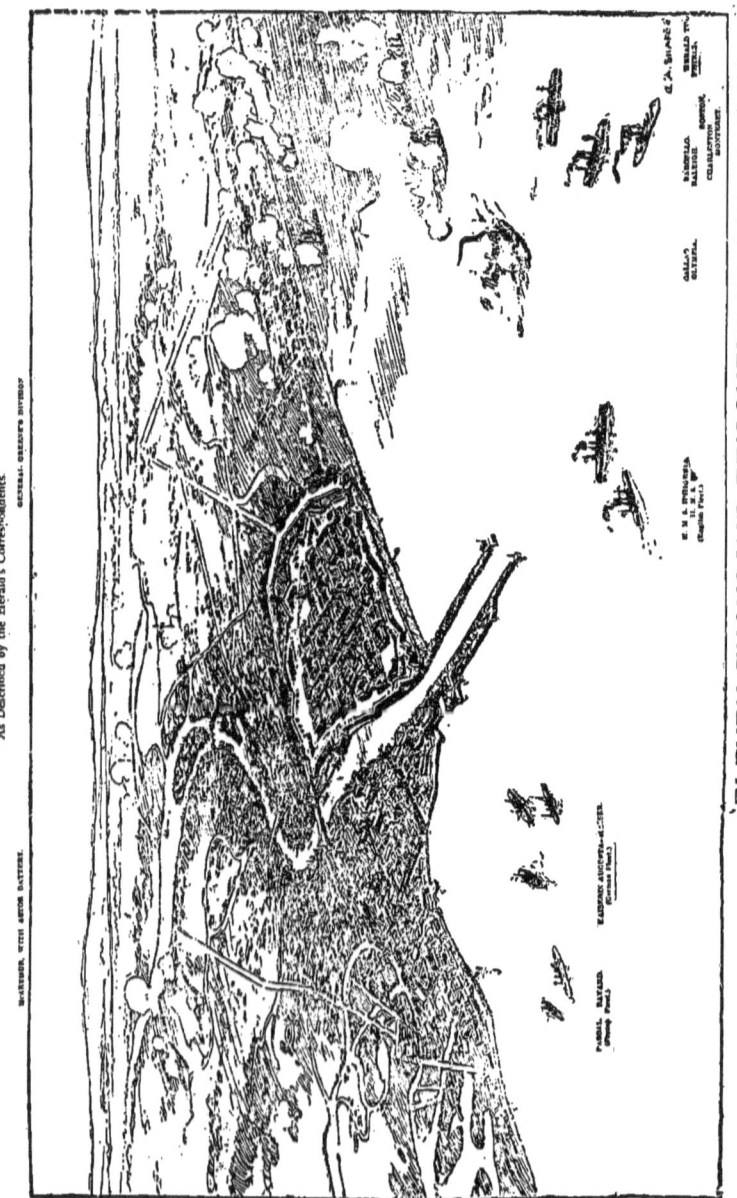

infantry and artillery on the night of July 31. The behavior of our troops during this night attack was all that could be desired, and I have, in cablegrams to the War Department, taken occasion to commend by name those who deserve special mention for good conduct in the affair. Our position was extended and strengthened after this and resisted successfully repeated night attacks, our forces suffering, however, considerable loss in wounded and killed, while the losses of the enemy, owing to the darkness, could not be ascertained.

"The strain of the night fighting and the heavy details for outpost duty made it imperative to re-enforce General Greene's troops with General MacArthur's brigade, which had arrived in transports on the 31st of July. The difficulties of this operation can hardly be overestimated. The transports were at anchor off Cavite, five miles from a point on the beach where it was desired to disembark the men. Several squalls, accompanied by floods of rain, raged day after day, and the only way to get the troops and supplies ashore was to load them from the ship's side into native lighters (called 'cascos') or small steamboats, move them to a point opposite the camp, and then disembark them through the surf in small boats, or by running the lighters head on to the beach. The landing was finally accomplished, after days of hard work and hardship; and I desire here to express again my admiration for the fortitude and cheerful willingness of the men of all commands engaged in this operation.

"Upon the assembly of MacArthur's brigade in support of Greene's, I had about 8,500 men in position to attack, and I deemed the time had come for final action. During the time of the night attacks I had communicated my desire to Admiral Dewey that he would allow his ships to open fire on the right of the Spanish line of intrenchments, believing that such action would stop the night firing and loss of life, but the Admiral had declined to order it unless we were in danger of losing our position by the assaults of the Spanish, for the reason that, in his opinion, it would precipitate a general engagement, for which he was not ready. Now, however, the brigade of General MacArthur was in position and the Monterey had arrived, and under date of August 6 Admiral Dewey agreed to my suggestion that we should send a joint letter to the Captain General notifying him that he should remove from the city all non-combatants within forty-eight hours."

The joint note of General Merritt and Admiral Dewey was as follows:

HEADQUARTERS U. S. LAND AND NAVAL FORCES,

Manila Bay, Philippine Islands, August 7, 1898.

The General in Chief Commanding Spanish Forces in Manila.

Sir: We have the honor to notify your excellency that operations of the land

and naval forces of the United States against the defenses of Manila may begin at any time after the expiration of forty-eight hours from the hour of receipt by you of this communication, or sooner if made necessary by an attack on your part.

This notice is given in order to afford you an opportunity to remove all non-combatants from the city. Very respectfully,

WESLEY MERRITT,
Major-General, United States Army,
Commanding Land Forces of the United States.
GEORGE DEWEY,
Rear-Admiral, United States Navy,
Commanding United States Naval Forces on Asiatic Station.

The notable words in this are those "against the defenses of Manila," instead of against the city itself—the usual way—the city was to be spared if possible.

Manila, August 7, 1898.

The Governor-General and Captain-General of the Philippines to the Major-General of the Army and the Rear Admiral of the Navy, commanding, respectively, the Military and Naval Forces of the United States.

Gentlemen: I have the honor to inform your excellencies that at half-past 12 to-day I received the notice with which you favor me, that after forty-eight hours have elapsed you may begin operations against this fortified city, or at an earlier hour if the forces under your command are attacked by mine.

As your notice is sent for the purpose of providing for the safety of non-combatants, I give thanks to your excellencies for the humane sentiment you have shown, and state that, finding myself surrounded by insurrectionary forces, I am without places of refuge for the increased numbers of wounded, sick, women, and children who are now lodged within the walls.

Very respectfully, and kissing the hands of your excellencies,

FORMIRE JAUDENES,
Governor-General and Captain-General of the Philippines.

The second paragraph of the Governor-General and Captain-General's letter indicates a sense of helplessness, and credits the insurgents with surrounding the city so that there was no refuge. August 9th there was a second joint note from Major-General Merritt and Rear Admiral Dewey, in the terms following:

"The Governor-General and Captain-General of the Philippines.

"Sir: The inevitable suffering in store for the wounded, sick, women, and children, in the event that it becomes our duty to reduce the defenses of the walled town in which they are gathered, will, we feel assured, appeal successfully to the sympathies of a general capable of making the determined and prolonged resistance which your excellency has exhibited after the loss of your naval forces and without hope of succor.

"We therefore, submit, without prejudice to the high sentiments of honor and duty which your excellency entertains, that surrounded on every side as you are by a constantly increasing force, with a powerful fleet in your front and deprived of all prospect of reinforcement and assistance, a most useless sacrifice of life would result in the event of an attack, and therefore every consideration of humanity makes it imperative that you should not subject your city to the horrors of a bombardment. Accordingly, we demand the surrender of the city of Manila and the Spanish forces under your command."

The Captain-General wanted time to hear from Madrid, and was refused.

The language of General Greene, in stating the fact that he took possession of the intrenchments of the insurgents, is in these words:

"On the morning of July 29, in compliance with verbal instructions received the previous day from the Adjutant-General of the Eighth Army Corps, I occupied the insurgent trenches, from the beach to the Calle Real, with one battalion Eighteenth United States Infantry, one battalion First Colorado Infantry, and four guns—two from each of the Utah batteries—these trenches being vacated at my request by the insurgent forces under Brigadier-General Noriel. As these trenches were badly located and insufficient in size and strength, I ordered another line constructed about 100 yards in advance of them, and this work was completed, mainly by the First Colorado, during the night of July 29-30. The length of this line was only 270 yards, and on its right were a few barricades, not continuous, occupied by the insurgents, extending over to the large rice swamp, just east of the road from Pasay to Paco (shown on the accompanying map). Facing these was a strong Spanish line, consisting of a stone fort, San Antonio de Abad, near the beach, intrenchments of sandbags and earth about seven feet high and 10 feet thick, extending in a curved direction for about 1,200 yards and terminating in a fortified blockhouse, known as No 14, beyond our right on the Pasay road. It faced our front and enveloped our right flank."

General Greene, reporting the fighting on his front, says of the Spanish position and first attack.

Mounted in and near the stone fort were seven guns in all, viz., three bronze field guns of 3.6 inches caliber, four bronze mountain guns of 3.2 inches caliber, and in the vicinity of Blockhouse No. 14 were two steel mountain guns of 3.2 inches caliber.

146   OFFICIAL HISTORY OF THE CONQUEST OF MANILA.

FORTIFICATIONS OF MANILA.

The line was manned throughout its length by infantry, with strong reserves at Malate and at the walled city in its rear.

Shortly before midnight of July 31-August 1 the Spaniards opened a heavy and continuous fire with both artillery and infantry from their entire line. Our trenches were occupied that day by the two battalions of the Tenth Pennsylvania Infantry, one foot battery (H), nearly 200 strong, of the Third Artillery, and four guns, two of Battery A and two of Battery B, Utah Artillery. For about an hour and a half the firing on both sides, with artillery and infantry, was very heavy and continuous, our expenditure of ammunition being 160 rounds of artillery and about 60,000 rounds of infantry. That of the Spaniards was nearly twice as much.

The American loss was ten killed and forty-three wounded.

General Greene says: "Major Cuthbertson. Tenth Pennsylvania, reports that the Spaniards left their trenches in force and attempted to turn our right flank, coming within 200 yards of his position. But as the night was intensely dark, with incessant and heavy rain, and as no dead or wounded were found in front of his position at daylight, it is possible that he was mistaken and that the heavy fire to which he was subjected came from the trenches near Block House 14, beyond his right flank, at a distance of about 700 yards. The Spaniards used smokeless powder, the thickets obscured the flash of their guns, and the sound of the Mauser bullets penetrating a bamboo pole is very similar to the crack of the rifle itself.

"This attack demonstrated the immediate necessity of extending our intrenchments to the right and, although not covered by my instructions (which were to occupy the trenches from the bay to Calle Real, and to avoid precipitating an engagement), I ordered the First Colorado and one battalion of the First California, which occupied the trenches at 9 a. m., August 1, to extend the line of trenches to the Pasay road. The work was begun by these troops, and continued every day by the troops occupying the trenches in turn, until a strong line was completed by August 12, about 1,200 yards in length, extending from the bay to the east side of the Pasay road. Its left rested on the bay and its right on an extensive rice swamp, practically impassable. The right flank was refused, because the only way to cross a smaller rice swamp, crossing the line about 700 yards from the beach, was along a cross-road in rear of the general line. As finally completed the works were very strong in profile, being five to six feet in height and eight to ten feet in thickness at the base, strengthened by bags filled with earth.

"The only material available was black soil saturated with water, and without the bags this was washed down and ruined in a day by the heavy and almost incessant rains. The construction of these trenches was constantly interrupted by the enemy's fire. They were occupied by the troops in succession, four battalions being usually sent out for a service of twenty-four hours, and posted with three battalions in the trenches, and one battalion in reserve along the crossroad to Pasay; Cossack posts being sent out from the latter to guard the camp against any possible surprise from the northeast and east. The service in the trenches was of the most arduous character, the rain being almost incessant, and the men having no protection against it; they were wet during the entire twenty-four hours, and the mud was so deep that the shoes were ruined and a considerable number of men rendered barefooted. Until the notice of bombardment was given on August 7, any exposure above or behind the trenches promptly brought the enemy's fire, so that the men had to sit in the mud under cover and keep awake, prepared to resist an attack, during the entire tour of twenty-four hours.

"After one particularly heavy rain a portion of the trench contained two feet of water, in which the men had to remain. It could not be drained, as it was lower than an adjoining rice swamp, in which the water had risen nearly two feet, the rainfall being more than four inches in twenty-four hours. These hardships were all endured by the men of the different regiments in turn, with the finest possible spirit and without a murmur of complaint."

This is a vivid picture of hard service. General Greene continues:

"August 7 the notice of bombardment after forty-eight hours, or sooner if the Spanish fire continued, was served, and after that date not a shot was fired on either side until the assault was made on August 13. It was with great difficulty, and in some cases not without force, that the insurgents were restrained from opening fire and thus drawing the fire of the Spaniards during this period.

"Owing to the heavy storm and high surf it was impossible to communicate promptly with the division commander at Cavite, and I received my instructions direct from the major-general commanding, or his staff officers, one of whom visited my camp every day, and I reported direct to him in the same manner. My instructions were to occupy the insurgent trenches near the beach, so as to be in a good position to advance on Manila when ordered, but meanwhile to avoid precipitating an engagement, not to waste ammunition, and (after August 1) not to return the enemy's fire unless convinced that he had left his trenches and was making an attack in force. These instructions were given daily in the most positive terms to the officer commanding in the trenches, and in the main they were faithfully carried out.

"More ammunition than necessary was expended on the nights of August 2 and 5, but in both cases the trenches were occupied by troops under fire for the first time, and in the darkness and rain there was ground to believe that the heavy fire indicated a real attack from outside the enemy's trenches. The total expenditure of ammunition on our side in the four engagements was about 150,000 rounds, and by the enemy very much more.

"After the attack of July 31-August 1, I communicated by signal with the captain of the U. S. S. Raleigh, anchored about 3,000 yards southwest of my camp, asking if he had received orders in regard to the action of his ship in case of another attack on my troops. He replied:

"Both Admiral Dewey and General Merritt desire to avoid general action at present. If attack too strong for you, we will assist you, and another vessel will come and offer help.

"In repeating this message, Lieutenant Tappan, commanding U. S. S. Callao, anchored nearer the beach, sent me a box of blue lights, and it was agreed that if I burned one of these on the beach the Raleigh would at once open fire on the Spanish fort."

General Merritt speaks of the Colorado skirmishers leaving their breastworks when the navy ceased firing on the 13th of August, and advancing swiftly, finding the Spanish trenches deserted, "but as they passed over the Spanish works they were met by a sharp fire from a second line, situated in the streets of Malate, by which a number of men were killed and wounded, among others the soldier who pulled down the Spanish colors still flying on the fort and raised our own."

General Greene is complimentary to the officers and who conducted the reconnaissances while he was at Camp Dewey twenty-five days, and states:

"Captain Grove and Lieutenant Means, of the First Colorado, had been particularly active in this work and fearless in penetrating beyond our lines and close to those of the enemy. As the time for attack approached, these officers made a careful examination of the ground between our trenches and Fort San Antonio de Abad, and, finally, on August 11, Major J. F. Bell, United States Volunteer Engineers, tested the creek in front of this fort and ascertained not only that it was fordable, but the exact width of the ford at the beach, and actually swam in the bay to a point from which he could examine the Spanish line from the rear. With the information thus obtained it was possible to plan the attack intelligently. The position assigned to my brigade extended from the beach to the small rice swamp, a front of about 700 yards.

"After the sharp skirmish on the second line of defense of the Spaniards, and after Greene's brigade moved through Malate, meeting a shuffling foe, the open space at the luneta, just south of the walled city, was reached about 1 p. m. A white flag was flying at the southwest bastion, and I rode forward to meet it under a heavy fire from our right and rear on the Paco road. At the bastion I was informed that officers representing General Merritt and Admiral Dewey were on their way ashore to receive the surrender, and I therefore turned east to the Paco road. The firing ceased at this time, and on reaching this road I found nearly 1,000 Spanish troops who had retreated from Santa Ana through Paco, and coming up the Paco road had been firing on our flank. I held the commanding officers, but ordered these troops to march into the walled city. At this point, the California regiment a short time before had met some insurgents who had fired at the Spaniards on the walls, and the latter in returning the fire had caused a loss in the California regiment of 1 killed and 2 wounded.

"My instructions were to march past the walled city on its surrender, cross the bridge, occupy the city on the north side of the Pasig, and protect lives and property there. While the white flag was flying on the walls yet, very sharp firing had just taken place outside, and there were from 5,000 to 6,000 men on the walls, with arms in their hands, only a few yards from us. I did not feel justified in leaving this force in my rear until the surrender was clearly established, and I therefore halted and assembled my force, prepared to force the gates if there was any more firing. The Eighteenth Infantry and First California were sent forward to hold the bridges a few yards ahead, but the second battalion, Third Artillery, First Nebraska, Tenth Pennsylvania, and First Colorado were all assembled at this point. While this was being done I received a note from Lieutenant-Colonel Whittier, of General Merritt's staff, written from the Captain-General's office within the walls, asking me to stop the firing outside, as negotiations for surrender were in progress."

And General Greene continues: "I then returned to the troops outside the walls and sent Captain Birkhimer's battalion of the Third Artillery down the Paco road to prevent any insurgents from entering. Feeling satisfied that there would be no attack from the Spanish troops lining the walls, I put the regiments in motion toward the bridges, brushing aside a considerable force of insurgents who had penetrated the city from the direction of Paco, and were in the main street with their flag expecting to march into the walled city and plant it on the walls. After crossing the bridges the Eighteenth United States Infantry was posted to patrol the principal streets near the bridge, the First California was sent up the Pasig to occupy Quiapo, San Miguel, and Malacanan, and with the First Nebraska I marched down the river to the Captain of the Port's office, where I ordered the Spanish flag hauled down and the American flag raised in its place."

The insurgents were disposed to disregard the white flag and the process of the capitulation, but "a considerable force" of them was "brushed aside." General

MURAT HALSTEAD, THE AUTHOR, AS HE APPEARED IN MANILA.

CATHEDRAL OF MANILA AFTER EARTHQUAKE.

SPANISH REINFORCEMENTS CROSSING BRIDGE OVER PASIG RIVER.

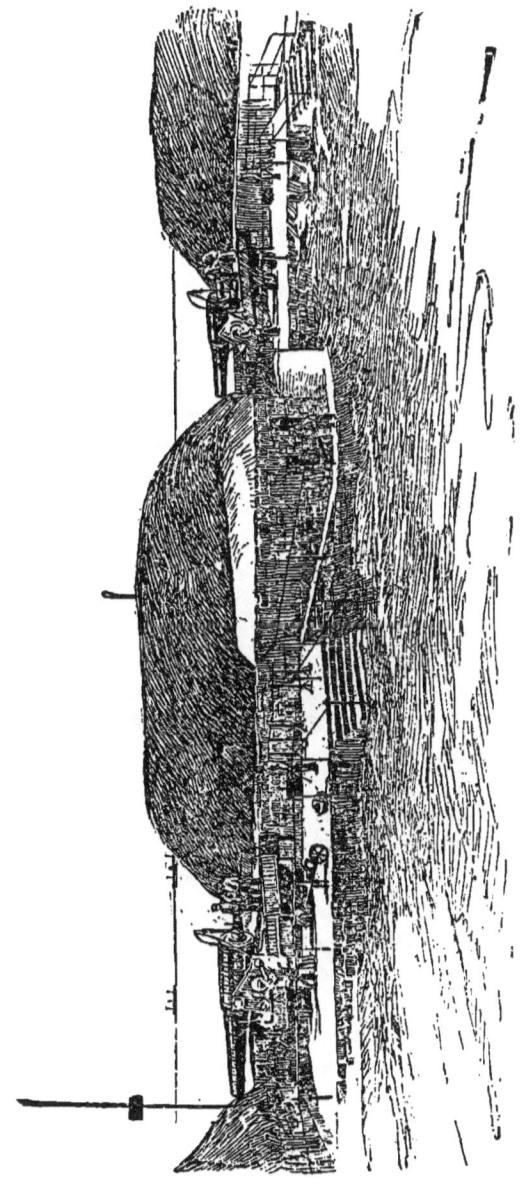

INTERIOR OF THE FORTIFICATIONS OF MANILA.

Greene's losses before Manila were 16 killed and 66 wounded; his force 5,100. He remarks: "The resistance encountered on the 13th was much less than anticipated and planned for, but had the resistance been greater the result would have been the same, only the loss would have been greater. Fortunately, the great result of capturing this city, the seat of Spanish power in the East for more than three hundred years, was accomplished with a loss of life comparatively insignificant."

Captain T. B. Mott, detached from General Merritt's temporarily, served on General Greene's staff, and received this mention:

"In posting troops in the trenches, in making reconnoissances, in transmitting orders under fire, and in making reports, he has uniformly exhibited courage, military ability, and sound judgment, the qualities, in short, which are most valuable in a staff officer."

Captain Bates, Lieutenant Schieflie, and Captain D. F. Millet, artist and author, are praised for activity, intelligence and valuable service. Millet was with Greene before Plevna, during the Russo-Turkish campaign. Greene was appointed the senior member of the committee to arrange the terms of the capitulation.

General Anderson had instructions to extend his line to crowd the insurgents out of their trenches with their consent, but this was not attempted, for that would have brought on an engagement prematurely. Anderson had purchased wire-cutters with insulated handles in San Francisco, and they were useful. Anderson had his trenches with the insurgents. McArthur's division was before a "circulated line of earthworks faced with sand bags," and the problem of the advance was made difficult because we could not be sure whether our first attack was to be tentative or serious, this depending on action of the navy; second, from our orders not to displace the insurgents without their consent from their position to the right of their guns on the Pasay road. This to the very last the insurgent leaders positively refused to give. Yet, if we could not go far enough to the right to silence their field guns and carry that part of their line, they would have a fatal cross fire on troops attacking blockhouse No. 14. I therefore directed General MacArthur to put the three 2.10 inch guns of Battery B, Utah Volunteer Artillery, in the emplacement of the insurgent gun and to place the Astor Battery behind a high garden wall to the right of the Pasay road, to be held there subject to orders.

"I assumed that when the action became hot at this point, as I knew it would be, that the insurgents would voluntarily fall back from their advanced position, and that the Astor Battery and its supports could take position without opposition."

General Anderson got a message from General MacArthur. "I knew from this that he wished to push the insurgents aside and put in the Astor Battery. I then authorized him to attack, which he did, and, soon after, the Twenty-third Infantry and the Thirteenth Minnesota carried the advance line of the enemy in the most gallant manner, the one gun of the Utah Battery and the Astor Battery lending most effective assistance."

It was General Anderson's opinion that MacArthur should counter march and go to Malate by the beach, but he had gone too far, for "the guns of the Astor Battery had been dragged to the front only after the utmost exertions, and were about being put into battery. At the same time I received a telegram stating that the insurgents were threatening to cross the bamboo bridge on our right; and to prevent this and guard our ammunition at Pasay, I ordered an Idaho battalion to that point."

Again the insurgents were making mischief, and General Anderson, as well as General Greene had the experience of the continuance of fire when the white flag was flying. The loss of General Anderson in the taking of the city was nineteen men killed and one hundred and three wounded. He concludes by saying:

"The opposition we met in battle was not sufficient to test the bravery of our soldiers, but all showed bravery and dash. The losses show that the leading regiments of the First Brigade—Thirteenth Minnesota, Twenty-third Infantry, and the Astor Battery—met the most serious opposition and deserve credit for their success. The Colorado, California, and Oregon regiments, the Regulars, and all the batteries of the Second Brigade showed such zeal that it seems a pity that they did not meet foemen worthy of their steel."

General MacArthur says: "Several hours before the operations of the day were intended to commence, there was considerable desultory firing from the Spanish line, both of cannon and small arms, provoked no doubt by Filipino soldiers, who insisted upon maintaining a general fusilade along their lines."

General MacArthur's personal mention is remarkably spirited, and makes stirring reading. We quote:

"The combat of Singalong can hardly be classified as a great military event, but the involved terrain and the prolonged resistance created a very trying situation, and afforded an unusual scope for the display of military qualities by a large number of individuals.

"The invincible composure of Colonel Ovenshine, during an exposure in dangerous space for more than an hour, was conspicuous and very inspiring to the troops; and the efficient manner in which he took advantage of opportunities as they arose during the varying aspects of the fight was of great practical value in determining the result.

"The cool, determined, and sustained efforts of Colonel Reeve, of the Thirteenth

Minnesota, contributed very materially to the maintenance of the discipline and marked efficiency of his regiment.

"The brilliant manner in which Lieutenant March accepted and discharged the responsible and dangerous duties of the day, and the pertinacity with which, assisted by his officers and men, he carried his guns over all obstacles to the very front of the firing line, was an exceptional display of warlike skill and good judgment, indicating the existence of many of the best qualifications for high command in battle.

"The gallant manner in which Captain Sawtelle, brigade quartermaster, volunteered to join the advance party in the rush; volunteered to command a firing line, for a time without an officer, and again volunteered to lead a scout to ascertain the presence or absence of the enemy in the blockhouse, was a fine display of personal intrepidity.

"The efficient, fearless, and intelligent manner in which Lieutenant Kernan, Twenty-first United States Infantry, acting assistant adjutant-general of the brigade, and Second Lieutenant Whitworth, Eighteenth United States Infantry, aid, executed a series of dangerous and difficult orders, was a fine exemplification of staff work under fire.

"The splendid bravery of Captains Bjornstad and Seebach, and Lieutenant Lackore, of the Thirteenth Minnesota, all wounded, and, finally, the work of the soldiers of the first firing line, too, all went to make up a rapid succession of individual actions of unusual merit."

Major General Merritt's account of the capture of the city must be given in full, for there are no words wasted, and he clears the field of all confusion.

"The works of the second line soon gave way to the determined advance of Greene's troops, and that officer pushed his brigade rapidly through Malate and over the bridges to occupy Binondo and San Miguel, as contemplated in his instructions. In the meantime the brigade of General MacArthur, advancing simultaneously on the Pasay road, encountered a very sharp fire, coming from the blockhouses, trenches, and woods in his front, positions which it was very difficult to carry, owing to the swampy condition of the ground on both sides of the roads, and the heavy undergrowth concealing the enemy. With much gallantry and excellent judgment on the part of the brigade commander and the troops engaged these difficulties were overcome with a minimum loss (see report of brigade commander appended), and MacArthur advanced and held the bridges and the town of Malate, as was contemplated in his instructions.

"The city of Manila was now in our possession, excepting the walled town, but

OFFICIAL HISTORY OF THE CONQUEST OF MANILA. 155

shortly after the entry of our troops into Malate a white flag was displayed on the walls, whereupon Lieutenant-Colonel C. A Whittier, United States Volunteers, of my staff, and Lieutenant Brumby, United States Navy, representing Admiral Dewey, were sent ashore to communicate with the Captain-General. I soon personally followed these officers into the town, going at once to the palace of the Governor-General, and there, after a conversation with the Spanish authorities, a preliminary agreement of the terms of capitulation was signed by the Captain-General and myself. This agreement was subsequently incorporated into the formal terms of capitulation, as arranged by the officers representing the two forces, a copy of which is hereto appended and marked.

"Immediately after the surrender the Spanish colors on the sea front were hauled down and the American flag displayed and saluted by the guns of the navy. The Second Oregon Regiment, which had proceeded by sea from Cavite, was disembarked and entered the walled town as a provost guard, and the colonel was directed to receive the Spanish arms and deposit them in places of security. The town was filled with the troops of the enemy driven in from the intrenchments, regiments formed and standing in line in the streets, but the work of disarming proceeded quietly and nothing unpleasant occurred.

"In leaving the subject of the operations of the 13th, I desire here to record my appreciation of the admirable manner in which the orders for attack and the plan for occupation of the city were carried out by the troops exactly as contemplated. I submit that for troops to enter under fire a town covering a wide area, to rapidly deploy and guard all principal points in the extensive suburbs, to keep out the insurgent forces pressing for admission, to quietly disarm an army of Spaniards more than equal in numbers to the American troops, and finally by all this to prevent entirely all rapine, pillage, and disorder, and gain entire and complete possession of a city of 300,000 people filled with natives hostile to the European interests, and stirred up by the knowledge that their own people were fighting in the outside trenches, was an act which only the law-abiding, temperate, resolute American soldier, well and skillfully handled by his regimental and brigade commanders, could accomplish.

The trophies of Manila were nearly $900,000,000, of which $240,000,000 were copper coin, 13,000 prisoners and 22,000 arms.

Three days after the surrender, General Merritt received news of the protocol, and soon was ordered to Paris. In parting he says of the insurgent chief that he had written communication with him on various occasions, and "he recognized my authority as military governor of the town of Manila and suburbs, and made professions of his willingness to withdraw his troops to a line which I might indicate, but at the same time asking certain favors for himself. The matters in this connection had not been settled at the date of my departure. Doubtless much dissatisfaction is felt by the rank and file of the insurgents that they have not been permitted to enjoy the occupancy of Manila, and there is some ground for trouble with them owing to that fact, but notwithstanding many rumors to the contrary, I am of the opinion that the leaders will be able to prevent serious disturbances, as they are sufficiently intelligent and educated to know that for them to antagonize the United States would be to destroy their only chance of future political improvement.

The Commanding General's personal acknowledgments are very handsome, as follows:

"Brigadier-General R. P. Hughes, my inspector-general at San Francisco, was especially noticeable in accomplishing the instruction of the green troops that came to the city, many of them without arms, clothing, or equipment of any kind. His services will undoubtedly be duly recognized by Major-General Otis, with whom I left him to continue the good work.

"I desire especially to express my acknowledgments to Brigadier-General Babcock, my adjutant-general and chief of staff, for his most valuable services from the inception of the campaign in San Francisco to the close of the work at the present time. This officer is too well known to require special mention of his services in any one direction. He was my right arm, not only in the office but in the field, and much of the success that has attended the expedition is due to his individual efforts.

"I desire especially to mention Major McClure and Major Whipple, of the pay department, who volunteered their services after they had completed their legitimate duties, and performed excellent work whenever called upon. Major McClure was especially important in his services immediately after the surrender, taking long rides under my orders to the Spanish lines, and bearing instructions to them which resulted in effecting their withdrawal in such manner as to prevent the incursion of the insurgents in the northern portions of the city. Other officers have been named in my special reports and have been recommended for brevets and promotion.

"I especially call attention to the services of Captain Mott, as mentioned in the report of Brigadier-General Greene. He was cheerful, willing, intelligent, and energetic in the discharge of the multifarious duties imposed upon him in connection with our troops and trenches during the rainy season, and in the final action showed those rare characteristics which stamp him as a very superior soldier."

OFFICIAL HISTORY OF THE CONQUEST OF MANILA. 157

FORT SANTIAGO AT MANILA, WHERE THE AMERICAN FLAG WAS RAISED.

158   OFFICIAL HISTORY OF THE CONQUEST OF MANILA.

THE TERMS OF CAPITULATION.

The undersigned having been appointed a commission to determine the details of the capitulation of the city and defenses of Manila and its suburbs and the Spanish forces stationed therein, in accordance with the agreement entered into the previous day by Major General Wesley Merritt, United States Army, American commander in chief in the Philippines, and His Excellency Don Fermin Jaudenes, acting General in chief of the Spanish Army in the Philippines, have agreed upon the following:

1. The Spanish troops, European and native, capitulate with the city and its defenses, with all the honors of war, depositing their arms in the places designated by the authorities of the United States, and remaining in the quarters designated and under the orders of their officers, and subject to the control of the aforesaid United States authorities, until the conclusion of a treaty of peace between the two belligerent nations.

All persons included in the capitulation remain at liberty, the officers remaining in their respective homes, which shall be respected as long as they observe the regulations prescribed for their government and the laws in force.

2. Officers shall retain their side arms, horses, and private property.

3. All public horses and public property of all kinds shall be turned over to staff officers designated by the United States.

4. Complete returns in duplicate of men by organizations, and full lists of public property and stores shall be rendered to the United States within ten days from this date.

5. All questions relating to the repatriation of officers and men of the Spanish forces and of their families, and of the expenses which said repatriation may occasion, shall be referred to the Government of the United States at Washington.   /

Spanish families may leave Manila at any time convenient to them.

The return of the arms surrendered by the Spanish forces shall take place when they evacuate the city or when the American Army evacuates.

6. Officers and men included in the capitulation shall be supplied by the United States, according to their rank, with rations and necessary aid as though they were prisoners of war, until the conclusion of a treaty of peace between the United States and Spain.

All the funds in the Spanish treasury and all other public funds shall be turned over to the authorities of the United States.

7. This city, its inhabitants, its churches and religious worship, its educational

establishments, and its private property of all descriptions are placed under the special safeguard of the faith and honor of the American Army.

F. V. GREENE,
Brigadier-General of Volunteers, United States Army.
B. P. LAMBERTON,
Captain, United States Navy.
CHARLES A. WHITTIER,
Lieutenant-Colonel and Inspector-General.
E. H. CROWDER,
Lieutenant-Colonel and Judge-Advocate.
NICHOLAS DE LA PETRA,
Auditor General Excmo.
CARLOS,
Coronel de Ingenieros.
JOSE,
Coronel de Estado Major.

The Spaniards wanted a long array of specifications as to what the Americans might and should not do, but finally were struck with the sufficiency of the shining simple words, "under the special safeguard of the faith and honor of the American Army."

CHAPTER XI.

THE ADMINISTRATION OF GENERAL MERRITT.

The Official Gazette Issued at Manila—Orders and Proclamations Showing the Policy and Detail of the Administration of Major-General Wesley Merritt, Who, as Commander of the Philippine Expedition, Became, Under the Circumstances of the Capture of Manila, the Governor of That City.

GENERAL MERRITT'S PROCLAMATION TO THE FILIPINOS.

Headquarters Department of the Pacific, August 14, 1898.

To the People of the Philippines:

1. War has existed between the United States and Spain since April 21 of this year. Since that date you have witnessed the destruction by an American fleet of the Spanish naval power in these islands, the fall of the principal city, Manila, and its defenses, and the surrender of the Spanish army of occupation to the forces of the United States.

II. The commander of the United States forces now in possession has instructions from his Government to assure the people that he has not come to wage war upon them, nor upon any part or faction among them, but to protect them in their homes, in their employments, and in their personal and religious rights. All persons who, by active aid or honest submission, co-operate with the United States in its efforts to give effect to this beneficent purpose, will receive the reward of its support and protection.

III. The government established among you by the United States is a government of military occupation; and for the present it is ordered that the municipal laws such as affect private rights of persons and property, regulate local institutions, and provide for the punishment of crime, shall be considered as continuing in force, so far as compatible with the purposes of military government, and that they be administered through the ordinary tribunals substantially as before occupation, but by officials appointed by the government of occupation.

IV. A Provost-Marshal-General will be appointed for the city of Manila and its outlying districts. This territory will be divided into sub-districts, and there will be assigned to each a Deputy-Provost-Marshal.

The duties of the Provost-Marshal-General and his deputies will be set forth in detail in future orders. In a general way they are charged with the duty of making arrests of military, as well as civil offenders, sending such of the former class as are triable by courts-martial to their proper commands, with statements of their offenses and names of witnesses, and detaining in custody all other offenders for trial by military commission, provost courts, or native criminal courts, in accordance with law and the instructions hereafter to be issued.

V. The port of Manila, and all other ports and places in the Philippines which may be in the actual possession of our land and naval forces, will be open, while our military occupation may continue, to the commerce of all neutral nations as well as our own, in articles not contraband of war, and upon payment of the prescribed rates of duty which may be in force at the time of the importation.

VI. All churches and places devoted to religious worship and to the arts and sciences, all educational institutions, libraries, scientific collections, and museums are, so far as possible, to be protected; and all destruction or intentional defacement of such places or property, of historical monuments, archives, or works of science and art, is prohibited, save when required by urgent military necessity. Severe punishment will be meted out for all violations of this regulation.

The custodians of all property of the character mentioned in this section will make prompt returns thereof to these headquarters, stating character and location, and embodying such recommendations as they may think proper for the full protection of the properties under their care and custody, that proper orders may issue enjoining the co-operation of both military and civil authorities in securing such protection.

VII. The Commanding General, in announcing the establishment of military government, and in entering upon his duty as Military Governor in pursuance of his appointment as such by the government of the United States, desires to assure the people that so long as they preserve the peace and perform their duties toward the representatives of the United States they will not be disturbed in their persons and property, except in so far as may be found necessary for the good of the service of the United States and the benefit of the people of the Philippines.

WESLEY MERRITT.

Major-General, United States Army, Commanding.

The general orders following are full of curious interest, as they declare the true intent and meaning of the Philippine Expedition, and define the situation at Manila, with extraordinary precision, and are in the strictest sense by authority:

HEADQUARTERS DEPARTMENT OF THE PACIFIC
AND
EIGHTH ARMY CORPS

Manila Bay, August 9th, 1898.

GENERAL ORDERS, No. 3.

1. In view of the extraordinary conditions under which this Army is operating, the Commanding General desires to acquaint the officers and men composing it, with the expectations which he entertains as to their conduct.

You are assembled upon foreign soil situated within the western confines of a vast ocean separating you from your native land. You have come not as despoilers and oppressors, but simply as the instruments of a strong free government, whose purposes are beneficent and which has declared itself in this war, the champion of those oppressed by Spanish misrule.

It is therefore the intention of this order to appeal directly to your pride in your position as representatives of a high civilization, in the hope and with the firm conviction that you will so conduct yourselves in your relations with the inhabitants of these islands, as to convince them of the lofty nature of the mission which you come to execute.

It is not believed that any acts of pillage, rapine, or violence will be committed by soldiers or other in the employ of the United States, but should there be persons with this command who prove themselves unworthy of this confidence, their acts will be considered not only as crimes against the sufferers, but as direct insults to the United States flag, and they will be punished on the spot with the maximum penalties known to military law.

By Command of Major-General Merritt:

J. B. BABCOCK,
Adjutant-General.

Official:
BENTLEY MOTT, Aid.

HEADQUARTERS DEPARTMENT OF THE PACIFIC
AND
EIGHTH ARMY CORPS.

Manila, P. I., August 15th, 1898.

GENERAL ORDERS, No. 4.

1. In addition to his duties as Division Commander, Brigadier-General T. M.

Anderson, U. S. Vols., is hereby assigned to the command of the District of Cavite and will remove his headquarters to that point. The garrison of the District of Cavite will be augmented upon the arrival of the next transports containing troops for this command.

2. In addition to his duties as Brigade Commander, Brigadier-General Arthur MacArthur, U. S. Vols., is hereby appointed Military Commandant of the walled city of Manila, and Provost-Marshal-General of the City of Manila, including all the outlying districts within the municipal jurisdiction. General MacArthur will remove his headquarters within the walled city and will bring with him one strong regiment of his command to take station within the walled town. The Commanding Officer of the 2nd Oregon Vol. Inf., now stationed in the walled city, will report to General MacArthur, and the Companies of the 2nd Oregon Vol. Inf., now at Cavite, will, upon being relieved by other troops, be sent to Manila to join the regiment. General MacArthur will relieve the Civil Governor of his functions, and take possession of the offices, clerks and all machinery of administration of that office, retaining and employing the present subordinate officers of civil administration until, in his judgment, it is desirable to replace them by other appointments.

3. Colonel James S. Smith, 1st California Vol. Inf., in addition to his duties as Regimental Commander, is appointed Deputy Provost-Marshal for the Districts of the city north of the Pasig River, and will report to General MacArthur. Colonel S. Ovenshine, 23rd U. S. Inf., is appointed Deputy Provost-Marshal for the districts of the city, including Ermita and Malate, outside of the walled town and south of the Pasig River, and will report to General MacArthur.

4. Under paragraphs "3" and "4" of the terms of capitulation, full lists of public property and stores, and returns in duplicate of the men by organizations, are to be rendered to the United States within ten days, and public horses and public property of all kinds are to be turned over to the staff officers of the United States designated to receive them. Under these paragraphs the Chief of Artillery at these headquarters, and the Chiefs of the Staff Departments, will take possession of the public property turned over as above, pertaining to their respective departments.

The returns of the prisoners will be submitted to the Military Commandant of the City, who will assign the men for quarters in such public buildings and barracks as are not required for the use of United States troops. The horses and private property of the officers of the Spanish forces are not to be disturbed. The Chief Paymaster at these headquarters will turn over such portion of the Spanish public funds received by him, by virtue of this order, to the administration of his office.

5. All removals and appointments of subordinate officers of civil administration,

and transfers of funds authorized by this order, must receive the approval of the Commanding General, before action is taken.

6. The Chief Quartermaster and Chief Commissary of Subsistence at these headquarters will establish depots of supply in Manila with as little delay as possible. Quartermaster and Subsistence depots will also be retained at Cavite.

By Command of Major-General Merritt:
J. B. BABCOCK,
Adjutant-General.

Official:
BENTLEY MOTT, Aid.

HEADQUARTERS DEPARTMENT OF THE PACIFIC
AND
EIGHTH ARMY CORPS.

Manila, P. I., August 17th, 1898.
GENERAL ORDERS No. 5.

1. In addition to the command of his Brigade, Brigadier-General F. V. Greene, U. S. Vols., will perform the duties hitherto performed by the Intendente General de Hacienda, and will have charge, subject to instructions of the Major General Commanding, of all fiscal affairs of the Government of Manila.

2. Lieutenant-Colonel C. A. Whittier, U. S. Vols., is appointed Collector of Customs, and the Chief Paymaster, Department of the Pacific, will designate a bonded officer of the Pay Department as custodian of all public funds. Both of these officers will report to Brigadier-General Greene for instructions.

By Command of Major-General Merritt:
J. B. BABCOCK,
Adjutant-General.

Official:
BENTLEY MOTT, Aid.

HEADQUARTERS DEPARTMENT OF THE PACIFIC
AND
EIGHTH ARMY CORPS.

Manila, P. I., August 17th, 1898.
GENERAL ORDERS, No. 6.

The Major-General Commanding desires to congratulate the troops of this command upon their brilliant success in the capture, by assault, of the defenses of Manila, on Saturday, August 13, a date hereafter to be memorable in the history of American victories.

After a journey of seven thousand miles by sea, the soldiers of the Philippine Expedition encountered most serious difficulties in landing, due to protracted storms raising high surf, through which it was necessary to pass the small boats which afforded the only means of disembarking the army and its supplies. This great task, and the privations and hardships of a campaign during the rainy season in tropical lowlands, were accomplished and endured by all the troops, in a spirit of soldierly fortitude, which has at all times during these days of trial, given the Commanding General the most heartfelt pride and confidence in his men. Nothing could be finer than the patient, uncomplaining devotion to duty which all have shown.

Now it is his pleasure to announce that within three weeks after the arrival in the Philippines of the greater portion of the forces, the capital city of the Spanish possessions in the East, held by Spanish veterans, has fallen into our hands, and he feels assured that all officers and men of this command have reason to be proud of the success of the expedition.

The Commanding General will hereafter take occasion to mention to the Home Government, the names of officers, men and organizations, to whom special credit is due.

By Command of Major-General Merritt:

J. B. BABCOCK,
Adjutant-General.

Official:
BENTLEY MOTT, Aid.

HEADQUARTERS OF THE PROVOST-MARSHAL-GENERAL
AND
MILITARY COMMANDANT.

City of Manila, P. I., August 18th, 1898.

GENERAL ORDERS, NO. 1.

1. In obedience to the provisions of General Orders, No. 3, dated Headquarters Department of the Pacific and Eighth Army Corps, Manila, P. I., August 15th, 1898, the undersigned hereby assumes the office and duties of Military Commandant of the walled city of Manila; Provost-Marshal-General of the city of Manila, including the outlying districts within the municipal jurisdiction, and also the functions of Civil Governor.

2. Until further orders the preservation of law and order throughout the city will be maintained according to the arrangements which now obtain.

3. The location of these Headquarters will be at the office of the Civil Governor, corner of San Juan de Letran and Anda Streets, and to the above address will be referred all papers requiring action by the undersigned. To insure prompt investigation, all claims, complaints, and petitions should be presented in the English language.

4. Major Harry C. Hale, Assistant Adjutant-General U. S. Volunteers; aide de camp to the Commanding General, having been assigned for temporary duty at these Headquarters, is hereby appointed Adjutant-General to the undersigned.

5. Colonel S. Overshine having been appointed by proper authority Deputy Provost-Marshal of the districts of the city (including Ermita and Malate) outside of the walled town and south of the Pasig river, will organize and establish his office as soon as possible, and report the location thereof to these Headquarters.

6. Colonel James S. Smith, 1st California Volunteer Infantry, having been appointed by proper authority Deputy Provost-Marshal of the districts of the city north of the Pasig river, will organize and establish his office as soon as possible and report location thereof to these Headquarters.

(Sgd.) ARTHUR MACARTHUR,
Brigadier-General U. S. Volunteers.
Military Commandant and Provost-Marshal-General.

The Official Gazette of Aug. 23 is a record of the organization of the Military Government of Manila.

OFFICE CHIEF OF POLICE.

MANILA, P. I.

ORDER No. 1.

By command of Brigadier-General MacArthur and Military Commandant, the Thirteenth Regiment Minnesota Volunteer Infantry is designated to perform the police duty of this city and the commanding officer thereof is appointed Chief of Police, and Major Ed. S. Bean, Inspector of Police.

Companies D, G, J and S are hereby detailed to at once take charge of the police stations and perform the necessary duties pertaining to the position of police and maintenance of order.

C. McC. REEVE,
Colonel 13th Regiment Minnesota Volunteer Infantry and Chief of Police.
Aug. 22d, 1898.

THE SULTAN OF JOLO IN MINDANAO.

A BEHEADED SPANIARD SIGN OF THE ORDER OF KATIPUNAN.

OFFICE CHIEF OF POLICE.
MANILA, P. I.
ORDER No. 2.

1. The following is published for the information of the police of this city:

2. Bulletin boards will be kept in all stations and all orders issued from this office will be posted thereon.

3. Armed native and Spanish soldiers must be disarmed before being allowed to pass through gates, either way.

4. Arrest drunk and disorderly persons.

5. Spanish officers are allowed to wear their side arms.

6. Commanding officers will have their respective districts patroled at least once each hour during the day and night.

7. Shoes must be blacked and all brasses bright and shining at all times.

8. Be courteous in your contact with both natives and Spaniards and see that all soldiers of other commands observe this rule.

9. Particular attention must be given by men at the gates to the saluting of officers in passing through, and particularly so to the general officers.

ED. S. BEAN,

Major 13th Regiment Minnesota Volunteer Infantry, and Inspector of Police.

Aug. 22d, 1898.

Approved,
REEVE,
Colonel 13th Regiment Minnesota Volunteer Infantry and Chief of Police.

HEADQUARTERS OF THE PROVOST-MARSHAL AND MILITARY COMMANDANT.

Adjutant-General's Office, City of Manila, P. I., August 22nd, 1898.

GENERAL ORDERS, No. 3.

Colonel McC. Reeve, 13th Minnesota Volunteer Infantry, is hereby directed to relieve the Commandante of the Guardia Civil Veterana of his functions, and will take possession of his office and will employ such officers and soldiers of his regiment as may be necessary for the adequate police protection of this city.

By Command of Brigadier-General MacArthur,
Provost-Marshal-General and Military Commandant,
HARRY C. HALE,
Assistant Adjutant-General.

ORDER No. 3.
OFFICE CHIEF OF POLICE.
MANILA, P. I.
To Commanding Officer.
STATIONS.

Notify all livery stables and other places in your districts, depositing large quantities of manure and other refuse in the streets, that they must cart it away daily, themselves.

Failure to do so will result in the arrest of the offending party.

ED. S. BEAN,
Major 13th Minnesota Volunteers, and Inspector of Police.
August 22d, 1898.
Approved
REEVE,
Colonel 13th Minnesota Volunteers, and Chief of Police.

HEADQUARTERS DEPARTMENT OF THE PACIFIC
AND
EIGHTH ARMY CORPS.

Manila, Philippine Islands, August 22nd, 1898.

GENERAL ORDERS, No. 8.

I. For the maintenance of law and order in those portions of the Philippines occupied or controlled by the Army of the United States, and to provide means to promptly punish infraction of the same, Military Commissions and Provost Courts, composed and constituted in accordance with the laws of war, will be appointed from time to time as occasion may require.

II. The local courts, continued in force for certain purposes in proclamation from these headquarters, dated August 14th, 1898, shall not exercise jurisdiction over any crime or offense committed by any person belonging to the Army of the United States, or any retainer of the Army, or person serving with it, or any person furnishing or transporting supplies for the Army; nor over any crime or offense committed on either of the same by any inhabitant or temporary resident of said territory. In such cases, except when Courts Martial have jurisdiction, jurisdiction to try and punish is vested in Military Commissions and the Provost Court, as hereinafter set forth.

III. The crimes and offenses triable by Military Commission are murder, manslaughter, assault and battery with intent to kill, robbery, rape, assault and battery with intent to rape, and such other crimes, offenses, or violations of the laws of war as may be referred to it for trial by the Commanding General. The punishment awarded by Military Commission shall conform, as far as possible, to the laws of the United States, or the custom of war. Its sentence is subject to the approval of the Commanding General.

IV. The Provost Court has jurisdiction to try all other crimes and offenses, referred to in Section II of this order; not exclusively triable by Courts Martial or Military Commission, including violations of orders or the laws of war, and such cases as may be referred to it by the Commanding General. It shall have power to punish with confinement, with or without hard labor, for not more than six (6) months, or with fine not exceeding Two Hundred and Fifty Dollars ($250.00) or both. Its sentence does not require the approval of the Commanding General, but may be mitigated or remitted by him.

V. The Judge of the Provost Court will be appointed by this Commanding General. When in the opinion of the Provost Court its power of punishment is inadequate, it shall certify the case to the Commanding General for his consideration and action.

By Command of Major-General Merritt:

J. B. BABCOCK,
Adjutant-General.

Official:
BENTLEY MOTT, Aid.

HEADQUARTERS DEPARTMENT OF THE PACIFIC.
AND
EIGHTH ARMY CORPS.

Manila, P. I., August 22nd. 1898.
SPECIAL ORDERS, No. 32.

1. Upon the recommendation of the Intendente General de Hacienda, Major R. B. C. Bement, Engineer Officer, U. S. Volunteers, is hereby appointed Administrator de Hacienda (Collector of Internal Revenue), and will report without delay to Brigadier-General F. V. Greene, U. S. Volunteers, Intendente General, Manila.

2. The following orders are confirmed: Special Orders No. 5, Headquarters Second Division, Eighth Army Corps, August 6th, 1898, placing First Lieutenant W. G. Haan, 3rd U. S. Artillery, in command of a separate battery to be organized

170 THE ADMINISTRATION OF GENERAL MERRITT.

by details from batteries of 3rd U. S. Artillery, to man the Hotchkiss revolving cannon brought on the transport Ohio.

3. Private H. J. Green, Company E, 2nd Oregon Volunteer Infantry, detailed on special duty at these headquarters, will be paid commutation of rations at the rate of seventy-five cents per diem, it being entirely impracticable for him to cook or utilize rations. He will also be paid commutation of quarters at the usual rate. Both commutations to be paid while this man is employed on his present duty and stationed in this city, and to date from and inclusive of the 10th inst.

4. Corporal Jerome Patterson, Company H, 23rd U. S. Infantry, Corporal James Maddy, Company F, 2nd Oregon Volunteer Infantry, Private Emmett Manley, Company D, 23rd U. S. Infantry, Private Robert M. Nichols, Company A, 1st Idaho Volunteer Infantry, Private P. H. Sullivan, Company F, 23rd U. S. Infantry, are hereby detailed on special duty at these Headquarters, and will report at once to the Adjutant-General for duty.

5. Lieutenant-Colonel Charles L. Jewett, Judge Advocate, U. S. Volunteers, is hereby appointed Judge of the Provost Court, for the city of Manila. He will hold the sessions of his court at the headquarters of the Provost-Marshal-General. The Quartermaster Department will provide the necessary offices and office furniture.

The Provost Court will be attended by one or more Assistant Provost-Marshal, to be detailed by the Provost-Marshal-General, who will be charged with the duty of enforcing its orders and executing its processes. The form of accusation in the Provost Court will be substantially the same as that used in Courts Martial, and a record of all cases tried, assimilated to that of the summary court, will be kept.

6. Upon the recommendation of the Chief Commissary of the Department of the Pacific, the issue to Spanish Prisoners by Major S. A. Cloman, C. S., U. S. Vols., Depot Commissary, Cavite, P. I., of one (1) box of soap (60 lbs. net) is hereby confirmed.

7. Sergeant Charles H. Burritt, Company C, 1st Wyoming Volunteer Infantry, will report to Lieutenant Morgareidge, 1st Wyoming Volunteer Infantry, on board Steamer Ohio, for temporary duty in unloading commissary supplies.

Upon completion of this duty Sergeant Burritt will rejoin his Company.

8. Lieutenant Charles H. Sleeper, 1st Colorado Volunteer Infantry, is hereby appointed Deputy Collector of Internal Revenue, and will report to Major R. B. C.

Bement, U. S. Vols., Administrator de Hacienda (Collector of Internal Revenue), for instructions.

9. Lieutenant-Colonel Charles L. Potter, U. S. Vols., Chief Engineer Officer, Eighth Army Corps, will assume charge of the water supply of this city, and will report to Brigadier-General Arthur MacArthur, U. S. Vols., Military Commandant of Manila, for instructions.

By Command of Major-General Merritt:

J. B. BABCOCK,
Adjutant-General.

Official:
BENTLEY MOTT, Aid.

The responsibilities of General Merritt in his Manila campaign were graver than the country understands, and his success was regarded as so much a matter of course that there has been forgetfulness to take into account the many circumstances that gave anxiety preceding decisions that seem easy now that they have been vindicated by events. The departure from San Francisco of the Major-General commanding the Philippine expedition was as well known to the Spanish as to the American cabinet, and there is reason to think there were no important particulars of the sailing of the third division of our Philippine soldiers unknown to enemies. There were in gold coin, a million and a half dollars in the strong box of Merritt's ship, the Newport. The Spanish spies were not as well posted as an average hackman, if they did not report the shipment of gold. It would have been a triumph for Spain to have captured the commanding general and the gold, the Astor Battery and the regular recruits with the headquarters ship. The Spanish were known to have a gunboat or two lurking in the islands within striking distance of our transports, unarmed vessels—except a few deck pieces of field artillery—with more than a thousand men on each. General Merritt wanted the escort of ships of war to make all secure, and application to Admiral Dewey to send one of his war boats, brought the statement that he could not spare a ship. Just at that time he heard of the run by Camara with the Cadiz fleet Eastward on the Mediterranean, and soon he had word that the Pelayo and her companions were in the Suez canal. General Greene had not arrived at Manila at that time, and the monitors Monterey and Monadnock were getting along slowly. Dewey knew he would have to evacuate the scene of his victory in case Camara was fully committed to go to Manila, and wait for the Monitors, and when he got them he said he would return and sink another Spanish fleet, but that was something it might be critical to explain, and General Merritt, after leaving San Francisco, did not get any news for twenty-six days. All that time he would have had no justification for surprise if he had been attacked by a Spanish gunboat, and if the Spaniards had pushed on their Rapide—the converted German liner the Normania—she could have been handled to cut off the American reinforcements on the way to the camps of the little American army already landed. When General Merritt reached Cavite, he found the situation difficult for the army and pushed things as the only way to get out of trouble. He had two armies to deal with, one the Spaniards, fiercely hostile, and the other, the Filipinos, factional and jealous, each outnumbering by five thousand the American forces with which the city was assailed and finally captured. There was no time lost, and if there had been any delay, even two days, the peace protocol would have found our army in the trenches, and the city belonging to the Spaniards. It was the energy of General Merritt, heartily shared by his division commanders, that prevented this embarrassment, which would have been a moral and military misfortune. We have given the General's orders to his troops and the Filipinos after the fall of the city— also his original statement of policy, and noted how cleverly they supported each other, and how smoothly the work of organization and administration is carried on the world is well aware. The orders deputing the officers to discharge certain duties are plain business. There was no departure from the strict, straight line of military government, and the threatened entanglements firmly touched passed away. There was nothing omitted, or superfluous, and the purpose and programme of policy was made clear by events. The confusion overcome by the genius of common sense there was order, all rights respected, the administration was a success from the beginning and continued, and is to be continued—security is established, there is public confidence in the air—the "faith and honor of the army" are inviolable, Manila is ours, and there is peace. If war comes in that quarter of the globe we shall stand on ground that earthquakes cannot shake.

CHAPTER XII.

THE AMERICAN ARMY IN MANILA.

Why the Boys Had a Spell of Home Sickness—Disadvantages of the Tropics—Admiral Dewey and his Happy Men—How Our Soldiers Passed the Time on the Ships—General Merritt's Headquarters—What Is Public Property—The Manila Water Supply—England Our Friend—Major-General Otis, General Merritt's Successor.

The American soldiers in the Philippines were most devoted and cheerful, patient under hardship and pleasantly satisfied that they were as far to the front as anybody and seeing all there was to see during the siege of Manila. They were out in tropical rains, and the ditches they waded were deep with mud unless filled with water. They were harassed by the Spanish with the long-range Mausers at night and insufficiently provided a part of the time with rations. At best they had a very rough experience, but kept their health and wanted to go into the city with a rush. They would rather have taken chances in storming the place than sleep in the mud, as they did for twenty days.

When the defenders of Manila concluded that the honor of Spain would be preserved by the shedding of only a little blood in a hopeless struggle and fell back from very strong positions before the advance of skirmish lines, and the American columns entered the city, keeping two armies—the Spaniards and the insurgents—apart, and, taking possession, restored order and were sheltered in houses. it soon began to occur to the boys, who came out of the wet campaign looking like veterans and feeling that they had gained much by experience, that they were doing garrison duty and that it was objectionable. The soldiers who arrived on the Peru, City of Pueblo and Pennsylvania were shocked that they had missed the fight and disgusted with the news of peace. They had made an immense journey to go actively into war, and emerged from the ocean solitude to police a city in time of peace. It was their notion that they lacked occupation; that their adventure had proved an enterprise that could not become glorious.

The romance of war faded. Unquiet sensations were produced by the stories that there was nothing to do but go home, and they would soon be placed aboard the transports and homeward bound. Besides, the climate was depressing. The days were hot and the nights were not refreshing. The rations were better and there were dry places to sleep, but there was no inspiring excitement, and it was not a life worth living. War—"the front"—instead of offering incomparable varieties, became tedious—it was a bore, in fact. How could a crowded city and thronged streets be attractive in a military sense, or the scene of patriotic sacrifice, when the most arduous duty was that of police? Was it for this they had left homes in Oregon, Montana, Pennsylvania, Wisconsin, Tennessee, Nebraska, Utah, California and Colorado?

There came an episode of homesickness. It was about time in a soldier's life to contrast it with the farms and the villages, the shops, mines and manufactories. They were kept busy on guard and in caring for themselves, in activities as the masters of a strange community, but the novelties of the tropics lost their flavor. What did a man want with oranges when there were apples? What was a rice swamp compared with a corn field? Think of the immeasurable superiority, as a steady thing, of an Irish potato to a banana, or a peach to a pineapple! What was a Chinese pony alongside a Kentucky horse, or a water buffalo with the belly of a hippopotamus and horns crooked as a saber and long as your arm to one who had seen old-fashioned cows, and bulls whose bellowing was as the roaring of lions? The miserable but mighty buffaloes were slower than oxen and, horns and all, tame as sheep—the slaves of serfs!

- As for the Chinese, if there were no other objection, they should be condemned because too numerous—faithful, perhaps, in a way, but appearing with too much frequency in the swarming streets. And the women, with hair hanging down their backs, one shoulder only sticking out of their dresses, the skin shining like a scoured copper kettle; a skirt tight around the hips and divided to show a petticoat of another tint, a jacket offering further contrasts in colors, slippers flapping under naked heels, faces solemn as masks of death heads—oh, for the rosy and jolly girls we left behind us in tears! How beautiful were the dear golden-haired and blue-eyed blondes of other days! The boys wanted at least tobacco and aerated waters to soothe themselves with, and if there was not to be any more fighting, what was the matter with going home?

They also serve, however, who only stand and wait—there are no soldiers or sailors in the world who are in a position of greater interest and usefulness than those of the American army and navy who hold fast with arms the capital city of the Philippines. The army, though much exposed, has not suffered severely from sickness. There has been an intense and protracted strain upon the men of the ships, but they have recovered from the amiable weakness for home, and they are not merely well; they are more than plain healthy—they are hearty and happy! There is the light of good times in their faces. One thing in their favor is they have not been allowed to eat unwholesome food, and the floors of the warboats and every piece of metal or wood that is in sight is polished and glistening with cleanliness. The soldiers will feel better when the postoffice is in working order and they will do better by their organs of digestion when they are not deluged with fizz—that is, pop, and beer made without malt, and the strange, sweetish fruits that at first were irresistible temptations.

"Come with me and see the men of the Olympia," said Admiral Dewey, "and see how happy they are, though they have been shut up here four months." And the men did look jolly and bright, and proud of the Admiral as he of them, and they were pleased when he noticed, kindly, the hostile little monkey, who is the mascot, and the other day bit the Captain.

The health of the boys was preserved at sea by systematic exercise. Not a transport crossed the Pacific that was not converted into a military school, and each floating schoolhouse had about 1,000 pupils. They were put through gymnastics and calisthenics when, as a rule, they were barefooted and wore no clothes but their undershirts and trousers. There was even a scarcity of suspenders. The drillmasters were in dead earnest, and their voices rang out until the manifestation of vocal capacity excited admiration. The boys had to reach suddenly for heaven with both hands and then bring their arms to their sides with swinging energy. Then they had to strike out right and left to the order "Right!" "Left!" until the sergeant was satisfied. Next each foot had to be lifted and put down quickly at the word of command; then it was needful that the legs should be widely separated in a jump and closed up with vigor; then the spinal columns swayed forward and back and all the joints and muscles had something to do. This was no laughing matter to any one, though it was funny enough from the ordinary standpoint of civil life. This medicine was taken day after day, and seemed to vindicate itself.

It was esteemed a good thing for the boys to perspire from exercise. There was no trouble, though, when south and west of Honolulu, in having substantially Turkish baths in the bunks at night, and there were queer scenes on deck—men by hundreds scantily clothed and sleeping in attitudes that artists might have chosen to advantage for life studies. It was necessary for those who walked about, during the hours thus given to repose, where the enlisted men took their rest with their undershirts and drawers around them, to be careful not to tramp on the extended limbs. Once I feared I had hit a soldier's nose with my heavy foot when stepping over him in a low light, and was gratified that my heel had merely collided with a big boy's thumb. He had gone to sleep with his head protected by his hand. I paused long enough to note that the sheltering hand if clinched would have been a mighty and smiting fist; and I was doubly pleased that I had not tramped on his big nose.

Not infrequently, when we were steaming along the 20th parallel of north latitude—that is to say, well in the torrid zone—and were wafted by the trade winds that were after us at about our own speed, heavy showers came up in the night and spoiled the luxurious content of those who were spread on the decks. The boys got in good form through the longest journey an army ever made—for the distance is greater from the United States to the Philippines than from Spain—and every week the skill of a soldier in acquiring the lessons of the climate and the best methods of taking care of himself will become more useful, and the tendency will be to settle down to the business of soldiering, make the best of it and accept it as educational—an experience having in it the elements of enduring enjoyments. "The days when I was in Manila, away down in the south seas, but a little way from the island from which came the wild man of Borneo," will be pleasant in remembrance, and there will be perpetually an honorable distinction in identification with an ambitious yet generous enterprise, one of the most remarkable a nation can undertake—not excepting the Roman conquests all around the Mediterranean, and that touched the northern sea, invading England.

In the later days of August there were in the prisons of Manila, which answer to the penitentiary and jail in the American States, 2,200 prisoners, one of whom was a Spaniard! The prisons are divided only by a high wall and contain many compartments to assist in classification. There are considerable spaces devoted to airing the prisoners, and one in which the privileged are permitted to amuse themselves with games. The guard consisted, when I visited the place, of sixty-three soldiers from Pennsylvania. There were many women imprisoned. One who had been shut up for more than a year was taken into custody because she had attempted rather informally to retake possession of a house of which she had been proprietor and out of which she had been fraudulently thrown. Her crime was a hysterical assertion of her rights and her uninvited tenants were Spaniards.

One of the buildings contained the criminals alleged to be desperate, and as they stood at the windows the chains on their right legs were in sight. It was plainly seen in several cases that the links of the chains used were about three inches long and that three or four turns were taken around the right ankle. In a group of prisoners waiting for supper to be handed them in pans in the open air a large number wore chains. Many of the prisoners were incarcerated as insurgents, having offended by refusing to espouse the Spanish cause or by some other capital criminality in that line of misconduct! A commission was investigating their cases and the Filipinos who had not satisfied the Spanish requirements were represented by an able lawyer, who was well informed and disposed to do justice. Sixty-two of the inmates of the penitentiary held for discontent with the Spanish system of government were to be discharged as soon as the papers could be made out.

Many most interesting questions arise in connection with the capitulation of the Spanish army. It was agreed that the Spaniards, upon surrendering and giving up the public property, should be entitled to the honors of war. It was expressly understood that the arms the troops gave up were to be retained. In case the Americans abandoned the islands or the Spaniards departed the rifles should be given them, and usage would seem to determine that this return of wapons must include the Mausers in the hands of the troops now prisoners of war and the cartridges they would carry if they took the field.

Then arises a difficulty as to the precise meaning of the words "public property." There were laid down by the Spaniards about 12,000 Mausers and Remingtons, and there were 10,000 in the arsenals—22,000 in all. It is admitted that 12,000 personally surrendered rifles go back to the Spaniards, whether they or we go away from the islands—as one or the other is sure to do—but the 10,000 stand of arms in the arsenals come under the head of "public property," and so should be retained permanently by the Americans. The number of ball cartridges a soldier starting out to make a march carries is 100. There were surrendered more than 500 rounds to the man. The public money was public property, of course, and General Greene demanded the keys to the vault containing it. The Spanish authorities objected, but yielded after presenting a written protest. The money consisted of Spanish and Mexican dollars, a lot of silver bars and change fused into one mass, and some gold in the same state, also $247,000 in copper coin, which was regarded, under the old dispensation, good stuff to pay poor wages to poor men and women.

There are some fine points about customs. The American flag floats over the city, and the importers and exporters want to know what the charges are and how much the private concessions must be. Some of these people ran around for several days with the object of placing a few hundred Mexican dollars in the hands of officials, where they would do the most good, and could not find anybody ready to confer special favors for hard cash. These pushing business men had been accustomed to meet calls for perquisites, and did not feel safe for a moment without complying with that kind of formality. They turned away embarrassed and disappointed, and were surprised to learn that they were on a ground floor that was wide enough to accommodate everybody.

It should be mentioned in this connection, also, a Mexican dollar passes in Manila for 50 cents American. The price of Mexican dollars in the banks of San Francisco and Honolulu is 46 and 47 cents. The way it works is illustrated in paying in a restaurant for a lunch—say for two. If the account is $2 you put down a $5 United States gold piece and receive in change eight Mexican dollars. If you buy cigars at $40 per 1,000 a $20 American gold piece pays the $40 bill. There is now pretty free coinage of Mexican dollars and they answer admirably as 50-cent coins. That is one of the ways in which free coinage of silver removes prejudices against the white metal; no one thinks of objecting to a Mexican dollar as a half-dollar, and our boys, paid in American gold, have a feeling that their wages are raised because all over the city one of their dollars counts two in the settlement of debts. These useful American dollars are admitted free of duty.

The headquarters of the American administration in Manila are in the city hall, situated in the walled city, with a park in front that plainly has been neglected for some time. It also fronts upon the same open square as the cathedral, while beyond are the Jesuit College and the Archbishop's palace. Just around the corner is a colossal church, and a triangular open space that has a few neglected trees and ought to be beautiful but is not. A street railroad passes between the church and the triangle, and the mule power is sufficient to carry at a reasonable rate a dozen Spanish officers and as many Chinamen. The fare is 1 cent American—that is, 2 cents Philippine—and the other side of the river you are entitled to a transfer, but the road is short and drivers cheap. There is a system of return coupons that I do not perfectly understand. The truth about the street railway system is that there is very little of it in proportion to the size of the city, but the average ride costs about 1 cent. If the Americans stay there is an opening for a trolley on a long line.

There is no matter of business that does not depend upon the question: Will the Americans stay? If they do all is well; if they do not all is ill, and enterprise not to be talked of.

The most important bridge across the Pasig is the bridge of Spain. The street railway crosses it. The carriages and the coolies, too, must keep to the left. It is the thoroughfare between the new and old cities, and at all hours of the day is thronged. It is a place favored by the native gig drivers to whip heavily laden coolies out of the way. A big Chinaman with powerful limbs, carrying a great burden, hastens to give the road to a puny creature driving a puny pony, lashing it with a big whip, and scrambles furiously away from a two-wheeler whirling along a man able to pay a 10-cent fare.

In other days when one passed this bridge he faced the botanical gardens, which had a world-wide reputation, an attraction being a wonderful display of orchids. There were also beautiful trees; now there are only stumps, disfigurements and desolation—some of the horrors of war. The gardens were laid waste by the Spaniards as a military precaution. As they seem to have known that they could not or would not put up a big fight for the city, what was the use of the destructiveness displayed in the gardens, parks and along the boulevards? The fashion of taking a garden and making a desert of it and calling it one of the military necessities of war is, however, not peculiar to the chieftains of Spain.

Crossing the bridge of Spain to the walled city and turning to the right there are well-paved streets bordered with strips of park beside the river, that is rushing the same way if you are going to headquarters; and the object that tells where to turn off to find the old gateway through the wall, with a drawbridge over the grassy moat, is a Monument to Alphonse, whose memory it is the habit of these people to celebrate. Approaching the city hall (headquarters) there is a white-walled hospital to note; then comes a heavy mass of buildings on a narrow street, and the small square already styled in this article a park, and we arrive at the grand entrance of the official edifice. The room devoted to ceremony is so spacious that one must consent that magnitude is akin to grandeur. There is the usual double stairway and a few stone steps to overcome. On the right and left under the second lift of stairs were corded the Spanish Mausers and Remingtons and many boxes of cartridges. I have several times noticed soldiers tramping on loose cartridges as though they had no objection at all to an explosion. You can tell the Mauser ammunition, because the cartridges are in clips of five, and the little bullets famous for their long flight are covered with nickel. The Remington bullets are bigger and coated with brass. Something has been said to the effect that the Remington balls used by the Spaniards are poisonous and that it is uncivilized to manufacture them. The object of the Mauser and Remington system in covering the bullets, the one with nickel and the other with brass, is not to poison, but to prevent the lead from fouling the rifles. The point is almost reached in modern guns of 2,000 and 3,000 yards range where the friction of the gun barrel and the speed of the missile at the muzzle are sufficient to fuse unprotected lead, and at any rate so much of the soft material would soon be left in the grooves as to impair accuracy and endanger the structure of the arm.

Right ahead when the first stairs are cleared is a splendid hall, with a pair of gilded lions on a dais, and some of the boys had adorned these beasts with crowns of theatrical splendor. The arms of Spain are conspicuous, and in superb medallions illustrious warriors, statesmen, authors, artists and navigators, look down from the walls upon desks now occupied by American officers. Above this floor the stairs are blocks of hardwood, the full width of the stairway and the height of the step, and this earthquake precaution does not detract from the dignity of the building, for the woodwork is massive and handsome. A marvelous effect might be produced in some of the marble palaces of private citizens in our American cities by the construction of stairways with the iron-hard and marble-brilliant wood that is abundant in Puerto Rico, Cuba and Luzon. The hall in which the city council met, now the place of the provost-marshal's court, is furnished in a style that puts to shame the frugality displayed in the council chambers of our expensively governed American cities, where men of power pose as municipal economists.

In the elevated chair of the President, faced by the array of chairs of the Spanish councilmen, or aldermen, sits the provost-marshal judge, and before him come the soldiers who have forgotten themselves and the culprits arrested by the patrol. On the wall above him is a full-length likeness of the Queen Regent—a beautiful, womanly figure, with a tender and anxious mother's solicitous face. She looks down with sad benignity upon the American military government. There is also a portrait of the boy king, who becomes slender as he gains height, and rather sickly than strong. It may be that too much care is taken of him.

In the corner room at the end of the corridor Major-General Otis received at his desk the news that Generals Merritt and Greene were ordered home, and that he was the major-general commanding and the chief of the civil, as well as the military department of the government. He had already found much to do and tackled the greater task with imperturbable spirit and a habit of hard work with, his friends say, no fault but a habit that is almost impracticable of seeing for himself almost everything he is himself held responsible for. If he has a weakness of that sort he has a rare opportunity to indulge it to the full extent of his personal resources. He certainly dispatches business rapidly, decides the controverted points quickly and has a clear eye for the field before him. His record is a good one. When the war of the States came on he was a New York lawyer—his home is at Rochester. Near the close of the war he was wounded on the Weldon road, along which Grant was extending his left wing to envelop Petersburg. He was struck by a musket ball almost an inch from the end of the nose, and the course of it was through the bones of the face under the right eye, passing out under the right ear. He was "shot through the head," and suffered intensely for a long time, but maintained his physical vitality and mental energy. His face is but slightly marked by this dreadful wound. He has been a hard student all his life, and is an accomplished soldier, as well as an experienced lawyer. His judicial services in court-martials have been highly estimated. Altogether he is well equipped for executing the various duties of his position. He will "hold the fort in good shape." In an adjacent room, Assistant Adjutant-General Strong, son of the ex-mayor of New York, a young man of much experience in the national guard and a sharp shooter, sticks to business with zeal and knowledge, and in a very few days established a reputation as a helper.

So much has been said in disparagement of the "sons of somebodies" that it is a pleasure to put in evidence the cleverness and intelligent industry of Captain Strong, late of the 69th New York, and of Captain Coudert, of New York.

General Merritt took possession of the palace of the governor-general, overlooking the river, a commodious establishment, with a pretentious gate on the street, a front yard full of shrubbery and rustling with trees, a drive for carriages and doors for their occupants at the side and a porte cochere, as the general said with a twinkle of his eye, for the steam launch which was a perquisite of the Governor. The commanding general of the Philippine expedition enjoyed the life on the river, along which boats were constantly passing, carrying country supplies to the city and returning. The capacity of canoes to convey fruit and vegetables and all that the market called for was an unexpected disclosure. There were unfailing resources up the river or a multitude of indications were inaccurate. The General's palace is more spacious than convenient; the dining room designed for stately banquets, but the furniture of the table was not after the manner of feasts, though the best the country afforded, and the supply of meat improved daily, while the fruit told of the kindly opulence of the tropics.

There was a work of art in the palatial headquarters that the commanding general highly appreciated—a splendid but somber painting of the queen regent in her widow's weeds, holding the boy king as a baby on her right shoulder, her back turned to the spectator, gloomy drapery flowing upon the carpet, her profile and pale brow and dark and lustrous hair shown, her gaze upon the child and his young eyes fixed upon the spectator. This picture has attracted more attention than any other in Manila, and the city is rich in likenesses of the queen mother and the royal boy, who, without fault have upon them the heavy sorrows of Spain in an era of misfortune and humiliation; and it will take some time for the Spanish people, highly or lowly placed, to realize that the loss of colonies, as they have held them, is a blessing to the nation and offers the only chance of recuperation and betterment in Spain's reputation and relations with the world.

The governor-general's palace, with General Merritt for General, was a workshop, and the highly decorated apartments, lofty and elaborate, were put to uses that had an appearance of being incongruous. The cot of the soldier, shrouded in a mosquito bar, stood in the midst of sumptuous furniture, before towering mirrors in showy frames, and from niches looked down marble statues that would have been more at home in the festal scenes of pompous life in the sleepy cities of dreamy lands.

There was no more striking combination than a typewriting machine mounted on a magnificent table, so thick and resplendent with gold that it seemed one mass of the precious metal—not gilt, but solid bullion—and the marble top had the iridescent glow of a sea shell. This was in the residence of the General, his dining and smoking rooms and bedrooms for himself and staff, the actual headquarters being next door in the residence of the secretary-general. Here was a brilliant exhibition of mirrors, upon some of which were paintings of dainty design and delicate execution, queerly effective. The tall glasses stood as if upon mantles. There were other glasses that duplicated their splendors; through the open doors down the street, which was the one for the contemplation of the gorgeous—and down the street means into the modern end of the city—was the residence of the Spanish Admiral of the annihilated fleet, Montijo. It had been the property of and was the creation of a German, who got rich and got away in good time with $1,000,000 or more, selling his house to one of the rich Chinese, who had the fortune, good, bad or indifferent, to become the landlord of the Admiral whose ships disappeared in a vast volume of white vapor on the May morning when the Americans came and introduced themselves.

General Greene's headquarters were in the house the German merchant built, the Chinese millionaire bought, and the Admiral, without a fleet since the 1st of May, rented. The furnishing was rich; there were frescoes that were aglow with the tropic birds and window curtains that were dreams. The vast mansions of the ex-officials were not, however, such as would have been sought as accommodations for the management of the military and other affairs, and there was much lacking to comfort; but as the hotels after the siege were not tolerable, the officers had to discover houses in which they could develop resources, and the public property was that of those who conquered to the extent to which it had belonged to those displaced.

The Americans got out of the chaotic hotels soon as possible, for there were some things in them simply not endurable. They rent houses and employ servants and set up housekeeping. The newspaper correspondents have been driven to this, and they are comparatively happy. They have found ponies almost a necessary of life, and food that is fair is attainable, while the flowing hydrants remove a good deal of privation and apprehension. The water is from an uncontaminated stream, and though slightly roiled after heavy rainfalls, it is not poisonous, and that is what many American and European cities cannot truthfully say of their water supplies. The demand for houses by the Americans has raised the views of the proprietors. The street on which the official Spaniards meant to flourish, as Weyler, Blanco and others had done before them, and had not time to reap a harvest of

MILITARY HEROES OF SANTIAGO AND PORTO RICO.
(Photo of Roosevelt Copyrighted by Rockwood.)
(Photo of Shafter Copyrighted by Chas. Parker.)

NAVAL HEROES OF SANTIAGO.
(Photo of Hobson Copyrighted by Falk.)

plunder before the days of doom came, would be called by the citizens of Cleveland, O., the Euclid avenue of the town. It runs out to the old fort where the Spaniards made their stand "for the honor of the arms of Spain." The English and German and Chinese successful men reside in this quarter. The majority of those who have provided themselves with houses by the river and fronting on the street most approved, looking out through groves and gardens, are Chinese half-castes, claiming Chinese fathers and Philippine mothers. These are the most rapacious and successful accumulators, and they would all be glad to see the Americans stay, now that they are there, and have shown themselves so competent to appreciate desirable opportunities and understand the ways and means, the acquirements and the dispensations of prosperity as our troops entered the city by the principal residence street, it was noticed that guards were left at all the houses that displayed the British flag—a reward for English courtesy, and the feeling of the troops that the British are our friends.

CHAPTER XIII.

THE WHITE UNIFORMS OF OUR HEROES IN THE TROPICS.

The Mother Hubbard Street Fashion in Honolulu, and That of Riding Astride—Spoiling Summer Clothes in Manila Mud—The White Raiment of High Officers—Drawing the Line on Nightshirts—Ashamed of Big Toes—Dewey and Merritt as Figures of Show—The Boys in White.

Recent experiences of the United States excite attention to the fashions of the tropics. In Florida our soldiers who invaded Cuba were in a degree and sense acclimated for the temperature of the island that has been for so long "so near, and yet so far," so wet and yet so hot. But the troops of the Philippine expedition were not prepared by the chilly blasts from the mountains of California for the exceedingly soft airs of Hawaii, though Honolulu was a pleasant introductory school to Manila. Our new possession two thousand miles from the continent, has been preparing for the destiny realized for two generations, and the American ladies who dwell in the islands of perpetual summer in the Pacific, have not submitted wholly to the dominion of the climate and composed themselves to languish in loose and gauzy garments when on the streets. But the Honolulu women, in general, who largely are in the possession of luxuriant proportions, are enveloped in the blandishments of Mother Hubbards, and do not even tie strings about themselves to show where they would have spectators to infer their waists ought to be. They go about flowing and fluttering in freedom, and have all the advantages due the total abandonment of corsets, and suffer none of the horrors of tight lacing recorded in medical publications. The Mother Hubbard gown is not without its attractions, but we can hardly say they are too obvious, and slender figures are lost in voluminous folds that are billowy in the various ways and means of embracing the evolutions of beauty. And the native singers seem fully justified in throwing the full force of their lungs and the rapture of their souls into the favorite chorus, "The Honolulu Girls Are Good Enough for Me." The refrains of the Hawaiian songs are full of a flavor of pathos, and there is the cry of sorrows, that seem to be in the very air, but belong to other ages. The Honolulu females of all races have flung away side saddles with their corsets, and bestride horses and mules with the confidence in the rectitude of their intentions that so besets and befits the riders of bicycles. People would stare with disapproval in Honolulu to see a woman riding with both legs on the same side of a horse, and those wandering abroad in the voluminous folds of two spacious garments disapprove the unusual and unseemly spectacle.

It is as hot in some parts of Texas, Arizona and California as in any of the islands of the seas of the South, but we had not been educated in the art of clothing armies for service in the torrid zone, until the Philippine expedition was undertaken, and we were making ready for challenging the Spaniards in their Cuban fastnesses, when it speedily was in evidence that we wanted something more than blue cloth and blankets. The Spanish white and blue stuff and straw hats were to our eyes unsightly and distasteful, and we began with a variety of goods. Our army hats were found good, but we tried nearly all things before holding onto anything as sufficient for trousers and coats. The officers on long journeys speedily resolved, if we may judge from the results, that the suit most natty and nice for wear within twenty degrees of the Equator was the perfect white, and so the snowy figures below shoulder straps became familiar. This did not, of course, indicate acute stages of active service. Never were campaigns more destructive of good looks in clothing, than those in assailing Santiago and Manila, in which the thin stuffs were tested in torrential rain and ditches full of mud. The compensation was that the volunteers fresh from the camps of instruction, put on in a few days the appearance of veteran campaigners. In Manila there was an edifying contrast between the Spaniards who had surrendered and the Americans who did not pause when the Mausers were fired into their ranks, not with the faintest hope of successful resistance, but for the "honor of Spain." The Spanish soldiers had been well sheltered and came out in fairly clean clothes, while the soldiers of our nation closed up dingy ranks, suited for hunting in swamps and thickets, their coats, hats and trousers the color of blasted grass and decayed leaves. The passage of the line from the new to the old clothes was sudden, and the gallant boys in blue were not in the least disconsolate over the discoloration of their uniforms, having reached the stage where it was a luxury to sleep on a floor or pavement, without wasting time to find a soft or quiet spot.

The sombre taste of the Spanish ladies in dress, so famous and effective that the black mantillas and skirts, and the fans that do such execution in the hands of the dark-eyed coquettes, as to have sway where empires have been lost and won—control Cuba, but does not dominate the Philippines. The Pope of the period, it will be remembered, divided the new worlds discovered by the navigators of Spain and Portugal, awarding to the best of his knowledge, by a line drawn south from the southern shore of the Caribbean Sea. Portugal holding that to the eastward and

Spain that to the westward. Hence the separation of South America between Brazil and the rest of the central and south American states, to await the inevitable end of the evolutions that were the revolutions of independence. Magellines, a Portuguese, who, being slighted in his own country, went over to the Spaniards, and pointed out that by sailing west the east would be attained, and so found the straits that bear his name, and the Ladrones and Philippines, annihilating the Papal boundary line by taking and breaking it from the rear.

The conquest of the Philippines by the Spaniards has not been complete as a military achievement or the enforcement of the adoption of customs and costumes according to the habits and taste of the conquerors, who have nibbled at the edges of the vast archipelago, greater in its length and breadth and its natural riches than the West Indies. The Spanish ladies in the Philippines are dressed as in the ancient cities of their own renowned peninsula. The Filipinos are of the varied styles that adorn Africans and the Asiatics. They are gay in colors and curious in the adjustment of stuffs, from the flimsy jackets to the fantastic skirts. The first essential in the dress of a Filipino is a jacket cut low, the decolette feature being obscured to some extent by pulling out one shoulder and covering the other, taking the chances of the lines that mark the concealment and disclosure of breast and back. There is no expression of immodesty. The woman of the Philippines is sad as she is swarthy, and her melancholy eyes are almost always introspective, or glancing far away, and revising the disappointed dreams of long ago. Profounder grief than is read in the faces of bronze and copper no mourning artist has wrought nor gloomy poet written. Below the jacket, the everlasting blazer, is a liberal width of cloth tightly drawn about the loins, stomach and hips, making no mistake in revelations of the original outline drawings, or the flexibilities which the activities display. There are two skirts, an outer one that opens in front, showing the tunic, which is of a color likely to be gaudy and showing strangely with the outer one. The feet are exposed, and if not bare, clothed only in clumsy slippers with toe pieces, and neither heels nor uppers. Women carry burdens on their heads, and walk erect and posed as if for snap photographs. The young girls are fond of long hair, black as cannel coal, and streaming in a startling cataract to the hips. It seems that the crop of hair is unusually large, and it shines with vitality, as the breeze lifts it in the sunshine. The Philippine boys are still more lightly clad than the girls, who have an eye to queer combinations of colors, and the revelation of the lines that distinguish the female form without flagrant disclosure. There is much Philippine dressing that may under all the surroundings be called modest, and the prevalent expression of the Filipino is that of fixed but bewildered grief. The males are rather careless, and display unstinted the drawings of legs, that are copper-colored and more uniform in tint than symmetry. Two or three rags do a surprisingly extensive service, and all the breezes cause the fluttering of fantastic but scanty raiment. It is a comfort to return to a country where people wear clothing not as a flimsy and inadequate disguise. What will be the influence of our armies sent to the tropics, upon the dress of Americans? It is a question that may be important. The "wheel" has introduced knickerbockers and promises to result in knee breeches. On the transports that have traversed the Pacific the soldiers were fond of taking exercise in undershirts and drawers only and they swarmed from their bunks at night, to sleep on deck, sometimes condescending to spread blankets to take the edge off the cruelty of the hard wood, but reluctant to be encumbered with undershirts. Their favorite night dress was drawers only, and they acted upon the false theory that one cannot take cold at sea. The authority of officers was often necessary to impress the average soldier that he ought to have an undershirt between his skin and the sky. The boys were during their long voyage very sparing in the use of shoes and stockings, and it has perhaps never before occurred in American experiences that there was such an opportunity to study the infinite variety of the big toe, and, indeed, of all the toes. In active army service the care of the feet is essential. The revelations on shipboard disclose the evils of ill-fitting shoes to be most distracting. One of the claims of West Point for high consideration is in teaching the beauty of white trousers, and our tropical army experiences will extend the fashion. When General Merritt and Admiral Dewey parted on the deck of the China in Manila harbor, both were clad in spotless white, their caps, coats and trousers making a showy combination. There was also a group of sea captains who had gathered to give the Captain of the China a good send-off, and they with the staff officers, were all in radiant white. There was not a boy in blue among them. The illustrious General and Admiral reminded me of Gabriel Ravel, when in his glory as The White Knight. It would be hard to say which wore the nattier cap, but that of the Admiral was of the more jaunty cut, while the General—gold cord for a band and gold buttons, especially became his blue eyes. If the officers of the army, navy and transports could be photographed as they stood in dazzling array, as if hewn from marble, the fashion plate resulting would be incomparably attractive, and in the summers to come we shall find among the influences of our tropical adventure and possessions a heightening of the colors worn by American ladies, and a whitening of the suits of gentlemen, involving the necessity of "calling in" white coats, as well as straw hats on stated days in early September.

CHAPTER XIV.

A MARTYR TO THE LIBERTY OF SPEECH.

Dr. Jose Rizal, the Most Distinguished Literary Man of the Philippines, Writer of History, Poetry, Political Pamphlets, and Novels, Shot on the Luneta of Manila—A Likeness of the Martyr—The Scene of His Execution, from a Photograph—His Wife Married the Day Before His Death—Poem Giving His Farewell Thoughts, Written in His Last Hours—The Works That Cost Him His Life—The Vision of Friar Rodriguez.

There is history, romance and tragedy in the martyrdom of Dr. Rizal, whose execution by shooting on the Luneta two years ago is a notable incident of the cruelties of Spanish rule. This was on account of the scholarship, the influence, the literary accomplishments, and the personal distinction of the man. Dr. Rizal was easily the foremost writer his race and country has produced. He was a poet, novelist, political essayist, and historian, and his execution was for the crime of loving his country, opposing the Spaniards, criticising and lampooning the priests. He is called the Tagalo Martyr, for he was of the tribe of Malay origin, the most numerous and rebellious in the Philippine Islands. His fate was shocking. He was an intelligent, learned man, an enthusiastic patriot, who had been educated in Spain and France. For writing a book against Spanish oppression he was exiled to the Island of Dapitan. There he met a young woman of Irish parentage, with whom he fell in love. They were engaged to be married, when, on some pretext, the Doctor was brought back to Manila, sent to Madrid to be tried, and then sent back to Manila. The unhappy girl to whom he was betrothed tells the rest of the story:

"Everyone knew that Dr. Rizal was innocent. All that could be brought against him was the publication of his book, and the Spanish officials who tried him had never even read it. Nevertheless, he was condemned to death. I then asked permission to be married to him, and they granted my request, thinking to add to the horror of his martyrdom. The marriage was celebrated by a friar the same day on which he was sentenced. I passed the whole night on my knees in prayer before the prison door, which shut my husband from me. When morning dawned, the Doctor came out, surrounded by soldiers, his hands bound behind his back. They took him to the Luneta, the fashionable promenade of the city, where all military executions take place. The lieutenant in command of the firing party asked my

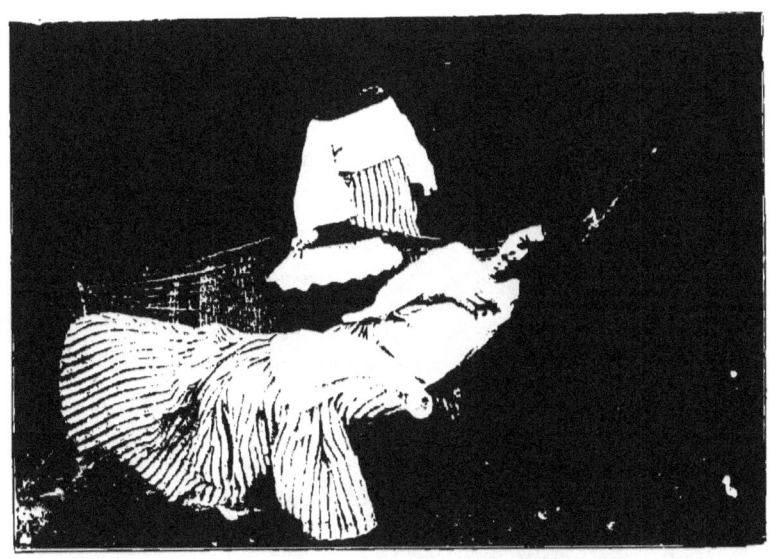

FILIPINA PREPARING FOR A SIESTA.

LOADING BUFFALOES IN LUZON WITH PRODUCE.

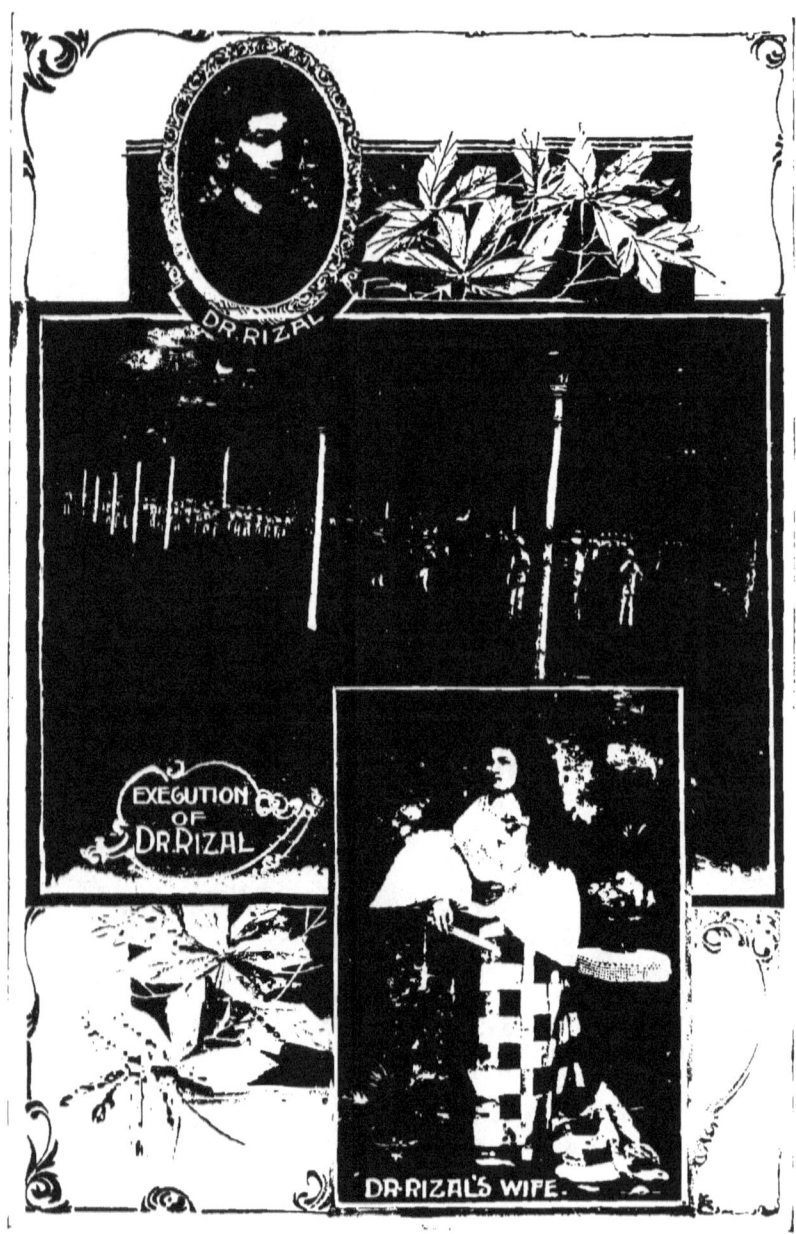

THE PHILIPPINE AUTHOR-MARTYR, HIS WIFE AND HIS EXECUTION.

husband where he would prefer to be shot. He replied 'Through the heart.' 'Impossible,' said the lieutenant. 'Such a favor is granted only to men of rank. You will be shot in the back.' A moment after my husband was dead. The soldiers shouted, 'Hurrah for Spain,' and I, 'Hurrah for the Philippines and death to Spain.' I asked for the body. It was refused me. Then I swore to avenge his death. I secured a revolver and dagger and joined the rebels. They gave me a Mauser rifle, and the Philippines will be free."

In his poem, filled with his last thoughts—his exalted dreams that had faded, his patriotic sentiments that were bloody dust and ashes, his love for the woman he was allowed to marry a few hours before he was shot, his woeful love for his troop of devoted friends, who would have died for him and with him if the sacrifice then and there had not been hopeless—it will be discovered that he was a true poet, and we give one of his stories that was hostile to the orders of the Church, and a satire on Spanish rule, showing why he was a martyr.

The following is a prose translation from the Spanish of the poem Dr. Rizal wrote the night before he was executed:

MY LAST THOUGHTS.

Farewell! my adored country; region beloved of the sun; pearl of the Orient sea; our lost Eden! I cheerfully give for thee my saddened life, and had it been brighter, happier and more rosy, I would as willingly give it for thy sake.

Unhesitatingly and without regret others give thee their lives in frenzied fight on the battlefield. But what matter the surroundings! Be they cypress, laurel or lilies, scaffold or open country, combat or cruel martyrdom, it is all the same, when for country and home's redress.

I die while watching the flushing skies announce through dark mantle the advent of a day. Should it need purple to tint its dawn, here is my blood; I gladly will shed it if only it be gilded by a ray of new-born light.

My dreams while only a boy, and when of vigor full, a youth, were always to see thee, jewel of the Orient sea! thy black eyes dry, thy frownless face uplifted, and spotless thine honor.

Dream of my life! My fervent anxiety! Shouts the soul that soon is to depart. Hail! It is glorious to fall to give thee flight; to die to give thee life; to die under thy skies, and in thy maternal bosom eternally to sleep.

Shouldst thou find some day over my grave, a lonesome, humble flower, blossoming through the dense foliage, take it to your lips and kiss my soul. Let me feel upon my forehead under the cold tomb your warm and tender breath.

Let the moon with her soft and silent light watch over me; let dawn spread its fulgent splendor; let the wind moan with solemn murmur. And should a bird descend and repose upon my cross, let it there proclaim a canticle of peace.

Let the burning sun evaporate the dew, spreading through space the notes of my songs. Let a friendly being mourn my early end, praying on calm evenings, when thou also, oh, dear country! should pray to God for me.

Pray for all those who died unhonored; for those who suffered unequaled torments; for our poor mothers who silently grieve; for orphans and for widows; for prisoners in torture; and pray for thyself that thou mayest attain thy final redemption.

And when the dark shades of night enwrap the cemetery, and the dead are left alone to watch, do not disturb their rest, do not disturb their mystery. Shouldst thou hear chords of a zither, it is I, beloved country! who sings to thee.

And when my grave, by all forgotten, is marked by neither cross nor stone, let the ploughman scatter its mould; and my ashes before returning to nothing will become the dust of your soil.

Then, I will not mind if thou castest me into oblivion. Thy atmosphere, thy space, thy valleys I will cross. A vibrating, limpid note I will be in your ear; aroma, color, rumor, song, a sigh, constantly repeating the essence of my faith.

My idolized country! grief of my griefs! My adored Philippines! Hear my last farewell. I leave them all with thee; my fathers and my loves. I go where there are no slaves, no oppressors, no executioners; where faith is not death; where He who reigns is God.

Farewell! fathers and brothers, parts of my soul! Friends of my infancy in the lost home. Give thanks that I should rest from the fatiguing day. Farewell, sweet stranger, my friend, my joy. Farewell, beloved beings. To die is to rest.

JOSE RIZAL.

THE VISION OF FRIAR RODRIGUEZ.

Comfortably seated in an arm chair one night, satisfied with himself as well as with his supper, Friar Jose Rodriguez dreamed of the many pennies that the sale of his little books was drawing from the pockets of the Filipinos, when suddenly, and as if by enchantment, the yellow light of the lamp gave a brilliant, white flash, the air was filled with soft perfume, and without his being able to explain how or wherefrom, a man appeared.

A MARTYR TO THE LIBERTY OF SPEECH.

This was an old man of medium height, dark complected and thin, whose white beard was a contrast to his glittering vivacious eyes, which gave his face extreme animation. Over his shoulder he wore a long cape; a mitre on his head and a crosier in his hand gave him the aspect of a Bishop.

At sight of him, Friar Rodriguez yawning, murmured:

"Dreams of my fertile imagin—!"

The vision did not permit him to finish the exclamation, but gave him a whack between the shoulders.

"Eh! This is no joke!" exclaimed Friar Rodriguez, stroking with one hand the afflicted part while with the other he rubbed his eyes.

"I see! It is no dream! But partner!"

Incensed at such familiarity, the strange personage began poking Friar Rodriguez severely with his crosier on the stomach. The latter, satisfied by this time that the thrashing was in earnest, exclaimed:

"Here! Here! Friar Pedro (Peter)—Is that the way you cancel indulgencies? That was not the agreement."

The strange Bishop, aroused to a high pitch of anger, stopped his poking and started to knock Friar Rodriguez on the head, believing it to be a more sensitive part. Unfortunately, Friar Rodriguez's head was too hard for anything, and the crosier fell, broken in two pieces. At last! said the poor friar, who, pale and deadly frightened, had fallen on his knees and was trying to creep away on all fours.

At sight of his pitiful condition, the stranger seemed satisfied, and, placing on a table the broken crosier, said with contempt:

"Homo sine homine, membra sine spiritu! Et iste appellatur filius meus!"

At the sound of that potent voice and language, unknown to him, Friar Rodriguez appeared confounded. The stranger could not be Friar Pedro (Peter) nor any brother in disguise! Impossible!

"Et tamen (the stranger continued), tanta est vanita vestra, ut ante me Patrem vestrum—sed video, loguor et non audis!"

And shaking in disgust his head, the vision continued speaking in Castillian, but with a foreign accent.

"And are you they who call themselves my sons? Has your haughtiness reached such a degree that you not only pretend to be feared and worshiped by governors and governed, but neither recognize nor respect me, whose name you dishonor, and whose condignity you abuse? How do I find you? Insolent with the unfortunate and cowardly towards those who do not fear you! Surge et audi!"

A MARTYR TO THE LIBERTY OF SPEECH.

His voice was so imperative and his command so expressive, that Friar Rodriguez, although shaking with tremor, made every effort to stand against a corner of the room.

Moved by this proof of obedience, so rarely found amongst those who make a vow of humility, the stranger, full of contempt, repressed a sigh and proceeded in a more familiar manner, but without losing dignity.

"For you and for your nonsense I have been obliged to leave that region, and come here! And what trouble I had to distinguish and find you amongst the others! With but little difference, you are all alike. 'Empty heads and replete stomachs!' UP THERE, they did not cease to tease me about you all and most especially on your account. It was useless to appear unconcerned. It was not only Lopez de Recalde (Ignatius of Loyola) who with his eternal smile and humble looks made fun of me; nor Domingo (Dominic) with his aristocratic pretensions and little stars of false jewelry on his forehead, who laughed at me; but even the great simpleton of Francisco (Francis), do you understand? tried to poke fun at me; at me, who has thought, argued and written more than all of them together!

"Your order is great and powerful," said Ignatius, bending his head. "It resembles one of the Egyptian pyramids; great at the base (you are the base), but the higher it goes the smaller it becomes—what a difference between the base and the apex!" he murmured, while walking away. "Doctor," said Dominic, "why did you not do with your science as I did with the nobility I left as inheritance to my sons? We would all be better off!"

"Mon ami, came and said Francis. If God should order me again to earth, to preach as before amongst brutes and animals, I would preach in your convents." And after saying this he roared in such a manner that although small and thin, it seemed as though he would burst.

"In vain I answered them that their sons were no better than you are, and that were we to look for skeletons in the closets, we had better wall every crevice. But of no use. How could I argue against three, moreover, having you to defend! Three, did I say? Why! Even Peter, the old fisherman, attracted by the laughter, left his porter's lodge and came to upbraid me for the trick you have played on his priests, taking away from them all their parishes, regardless of the fact that they had been in these islands long before you, and that they were the first to baptise in Cebu and in Luzon.

"Of course," he said, "as my sons are lazy and in dissension among themselves,

A MARTYR TO THE LIBERTY OF SPEECH.

and yours lie and shout louder, they make themselves believed by the ignorant. But I shall be glad when my descendants are extinct."

"And so shall I! And I! I wish it was all over with mine!" shouted at once several voices.

"But old Peter's revenge did not stop at that. Yesterday he played a hard joke on me. He not only confiscated a package that a Tagalo (*) brought with him, but instead of directing him to the imbecile's department, he took him where we all were. The poor Tagalo carried with him a large collection of little books written by you, which were given him by his Priest, who told him they represented so much indulgency for his next life. As soon as the Indian had arrived everyone UP THERE knew he had brought books written by an Augustinian monk, and they were snatched away. I tried to hide myself, but I could not. What laughter and what jokes! The little angels came in a body; the Celestial Father's Orchestra lost its time; the Virgins, instead of watching their music sheets read the books and sang most discordantly, and even old Anthony's little pig began grunting and twisting his tail.

"I felt ashamed; I could see every one point their finger at me and laugh. But, in spite of all this Zarathustra, the grave and serious Zarathustra, did not laugh. With a humiliating pride he asked me:

"'Is that your son, he who pretends that my religion is paganish, and that I am a pagan? Have your sons degenerated to such a degree as to confound my pure religion, root of the most perfect creeds, with Polytheism and Idolatry? Do they know that paganism is derived from pagani, which means inhabitant of the fields, who always were faithful to the Greek and Roman Polytheism? You may answer that they do not know Latin! If so, make then speak more modestly. Tell them that paganus comes from pagus, from which the words pages, payes, paien, paese, pais (country), are derived. Tell those unfortunate that the Zend-Avesta religion was never professed by the rural inhabitants of the Roman country. Tell them that my religion is monotheist, even more so than the Roman Catholic religion, which not only accepted the dualism of my creed, but has deified several creatures. Tell them that Paganism in its widest and most corrupted sense, duly meant Polytheism; that neither my religion nor that of Moses nor Mohammed were ever Pagan religions. Tell them to read your own works, where in every page you refer to the Pagans. Repeat to them that which you said in speaking of the religion of the Manechees (a

---

(*) Tagalo.—Name of one of the tribes of Indians inhabiting the Philippine Islands.—Trans. Note.

corruption of my doctrine by you professed) which influenced your works and prevails yet in your religion, and which at one time caused the Roman Catholic Church to vacillate. Yes; I linked the principle of Good and Evil together—Ahura-Mazda; God! But this is not to admit of two Gods, as you, yourself said. To speak of health and sickness is not to admit two healths. And what? Have they not copied my principle of evil in Satan, prince of darkness? Tell them that if they do not know Latin to at least study the religions, since they fail to recognize the true one!'

"Thus spoke Zarathustra, or Zoroaster. Then, Voltaire—Voltaire, who had heard what you were saying about his death, accosted me, and grasping me by the hand, effusively thanked me.

" 'Why so?' I asked him.

" 'Your sons, mon cher Docteur de l'Eglise,' he answered, 'have proved and continue proving by facts, that which I maintained. And what was it that you maintained? That besides being ignorant, they were liars.

"To this I could not reply, for he was right. You should know that he died when 84 years of age, possessed of all his faculties, and with so lucid a mind that when nearing his end and being importuned to make confession, he said: 'Let me die in peace'—and died. But the worst of it all is, that Voltaire has been pleading with God to take you to Heaven alive and clothed, and when asked why so, he answered 'So that we may have some fun.'

"On learning of all the indulgences that the Archbishop had allowed on your books, to allure buyers, old Peter, thumping his bald head, exclaimed:

" 'Why did I not think of granting indulgencies with the fish I sold, when a fisherman? We would have been rich, and Judas, instead of selling the Master, would have sold sardines and tinapa! (*) I would not have been obliged to cowardly apostatize, and would not have suffered martyrdom. Verily, I say, that my friend down BELOW leaves me behind in the matter of knowing how to make money; and yet I am a Jew.'

" 'Of course, don't you know that your friend BELOW is a Gallego?' (*) Said a

---

(*) Tinapa.—Small white-bait fish, which, mixed with rice, constitutes the daily diet of the lower class of natives in the Philippine Islands.—Trans. Note.

(*) Gallego.—Native of Galicia, northwestern Province in Spain. On account of their healthy and robust constitution, the lower class of Gallego are found employed in the hardest work throughout the country, where physical strength is necessary, although they are considered slow and lazy. Their predominant characteristic seems to be an insatiable greed of hoarding money.—Trans. Note.

little old man who had been UP THERE but a few years. His name was Tasio, and, addressing himself to me, he continued:

" 'You are a great Doctor, and although you have contradicted yourself many times, I hold you as a privileged character of vast erudition, for, having written your books, Retractationum, and Confesiones; and since you are so different from your sons who try, when defending themselves, to make black appear white, and white green, I will state my complaints, so that you, as their Father, may put a stop to it all.

" 'There exists on earth an unfortunate, who, amongst many foolish acts, has committed the following:

" '1st. He holds solidary of all that I have said during my earthly life, an Indian called Rizal, only because said Indian has quoted my words in a book that he wrote. As you can see, should we follow such a system of reasoning, Rizal would also agree with the views expressed by friars, policemen, etc., and you, yourself, Holy Doctor, would also be solidary of all that you ascribe to heretics, Pagans, and above all, to Manichees.

" '2nd. He wants me to think as he himself does, since he quotes me as saying 'The Bible and the Holy Gospel.' It may be well that he, as all fanatics, should believe that these are one and the same thing. But I, having studied the original Hebraic Bible, know, that it does not contain the Gospel. That the Jewish Bible, being a history of creation, treasure and patrimony of Jewish people, the Jews, who do not accept the Gospel, should be authority. That as the Latin translation is incorrect, the Catholics could not lay down the Law, notwithstanding their habit of appropriating everything to themselves, and of misconstruing to their advantage the translation of the original text. Besides, the Gospels, with the exception of that written by Saint Mathew, were written in Greek later than the Bible, and conflict in every respect with the Law of Moses, as proved by the enemity between Jews and Christians. How, then, could I, knowing all this, express myself as a fanatic, or as an ignorant monk? I do not exact from any monk the speech of a free-thinker and therefore, they should not exact that I express myself as a monk would. Why do they want me to consolidate under one name two distinct things, which, to a certain extent contradict each other? Let the Christians do so, but I must not, and cannot. If I call them separately, it is in accordance with the thought inspiring two works, two legislations, two religions, on which they want to found the Catholic Religion. Your son, moreover, reasons finely, when he says: 'I did not know that the Gospels were different from the Bible, and not a principal part of it.' Tell him, Holy Father, that in every country a part, no matter how principal may it be, is always different from the whole, for instance: The principal thing in Friar Rodriguez is his habit; but his habit is different from Friar Rodriguez, as otherwise there would be one dirty Friar Rodriguez, another shining, another creased, another wide, short, long, greasy, etc. On the other hand, the habit is different from the monk, because a piece of cloth, no matter how dirty, could never be presumptuous, despotic, ignorant or obscurautistic.

"'3d. To prove the existence of a Purgatory, he quotes: 'Saint Mathew says in Chapter twelfth, thirty-sixth verse——.' But he quotes wrongly, as from that verse cannot be derived the existence of a Purgatory, nor anything of its kind. The Hebrew text says: 'Wa 'ebif 'omar lakam kij 'al kal abar reg ashar idabbru 'abaschim yittbu heschboun biom hammischphat'; the Greek text, 'Lego de hynun hote pan rema argon, ho ean lalesosin hoi anthropoi, apodosousi peri auton logon en hemera kriseos.' All these translated into Latin say: 'Dicto autem vobis, quoniam omne verbum otiosum quod locuti fuerint homines, reddent rationem de eo in die judicii,' which, translated into English means, 'AND I SAY TO YOU, THAT ON THE DAY OF JUDGMENT, MEN SHALL HAVE TO ACCOUNT FOR EVERY IDLE WORD.' From all these texts, you can see, Holy Doctor, that the only thing to be derived is that on the Day of Judgment, Friar Rodriguez will have to give such an account of himself, that very likely it will take him two days to account for all the nonsense he has said.

"I imagine that your son, instead of the thirty-sixth verse, meant to quote the thirty- second, which says: "And all who shall say word against the son of man will be forgiven; but he who says word against the Holy Ghost, shall not be pardoned; neither in this life nor in the next." From this they have tried to derive the existence of a Purgatory. What a fertile imagination!

"'4th. Because Saint Ireneus, St. Clement of Alexandria, and Origenes, three in all, although not being the first Christian, had some remote idea of Purgatory, it does not follow that the Christians of the first century did believe in it, unless it could be previously established that three persons represent a totality, even if amongst such a totality existed, contradictory ideas. But, as a proof that was it not so, you, yourself, Holy Doctor, being their father, having flourished in the fourth and fifth century, and supposed to be the greatest amongst the Fathers of the Church, denied most emphatically, in various instances, the existence of a Purgatory. In your CCXCV cermon, beginning by: 'Frecuenter charitatem vestra,' etc., you said very decidedly: 'Nemo se slecipiat fratres; DUO enim LOCA sunt et TERIUS non est ullus. Qui cum Christo reguare non meruerit, cum diabolo ABSQUE DUBITATIONE ULLA perebit.' This translated means, 'Do not deceive yourselves, brethren; there are but two places for the soul and there is no third place. He who should not deserve to live with Christ, UNDOUBTEDLY will perish.'

" 'Further on, in de Consolatione mortuorum, you say: 'Sed recedus anima quoe carnalibus oculis non videtur, ab angelis susciptur et collocatur, aut in sinu, Abrahae, si fidelis est, aut in carcerio inferni custodia si peccatrix est.' This means, *But at the departure of that soul which the eyes of the flesh cannot see, the angels will receive and carry it to the Bosom of Abraham, if it has been faithful; or to Hell, if sinful.' On the other hand, I could quote a large number of your own texts showing that for you, Purgatory was not an impossibility. Add to all this what Saint Fulgentius, who flourished after you during the fifth and sixth century, says in Chapter XIV., of his 'de incarnatione et gratia,' etc.: 'Quicumque regnum Dei non ingreditur, poenis oeternis cruciatur.' That is to say, 'He who could not enter the Kingdom of God, will suffer eternal punishment.'

" '5th. Your son either cannot read, or else acts in bad faith; otherwise, how could he, from my estatement, 'The Protestants DO NOT BELIEVE in it; neither do the Greek Fathers, because they miss,' etc., try to make 'The Greek Fathers DID NOT believe in a Purgatory?'

" 'How could he deduct from a present, a past tense and twist the sentences to make from it 'The Holy Greek Fathers?'

" 'I used 'BELIEVE,' the present tense, although in my time the HOLY GREEK FATHERS did not exist, but simply the fathers belonging to the Greek Church. Moreover, as I was following an historical order, how could I refer to the Protestants, first, and to the HOLY GREEK FATHERS afterwards, who believed what they wished, and who at the time of my earthly life were a past to me?

" 'And enwrapped in such bad faith, he dares to qualify as a slanderer, imposter and ignoramus, the man who only quoted me!

" 'But such proceeding is worthy of Friar Rodriguez, who, following his system of confusing a part with the whole, tries to condemn another's book, and mistakes the rays of the sun for the sun itself, all with the purpose of slandering the author and calling him Freemason.

" 'Tell me, Holy Doctor, after what I have told you, who is the real ignoramus, impostor and slanderer?

" '6th. Instead of accusing others of ignorance, and presuming to know everything, he should be careful, because he has not even read your books, notwithstanding you are his father, and that it is his duty to know what you have said. Should he have done so, he would neither have written so much nonsense nor would he have shown the shallowness of his knowledge, which, by the way, he derives from some little books, which, to propagate and maintain obscurantism, were published in Cataluna, (*) by Sarda y Salvany.'

"Thus was old Tasio expressing himself, when the voice of the Almighty was heard summoning me to His presence.

"Trembling, I approached, and prostrated myself at His feet.'

" 'Go to Earth,' said the voice, 'and tell those who call themselves your sons that I, having created millions of suns, around which, thousands of worlds, inhabited by millions of millions of beings, created by my infinite Mercy, gyrate, cannot be an instrument to the fulfilment of a few ungrateful creatures' passions, simply handfuls of dust caried away by a gust of wind; insignificant particles of the inhabitants of one of my smallest worlds!

" 'Tell them that my Name must not be used to extend the misery or ignorance of their brothers, nor shall they restrain in my Name, intelligence and thought, which I created free. That they must not commit abuses in my Name, cause a tear, nor a single drop of blood to be shed. That they must not represent me as being cruel, revengeful, subject to their whims and executor of their will. Not to represent me, The Fountain of Goodness, as a tyrant, or an unkind Father, pretending that they are the only possessors of Light and Eternal Life. How? I, who have given to each being air, light, life and love, that he may be happy, could I deny to one of the most transcendental, true happiness, for the sake of others? Impious! Absurd! Tell them that I, who am All, and apart from whom nothing exists, nor could exist, I have not and cannot have enemies. Nothing equals me, and no one can oppose my will!

" 'Tell them that their enemies are not my enemies; that I have never identified Myself with them, and that their maxims are vain, insensible, blasphemous! Tell them that I pardon error, but punish iniquity; that I will forgive a sin against me, but will prosecute those who should torture an unfortunate. That being infinitely Powerful, all the sins of all the inhabitants of all the worlds, thousands of times centuplicated, can never dim an atom of my glory. But the least injury to the poor and oppressed I will punish, for I have not created man to make him unhappy nor the victim of his brothers. I am the Father of all existent; I

(*) Cataluna.—Province of Spain, which capital is Barcelona.—Trans. Note.

DINING ROOM IN GENERAL MERRITT'S PALACE AT MANILA.

VICTIMS REPORTED DEAD AFTER AN EXECUTION.

AN EXECUTION ENTERTAINMENT ON THE LUNETA.

A MARTYR TO THE LIBERTY OF SPEECH.

know the destiny of every atom; let me love all men, whose miseries and needs I know. Let each one perform his duty, that I, The God of Mercy, know my own will.'

"Thus spoke the Almighty; and I came here to fulfill his command. Now, I say to you:

"That the miseries of the unhappy Indian whom you have impoverished and stupefied, have reached the Throne of the Highest. THERE have arrived so many intelligences obscured and impaired by you! The cry of so many exiles, tortured, and killed at your instigation! The tears of so many mothers and the miseries of so many orphans, combined with the noise of your orgies! Know that there is a God, (perhaps you doubt His existence, and only use His name to advance your ends) who will some day call you to account for all your iniquities. Know that He needs not the money of the poor, nor is it necessary to worship Him by burning candles and incense, saying masses or believing blindly what others say, contrary to common sense.

"No! His luminary is greater than your own sun; His flowers more fragrant than those on earth. He suffices to Himself. He created intelligence for no subservient purpose; but that with its use, man could be happy in raising himself to Him. He needs no one. He created man, not for His sake, but for man's own. He is happy for all eternity!

"You obstinately uphold the existence of a Purgatory, using even the most ignoble weapons and means to defend your belief. Why, instead of wasting your time in affirming the existence of that which you never saw, do you not preach and practice love and charity amongst yourselves? Why not preach words of comfort and hope, to somewhat soothe the miseries of life, instead of frightening your brothers by tales of future punishment? Why? Because Christ's True Doctrine would bring you no earthly wealth, and all that you look for is gold, and gold! And to satisfy your end and bleed the timid souls, of money, you have invented a Purgatory! Why afflict orphans and widows with dreadful tales of the next life, only to extort from them a few cents? Have you forgotten what the Apostle said? 'Nolo vos ignorare, fratres, de dormientibus, ut non contristenuni, sicut qui spem non habent,' which means, 'I do not wish you to ignore, brethren, that which concerns those who sleep, that you may not be saddened, like those who have lost all hope.' Also, that I, myself, have said? 'Hoec enim est Christianoe fidei summa: vitam veram expectare post mortem,' that is 'Here is then the summary of the Christian faith: to hope for a true life after death.' But you, lacking in charity, and for a vile, greedy interest, live in opposition to Christ, and pretend to be able to mould Divine Judgment. All the strength of your philosophy seems to be derived from your own theory, which denies the existence of souls sufficiently sinners to be condemned, or pure enough to enter the Kingdom of God! By whose authority do you pretend to oppose the judgment of Him who weighs and considers the smallest thought? Who knows it is impossible to expect perfection from beings made of clay, subject to the miseries and oppressions of earthly life? Who told you that He will judge as you, with your narrow, limited intelligence, do? That the miseries of this life are not expiations of sins?

"Cease in your avaricious hoarding of wealth! You have now enough. Do not wrench from the poor his last mouthful of bread.

"Remember what Saint Fulgentius said: 'Et si mithetur in stagnum ignis et sulphuris qui nudum vestimento non tegit, quid passures est qui vestimento crudelis expoliat? Et si rerum suarem avarus possessor requiem non habebit, quomodo aliaenarum rerum insatiabilis raptor?' Meaning, 'And if he who never clothed the naked is sent to the pond of fire and sulphur, where will he, who cruelly stripped them, go? And if the greedy possessor of his own wealth may never rest, how shall it be with the thief, insatiable in his greed for the wealth of others?'

"Preach then, the religion of Hope and Promises, as you, above all, are in need of pardon and forgiveness. Do not speak of rigor, nor condemn others, lest God should hear and judge you according to the laws by you formulated. Bear always in mind Christ's words, 'Vae vobis scribae et Pharisae hypocrite qui clauditis regnum coelorum ante homines; vos non intratis, nec introeunts sinitis intrare!' This means, 'Woe to you, Scribes and Pharisees, who close to men the Kingdom of God, and neither enter nor allow others to enter!'

"Now, to you personally, I will say: You are an unfortunate fool, who speak numberless absurdities, although I could not expect aught else from you, and would not punish you for them. But you have had the audacity of not only insulting others, by which you forgot truth and charity, but praised yourself and called attention to your own praise.

"Referring to yourself, you said. This Father, whom I well know (liar, you do not even know yourself), although he may appear a little hard headed (a little hardheaded? Ask my crosier if your head is not harder than stone), never speaks in vain (this is true; every word you say causes as much laughter on earth as in Heaven), nor uses words without first thinking (if such is true, your intelligence is very limited).

"For such foolish vanity I ought to punish you severely, so that you would stop forever your senseless writings, saving me the trouble of coming to reprimand you at every instance.

"Were I to judge you according to your own theory, you should at least go to your Purgatory. But, after all, you are not so bad, as many learned persons are made to laugh at your writings.

"It would be well for your pride if you allowed the Indians to pass by you without taking off their hats or kissing your hand. But then, they would be imprisoned or exiled, and it would not do to increase the wrong you do them.

"Shall I make you lame and dumb? No! Your brothers would claim it was a trial of your forbearance, to which God had submitted you. No; you won't catch me on that!

"What shall I do with you?"

The old Bishop meditated for a few moments, and then, he exclaimed:

"Ah! Now I know! Your own sin shall be your punishment!

"I condemn you to continue saying and writing nonsense for the rest of your life, so that the world may laugh at you, and also, that on the Day of Judgment you may be judged according to your deserts!"

"Amen!" replied Friar Rodriguez.

The vision then disappeared; the light of the lamp regained its yellowish flame, and the soft perfume dispersed.

On the following day Friar Rodriguez started writing greater nonsense, with renewed energy.

Amen!

JOSE RIZAL.

Note.—The foregoing admirable translations from the writings of Dr. Rizal were made by Mr. F. M. de Rivas, of Chicago.

CHAPTER XV.

EVENTS OF THE SPANISH-AMERICAN WAR.

No Mystery About the Cause of the War—The Expected and the Inevitable Has Happened—The Tragedy of the Maine—Vigilant Wisdom of President McKinley—Dewey's Prompt Triumph—The Battles at Manila and Santiago Compared—General Shafter Tells of the Battle of Santiago—Report of Wainwright Board on Movements of Sampson's Fleet in the Destruction of Cervera's Squadron—Stars and Stripes Raised Over Porto Rico—American and Spanish Fleets at Manila Compared.—Text of Peace Protocol.

The war between Spain and the United States was a long time coming, and there is no more mystery about its cause than doubt as to its decisions. It was foretold in every chapter of the terrible stories of the conflicts between the Spaniards and their colonists, largely of their blood, in Central and South America. The causes of war in Cuba, and the conduct of warfare by Spain in that island were the same that resulted in revolutionary strife in Mexico and Peru, and, indeed, all the nations in the Americas that once were swayed by the sovereignty of Spain. The last of the islands of the Spanish possessions in the hemisphere introduced to the civilized world by Columbus were lost by the western peninsula of Europe, symbolized and personified in the Crown, as the first crumbling fragments of the colonial empires of Spain fell away from her. Only in the case of Cuba there was the direct intervention of the United States to establish "a stable government" in the distracted island, desolated by war, pestilence and famine, that had evolved conditions, of terrible misery incurable from within, and of inhumane oppression that should be resented by all enlightened people. It had long been realized by the thoughtful men of Spain capable of estimating the currents of events, that the time must come, and was close at hand, when the arms of the United States would be directed to the conquest of Cuba. It was not only in the air that this was to be, it was written in the history of Spanish America, and more than that, there was not an Atlas that did not proclaim in the maps of the continents of the Western world, that Cuba would and in the largest sense of right should, become a part of the United States, and must do so in order to be redeemed from the disabilities deeply implanted, and released from having the intolerable burdens imposed by the rule of Spain. The consciousness of the Spaniards, that the shadow of the United States lowered over the misgovernment of Cuba, and that there was a thunder-cloud in the north that must burst—with more than the force of the hurricanes that spin on their dizzy way of destruction from the Caribbean Sea—aroused the fury of passion, of jealous hatred and thirst for revenge, in anticipation of the inevitable, that caused the catastrophe of the blowing up of the Maine, and kindled with the flame of the explosion, the conflagration of warfare in the Indies West and East, that has reddened the seas and the skies with the blood of Spain and the glow of America's victory both in the Antilles and the Philippines, wiping from the face of the earth the last vestiges of the colonial imperialism of Spain that gave her mediaeval riches and celebrity, for which—as the system always evil became hideous with malignant growth, so that each colony was a cancer on the mother country—there has been exacted punishment of modern poverty, and finally the humiliation of the haughty, with no consolation for defeat, but the fact that in desperate and forlorn circumstances there were seen glimpses of the ancient valor in Spanish soldiers, that was once their high distinction among the legions of embattled Europe.

The United States was not ready for war. Our regular army was a 16 to 120 Spanish troops in Cuba, our field guns 1 to 6 of Blanco's batteries, our siege train nowhere, and fortified cities to assail; and the ability and industry of the Spaniards as well as their skill and strength in surveying and fortifying military lines, and their food resources were dangerously undervalued. The war was rushed upon the country, contrary to the calm executive judgment of the President. The army and navy were admirable but faulty in hasty equipment, the navy a perfect machine in itself, but without docks and arsenals in the right place for the supply of a fleet in the old battle field of European navies, the West Indies. The energies of the Government were put forth as soon as the war was seriously threatened, and the mighty people arose and swiftly as the aptitudes of Americans in emergencies could be applied, deficiencies were supplied. The first stroke of arms came as a dazzling flash from the far southwest, in the story of the smashing victory of Dewey at Manila. That splendid officer, gentleman and hero did not signal his fleet as Nelson at Trafalgar, that every man was expected to do his duty, but he reported that every man did his duty; and the East Indian fleet of Spain vanished, smashed, burned and sunken by a thunderbolt! The theory of war countenanced by the impetuous and demanded by the presumptuous, was that our aggressive forces must attack Havana. In and around that city were an enormous garrison, abundant military stores, forty miles of trenches defended by sixty thousand men; and far more to be dreaded the deadly climate, the overwhelming rains, the deep rank soil soaked under the tropical sun and the dense vegetation, and still more the pestilence—the ghastly Yellow Fever, and scarcely less poisonous and fatal pernicious malarial fevers, and dysenteries that exhausted as fast as fever consumed. Fortunately, it was decided that the place to attack Havana was Santiago, and there the regular army, with the exception of the regiments sent to the Philippines, was ordered and in due time reinforced by volunteers, safely embarked and disembarked, to become the winners on bloody fields and receive the surrender of the Spanish garrisons of the city and province of Santiago. The vaunted fleet of Cervera, having attempted flight, perished—the wrecks of his fine ships strewing the southern coast of Cuba, where they remain as memorials, like and unlike the distorted iron that was the Maine, in the harbor of Havana, and as the shattered and charred remnants of the fleet of Montejo, at Manila, still cumber the waters of the bay off Cavite, telling the story of the glory of our victorious heroes there.

The responsibility of the Chief Magistrate of the United States in the late war was remarkable. Everything of moment was referred to him from the Cabinet officers of the Government, and he gave all the closest attention, making, after conscientious consideration, the decisions that determined the course of action taken. This was true in unusual measure of the Treasury, State, War and Navy Departments.

It is well the President resisted while he could the "rush line" in Congress, that strove headlong for war, and strenuously urged in the time gained essential preparations, and that he pressed the war the day it was declared with a hurry message to Admiral Dewey, who won his immortal victory on the other side of the world within a week of his orders by cable to "destroy" the squadron of the enemy that might be found somewhere on the west coast of Luzon.

Nearer home there was a harder task. The Spanish army in Cuba was much more formidable on the defensive than in the offensive. There were greater numbers of soldiers of a better class in the service of Spain on the island, than had been supposed, and they did not lack, in the degree believed, discipline, ammunition or provisions. The Spaniards had an effective field artillery, more than one hundred guns, and their Mauser rifles were excellent, far-reaching; and, in field ammunition, they were ahead of us in smokeless powder. Our regiments would have given way before the Spanish rifles, that told no tales except with bolts, that flew invisible, fatal arrows, from the jungles, if the American soldier had not been of stuff that was like pure steel, and marched unflinchingly through the deadly hail, regarding the bitter pelting as a summons to "come on" and carry the trenches and ambuscades by storm. The incapacity of the Spaniards to put down the Cuban Rebellion caused grave misapprehensions, both as to the Spanish and Cuban soldiery, for few Americans understand the conditions of the interminable guerilla warfare, the particular military accomplishment of the Spanish race, impotent in all save the destructive effect upon those not engaged in it. In Congress no impression could be made of the real feebleness of the Cubans, except in bushwhacking, and it is still a puzzle that the immense masses of Spanish troops should be so helpless against the insurgents, and yet so troublesome in harassing invaders. The Cuban army was not a myth, certainly, but it has been a disappointment to those who were swift in shouting its praises, upon information given by the Cuban Key West Bureau of News novelettes. It was well that the attack on Spain in the West Indies was directed upon Santiago and Porto Rico. The former manifestly was a point that commanded the central waters of the West Indies; recently there have been expressions of surprise that the expedition to Porto Rico, finally and handsomely led by Major General Miles, commanding the army of the United States, was so delayed. Investigation from the inside will duly determine that no harm was done in that case by loss of time. Santiago was pointed out by many circumstances as the vital spot of Spanish power in America, where a mortal blow might be delivered. It was in the province where the insurgents had greater strength than in any other part of the island. It was so situated that our fleet in that locality was close to the Windward Passage, east of Cuba, where Columbus was at once perplexed and triumphant, and to Hayti, Jamaica and Porto Rico; and there were several landings where it would be possible to disembark troops, protected by the fire of our ships. More than that, Santiago is the old capital of Cuba, the place where the head of the Cuban church abides, and the scene of the Virginius Massacre—altogether having a place in history almost equal to that of Havana. It was not doubted the sanitary situation of the east end of Cuba was better than that of the west end. Experience shows that this easy assumption was questionable. If we omit the great plague spot, the city of Havana, it will appear that Santiago is in a region as pestilential as can be found in the provinces of Havana and Pinar del Rio. More than all other associations and conspicuities, the attention of the world was directed to Santiago because Cervera's elusive fleet, short of coal and provisions, and overmatched by the United States navy, took refuge in the deep harbor, hoping to clean his ships, get supplies and escape with coal enough to open a new career. The Spaniards were too slow, and the only ships of Spain that showed a sign of the spirit of enterprise and the capacity of adventure, were bottled up by a relentless blockade. Lieutenant Hobson became famous in a night in his most hazardous effort to use the Merrimac as a cork for the bottle, but fortunately left a gap through which the Spaniards made haste to their doom. When the second fleet of Spain was destroyed, all chance of disputing our supremacy at sea, or of doing anything to guard Spanish interests either in the East or West Indies, was extinguished.

There has been no marked features of contention as to the battles of Manila, except in the case of the gratuitous observations of critical persons, whose feelings have been disturbed, that the storming of the town was not bloody enough. The victory, however, was all the greater, for the casualty lists were not long, owing to the management of the Commanding General and the heroic Admiral, who won a battle famous as that at New Orleans, with less bloodshed, but as Jackson's victory was not belittled because he lost but half a dozen men killed, the victories at Manila should not be slighted. The Santiago battles, however, have stirred controversies, and there is a great mass of literature, official and other, subject to endless examination, and perhaps so voluminous as to confuse readers for some generations. The leading and indisputable facts are, that the Spaniards fought well on land, but were ineffectual afloat, in their attempts to inflict injuries, though they put to sea in dashing style, and did not flinch in efforts to evade a superior force, until the fire of the Americans crushed them. In the incidents of warfare on the hills around and the waves before Santiago, it is fair to say that the Spaniards redeemed themselves from imputation of timidity, and fought in a manner not unworthy of the countrymen of the Garrison of Morro Castle, Havana, whose gallantry in resisting the army and fleet of England, in 1762, commanded the respectful regard of their conquerers, and is a glorious chapter in the story of Spain. The Santiago events were most honorable to American arms, and it would lessen the splendor of the reputation of the American soldiers if one failed to do justice to the sturdy fighters they overcame. It is too early or too late for participation in the debates whether civil or acrimonious, as to the merits or faults of those engaged at Santiago, further than to quote that golden sentence from the report of Commodore Schley, that there was "glory enough to go around." We, whatever is said, remember what was done on those hills that have an everlasting place in history. There forever is to be application of marvelous propriety, of the mournful and noble lines of Kentucky's poet, Theodore O'Hara:

> "On Fame's eternal camping ground
> Their silent tents are spread,
> And Glory guards with solemn round
> The bivouac of the dead."

There was a speedy realization by the country, and all the intelligent peoples

EVENTS OF THE SPANISH-AMERICAN WAR. 207

of the earth, when our troops were embarked for the Santiago campaign, that the crisis of the war was at hand. No American thought of failure. The only questions were as to the power of the defense of Cuba by Spain, and the cost to us in men and money to overcome the defenders. Those who knew the most about the conditions in Cuba had the least confidence in the efficiency of the Cuban Army. The only body of organized Cubans of importance was that under command of Garcia, and it was the province of which he was in partial occupation that we invaded in force. The public had been considerably interested and entertained by the rousing accounts of the various naval bombardments of Spanish shore fortresses. But the firing from our ships had not materially shaken the Spanish defenses. The sea power had not shattered the shore lines, but found abundant occupation in guarding transports and protecting the troops when landing. It would have been an act of the most gross imprudence and incompetency to have put an army ashore unless the supremacy of the navy on the sea was absolute. More than that, our own cities had to be assured that they were secure from attack. On the 31st of May orders were issued for the embarkation of the army of invasion as follows:

1. The Fifth Army Corps.

2. The Battalion of Engineers.

3. The detachment of the Signal Corps.

4. Five squadrons of cavalry, to be selected by the commanding general of the cavalry division, in accordance with instruction previously given.

5. Four batteries of light artillery, to be commanded by a major, to be selected by the commanding officer of the light artillery brigade.

6. Two batteries of heavy artillery, to be selected by the commanding officer of the siege artillery battalion, with eight (8) siege guns and eight (8) field mortars.

7. The Battalion of Engineers, the infantry, and cavalry, will be supplied with 500 rounds of ammunition per man.

8. All troops will carry, in addition to the fourteen (14) days' field rations now on hand, ten (10) days' travel rations.

9. The minimum allowance of tentage and baggage as prescribed in General Orders 54, A. G. O., current series, will be taken.

10. In addition to the rations specified in paragraph 8 of this order, the chief commissary will provide sixty (60) days' field rations for the entire command.

11. All recruits and extra baggage, the latter to be stored, carefully piled and covered, will be left in camp, in charge of a commissioned officer, to be selected by

the regimental commander. Where there are no recruits available the necessary guard only will be left.

12. Travel rations will be drawn, at once, by the several commands, as indicated in paragraph 8.

This was by command of Major-General Shafter. There were delays on account of inadequate facilities for embarkation at Tampa and Port Tampa. Orders for General Shafter to move with not less than 10,000 men were issued on the 7th, and there was delay on account of reports of Spanish ships of war ready to strike a blow at the transports. Twelve squadrons of cavalry not mounted were added to the troops designated in the general order, and June 14th the expedition sailed with 815 officers and 16,072 enlisted men, and had a smooth and uneventful passage. There were several demonstrations for the deception of the enemy, in one of which 500 Cubans were employed. General Shafter was committed by the movements and the ground, as he says in his official report:

"To approach Santiago from the east over a narrow road, at first in some places not better than a trail, running from Daiquiri through Siboney and Sevilla, and making attack from that quarter, was, in my judgment, the only feasible plan, and subsequent information and results confirmed my judgment."

The disembarkation commenced June 22nd, and all men were ordered to carry "on the person the blanket roll (with shelter tent and poncho), three days' field rations (with coffee, ground), canteens filled, and 100 rounds of ammunition per man. Additional ammunition, already issued to the troops, tentage, baggage, and company cooking utensils left under charge of the regimental quartermaster, with one non-commissioned officer and two privates from each company."

Two days were occupied in getting the troops ashore, and the first engagement was on the morning of the 24th, General Young's brigade taking the advance, and finding a Spanish force strongly intrenched on the Santiago road three miles from Siboney. Young's force was 964 officers and men. The enemy were driven from the field. Our loss, 1 officer and 15 men killed, and 6 officers and 46 men wounded. Spanish loss reported 9 killed and 27 wounded. General Shafter says the engagement had "an inspiring effect" upon the men, and "gave us a well-watered country further to the front, on which to encamp our troops," and the rest of the month was occupied in attempting to land rations enough to have a reserve, and "it was not until nearly two weeks after the army landed that it was possible to place on shore three days' supplies in excess of those required for the daily consumption."

General Shafter reconnoitered, and formed his plan of battle June 30th, and reports that in the opening of the engagement on July 1st "the artillery fire from El Pozo was soon returned by the enemy's artillery. They evidently had the range of this hill, and their first shells killed and wounded several men. As the Spaniards used smokeless powder it was very difficult to locate the position of their pieces, while, on the contrary, the smoke caused by our black powder plainly indicated the position of our battery."

The advantages the Spaniards had in the use of smokeless powder were conspicuous throughout the scenes of fighting both at Santiago and Manila. We had, however, at Santiago a war balloon of the actual service, of which General Shafter says: "General Kent forced the head of his column alongside of the cavalry column as far as the narrow trail permitted, and thus hurried his arrival at the San Juan and the formation beyond that stream. A few hundred yards before reaching the San Juan the road forks, a fact that was discovered by Lieutenant-Colonel Derby of my staff, who had approached well to the front in a war balloon. This information he furnished to the troops, resulting in Sumner moving on the right-hand road, while Kent was enabled to utilize the road to the left."

General Shafter officially makes the following reference to his illness at the time:

"My own health was impaired by overexertion in the sun and intense heat of the day before, which prevented me from participating as actively in the battle as I desired; but from a high hill near my headquarters I had a general view of the battlefield, extending from El Caney on the right to the left of our lines on San Juan Hill. My staff officers were stationed at various points on the field, rendering frequent reports, and through them by the means of orderlies and the telephone, I was enabled to transmit my orders.

"After the brilliant and important victory gained at El Caney, Lawton started his tried troops, who had been fighting all day and marching much of the night before, to connect with the right of the cavalry division. Night came on before this movement could be accomplished. In the darkness the enemy's pickets were encountered, and the Division Commander being uncertain of the ground and as to what might be in his front halted his command and reported the situation to me. This information was received about 12:30 a. m., and I directed General Lawton to return by my headquarters and the El Pozo House as the only certain way of gaining his new position.

"This was done, and the division took position on the right of the cavalry early next morning, Chaffee's brigade arriving first, about half-past 7, and the other brigades before noon."

Of the hottest of the fight on the 1st of July, General Shafter reports: "Great credit is due to Brigadier-General H. S. Hawkins, who, placing himself between his regiments, urged them on by voice and bugle calls to the attack so brilliantly executed.

"In this fierce encounter words fail to do justice to the gallant regimental commanders and their heroic men, for, while the generals indicated the formations and the points of attack, it was, after all, the intrepid bravery of the subordinate officers and men that planted our colors on the crest of San Juan Hill and drove the enemy from his trenches and blockhouses, thus gaining a position which sealed the fate of Santiago.

"In this action on this part of the field most efficient service was rendered by Lieutenant John H. Parker, Thirteenth Infantry, and the Gatling gun detachment under his command. The fighting continued at intervals until nightfall, but our men held resolutely to the positions gained at the cost of so much blood and toil.

"I am greatly indebted to General Wheeler, who, as previously stated, returned from the sick list to duty during the afternoon. His cheerfulness and aggressiveness made itself felt on this part of the battlefield, and the information he furnished to me at various stages of the battle proved to be most useful."

The report of the General Commanding of the further fighting is a model of forcible brevity, in these paragraphs:

"Soon after daylight on July 2 the enemy opened battle, but because of the intrenchments made during the night, the approach of Lawton's division, and the presence of Bates' brigade, which had taken position during the night on Kent's left, little apprehension was felt as to our ability to repel the Spaniards.

"It is proper here to state that General Bates and his brigade had performed most arduous and efficient service, having marched much of the night of June 30-July 1, and a good part of the latter day, during which he also participated in the battle of El Caney, after which he proceeded, by way of El Pozo, to the left of the line at San Juan, reaching his new position about midnight.

"All day on the 2d the battle raged with more or less fury, but such of our troops as were in position at daylight held their ground, and Lawton gained a strong and commanding position on the right.

"About 10 p. m., the enemy made a vigorous assault to break through my lines, but he was repulsed at all points.

"On the morning of the 3d the battle was renewed, but the enemy seemed to have expended his energy in the assault of the previous night, and the firing along the lines was desultory;" and this was stopped by a letter sent by General Shafter, saying he would be obliged to "shell Santiago," if not surrendered, and non-combatants would be given until 10 o'clock July 4th to leave the city. The reply of the Spanish General was that he would not surrender. Then foreign consuls came within our lines asking more time to remove the women and children. The language of General Shafter reporting the situation at the time and the events following, is here reproduced as of permanent interest:

"My first message went in under a flag of truce at 12:30 p. m. I was of the opinion that the Spaniards would surrender if given a little time, and I thought this result would be hastened if the men of their army could be made to understand they would be well treated as prisoners of war. Acting upon this presumption, I determined to offer to return all the wounded Spanish officers at El Caney who were able to bear transportation, and who were willing to give their paroles not to serve against the forces of the United States until regularly exchanged. This offer was made and accepted. These officers, as well as several of the wounded Spanish privates, 27 in all, were sent to their lines under the escort of some of our mounted cavalry. Our troops were received with honors, and I have every reason to believe the return of the Spanish prisoners produced a good impression on their comrades.

"The cessation of firing about noon on the 3d practically terminated the battle of Santiago.

"A few Cubans assisted in the attack at El Caney, and fought valiantly, but their numbers were too small to materially change the strength, as indicated above. The enemy confronted us with numbers about equal to our own; they fought obstinately in strong and intrenched positions, and the results obtained clearly indicate the intrepid gallantry of the company, officers and men, and the benefits derived from the careful training and instruction given in the company in recent years in rifle practice and other battle exercises. Our losses in these battles were 22 officers and 208 men killed, and 81 officers and 1,203 men wounded; missing, 79. The missing, with few exceptions, reported later.

"The arrival of General Escario on the night of July 2, and his entrance into the city was not anticipated, for although it was known, as previously stated, that General Pando had left Manzanillo with reinforcements for the garrison of Santiago, it was not believed his troops could arrive so soon. General Garcia, with between four and five thousand Cubans, was intrusted with the duty of watching for and intercepting the reinforcements expected. This, however, he failed to do, and Escario passed into the city along on my extreme right and near the bay."

On the 11th, when the firing ceased and was not resumed "the sickness in the army was increasing very rapidly, as a result of exposure in the trenches to the intense heat of the sun and the heavy rains. Moreover, the dews in Cuba are almost equal to rains. The weakness of the troops was becoming so apparent I was anxious to bring the siege to an end, but in common with most of the officers of the army I did not think an assault would be justifiable, especially as the enemy seemed to be acting in good faith in their preliminary propositions to surrender.

"July 12 I informed the Spanish Commander that Major-General Miles, Commander-in-Chief of the American army, had just arrived in my camp, and requested him to grant us a personal interview on the following day. He replied he would be pleased to meet us. The interview took place on the 13th."

The Spanish raised many points, as is their habit, and were tenacious about retaining their arms, but yielded, and "the terms of surrender finally agreed upon included about 12,000 Spanish troops in the city and as many more in the surrendered district."

July 17th "we met midway between the representatives of our two armies, and the Spanish Commander formally consummated the surrender of the city and the 24,000 troops in Santiago and the surrendered district.

"After this ceremony I entered the city with my staff and escort, and at 12 o'clock noon the American flag was raised over the Governor's palace."

The men and material surrendered by the Spaniards at Santiago largely exceeded the two English armies and their equipments at Saratoga and Yorktown.

The yellow fever appeared in the American camp at Siboney July 4th, and the fact was soon known to the army. General Shafter says of the wounded and sick: "They received every attention that it was possible to give them. The medical officers without exception worked night and day to alleviate the suffering, which was no greater than invariably accompanies a campaign. It would have been better if we had more ambulances, but as many were taken as was thought necessary, judging from previous campaigns."

General Joe Wheeler's report of the action of July 1st is a paper full of striking points. The movement into battle began in wading the San Juan river under heavy fire, and the General says:

"We were as much under fire in forming the line as we would be by an advance, and I therefore pressed the command forward from the covering which it was formed.

It merged into open space, in full view of the enemy, who occupied breastworks and batteries on the crest of the hill which overlooked Santiago, officers and men falling at every step. The troops advanced gallantly, soon reached the foot of the hill and ascended, driving the enemy from their works and occupying them on the crest of the hill.

"Colonel Carroll and Major Wessels were both wounded during the charge, but Major Wessels was enabled to return and resume command. General Wyckoff, commanding Kent's Third Brigade, was killed at 12:10. Lieutenant-Colonel Worth took command and was wounded at 12:15. Lieutenant-Colonel Liscum then took command and was wounded at 12:20, and the command then devolved upon Lieutenant-Colonel Ewers, Ninth Infantry.

"Upon reaching the crest I ordered breastworks to be constructed, and sent to the rear for shovels, picks, spades, and axes. The enemy's retreat from the ridge was precipitate, but our men were so thoroughly exhausted that it was impossible for them to follow. Their shoes were soaked with water by wading the San Juan River; they had become drenched with rain, and when they reached the crest they were absolutely unable to proceed further. Notwithsatnding this condition these exhausted men labored during the night to erect breastworks, furnished details to bury the dead and carry the wounded back in improvised litters."

Wheeler's loss was 6 officers and 40 men killed, 29 officers and 288 men wounded, and 10 men missing—total 372, out of a force of 127 officers and 2,536 men.

General Bates says that after his brigade remained for some time in the first cross road after wading the San Juan river: "We moved to the right to assault a small hill, occupied upon the top by a stone fort and well protected by rifle pits. General Chaffee's brigade charged them from the right, and the two brigades, joining upon the crest, opened fire from this point of vantage, lately occupied by the Spanish, upon the village of El Caney.

"From this advantageous position the Spanish were easily driven from place to place in the village proper, and as fast as they sought shelter in one building were driven out to seek shelter elsewhere. The sharp-shooters of my command were enabled to do effective work at this point. The town proper was soon pretty thoroughly cleaned out of Spanish, though a couple of blockhouses upon the hill to the right of the town offered shelter to a few, and some could be seen retreating along a mountain road leading to the northwest. A part of these made a stand in a field among some bowlders.

General Lawton observes: "The light battery first opened on a column of Spanish troops, which appeared to be cavalry moving westward from El Caney, and about 2 miles range, resulting, as was afterwards learned, in killing 16 in the column."

The General has much to say of a pleasing personal nature.

The report of General Kent is of extraordinary merit for the exact detail and local color. Colonel McClernand, he says, "pointed out to me a green hill in the distance which was to be my objective on my left," and as he moved into action, "I proceeded to join the head of my division, just coming under heavy fire. Approaching the First Brigade I directed them to move alongside the cavalry (which was halted). We were already suffering losses caused by the balloon near by attracting fire and disclosing our position.

"The enemy's infantry fire, steadily increasing in intensity, now came from all directions, not only from the front and the dense tropical thickets on our flanks, but from sharpshooters thickly posted in trees in our rear, and from shrapnel apparently aimed at the balloon. Lieutenant-Colonel Derby, of General Shafter's staff, met me about this time and informed me that a trail or narrow way had been discovered from the balloon a short distance back leading to the left to a ford lower down the stream. I hastened to the forks made by this road, and soon after the Seventy-first New York Regiment of Hawkins' brigade came up. I turned them into the by path indicated by Lieutenant-Colonel Derby, leading to the lower ford, sending word to General Hawkins of this movement. This would have speedily delivered them in their proper place on the left of their brigade, but under the galling fire of the enemy the leading battalion of this regiment was thrown into confusion and recoiled in disorder on the troops in the rear."

The Second and Third Battalions "came up in better order," but there was some delay, and General Kent says:

"I had received orders some time before to keep in rear of the cavalry division. Their advance was much delayed, resulting in frequent halts, presumably to drop their blanket rolls and due to the natural delay in fording a stream. These delays under such a hot fire grew exceedingly irksome, and I therefore pushed the head of my division as quickly as I could toward the river in column files of twos parallel in the narrow way by the cavalry. This quickened the forward movement and enabled me to get into position as speedily as possible for the attack. Owing to the congested condition of the road, the progress of the narrow columns was, however, painfully slow. I again sent a staff officer at a gallop to urge forward the troops in rear."

The Second Brigade and Third "moved toward Fort San Juan, sweeping through a zone of most destructive fire, scaling a steep and difficult hill, and assisting in

AGUINALDO AND HIS COMPATRIOTS.

SAVAGE NATIVE HUNTERS.

GIRL'S COSTUME TO SHOW ONE SHOULDER.

capturing the enemy's strong position (Fort San Juan) at 1:30 p. m. This crest was about 125 feet above the general level, and was defended by deep trenches and a loopholed brick fort surrounded by barbed-wire entanglements."

General Hawkins, after General Kent reached the crest, "reported that the Sixth and Sixteenth Infantry had captured the hill, which I now consider incorrect. Credit is almost equally due the Sixth, Ninth, Thirteenth, Sixteenth, and Twenty-fourth regiments of infantry. Owing to General Hawkins' representations, I forwarded the report sent to corps headquarters about 3 p. m. that the Sixth and Sixteenth infantry regiments captured the hill. The Thirteenth Infantry captured the enemy's colors waving over the fort, but, unfortunately, destroyed them, distributing the fragments among the men, because, as was asserted, 'It was a bad omen,' two or three men having been shot while assisting private Arthur Agnew, Company H, Thirteenth Infantry, the captor. All fragments which could be recovered are submitted with this report.

"I have already mentioned the circumstances of my Third Brigade's advance across the ford, where in the brief space of ten minutes it lost its brave commander (killed) and the next two ranking officers by disabling wounds. Yet, in spite of these confusing conditions the formations were effected without hesitation, although under a stinging fire, companies acting singly in some instances, and by battalion and regiments in others, rushing through the jungle, across the stream waist deep, and over the wide bottom thickly set with barbed wire."

General Kent says:

"The bloody fighting of my brave command can not be adequately described in words. The following list of killed, wounded, and missing tells the story of their valor:

"July 1st the loss was 12 officers and 77 men killed, 32 officers and 463 men wounded, 58 men missing. Total loss, 642."

The following day the Spaniards resumed the battle, and the losses of Kent's command on the 2nd and 3d of July made up a total loss in three days of 99 killed and 597 wounded, and 62 missing. General Shafter said that before closing his report he desired to dwell upon "the natural obstacles I had to encounter, and which no foresight could have overcome or obviated. The rocky and precipitous coast afforded no sheltered landing places, the roads were mere bridle paths, the effect of the tropical sun and rains upon unacclimated troops was deadly, and a dread of strange and unknown diseases had its effect on the army.

"The San Juan and Aguadores rivers would often suddenly rise so as to prevent the passage of wagons, and then the eight pack trains with the command had to be depended upon for the victualing of my army, as well as the 20,000 refugees, who could not in the interests of humanity be left to starve while we had rations."

During the Chicago Peace Jubilee, General Shafter made an address at the Armory of the First Illinois Volunteers, and, released from the continual forms of official reports, added much of interest to the story of Santiago. He says of the send-off:

"We were twice embarked and twice taken back to Tampa and disembarked. On the first occasion the cause was the appearance of Admiral Cervera's fleet; it requiring the entire navy that was disposable to go after that fleet, and the second time by a report that afterwards turned out to be incorrect, that in the St. Nicholas channel, through which we would have to go, some Spanish cruisers had been seen."

When ordered to Tampa to command the first Cuban expedition, he continued:

"I took the troops that I thought best fitted and prepared for that service. There were some magnificent regiments of volunteers, but to part of them I had issued arms only two or three days before. They were not properly equipped, and lacked experience. As I had the choice, I took all of the regulars that were there, and with them three regiments of volunteers. They were magnificent men, as perfect as men could be, but, as you know who served in '61, poorly prepared to take care of themselves at first. You recollect it was months before we were prepared, and we made numerous mistakes that led to sickness and death. The same things have occurred again, and they always will continue with troops that are not used to the field, and in this campaign men were taken directly from their camps immediately after being mustered in, and put into the most difficult campaign of modern military history.

"I practically had the entire regular army of the United States, twenty of the twenty-five regiments of infantry, five of the ten regiments of cavalry, and five batteries of artillery, with three regiments of volunteers, the Seventy-first New York, the Second Massachusetts, and the regiment known as Roosevelt's rough riders. The last were practically seasoned soldiers. They were men from the frontier, men who had been accustomed for years to taking a little sack of corn meal on their saddles, and a blanket, and going out to sleep out of doors for a week or a month at a time. Of course, they knew how to care for themselves in camp.

"Early in June I was called to the telephone in Tampa, and told from the President's mansion in Washington to proceed immediately with not less than 10,000 men to Santiago; that news had been received that day that the fleet of Cervera was surely within that harbor, and that if 10,000 men could be placed there at once the fleet and the city could be captured in forty-eight hours. The horses and mules had been taken off from the ships as well as the men, and the time consumed in reloading the horses and mules allowed me to embark 17,000 men nearly. That was very fortunate for me and our cause."

On arrival off Santiago, he, "with Admiral Sampson, went down the coast about twenty miles, and saw General Garcia, and asked him his opinion of the country, what his force was, and whether he was disposed to assist. I found him very willing and very glad to offer his services at once, with 3,000 men that he had with him and another thousand that he had up the country a little further, which were to join us immediately. In sailing along the coast, looking for a landing place, I selected two places—Siboney, a little indentation in the coast about twelve or thirteen miles east of Santiago, and another little bay about eight miles further east, where small streams entered into the sea, making a valley and a sandbar about 150 to 200 yards in extent. All the rest of the coast is abrupt, perpendicular walls of rock from ten to thirty feet high, against which the waves were dashing all the time, and where it is utterly impossible to land.

"We had the earnest and able support of the navy and their assistance in disembarking, and the next morning were bombarding the two little places and driving the few hundred Spanish soldiers that were there away. We began disembarking, and before the end of the day the men were on shore, with 2,000 horses and mules that we had to throw overboard to get ashore, and the artillery."

The General noted the loss of 17,000 troops out of 24,000 in the English army that besieged Havana in 1762, at the same time of year that he landed at Santiago, and remarked:

"I knew that my entire army would be sick if it stayed long enough; that it was simply a question of getting that town just as soon as possible. I knew the strength, the courage, and the will of my men, or I thought I did, and the result shows that I was not mistaken. It was a question of starting the moment we landed and not stopping until we reached the Spanish outposts, and, therefore, as soon as a division was put on shore it was started on the march.

"On the 24th the first engagement took place, in which we had between 800 and 900 men on the American side and probably 1,000 or 1,200 on the Spanish. The enemy was strongly intrenched, showing only their heads, while the American forces had to march exposing their whole bodies to the fire of the enemy.

"It is announced by military experts as an axiom that trained troops armed with the present breech-loading and rapid-firing arm cannot be successfully assailed by any troops who simply assault. Of course you can make the regular approaches and dig up to them. The fallacy of that proposition was made very manifest that day when the men composing the advance marched as deliberately over those breastworks as they ever did when they fought with arms that you could only load about twice in a minute and of the range of only 200 or 300 yards.

"This army was an army of marksmen. For fifteen years the greatest attention has been paid to marksmanship, and I suppose four-fifths of all the men in that army wore on their breasts the marksman's badge. I had given orders, knowing that the noise of firing is harmless and that shots put in the air are harmless—I had given the strictest orders to all officers that their men should be told not to fire a shot unless they could see something moving, and the firing was to be by individuals, what is called file firing, individual firing. The Spanish troops, not so well drilled in firing as ours, used volley firing, which is very effective against large bodies of troops massed and moving over a plain, but utterly inefficient when used against skirmishers moving over a rough country. In that battle, which lasted two hours, less than ten rounds of ammunition per man was fired by my men, and the losses, notwithstanding my men were exposed, their whole bodies, while the enemy were in trenches, where only their heads could be seen, were about equal.

"I saw the commander of that force a few days later in Santiago, and in talking about it he said to me: 'Your men behaved very strange. We were much surprised. They were whipped, but they didn't seem to know it; they continued to advance (laughter and applause), and we had to go away.' He was quite right about it. They did have to go away.

"On the 29th we had reached the immediate vicinity of the peaks in front of Santiago, about a mile and a half from the city. On the 30th I carefully reconnoitered the ground as much as one could in the dense undergrowth, and determined where I would make my attack, which was simply directed in front, and to make a direct assault. There was no attempt at strategy, and no attempt at turning their flanks. It was simply going straight for them. In that I did not misjudge my men, and that is where I succeeded so well. (Applause.) If we had attempted to flank them out or dig them out by regular parallels and get close to them my men would have been sick before it could have been accomplished, and the losses would have been many times greater than they were.

"The only misfortune, as I judged it, of the first day's fight, but which I have since learned was for the best, was that immediately on our right, and what would be in

PUBLIC BUILDINGS IN MANILA.

FORT WEYLER BUILT BY GENERAL WEYLER WHILE GOVERNOR OF THE PHILIPPINES.

our rear when we attacked the town, was a little village called El Caney, four miles and a half from Santiago, and whence the best road in the country connected with Santiago. I did not know the exact force there, but it was estimated to be 1,000, and perhaps a little more, and it would, of course, have been very hazardous to have left that force so near in our rear.

"Instead of finishing the affair by 9 o'clock, as we expected, it took until 4:30 o'clock in the afternoon before the last shot was fired, and then after a loss of nearly a hundred killed and 250 wounded on our side and the almost total annihilation of the force opposed to us. They had an idea that they would be killed, and when men believe that it is hard to capture them. Just at the close of the battle three or four hundred did attempt to escape, but ran out in front of a brigade that they did not see, and in the course of about three or four hundred yards most of them were dead or mortally wounded, so that probably not more than twenty men on the other side escaped from that battle. It was a most desperate struggle.

"Men were killed in the trenches by being knocked on the head with muskets, and one man I was shown two days later with what would be called a tremendous head on him, and the interpreter asked him how that had occurred, and he doubled up his fist and spoke of the soldier that had hit him as a black man, that he had dropped his gun and hit him in the head with his fist. That was pretty close work.

"Meanwhile the battle in front of Santiago progressed, with three divisions on our side, one of dismounted cavalry and two of infantry. It was beautifully fought. Every man knew what he had to do, and so did every officer. The orders were that immediately upon being deployed they were to attack. They did it. Every man kept going, and when one's comrade dropped the rest kept going. The result was that in about two hours the line was taken, and practically that afternoon the battle of Santiago was ended, for those men never advanced beyond that point.

"During the night I brought up the division of General Lawton that had been on the right at Caney and put them on the extreme right, where I had intended to have them the day before, and where, had they been, we should probably have taken the town and have gotten only the men that were there, and not the 12,000 that were far beyond our reach who were surrendered a few days later.

"On the morning of the 2d a weak attempt was made upon our lines. In that the Spaniards had to expose themselves, while my men were covered. The fight lasted but a little while, and they retreated.

"On the morning of July 3 I thought we had so much of an advantage that I could notify the enemy, first, that I wanted a surrender and, second, if they declined to surrender that they could have twenty-four hours to get the women and children out of town. Of course, civilized people do not fire on towns filled with women and children if they will come out if it can be avoided. The Spanish commander declined very promptly to surrender, but said he would notify the women and children and those that desired to go, but he wanted twenty-four hours more, and said there were a great many people to go out. They began to stream out at once, and for forty-eight hours old men, women, and children poured out until it was estimated that at least 20,000 people passed through our lines and out into the woods in the rear. Of course, there was an immense amount of suffering, and numbers died, especially of the old. Fortunately we were enabled to give them some food, enough so that they existed, but at that time, with the Cuban forces that I had, I was issuing daily 45,000 rations. Forty-five thousand people are a good many to feed when you have such fearful roads and food could only be carried on the backs of mules.

"On that morning of the 3d, about an hour after the time for surrendering, Cervera's fleet left the harbor, and went out, as you know, to total annihilation. It was not more than twenty or thirty minutes after they left the mouth of the harbor before, so far as we could hear, the firing had ceased, and 1,700 men were prisoners, 600 were killed, and three or four battleships and some torpedo boats were either on the rocks or in the bottom of the sea—a most wonderful victory, never equaled before in naval history, and due mainly to the magnificent marksmanship of our men, which covered the Spanish decks with such a hail of iron that no sailors on earth could stand against it.

"Two days after this I saw General Toral, and I was convinced from conversation with him that he was going to surrender. I had no one but myself to take the responsibility, in fact, I did not want anyone else to do it, but while I was convinced myself it was hard to convince others. I knew that we could capture the town at any time, that we had it surrounded so that they could not possibly get away, although on the night of July 2 2,800 men marched in. I had understood there were 8,000, but when we counted them a few days afterward there were only 2,800. I knew that if we carried that town by force a thousand men at least would be lost to the American army, and a thousand good American men are a good many to expend in capturing a Spanish town (applause), and I did not propose to do it if I could possibly talk them out of it.

"General Toral knew just as well as I did that I knew just what he had—that he was on his last rations, and that nothing but plain rice, that we had his retreat cut off, that we had the town surrounded, that he could not hurt us, while we could bombard him and do some little damage, perhaps, and that it was only a question of a few days.

"I found out a few days later what the hitch was which caused the delay, for General Toral had told me that he had been authorized by Blanco, the Governor-General, to enter into negotiations and make terms for surrender, and in Cuba you know General Blanco was in supreme command. His authority was such that he could even set aside a law of Spain. Knowing that, I felt sure that after very little delay they would surrender. They desired to get permission from the Madrid government to return to Spain. It was that that delayed them. Immediately upon receiving the permission to return to Spain they surrendered.

"I had in line when the fighting was going on, about 13,000 men—not more than that at any time. Inside the Spanish trenches there were about 10,000. There were 11,500 surrendered, and I think about 1,500 of them were sick. The disproportion, considering the difference of situation, is not very great. In fact, I think that 10,000 American soldiers could have kept 100,000 Spaniards out had they been in the same position (applause), although I do not wish to disparage the bravery of the Spanish troops. They are gallant fellows, but they have not the intelligence and do not take the initiative as do the American soldiers; and they have not the bull-dog pluck that hangs on day after day.

"Toral made the first proposition to surrender. He said if I would let him take his men and such things as they could carry on their persons and on a few pack mules that they had and guarantee him safe conduct to Holguin, which was fifty-two miles away to the north and in the interior, they would march out. I told him, of course, that was out of the question; that I could not accept any such terms as that, but I would submit it to the President. I did so, and was very promptly informed that only unconditional surrender would be received, but I was at liberty to say to General Toral that if they would surrender they would be carried, at the expense of the United States government, back to Spain. When that proposition was made to him I could see his face lighten up and the faces of his staff, who were there. They were simply delighted. Those men love their country intensely, they had been brought to Cuba against their will, and had stayed there three years, poorly clad, not paid at all, and not well fed, and the prospect of going back to their homes had as much to do with conforming their views to our wishes as anything that was done during the campaign.

"Meanwhile ten or twelve days had elapsed and I had received quite a number of volunteer regiments—two from Michigan, the First District of Columbia, a Massachusetts regiment, and an Ohio regiment, the Eighth Ohio—all splendid troops and well equipped, and while they were not there at the hardest of the fighting they were there during the suffering, and everything that soldiers were called upon to do they did like men.

"It is a great deal harder to stand up day after day and see companions go from sickness and disease than it is to face the perils of battle.

"When I told General Toral that we would carry his men back he said: 'Does that include my entire command?' I said: 'What is your command and where are they?' He replied the Fourth Army Corps; 11,500 men in the city, 3,000 twenty miles in the rear of us; 7,500 he said were up the coast less than sixty miles, and about 1,500 125 to 150 miles off on the northeastern coast.

"There were 3,440 odd, and at a place less than sixty miles east there were 7,500 and a few over, because we counted them and took their arms. The result of that surrender was as unexpected to us as probably it was to every person in the United States. There was simply a little army there, which had gone down to assist the navy in getting the Spanish fleet out and capturing that town, and we expected no other result from it than victory at the spot at the utmost, but in attacking the limb we got the whole body. It was expected that, beginning about the first of October, the objective point of the campaign was to be Havana, where we knew there were from 125,000 to 150,000 men, and it was expected that about the first of October a large army would be sent over there, and the battle that would decide the war would be fought in the vicinity of Havana. I think that was the universal feeling. The loss of that city and of those 24,000 men—23,376, to be accurate—so dispirited them that within a week the proposition of Spain to close the war was made, and, happily, the war was ended.

"The difficulties of that campaign were not in the fighting. That was the easiest part of it. The difficulties were in getting food and medicine to the front. There was but a single road, a muddy and terrible road, and with five or six wagons going over it the sixth wagon would be on the axle tree, and in taking up some artillery I had fourteen horses on one battery that was usually drawn by four, and even with that number it went out of sight, and we had to leave it and dig it out after the water had subsided."

Admiral Sampson's report, dated August 3d, was published October 23d, and covers the conduct of the fleet under his command, in its operations in the West Indies, for about two months prior to the destruction of Admiral Cervera's ships on July 3. It was made up largely of official dispatches and the movements of the fleet, with explanations and comment by the Admiral, and begins with a statement of the determination reached by the Navy department to send a squadron to the Windward Passage for the purpose of observation, because of the information received of the sailing, on April 29, of Admiral Cervera's squadron from the Cape Verde Islands.

On the voyage eastward from the naval base at Key West, which began on May 4, Admiral Sampson reports there was experienced endless trouble and delay because of the inefficiency of the two monitors accompanying the other ships, and which had to be taken in tow. Their coal supply was so small that it was at once evident that they must either frequently coal or be towed. The Admiral says:

"Had the sea been rough, or had the enemy appeared at this juncture, the squadron would have been in a much better position for an engagement had the monitors been elsewhere. Subsequently, when engaging the batteries of San Juan, it was evident that their shooting was bad.

"Owing to the quick rolling of these vessels, even in a moderate sea, they were unable to fire with any degree of accuracy."

Among the telegrams received by the Admiral from the department at Washington when off Cape Haytien was the following:

Washington, D. C., May 6.—Do not risk or cripple your vessels against fortifications as to prevent from soon afterwards successfully fighting Spanish fleet, composed of Pelayo, Carlos V., Oquendo, Vizcaya, Maria Teresa, Cristobal Colon, four deep sea torpedo boats, if they should appear on this side. LONG.

It was determined to go to Porto Rico, and the squadron arrived off San Juan on the morning of the 12th and the bombardment of that place ensued. Regarding his action at this place the Admiral says:

"It was clear to my own mind that the squadron would not have any great difficulty in forcing the surrender of the place, but the fact that we should be held several days in completing arrangements for holding it; that part of our force would have to be left to await the arrival of troops to garrison it; that the movements of the Spanish squadron, our main objective, were still unknown; that the flying squadron was still north and not in a position to render any aid; that Havana, Cervera's natural objective, was thus open to entry by such force as his, while we were a thousand miles distant, made our immediate movement toward Havana imperative.

"I thus reluctantly gave up the project against San Juan and stood westward for Havana."

Several telegrams are here presented, based on reports that Cervera's squadron had returned to Cadiz and they had in view "to return and capture San Juan, the desire to do so and occupy the place being assured in the event of Admiral Cervera's failure to cross the Atlantic."

Shortly after news was received that the Spanish fleet had appeared off Curacoa, West Indies, and the squadron under orders from the department proceeded to Key West, to which place the flying squadron under Commodore (now Admiral) Schley had already been ordered.

Arrangements were then hurriedly made and the flying squadron, augmented by the other vessels under Commodore Schley, was sent off Cienfuegos, where it was believed the enemy would go, in which case an effort was to be made to engage and capture him. Sampson was given the choice either of the command of the blockading squadron off Havana or at Cienfuegos, Schley in either case to remain with his own squadron.

From messages received by the Admiral from the department about May 20 it appears that reports had reached the United States that the Spanish fleet was at Santiago, so the department advised Sampson to send immediately word to Schley to proceed to that place, leaving one small vessel off Cienfuegos.

On May 21 instructions were written by Sampson for Commodore Schley and sent to him via the Marblehead regarding the possibility of the Spanish fleet being at Santiago. They are in part as follows:

United States Flagship New York, First Rate, Key West, Fla., May 21.—Sir: Spanish squadron is probably at Santiago de Cuba—four ships and three torpedo boat destroyers. If you are satisfied they are not at Cienfuegos proceed with all dispatch, but cautiously, to Santiago de Cuba, and if the enemy is there blockade him in port. You will probably find it necessary to establish communication with some of the inhabitants—fishermen or others—to learn definitely that the ships are in port, it being impossible to see into it from the outside.

The Admiral said he felt much concerned as to the delivery of these orders and sent a duplicate by the Hawk with an additional memorandum. The Admiral suggested that if the information did not reach Commodore Schley before daylight of May 23 to mask the real direction he should take as much as possible. He adds: "Follow the Spanish squadron whichever direction they take."

The Admiral off Havana gives copies of orders of battle which were to be followed in the event that Cervera left Santiago on the approach of Schley's fleet from Cienfuegos and attempted to cruise around the coast to Havana, in which case the Havana squadron would attempt to intercept him by going east about 200 miles beyond the junction of Santiren and Nicholas Channels. Strict orders were given for screening lights and to see that none were accidentally shown.

The squadron was to cruise generally to the eastward in the day and westward during the night.

On May 23, as shown by the report, Commodore Schley expressed the belief that the Spaniards were at Cienfuegos. On the 27th the Admiral sent word to Schley, directing him to proceed with all possible speed to Santiago because of information received that the Spaniards were there. The same time orders were sent to have the collier Sterling dispatched to Santiago with an expression of opinion that the Commodore should use it to obstruct the channel at its narrowest part leading into the harbor.

The details of the plan were left to the Commodore's judgment, as he (Sampson) had "the utmost confidence in his ability to carry this plan to a successful conclusion, and earnestly wished him good luck."

Sampson apparently felt certain of the presence of the Spaniards at Santiago and urged that the harbor must be blockaded at all hazards. Schley in the meantime had proceeded to Santiago, although it appears not the same day Admiral Sampson expected.

At one time Commodore Schley contemplated going to Key West with the squadron for coal, but this was abandoned, his collier having been temporarily repaired, and the necessity for a trip to Key West being avoided Santiago was then blockaded.

Admiral Sampson arrived at Santiago June 1st. June 8 the Admiral urged upon the department, as he had previously done, to expedite the arrival of the troops for Santiago, the difficulty of blockading the Spanish ships daily increasing.

In a memorandum dated June 15, the Admiral says:

"The Commander-in-Chief desires again to call the attention of the commanding officers to the positions occupied by the blockading fleet, especially during the daytime, and it is now directed that all ships keep within a distance of the entrance to Santiago of four miles, and this distance must not be exceeded.

"If the vessel is coaling or is otherwise restricted in its movements it must nevertheless keep within this distance. If at any time the flagship makes signal which is not visible to any vessel, such vessel must at once approach the flagship or retreating vessel to a point where it can read the signal.

"Disregard of the directions which have already been given on this head has led to endless confusion. Many times during the day the fleet is so scattered that it would be perfectly possible for the enemy to come out of the harbor and meet with little opposition.

"The Commander-in-Chief hopes that strict attention will be given this order."

In the order of battle incidental to the landing of Shafter's army corps June 22, when ships were sent to shell the beach and cover the landing of the men, the following occurs:

"The attention of commanding officers of all vessels engaged in blockading Santiago de Cuba is earnestly called to the necessity of the utmost vigilance from this time forward, both as to maintaining stations and readiness for action and as to keeping a close watch upon the harbor mouth. If the Spanish Admiral ever intends to attempt to escape that attempt will be made soon."

The Admiral says trouble was experienced in the landing of Shafter's army on account of the wandering proclivities of some of the transports. The progress of the disembarkation was rendered somewhat difficult by a heavy sea, the heaviest during the three weeks the fleet had been stationed there, owing to a stiff blow off the coast of Jamaica.

According to a dispatch to Secretary Long, dated June 26, the channel at Santiago not having been obstructed by the sinking of the Merrimac, Admiral Sampson was preparing a torpedo attack to hasten the destruction of the Spanish vessels, although he regretted resorting to this method because of its difficulties and small chance of success. He would not do this, he says, were the present force to be kept there; as it then insured a capture, which he believed would terminate the war.

There was contemplated at this time sending a fleet to the Spanish coast; and this expedition was to consist of the Iowa, Oregon, Newark, Yosemite, Yankee, and Dixie, and they were to go to the Azores for orders, en route to Tangier, Morocco. The colliers were to join the fleet at the Azores.

On June 30 the Admiral received a communication from Major-General Shafter announcing that he expected to attack Santiago the following morning, and asking that he (Sampson) bombard the forts at Aguadores in support of a regiment of infantry, and make such demonstrations as he thought proper at the harbor's mouth, so as to keep as many of the enemy there as possible.

This request was complied with, and on July 1 General Shafter asked that the Admiral keep up his fight on the Santiago water front. On July 2 the following was received from General Shafter.

"Terrible fight yesterday, but my line is now strongly intrenched about three-fourths of a mile from town. I urge that you make effort immediately to force the

THE DESTRUCTION OF CERVERA'S SQUADRON AT SANTIAGO.

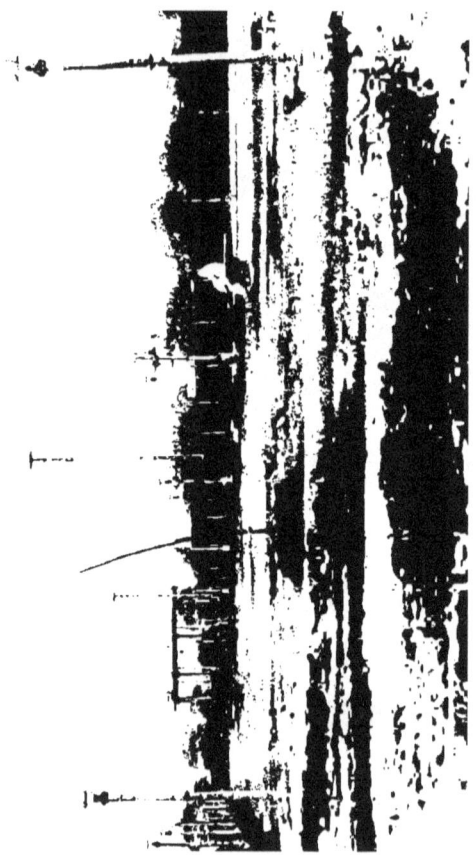

entrance to avoid future losses among my men, which are already heavy. You can now operate with less loss of life than I can. Please telephone answer."

A reply was telephoned General Shafter from Admiral Sampson, through Lieutenant Stanton, which said the Admiral had bombarded the forts at the entrance of Santiago and also Punta Gorda battery inside, silencing their fire, and asked whether he (Shafter) wanted further firing on the Admiral's part. The explanation was made that it was impossible to force an entrance until the channel was cleared of mines —a work of some time after the forts were taken possession of by the troops. To this General Shafter replied:

"It is impossible for me to say when I can take batteries at entrance of harbor. If they are as difficult to take as those which we have been pitted against it will be some time and at great loss of life. I am at a loss to see why the navy cannot work under a destructive fire as well as the army. My loss yesterday was over 500 men. By all means keep up fire on everything in sight of you until demolished. I expect, however, in time and with sufficient men to capture the forts along the bay."

On the 2nd of July, Sampson wrote to Shafter.

"An officer of my staff has already reported to you the firing which we did this morning, but I must say in addition to what he told you that the forts which we silenced were not the forts which would give you any inconvenience in capturing the city, as they cannot fire except to seaward. They cannot even prevent our entrance into the harbor of Santiago. Our trouble from the first has been the channel to the harbor is well strewn with observation mines, which would certainly result in the sinking of one or more of our ships if we attempted to enter the harbor, and by the sinking of a ship the object of attempting to enter the harbor would be defeated by the preventing of further progress on our part.

"It was my hope that an attack on your part of these shore batteries from the rear would leave us at liberty to drag the channel for torpedoes.

"If it is your earnest desire that we should force our entrance I will at once prepare to undertake it. I think, however, that our position and yours would be made more difficult if, as is possible, we fail in our attempt.

"We have in our outfit at Guantanamo forty countermining mines, which I will bring here with as little delay as possible, and if we can succeed in freeing the entrance of mines by their use I will enter the harbor.

"This work, which is unfamiliar to us, will require considerable time.

"It is not so much the loss of men as it is the loss of ships which has until now deterred me from making a direct attack upon the ships within the port."

The Admiral says he began making preparations to countermine, and, with the object of arranging an attack upon the batteries at the entrance a visit was arranged to General Shafter, so that the matter might be thoroughly discussed, and combined action take place.

He adds: "I had in view the employment of the marines for an assault on either the Morro or Socapa battery, while at the same time assaulting the defenses at the entrance with the fleet."

The Admiral says of the sortie and destruction of Cervera's fleet:

"This event closes the purely naval campaign, crowning with complete success the anxious work of almost exactly two months."

The error of Commodore Schley as to the location of Cervera's fleet, his hesitation in accepting the report of the Spaniards' presence at Santiago, appears to have caused the advancement of Admiral Sampson and subordinated Schley. Out of this came differences of opinion about facts among the close friends of the two distinguished officers. Schley was close at hand when Cervera's run from Santiago took place, while Sampson was out of the way on other duty, and Schley has been charged with an evasive movement of the New York just then that lost valuable time. It is related by the Washington staff correspondent of the Chicago Times-Herald that just after the battle of Santiago, Commodore Schley went aboard the Iowa and hailed Captain Evans with the remark that it had been a great day for the American navy.

"But why didn't you obey orders and close in on the mouth of the harbor instead of heading out to sea?" inquired Evans.

Commodore Schley's reply was that he was afraid the Vizcaya would ram the Brooklyn. This colloquy referred to a striking maneuver of the flagship Brooklyn early in the engagement at Santiago, which has been commented on before. In justice to Commodore Schley the navy department officers admit the Spanish officers after the battle said that it had been their purpose, on emerging from the harbor, to have the Vizcaya ram the Brooklyn, believing that the Spanish cruisers could outrun the remaining vessels in the American fleet, most of which were battleships, supposed to be of a lower rate of speed than the Spanish cruisers.

The action of the Vizcaya as she headed toward the Brooklyn indicated her determination to carry out this programme. But the remark of Captain Evans to the nominal commander of the squadron would under ordinary circumstances have been an act of insubordination and only illustrates the feeling of some of the captains of the fleet toward the Commodore.

EVENTS OF THE SPANISH-AMERICAN WAR. 29

It has been said that Schley, being ordered to Key West when Cervera appeared in Cuban waters, "proceeded to Cienfuegos, which was thought to be the destination of the Spanish warships. That port commanded the only direct railroad connection with Havana, and had the Spanish fleet gone there Admiral Cervera could have relieved General Blanco with money and munitions of war and received in return supplies necessary for his squadron. It is believed even now that had the Spanish ships been properly supplied and equipped they would have gone to Cienfuegos instead of to Santiago. But subsequent developments have shown that Admiral Cervera was permitted to take only enough coal to carry him to the nearest port, Santiago."

Schley credited Cervera with knowing enough to know that Cienfuegos was the better port for his purposes, and therefore adhered to his opinion, and Sampson was made his superior officer. So important have the differences seemed that the Wainwright Board was convened to investigate the parts taken in the Santiago naval battle respectively by Admiral Sampson and Admiral Schley. But in official phrase this board was convened for the purpose of determining the position and courses of the ships engaged in the action at Santiago July 3, and reporting to the Secretary of the Navy.

The report is:

"U. S. F. S. New York, First Rate, Navy Yard, New York, Oct. 8, 1898.—Sir: In obedience to your order of Sept. 2, 1898, appointing us a board to plot the positions of the ships of Admiral Cervera's squadron and those of the United States fleet in the battle of July 3, off Santiago de Cuba, we have the honor to submit the following report, accompanied by a chart, showing the positions of the ships at seven different times.

"These times, as taken by the United States ships engaged, with the incidents noted, are as follows:

"No. 1, 9:35 a. m.—Maria Teresa came out of the harbor.

"No. 2, 9:50 a. m.—Pluton came out.

"No. 3, 10:15 a. m.—Maria Teresa turned to run ashore.

"No. 4, 10:20 a. m.—Oquendo turned to run ashore.

"No. 5, 10:30 a. m.—Furor blew up and Pluton turned to run ashore.

"No. 6, 11:05 a. m.—Vizcaya turned to run ashore.

"No. 7, 1:15 p. m.—Colon surrendered.

"The chart selected by the board for plotting is H. O. chart No. 716, 1885, West Indies, eastern part of Bahama Islands, with part of Cuba and north coast of San

Domingo. This selection was made after a careful comparison with all other charts at hand, as the positions of the principal headlands and inlets and the distances between them on it agree more nearly with the observation of members of the board than those given by any other.

"The positions of the United States ships were established by known bearings and distances from the Morro at No. 1, with the exception of the New York, whose position is plotted by the revolutions of its engines during a run of forty-five minutes east from its position, southeast half south of the Morro, 6,000 yards. Position at No. 2 is plotted by all ships according to their relative bearings from each other, the operations of their engines from 9:35 to 9:50, the evidence of the officers on board them, and the ranges used in firing at the Spanish ships. Position No. 3 is plotted from observations of the officers of the United States ships, with regard to their nearness to each other, and relative bearings of themselves from Teresa, with ranges in use at the time, the performance of the engines, and general heading of the ships. Position No. 4 same as No. 3, substituting Oquendo for Teresa. Position Nos. 5, 6, and 7 are plotted on the same general plan.

"Before plotting these positions the board took each ship separately and discussed the data for the position under consideration—this data being obtained from the report of the commanding officers, notes taken during the action, and the evidence of the members of the board. In reconciling differences of opinion in regard to distances, bearings, ranges, etc., full liberty was given to the representative of the ships under discussion to bring in any argument or data he considered necessary, and the board submits this report with a feeling that, under the circumstances, it is as nearly correct as is possible so long after the engagement. Very respectfully,

"RICHARD WAINWRIGHT,
"Lieutenant Commander, U. S. N., Senior Member.
"S. P. COMLY,
"Lieutenant, U. S. N.
"L. C. HEILNER,
"Lieutenant, U. S. N.
"W. H. SCHUETZE,
"Lieutenant, U. S. N.
"A. C. HODGSON,
"Lieutenant, U. S. N.
"W. H. ALLEN,
"Lieutenant, U. S. N.
"EDWARD E. CAPEHART,
"Lieutenant, U. S. N.

"To the Commander-in-Chief."

EVENTS OF THE SPANISH-AMERICAN WAR. 231

Measurements upon the chart showing the positions of the vessels at the specified times named in the report will give as fair an idea of the work of the board as can be made without the chart itself.

"Position No. 1, 9:35 a. m. When the Maria Teresa came out of the harbor the New York was nine miles east of Morro, accompanied by the Hist and Ericsson. The Brooklyn was three miles southwest of Morro, being two and two-tenths miles from the shore west of the mouth of the harbor. The Texas was eight-tenths of a mile east of the Brooklyn; the Iowa one and eight-tenths miles east and south of the Brooklyn, and the Oregon a half mile east of the Iowa, the Iowa being three miles directly south of Morro. The Indiana was two and two-tenths miles southwest of Morro and the Gloucester one mile almost directly north of the Indiana, a mile and four-tenths from Morro.

"Position No. 2, 9:50 a. m. When the Pluton came out all the Spanish vessels had come out of the harbor and their positions were: Maria Teresa two and a half miles southwest of Morro, the Vizcaya, Colon and Oquendo, in the order named, behind the Teresa and from four-tenths to half a mile apart. The position of the American vessels were: The New York had moved up two and one-tenth miles westward. The Brooklyn had started north, swerved to the northeast and toward the mouth of the harbor, and was turning east on the swing it made to the right and around to the westward course; it was eight-tenths of a mile from the Vizcaya. At position No. 2 the Texas first went east a half mile, swinging toward the harbor, then turning to the left it is at No. 2 a half mile directly north of the first position. The Iowa moved by a varying course northwest and was a mile and four-tenths from the Vizcaya, the Oregon being two-tenths of a mile behind the Iowa, the Indiana three-tenths behind the Iowa. The Gloucester's first start was half a mile directly away from the harbor, but swinging to the right, had advanced toward the Spanish ships, being one and seven-tenths miles from the nearest, the Oquendo.

"Position No. 3, 10:15 a. m. Maria Teresa turned to run ashore. It was five and one-half miles from Morro. The Vizcaya was two and three-tenths miles westward from the Teresa, the Oquendo one and two-tenths miles, and the Colon one and four-tenths miles in advance of the Teresa. The American vessels were as follows: The New York had come within three miles of Morro, being southeast of that point. The Brooklyn had made its swing to the westward, crossing its track, and was two and one-half miles south and west of the Teresa, and one and three-tenths miles directly south of the Colon, and one and one-tenth miles and a little behind the Vizcaya, one and three-tenths miles and a little in advance of the Oquendo. The

Texas was one and two-tenths miles from the Teresa, a little behind it, and one and four-tenths miles from and behind the next Spanish ship, the Oquendo. The Iowa was one and one-tenth miles from the Teresa and a little closer in, but not quite as far west as the Texas. The Oregon had pulled up and passed the Texas and Iowa, being a little further in shore than the Texas and a little further out than the Iowa. It was in advance of the Teresa, being one and seven-tenths miles from that vessel, six-tenths of a mile from and directly in the line of the Oquendo, seven-tenths of a mile from the Colon, and one and two-tenths miles behind the Vizcaya. The Indiana was two miles from the Texas and two and six-tenths miles from the Oquendo, the nearest Spanish vessel. The Gloucester had moved up six-tenths of a mile and was just a mile directly south of Morro.

"Position No. 4, 10:20 a. m. Oquendo turned to run ashore. Only five minutes elapsed from position No. 3. All vessels had been running westward without material changes in their positions. The Colon had run one and three-tenths miles, the Vizcaya about one-tenth of a mile less, and swerved to the left, bringing it to within one and one-tenth miles of the Brooklyn. The Iowa was the same distance, but almost directly astern, and the Oregon was one and three-tenths miles from the Vizcaya, but farther out to sea. The Iowa was eight-tenths of a mile from the Oquendo, the Oregon nine-tenths of a mile from the same vessel, and both somewhat in advance of the doomed Spanish ship. The Indiana had advanced eight-tenths of a mile and was two and six-tenths miles away from the Oquendo, the nearest Spanish ship. The New York had advanced nearly a mile, but was not yet abreast of Morro. The Gloucester had run over two miles and was now well west of Morro, but five miles east of the Oquendo.

"Position No. 5, 10:30 a. m. Furor blew up and Pluton turned to run ashore. This is ten minutes later than position No. 4. The Gloucester had run a little more than two miles, and was four-tenths of a mile from the Furor and but little further from the Pluton. The New York had run two and two-tenths miles, and was three and three-tenths miles from the Furor, the nearest Spanish ship, and two and two-tenths miles south and a little west of Morro. The Colon had run two and nine-tenths miles, and the Vizcaya two and seven-tenths miles. The Brooklyn had run two and three-tenths miles, and was one and two-tenths miles from the Vizcaya and one and six-tenths miles from the Colon, which was running nearer the shore. The Oregon had sailed two and a half miles, and was one and one-half miles from the Vizcaya, and about the same distance from the Colon. The Texas was one and two-tenths miles astern of the Oregon, two and four-tenths miles from the Oregon. The Indiana was one and one-half miles astern of the Texas.

"Position No. 6, 11:05 a. m. Vizcaya turned to run ashore. In thirty-five minutes the Vizcaya had sailed about seven miles, and was off the mouth of the Aserradero River. The Colon had run five and one-half miles further, and was more than that distance in advance of any of the American vessels. The Brooklyn was one and three-tenths miles distant from the Vizcaya and slightly behind it. The Oregon was one and a half miles from the Vizcaya, but nearer the shore and somewhat more astern of the enemy. The Texas was two and seven-tenths miles from the Vizcaya and directly astern of the Oregon. The Iowa was three and two-tenths miles directly astern of the Vizcaya. The New York was five miles behind the Iowa. The Ericsson had kept along with the New York all the time, and was, at this position, one-half a mile in advance of it. The Indiana was nearly four miles behind the Iowa.

"Position No. 7, 1:15 p. m. The Colon surrendered. In the two hours and ten minutes from the last position given the vessels had coursed westward a great distance. The Colon had run twenty-six and one-half miles and was off the Tarquino River. The Brooklyn was the nearest American vessel. It had sailed twenty-eight and one-half miles and was three and four-tenths miles from the Colon. The Oregon was four and one-half miles from the Colon and more in shore than the Brooklyn. The Texas was three and four-tenths miles behind the Oregon. The New York was nine and one-half miles from the Colon. No one of the other vessels had come up save the Vixen, which was abreast of the New York. This little vessel in the beginning of the fight steamed out to sea and sailed westward on a course about two and one-quarter miles from that of the nearest Spanish ships.

"The tracings of the chart show that the Spanish vessels sailed on courses not more than three-tenths of a mile apart until the Oquendo ran ashore. Then the Vizcaya veered out to sea and the Colon kept nearer the shore, their courses being about seven-tenths of a mile apart. Up to the time the Oquendo went ashore the Iowa, Indiana, Oregon, and Texas sailed on courses within three-tenths of a mile of each other, the Iowa being the nearest and the Texas the farthest from the course of the Spanish ships. The Brooklyn's course was from three-tenths to one-half of a mile outside that of the Texas. The swing to the right which the Brooklyn made at the beginning of the engagement shows an oval four-tenths of a mile across. It crossed the courses of the Texas, Oregon, and Indiana twice while making the turn, but before these vessels had gone over them. The course of the New York after passing Morro was nearer the shore than any other United States vessel except the Gloucester, and a mile behind where the Oquedo turned to run ashore it passed inside the courses of the Spanish vessels. Ten miles west of the Vizcaya disaster it crossed the Colon's track, but followed close the course of that vessel until the latter surrendered.

"The Iowa, Indiana, and Ericsson did not go further west than where the Vizcaya ran ashore. The Gloucester stopped by the Maria Teresa and Oquendo, as also did the Hist. The latter vessel was not able to keep pace with the New York and Ericsson, the vessels it was with at the beginning of the battle."

Major General Nelson A. Miles was carrying on, as a master of the art and science of war, a prospering campaign in Porto Rico, when the protocol of peace between the United States and Spain was signed, and "the war drum throbbed" no longer. It is the testimony of those who have studied the management of the invasion of Porto Rico by the military head of the army, that it was going on guided with consummate skill when the war closed. The American forces had the pleasure in Porto Rico of moving in a country that had not been desolated as Cuba was. The island was a tropical picture of peace, only the glitter of armies breaking the spell. The defenders had the help of good roads, by which they could, on the inner lines, shift their columns with rapidity and ease. But the Porto Rico people were largely favorable to United States sovereignty—just as the Cubans would be if it were not for the selfishness and jealousies, hatreds and scheming, regardless of the favor or prosperity of the people, that the most deplorable warfare known in the later years of the earth has engendered. It was on October 18, 1898, that the American flag was raised over San Juan de Porto Rico. The telegram of the Associated Press contained this announcement of the ceremony and symbol by which was announced the glorious initial chapter of a new dispensation that adds to America's territory one of the loveliest islands of the sea:

San Juan de Porto Rico, Oct. 18.—Promptly at noon to-day the American flag was raised over San Juan. The ceremony was quiet and dignified, unmarred by disorder of any kind.

The Eleventh Regular Infantry, with two batteries of the Fifth Artillery, landed this morning. The latter proceeded to the forts, while the infantry lined up on the docks. It was a holiday for San Juan, and there were many people in the streets.

Rear Admiral Schley and General Gordon, accompanied by their staffs, proceeded to the palace in carriages. The Eleventh infantry Regiment and band, with Troop H of the Sixth United States Cavalry, then marched through the streets and formed in the square opposite the palace.

At 11:40 a. m. General Brooke, Admiral Schley, and General Gordon, the United States Evacuation Commissioners, came out of the palace, with many naval officers, and formed on the right side of the square. The streets behind the soldiers were thronged with townspeople, who stood waiting in dead silence.

At last the city clock struck the hour of 12 and the crowds, almost breathless and with eyes fixed upon the flagpole, watched for developments. At the sound of the first gun from Fort Morro, Major Dean and Lieutenant Castle, of General Brooke's staff, hoisted the Stars and Stripes, while the band played the "Star Spangled Banner."

All heads were bared and the crowds cheered. Fort Morro, Fort San Cristobal, and the United States revenue cutter Manning, lying in the harbor, fired twenty-one guns each.

Senor Munoz Rivera, who was President of the recent autonomist council of secretaries, and other officials of the late insular government, were present at the proceedings.

Congratulations and handshaking among the American officers followed, Ensign King hoisted the Stars and Stripes over the intendencia, but all other flags on the various public buildings were hoisted by military officers. Simultaneously with the raising of the flag over the Captain General's palace many others were hoisted in different parts of the city.

Washington, D. C., Oct. 18.—The War Department has received the following to-day:

"San Juan, Porto Rico, Oct. 18.—Secretary of War, Washington, D. C.: Flags have been raised on public buildings and forts in this city and saluted with national salutes. The occupation of the island is now complete.

"BROOKE, Chairman."

The two Spanish fleets—of the East and West Indies, were annihilated, the former May 1st, and the latter July 2nd, two months and two days between the events. The respective fleets in Manila bay were as follows:

AMERICAN FLEET.

Name.	Class.	Armament.	Men and Officers
Olympia	Protected Cruiser	Four 8-in., ten 5-in., 24 R. F.	466
Baltimore	Protected Cruiser	Four 8-in., six 6-in., 10 R. F.	395
Boston	Par. Ptd. Cruiser	Two 8-in., six 6-in., 10 R. F.	272
Raleigh	Protected Cruiser	One 6-in., ten 5-in., 14 R. F.	295
Concord	Gunboat	Six 6-in., 9 R. F.	150
Petrel	Gunboat	Four 6-in., 7 R. F.	100
McCulloch	Revenue Cutter	Four 4-in	180

EVENTS OF THE SPANISH-AMERICAN WAR.

SPANISH FLEET.

Name.	Class.	Armament.	Men and Officers
*Reina Cristiua	Steel Cruiser	Six 6.2-in., two 2.7., 13 R. F.	370
Castilla	Wood Cruiser	Four 5.9, two 4.7, two 3.4, two 2.9, 12 R. F.	300
Don Antonio de Ulloa	Iron Cruiser	Four 4.7, 5 R. F.	173
Don Juan de Austria	Iron Cruiser	Four 4.7, two 2.7, 21 R. F.	173
Isla de Luzon	Steel Ptd. Cruiser	Six 4.7, 8 R. F.	164
Isla de Cuba	Steel Ptd. Cruiser	Six 4.7, 8 R. F.	164
Velasco	Iron Cruiser	Three 6-in., two 2.7, two R. F.	173
Marques del Duero	Gunboat	One 6.2, two 4.7, 1 R. F.	98
General Lezo	Gunboat	One 3.5, 1 R. F.	97
El Correo	Gunboat	Three 4.7, 4 R. F.	116
Quiros	Gunboat	4 R. F.	60
Villalobos	Gunboat	4 R F.	60

Two torpedo boats and two transports.

The American squadron was thus officered:

Acting Rear Admiral George Dewey, Commander-in-Chief.

Commander B. P. Lamberter, Chief-of-Staff.

Lieutenant L. M. Brumby, Flag Lieutenant.

Ensign H. H. Caldwell, Secretary.

OLYMPIA (Flagship).

Captain, Charles V. Gridley.

Lieutenant-Commander, S. C. Paine.

Lieutenants: C. G. Calkins, V. S. Nelson, G. S. Morgan, S. M. Strite.

Ensigns: M. M. Taylor, F. B. Upham, W. P. Scott, A. G. Kavanagh, H. V. Butler.

Medical Inspector, A. F. Price; Passed Assistant Surgeon, J. E. Page; Assistant Surgeon, C. H. Kindleberger; Pay Inspector, D. A. Smith; Chief Engineer, J. Entwistle; Assistant Engineer, S. H. DeLany; Assistant Engineer, J. F. Marshall, Jr.; Chaplain, J. B. Frazier; Captain of Marines, W. P. Biddle; Gunner, L. J. G. Kuhlwein; Carpenter, W. Macdonald; Acting Boatswain, E. J. Norcott.

THE BOSTON.

Captain, F. Wildes.

Lieutenant-Commander, J. A. Norris.

Lieutenants: J. Gibson, W. L. Howard.

Ensigns: S. S. Robinson, L. H. Everhart, J. S. Doddridge.

Surgeon, M. H. Crawford; Assistant Surgeon, R. S. Balkeman; Paymaster, J. R. Martin; Chief Engineer, G. B. Ransom; Assistant Engineer, L. J. James; First Lieutenant of Marines, R. McM. Dutton; Gunner, J. C. Evans; Carpenter, I. H. Hilton.

U. S. STEAMSHIP BALTIMORE.

Captain, N. M. Dyer.
Lieutenant-Commander, G. Blocklinger.
Lieutenants: W. Braunersreuther, F. W. Kellogg, J. M. Ellicott, C. S. Stanworth.
Ensigns: G. H. Hayward, M. J. McCormack, U. E. Irwin.
Naval Cadets, D. W. Wurtsbaugh, I. Z. Wettersoll, C. M. Tozer T. A. Karney; Passed Assistant Surgeon, F. A. Heiseler; Assistant Surgeon, R. K. Smith; Pay Inspector, E. Bellows; Chief Engineer, A. C. Engard; Assistant Engineers, H. B. Price, H. I. Cone; Naval Cadet (engineer), C. P. Burt; Chaplain. T. S. K. Freeman; First Lieutenant of Marines, D. Williams; Acting Boatswain, H. R. Brayton; Gunner, L. J. Connelly; Acting Gunner, L. J. Waller; Carpenter, O. Bath.

U. S. STEAMSHIP RALEIGH.

Captain, J. B. Coghlan.
Lieutenant-Commander, F. Singer.
Lieutenants: W. Winder, B. Tappan, H. Rodman, C. B. Morgan.
Ensigns: F. L. Chidwick, P. Babin.
Surgeon, E. H. Marsteller; Assistant Surgeon, D. N. Carpenter; Passed Assistant Paymaster, S. R. Heap; Chief Engineer, F. H. Bailey; Passed Assistant Engineer, A. S. Halstead; Assistant Engineer, J. R. Brady; First Lieutenant of Marines, T. C. Treadwell; Acting Gunner, G. D. Johnstone; Acting Carpenter, T. E. Kiley.

THE CONCORD.

Commander, A. S. Walker.
Lieutenant-Commander, G. P. Colvocoreses.
Lieutenants: T. B. Howard, P. W. Hourigan.
Ensigns: L. A. Kiser, W. C. Davidson, O. S. Knepper.
Passed Assistant Surgeon, R. G. Broderick; Passed Assistant Paymaster, E. D. Ryan; Chief Engineer, Richard Inch; Passed Assistant Engineer, H. W. Jones; Assistant Engineer, E. H. Dunn.

THE PETREL.

Commander, E. P. Wood.
Lieutenants: E. M. Hughes, B. A. Fiske, A. N. Wood, C. P. Plunkett.
Ensigns: G. L. Fermier, W. S. Montgomery.
Passed Assistant Surgeon, C. D. Brownell; Assistant Paymaster, G. G. Siebals; Passed Assistant Engineer, R. T. Hall.

The marvel of the naval engagements that disarmed Spain in both the Indies, is that only one American was killed in the Santiago action, and the only man who lost his life on Dewey's fleet was overcome by heat. The Spaniards were deceived as well as surprised at Manila, the deception being their dependence upon the belief that the Americans would take it for granted that the falsified official charts were correct, and stand off. The course of the American fleet, finding with the lead on the first round 32 feet of water where the chart said 15, dismayed the enemy. The Spanish had but one chance to cripple Dewey, and that was by closing with him, but they never seem, except in the case of the flagship, to have contemplated taking the offensive.

In the course of the war crowded with victory, two Spanish fleets were destroyed, two Spanish armies surrendered, thirty-six thousand soldiers and sailors of Spain made prisoners of war, the only heavy losses of Americans were at Santiago, and they happened because in the terrible climate of Cuba in summer, for those unaccustomed to it and forced to be in the rain and sleep on the ground, it was necessary to carry the enemy's lines of defense by assault, because it was certain that delay would be destruction of the troops. The campaign was hurried and short, but such was the effect of the few weeks spent in Cuba that, bloody as were the first days of July, the weeks succeeding witnessed the death from sickness of more soldiers than fell in battle.

Not until November 5, 1898, did the State Department make public the complete text of the Protocol between the United States and Spain for the preliminary settlement of the war. A copy was cabled to this country from the French translation, but the department here never gave out the text of the document in official form. The Protocol textually is as follows:

"Protocol of agreement between the United States and Spain, embodying the terms of a basis for the establishment of peace between the two countries, signed at Washington Aug. 12, 1898. Protocol: William R. Day, Secretary of State of the United States, and his Excellency, Jules Cambon, Ambassador Extraordinary and Plenipotentiary of the Republic of France at Washington, respectively possessing for this purpose full authority from the government of the United States and the government of Spain, have concluded and signed the following articles, embodying the terms on which the two governments have agreed in respect to the matters hereinafter set forth, having in view the establishment of peace between the two countries —that is to say:

ARTICLE I.

"Spain will relinquish all claim of sovereignty over and title to Cuba.

ARTICLE II.

"Spain will cede to the United States the Island of Porto Rico and other islands now under Spanish sovereignty in the West Indies, and also an island in the Ladrones, to be selected by the United States.

ARTICLE III.

"The United States will occupy and hold the City, Bay, and Harbor of Manila, pending the conclusion of a treaty of peace, which shall determine the control, disposition, and government of the Philippines.

ARTICLE IV.

"Spain will immediately evacuate Cuba, Porto Rico, and other islands now under Spanish sovereignty in the West Indies, and to this end each government will, within ten days after the signing of this protocol, appoint commissioners, and the commissioners so appointed shall, within thirty days after the signing of this protocol, meet at Havana for the purpose of arranging and carrying out the details of the aforesaid evacuation of Cuba and the adjacent Spanish islands; and each government will, within ten days after the signing of this protocol, also appoint other commissioners, who shall, within thirty days after the signing of this protocol, meet at San Juan, Porto Rico, for the purpose of arranging and carrying out the details of the aforesaid evacuation of Porto Rico and other islands now under Spanish sovereignty in the West Indies.

ARTICLE V.

"The United States and Spain will each appoint not more than five commissioners to treat of peace, and the commissioners so appointed shall meet at Paris not later than Oct. 1, 1898, and proceed to the negotiation and conclusion of a treaty of peace, which treaty shall be subject to ratification according to the respective constitutional forms of the two countries.

ARTICLE VI.

"Upon the conclusion and signing of this protocol hostilities between the two countries shall be suspended, and notice to that effect shall be given as soon as possible by each government to the commanders of its military and naval forces.

"Done at Washington in duplicate, in English and in French, by the undersigned, who have hereunto set their hands and seals, the 12th day of August, 1898.

"WILLIAM R. DAY.
"JULES CAMBON."

CHAPTER XVI.

THE PEACE JUBILEE.

The Lessons of War in the Joy Over Peace in the Celebrations at Chicago and Philadelphia—Orations by Archbishop Ireland and Judge Emory Speer—The President's Few Words of Thrilling Significance—The Parade of the Loyal League, and Clover Club Banquet at Philadelphia—Address by the President—The Hero Hobson Makes a Speech—Fighting Bob Evans' Startling Battle Picture—The Destruction of Cervera's Fleet—The Proclamation of Thanksgiving.

The lessons of war—that which has been through it accomplished for the country—the new lands over which our sovereignty is established—the gain in the national character—the increased immensity of the outlook of destiny, found impressive expression in the peace jubilee, the President of the United States participating, and interpreting history with dignity, in great Chicago, the giant of the West and North, and Philadelphia, the holy city of Independence Hall and the liberty bell.

Of the celebrations of Peace with honor and victory, the first was that at Chicago, and it will be memorable for remarkable speeches in which many orators rose to the height of the occasion, their speeches worthy of celebrity and certain to give imperishable passages to the school books of the future. We have to pass over much of meritorious distinction, and confine ourselves in the selections for these pages, to the utterances of the President—Archbishop Ireland, whose golden periods of Americanism ring through the land, and the Southern orator, Judge Emory Speer, of Georgia, whose patriotism springs forth and elevates the nobility of his thought, and touches with sacred fire the ruddy glow of his eloquence.

"Lead, my country, in peace!" was Archbishop Ireland's passionate exclamation, the key-note of his oration. He said:

"War has passed; peace reigns. Stilled over land and sea is the clang of arms; from San Juan to Manila, fearless and triumphant, floats the star spangled banner. America: 'Be glad and rejoice, for the Lord hath done great things.' America, with whole heart and soul, celebrate thy jubilee of peace.

"Welcome to America, sweet, beloved peace; welcome to America, honored, glorious victory. Oh, peace, thou art heaven's gift to men. When the Savior of humanity was born in Bethlehem the sky sang forth, 'Glory to God in the highest, and on earth peace and good will to men.' Peace was offered to the world through

Christ, and when the spirit of Christ is supreme, there is universal peace—peace among men, peace among nations.

"Oh, peace, so precious art thou to humanity that our highest ideal of social felicity must ever be thy sovereignty upon earth. Pagan statesmanship, speaking through pagan poetry, exclaims: 'The best of things which it is given to know is peace; better than a thousand triumphs is the simple gift of peace.' The regenerated world shall not lift up sword against sword; neither shall they be exercised any more in war.

"Peace is the normal flow of humanity's life, the healthy pulsation of humanity's social organism, the vital condition of humanity's growth and happiness.

" 'O first of human blessings and supreme,
Fair Peace! how lovely, how delightful thou.
* * * * *
Oh peace! thou soul and source of social life,
Beneath whose calm inspiring influence
Science his views enlarges, art refines,
And swelling commerce opens all her ports.
Blessed be the man divine who gave us thee.'

"The praise of peace is proclaimed beyond need of other words, when men confess that the only possible justification of war is the establishment of peace. Peace, we prize thee.

" 'But the better thou,
The richer of delight, sometime the more
Inevitable war.'

" 'Pasis imponero morem'—to enforce the law of peace: this, the sole moral argument which God and humanity allow for war. O peace, welcome again to America.

"War—how dreadful thou art! I shall not, indeed, declare thee to be immoral, ever unnecessary, ever accursed. No; I shall not so arraign thee as to mete plenary condemnation to the whole past history of nations, to the whole past history of my own America. But that thou art ever dreadful, ever barbarous, I shall not deny. War! Is it by cunning design—in order to hide from men thy true nature—that pomp and circumstance attend thy march; that poetry and music set in brightest colors, the rays of light struggling through thy heavy darkness, that history weaves into threads of richest glory the woes and virtues of thy victims? Stripped of thy show and tinsel, what art thou but the slaying of men?—the slaying of men by the thousands, aye, often by the tens, by the hundreds of thousands.

"With the steady aim and relentless energy tasking science to its utmost ingenuity, the multitudes of men to their utmost endurance, whole nations work day and night, fitting ourselves for the quick and extensive killing of men. This preparation for war. Armies meet on the field of battle; shot and shell rend the air; men fall to the ground like leaves in autumnal storms, bleeding, agonizing, dying; the earth is reddened by human blood; the more gory the earth beneath the tread of one army the louder the revel of victory in the ranks of the other. This, the actual conflict of war. From north to south, from east to west, through both countries whose flags were raised over the field of battle, homes not to be numbered mourned in soul-wrecking grief, for husband, father, son or brother who sank beneath the foeman's steel or yielded life within the fever tent, or who, surviving shot and malady, carries back to his loved ones a maimed or weakened body. This, the result of war.

"Reduced to the smallest sacrifice of human life the carnage of the battlefields, some one has died and some one is bereft. 'Only one killed,' the headline reads. The glad news speeds. The newsboys cry: 'Killed only one.' 'He was my son. What were a thousand to this one—my only son.'

"It was Wellington who said: 'Take my word for it, if you had seen but one day of war you would pray to Almighty God that you might never see such a thing again.' It was Napoleon who said: 'The sight of a battlefield after the fight is enough to inspire princes with a love of peace and a horror of war.'

"War, be thou gone from my soul's sight! I thank the good God that thy ghastly specter stands no longer upon the thresholds of the homes of my fellow countrymen in America, or my fellow beings in distant Andalusia. When, I ask heaven, shall humanity rise to such heights of reason and of religion that war shall be impossible, and stories of battlefields but the saddening echoes of primitive ages of the race?

"And yet, while we await that blessed day, when embodied justice shall sit in judgment between peoples as between individuals, from time to time conditions more repellant than war may confront a nation, and to remove such conditions as the solemn dictates of reason and religion impose was as righteous and obligatory. Let the life of a nation or the integrity of its territory be menaced, let the honor of a nation be assailed, let the grievous crime against humanity be perpetrated within reach of a nation's flag or a nation's arm, reiterated appeals or argument and diplomacy failing, what else remains to a nation which is not so base as to court death or dishonor but to challenge the fortunes of war and give battle while strength remains in defense of 'its hearthstones and its altars'? War, indeed, is dreadful; but let it come; the sky may fall, but let justice be done. War is no longer a repudiation of

THE PEACE JUBILEE.

peace, but the means to peace—to the soul peace a self-sacrificing people may enjoy —peace with honor.

"A just and necessary war is holy. The men who at country's call engage in such a war are the country's heroes, to whom must be given unstinted gratitude and unstinted praise. The sword in their hands is the emblem of self-sacrifice and of valor; the flag which bears them betokens their country and bids them pour out in oblation to purest patriotism the life blood of their hearts; the shroud which spreads over the dead of the battlefield is the mantle of fame and of glory.

"Happy the nation which has the courage of a just war, no less than that of a just peace, whose sons are able and willing to serve her with honor alike in war and in peace. Happy the nation whose jubilee of peace, when war has ceased, is also a jubilee of victory.

"'We love peace, not war, but when we go to war we send it the best and bravest of the country.' These words, spoken a few days ago by the chief magistrate of America, embody a great principle of American life.

Six months ago the congress of the United States declared that in the name of humanity war should be waged in order to give to the island of Cuba a stable and independent government. Magnificent patriotism of America. The people of the United States at once rose in their might. They argued not, they hesitated not. America had spoken; theirs was not to judge but to obey. In a moment the money of America, the lives of America, were at the disposal of the chief magistrate of the nation, whose embarrassment was the too generous response to his appeal for means to bring victory to the nation's flag. America had spoken. Partisan politics, sectional disputes instantly were stilled beneath the majesty of her voice. Oft it had been whispered that we had a North and a South. When America spoke we knew that we were but one people; that all were Americans. It had been whispered that social and economic lines were hopelessly dividing the American people, and that patriotism was retreating before the growth of class interests and class prejudices.

"But when America spoke there was no one in the land who was not an American; the laborer dropped his hammer; the farmer turned from his plow; the merchant forgot his counting-room; the millionaire closed the door of his mansion; and side by side, equal in love of country; their resolve to serve her, they marched to danger and to death. America can never doubt the united loyalty of her whole population, nor the power which such united loyalty puts into her hand.

"And what may I not say in eulogy of the sentiment of humanity, that in union with their patriotism swayed the hearts of the American people, and in their vision invested the war with the halo of highest and most sacred duty to fellow-men? I speak of the great multitude, whom we name the American people. They had been told of dire suffering by neighboring people—struggling for peace and liberty; they believed that only through war could they acquit themselves of the sacred duty of rescuing that people from their sufferings. I state a broad, undeniable fact. The dominating, impelling motive of the war in the depths of the national heart of America was the sentiment of humanity. The people of America offered their lives through no sordid ambition of pecuniary gain, of conquest of territory, of national aggrandizement. Theirs was the high-born ambition to succor fellowmen.

"What strength and power America was found to possess. When war was declared, so small was her army, so small her navy that the thought of war coming upon the country affrighted for the moment her own citizens and excited the derisive smiles of foreigners. Of her latent resources no doubt was possible; but how much time was needed to utilize them, and, meanwhile, how much humiliation was possible. The President waved his wand; instantly armies and navies were created as by magic. Within a few weeks a quarter of a million of men were formed into regiments and army corps; vessels of war and transport ships were covering the seas; upon water and land battles were fought and great victories won, from one side of the globe to the other. I know not of similar feats in history. What if in this bewildering rush of a nation to arms one department or another of the national administration was unable to put in a moment its hand upon all the details which a thoroughly rounded equipment required? The wonder is that the things that were done could at all have been done, and that what was done so quickly could have been done so well. The wonder is that this sudden creation of such vast military forces was possible, even in America

"What prowess in action, what intellect in planning, what skill in execution, were displayed by soldiers and seamen, by men and officers. Magnificent the sweep of Dewey's squadron in Manila harbor. Magnificent the broadsides from Sampson's fleet upon Cervera's fleeing ships. Magnificent the charge of regiments of regular infantry, and of Roosevelt's riders up the hills of El Caney. Never daunted, never calculating defeat, every man determined to die or conquer, every man knowing his duty, how to do it—the soldiers and seamen of America were invincible. Spanish fleets and Spanish armies vanished before them as mists before the morning sun; the nations of the earth stood amazed in the presence of such quick and decisive triumphs, at what America had done and at what, they now understood, America could do.

THE PEACE JUBILEE.

"The war is ended. It would ill become me to say what details shall enter into the treaty of peace which America is concluding with her vanquished foe. I stand in the presence of the chief magistrate of the republic. To him it belongs by right of official position and of personal wisdom to prescribe those details. The country has learned from the acts of his administration that to his patriotism, his courage, his prudence, she may well confide her safety, her honor, her destiny, her peace. Whatever the treaty of Sapin, America will be pleased when appended to this treaty is the name of William McKinley.

"What I may speak of on this occasion is the results of the war, manifest even in this hour to America and to the world, transcending and independent of all treaties of peace, possessing for America and the world a meaning far mightier than mere accumulation of material wealth or commercial concessions or territorial extension.

"To do great things, to meet fitly great responsibilities, a nation, like a person, must be conscious of its dignity and its power. The consciousness of what she is and what she may be has come to America. She knows that she is a great nation. The elements of greatness were not imparted by the war; but they were revealed to her by the war, and their vitality and their significance were increased through the war.

"To take its proper place among the older nations of the earth a nation must be known as she is to those nations. The world to-day as ne'er before knows and confesses the greatness and the power of America. The world to-day admires and respects America. The young giant of the West, heretofore neglected and almost despised in his remoteness and isolation, has begun to move as becomes his stature; the world sees what he is and pictures what he may be.

"All this does not happen by chance or accident. An all-ruling Providence directs the movements of humanity. What we witness is a momentous dispensation from the master of men. 'Magnus ab integro saeclorum nascitur ordo—with the revolution of centuries there is born to the world a new order of things,' sang the Mantuan poet at the birth of the Augustan age. So to-day we proclaim a new order of things has appeared.

"America is too great to be isolated from the world around her and beyond her. She is a world power, to whom no world interest is alien, whose voice reaches afar, whose spirit travels across seas and mountain ranges to most distant continents and islands—and with America goes far and wide what America in the grandest ideal represents—democracy and liberty, a government of the people, by the people, for the people. This is Americanism more than American territory, or American

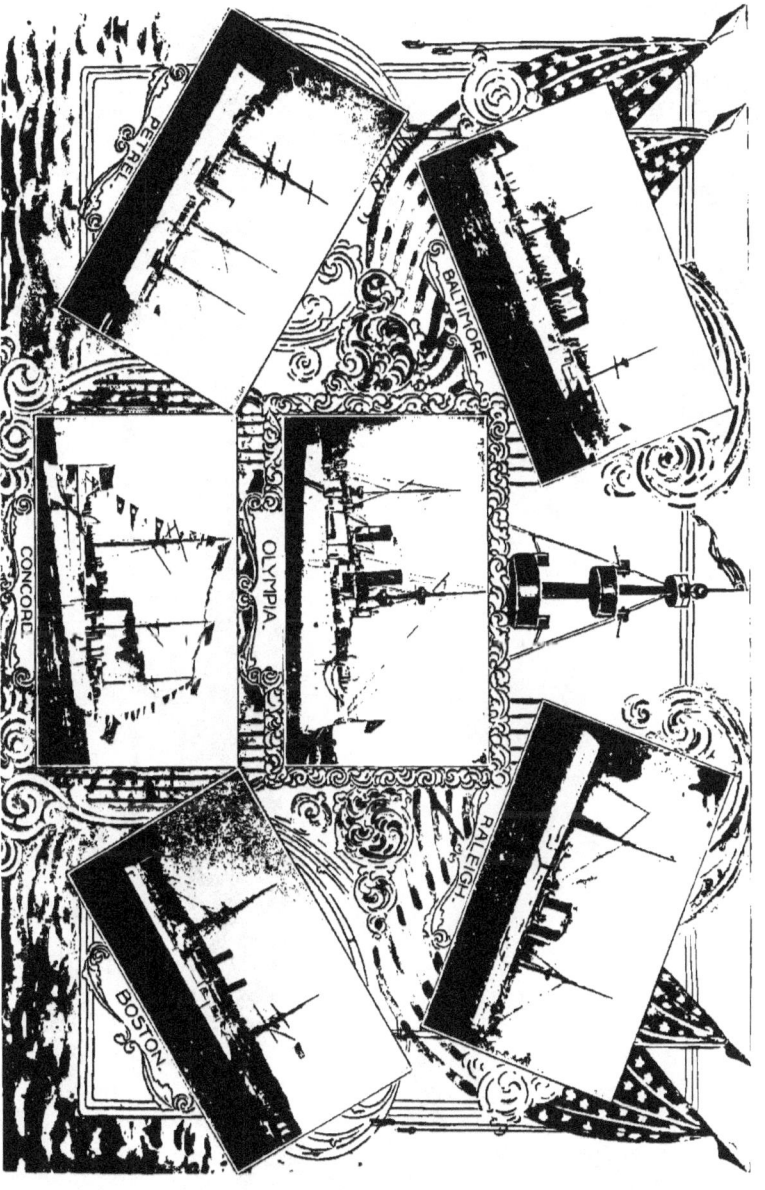

ADMIRAL DEWEY'S FLEET THAT WON THE BATTLE OF MANILA BAY.

THE MONUMENT OF MAGELLINS IN THE WALLED CITY.

shipping, or American soldiery. Where this grandest ideal of American life is not held supreme America has not reached, where this ideal is supreme America reigns. The vital significance of America's triumphs is not understood unless by those triumphs is understood the triumph of democracy and of liberty.

"If it was ever allowed to nations to rejoice over the result of their wars, America may rejoice to-day. Shall we then chant the praises of war and change this jubilee of peace into a jubilee of war? Heaven forbid!

"'We love peace, not war.' The greatness of America makes it imperative upon her to profess peace—peace to-day, peace to-morrow. Her mission as a world power demands that she be a messenger, an advocate of peace before the world. Fain would we make her jubilee of peace a jubilee of peace for all nations. At least the message from it to the world shall be a message of peace.

"That at times wonderful things come through war, we must admit; but that they come through war and not through the methods of peaceful justice, we must ever regret. When they do come through war, their beauty and grandeur are dimmed by the memory of the sufferings and carnage which were their price.

"We say in defense of war that its purpose is justice; but is it worthy of Christian civilization that there is no other way to justice than war, that nations are forced to stoop to the methods of the animal and savage? Time was when individuals gave battle to one another in the name of justice; it was the time of social barbarism. Tribunals have since taken to themselves the administration of justice, and how much better it is for the happiness and progress of mankind.

"It is force, or chance, that decides the issue of the battle. Justice herself is not heard; the decision of justice is what it was before the battle, the judgment of one party. Must we not hope that with the widening influence of reason and of religion among men, the day is approaching when justice shall be enthroned upon a great international tribunal, before which nations shall bow, demanding from it judgment and peace? Say what we will, our civilization is a vain boast.

> " 'Till the war drum throbs no longer, and the battle flags are furled
> In the parliament of man, the federation of the world.
> There the common sense of most shall hold a fretful realm in awe,
> And the kindly earth shall slumber, wrapt in universal law.'

"It is America's great soldier who said:

" 'Though I have been trained as a soldier, and have participated in many battles, there never was a time when, in my opinion, some way could not have been found of preventing the drawing of the sword. I look forward to an epoch when a court, recognized by all nations, will settle international differences, instead of keeping large standing armies, as they do in Europe.' Shall we not allow the words of General Grant to go forth as the message of America?

"Some weeks ago the Czar of Russia said: 'The maintenance of general peace and possible reduction of the excessive armaments which weigh upon all nations present themselves in the existing condition of the whole world as an ideal towards which the endeavors of all governments should be directed,' and in accordance with those views he invited all nations to send representatives to an international peace congress, in which the question of reducing the armaments of the several countries of the world and otherwise preparing some plan for the prevention of wars might be discussed.

"Shall not America send to St. Petersburg a message of good will, a promise of earnest co-operation? America, great and powerful, can afford to speak of peace. Words of peace from her will be the more gracious and timely, as they who do not know her say that, maddened by her recent triumphs, she is now committed beyond return to a policy of militarism and of conquest.

"Lead, my country, in peace—in peace for thyself, in peace for the world. When war is necessary, lead, we pray thee, in war; but when peace is possible, lead, we pray thee yet more, lead in peace; lead in all that makes for peace, that prepares the world for pecae.

"America, the eyes of the world are upon thee. Thou livest for the world. The new era is shedding its light upon thee, and through thee upon the whole world. Thy greatness and thy power daze me; even more, thy responsibilities to God and to humanity daze me—I would say affright me. America, thou failing, democracy and liberty fail throughout the world.

"And now know, in the day of thy triumphs and victories, what guards democracy and liberty, what is thy true grandeur. Not in commerce and industry, not in ships and in armies, are the safety and the grandeur of nations, and, more especially, of republics. Intelligence and virtue build up nations and save them; without intelligence and virtue, material wealth and victorious armies bring corruption to nations and precipitate the ruin of liberty.

"And now, America, the country of our pride, our love, our hope, we remit thee for to-day and for to-morrow into the hands of the Almighty God, under whose protecting hand thou canst not fail, whose commandments are the supreme rules of truth and righteousness."

The Archbishop was followed by Judge Speer, of Georgia:

THE PEACE JUBILEE. 249

"Mr. President, Ladies and Gentlemen: Spain had long been our near and dangerous neighbor. Its people have a degree of reverence almost superstitious for monarchy, and regard republican institutions with great disfavor. It has been said of Spain that some incurable vice in her organization, or it may be in the temper of her people, neutralizes all of the advantages she ought to derive from her sturdy hardihood, her nearly perfect capacity for endurance and the somber genius alike for war, for art and for literature, which has so often marked her sons. While this seems to be true, the Spaniard is not only a formidable antagonist, but there is a wealth of interest and charm in his rich, romantic history which commands the admiration of a generous foeman. This must be accorded, whether we contemplate that ancient people as they alternately resist the aggressions of Carthage and of Rome, the fierce cavalry of Hamilcar, the legions of Scipio, of Pompey and of Caesar, or in more recent times the achievements of their renowned infantry which broke to fragments the best armies of Europe, or the infuriated people in arms against the hitherto unconquered veterans of Napoleon, or but now as with patient and dogged courage, with flaming volleys, they vainly strive to hold the works of Caney and San Juan against the irresistible and rushing valor of the American soldier. In art the Spaniard has been not less famous. In the royal collection of Madrid, in the venerable cathedrals of Seville, in the Louvre, in the London National Gallery, the lover of the beautiful may be charmed by the warmth of color, the accuracy of technique, the rounded outline and saintly salvation of Murillo.

"Many a quaint moralist, many a stately poet, many a priestly chronicler attests the genius of Spanish literature, but if these had not been, Don Quixote and Sancho Panza had been its title to immortality. The admirable attributes of Spanish character nowhere found warmer appreciation than with our own countrymen. What Prescott did for the statecraft, and stern martial renown of the Spaniards, Washington Irving, with melodious prose and gentle humor, surpassed in his kindly portrayal of Spanish character in his charming romance, The Conquest of Granada. It is perhaps due to the drollery and Addisonian humor of that gifted American that we have never been able to estimate the Spaniard quite so seriously as he estimates himself, or, indeed, as his stern and uncompromising nature deserves. The truth is, Spanish policy has ever been insidiously and persistently inimical to the American people, and has culminated in deeds more atrocious than those which have rendered infamous the baleful memory of Pedro the Cruel.

"We all know how in 1492 his holiness, Alexander VI., in order to prevent unseemly collisions between Christian princes, published a bull by which he as-

THE PEACE JUBILEE.

signed to Spain all discoveries lying west of an imaginary line drawn 300 leagues to the westward of the Cape Verde islands. All discoveries to the east were confined to Portugal.

"All of South America save Brazil and the two Guineas, all Central America, Mexico, the entire territory west of the Mississippi, now embraced by the United States, beautiful Cuba, from whose eastern province of Santiago Ponce de Leon across the lucent waves of the tropical sea coveted the ambrosial forests and fertile meadows of Porto Rico, whence he was to sail to the floral empire of Florida. But this was not all of Spain's magnificent domain. Far across the waters of the South Pacific was the now famous cluster of islands bearing the name of the Spanish king. And from their great cities, via Guam, and Hawaii ,and San Francisco, to Acapulco, sailed the famous Manila fleet, huge galleons, loaded to the gunwales with the silken and golden wealth of the orient. Where are her colonies now? The declaration of the senior senator from the noble state of Illinois has been fulfilled: No race outside of her own borders, even if Spanish by origin, has ever been able to endure her reign, and every race which has resisted her ultimately succeeded in withdrawing from her control.

"In the meantime the Americans, as declared by the German philosopher, Lessing, were building in the new world the lodge of humanity. The determined malignity of the Spaniard toward the adventurous men of our race who were fringing the Atlantic coast with sparsely peopled and widely separated settlements was promptly disclosed. They had threatened to send an armed ship to remove the Virginia planters. They laid claim to Carolina, and they directed powerful armed expeditions against the young colony of Georgia. They were now to meet, not the helpless savages who had been their victims, but men of that same fighting strain who in this good year breasted the hail of death, swarmed up the heights and planted the colors on the intrenchments of Santiago.

"That field where the Georgian and Spaniards on that momentous day in 1742 met is yet called the Blood Marsh. The commander of our colonial forces was James Edward Oglethorpe. To his military genius and the heroism of his slender force is due the fact that the southern territory of the United States was not added to the dependencies of Spain. That illustrious Englishman should ever live in the memory and veneration of the American people. He did more to exclude the Spaniards from American soil than any other man of the English speaking race, save that successor of Washington, the president, who evinces his fervid love of country and graces the occasion by his presence to-day.

"Defeated in their scheme of invasion, the Spaniards remained intensely inimical to our fathers. What more striking demonstration of that superintending providence, which administers justice, not only to individuals, but to nations, than the spectacle in this mighty city, builded on the heritage of which Spain would have deprived this people of this gathering of Americans to mark the epoch when the last Spanish soldier has been driven from the last foot of soil of that hemisphere discovered by Columbus. May we not justly exclaim with the psalmist of old: 'Oh, clap your hands, all ye people; shout unto God with the voice of triumph.'

"It is perhaps impossible for Americans of this day and time to conceive how vast was the control Spain might have exerted over the destinies of our republic. The independence of the United States had been recognized, the constitution had been adopted and the government organized, and yet for many years she claimed without dispute the peninsula of Florida, thence a strip along the gulf extending to and including the city of New Orleans, and she held all of that territory west of the Mississippi extending from the Father of Waters to the Pacific ocean, and from the Gulf of Mexico northward to the undefined boundaries of the British possessions.

"Even as it is to-day, that empire mentioned in Bishop Berkely's prophetic stanza, 'Westward the course of empire takes its way,' which sprang into being with the first shot of the simple, God-fearing husbandmen on the green at Lexington extends more than half way across the Pacific ocean, and the miner or the fisherman standing on the ultimate island of Alaska and gazing eastward across the icy waters may with the naked eye behold the dominions of the czar. Nor in this do we include those distant islands, where one May morning, ever to be famous in the annals of our race, the spicy breezes that blow o'er Manila bay were rent by the guns of the noble Dewey as they proclaimed that the genius of liberty had come to rid of cruelty and avarice and crime that charming land 'where every prospect pleases and only man is vile.'

"In this connection may it not be well for us and for some of our distinguished representatives now in Paris to consider if it can be ever possible for men with the American and Spanish ideas of government to live in proximity and in peace? Contrast the character of the average American citizen with that of the Spaniard. The native and distinctive modesty of the national character forbids me to pronounce an extravagant eulogium upon the American citizen, but behold him and see what he has done and can do.

"While the human intellect has been making prodigious and unheard-of strides, while the world is ringing with the noise of intellectual achievements, Spain sleeps on untroubled, unheeding, impassive, receiving no impression upon it. There she lies at the farther extremity of the continent, a huge and torpid mass, the sole representative now remaining of the feelings and knowledge of the middle ages. And, what is the worst symptom of all, she is satisfied with her own condition. Though she is the most backward country in Europe she believes herself to be the foremost. She is proud of everything of which she ought to be ashamed.

"How incompatible is the temperament of the American and the Spaniard.

"May the worn and wasted followers of Gomez and Garcia come to appreciate the blessings of liberty under the law. No other wish is in consonance with the aims of the American people. We would not, if we could, be their masters. The gigantic power of the country has been put forth for their salvation and for their pacification. Connected with them by bonds of genuine sympathy and indissoluble interest, we will labor with them to secure for them established justice, domestic tranquility, general welfare and the blessings of liberty to themselves and to their posterity. For the common defense, in the blue ether above the beautiful island of Cuba is poised the eagle.'

'Whose golden plume
Floats moveless on the storm and in the blaze
Of sunrise gleams when earth is wrapt in gloom.'

"It was not enough, however, for the American people to recognize the independence of the Spanish-American republics. It soon became our duty to notify the world that in certain eventualities it was our purpose to defend their national existence. The holy alliance, as it was termed, had been formed. The great powers who signed the famous compact declared its purpose to maintain as Christian doctrine the proposition that useful or necessary changes in legislation, or in the administration of states, can only emanate from the free will and well-weighed convictions of those whom God has rendered responsible for power. Whom had God made responsible for power? What is a well-weighed conviction? These are questions about which the irreverent Americans might perchance differ with royalty. We had been lead to believe, and yet believe, that the voice of the people is the voice of God. When, therefore, the absolution of the holy alliance, not content with smothering a feeble spark of liberty in Spain, initiated a joint movement of their arms against the Spanish-American republics, it gave the people of our country the gravest concern. In the meantime our relations with Great Britain had grown cordial. That they may grow ever stronger and more cordial should be the prayer of every man of the English speaking race. An unspeakable blessing to mankind of the struggle from which we are now emerging is the genuine brotherly sympathy for the people of the United States flowing from that land.

"And it is returned in no unstinted measure. But two months ago the flagship of Admiral Dewey steamed slowly into the battle line at Manila. As she passed the British flagship Immortalite its band rang out the inspiring air 'See the Conquering Hero Comes,' and as the gorgeous ensign of the republic was flung to the breeze at the peak of the Olympia there now came thrilling o'er the waters from our kinsmen's ship the martial strains of the 'Star Spangled Banner.'

"Finally, when our gallant seamen, reposing in fancied security in the scorching blast of the treacherous explosion were cruelly and remorselessly slain, and calm investigation had developed the truth, we had been despicable on the historic page had we not appealed to the god of battle for retribution. The pious rage of seventy millions of people cried aloud to heaven for the piteous agony, for the shameful slaughter of our brethren. Our noble navy was swiftly speeding to its duty. Poetic genius bodied forth the spirit of our gallant seamen as the mighty ships sped on their way.

"Let the waters of the orient as they moan through the shell-riven wrecks at Cavite, the booming waves of the Caribbean as fathoms deep it sweeps over Pluton and Furor and breaks into spray on the shapeless and fire-distorted steel of Vizcaya and Oquendo, tell how the navy has paid our debt to Spain. Nor is the renown which crowns the standards of our army one whit less glorious. Nothing in the lucid page of Thucydides nor in the terse commentaries of Caesar, nothing in the vivid narrative of Napier or the glowing battle scenes of Allison, can surpass the story how, spurning the chapparal and the barbed wire, pressing their rifles to their throbbing hearts, toiling up the heights, and all the while the machine guns and the Mausers mowing the jungle as if with a mighty reaper, on and yet right on, they won the fiery crests, and Santiago fell. Well may we exclaim with the royal poet of Israel:

"'Oh, sing unto the Lord a new song, for he hath done marvelous things; his right hand and his holy arm hath gotten him the victory.'

"America! Humane in the hour of triumph, gentle to the vanquished, grateful to the Lord of Hosts, a reunited people forever:

"'Great people. As the sands shalt thou become;
Thy growth is swift as morn, when night must fade
The multitudinous earth shall sleep beneath thy shade.'"

The band burst into the strains of "Dixie" in honor of the Southern birth of Judge Speer, as he concluded his oration. President McKinley, as on other occasions during the program, joined in the hearty applause. Cries of "McKinley," "Mc-

Kinley," "The President," "The President," were heard all over the hall, and in a moment it was seen that the President was going to respond. Every one stood up. Ex-Governor Oglesby approached the front of the box, and said, "I have the honor to introduce the guest of the occasion, the President."

"Leaning forward," we quote the Tribune, "from his box in the earnestness of his utterance, speaking in the tones of emotion having birth in the fullness of heart, President William McKinley, at the Auditorium jubilee meeting yesterday morning gave to the people a message of simple thanks and significant augury. Save for a wave of applause at the mention of American charity, the terse, reverent address was heard in silence. An added hush fell upon the intent throng when the President began the portentous concluding paragraph, and when he ceased speaking and stood before them grave and masterful, the quiet was breathless, tense under the force of repression. Then the meaning of the words of the Executive coursed from heart to brain, and men's minds grasped the fact that they had heard the President's lips declare that he had seen the direction of the flow of the currents of destiny, that he recognized their majesty, and that his purpose was in harmony with the common will—the force working for the retention of the conquered islands in the distant Pacific and for the policy of national growth.

"The applause broke the louder for the preceding calm and the deeper for the inspiring motive. Hats were swung and handkerchiefs waved. Men climbed on chairs to lead the cheering and women forgot gloved hands and applauded with energy. At the last, ex-Governor Richard J. Oglesby, who had a seat in the President's box, led in three cheers."

The message of the President was:

"My Fellow Citizens: I have been deeply moved by this great demonstaration. I have been deeply touched by the words of patriotism that have been uttered by the distinguished men so eloquently in your presence. It is gratifying to all of us to know that this has never ceased to be a war of humanity. The last ship that went out of the harbor of Havana before war was declared was an American ship that had taken to the suffering people of Cuba the supplies furnished by American charity, and the first ship to sail into the harbor of Santiago was another American ship bearing food supplies to the suffering Cubans.

"I am sure it is the universal prayer of American citizens that justice and humanity and civilization shall characterize the final settlement of peace as they have distinguished the progress of the war.

"My countrymen, the currents of destiny flow through the hearts of the people.

THE PEACE JUBILEE. 255

Who will check them? Who will divert them? Who will stop them? And the movements of men, planned by the master of men, will never be interrupted by the American people."

The Philadelphia celebration was a scene of a demonstration of popular interest and patriotic feeling amazing in its multitudinous enthusiasm. The Loyal League was out in full force, the parade was a prodigy of display, and the Clover Club gave a brilliant dinner, and the cleverness of the President's speech carried the club by storm. He said:

"I cannot forego making acknowledgment to this far-famed club for the permission it has granted me to meet with you here to-night. You do not seem half so bad at this stage as you have been pictured. No one can unfold the future of the Clover Club. (Laughter.)

It has been so gratifying to me to participate with the people of the city of Philadelphia in this great patriotic celebration. It was a pageant the like of which I do not believe has been seen since the close of the great Civil War, when the army of Grant, Sherman and Sheridan, and the navy of Dupont, Dahlgren and Porter gave the great review in the capital city of the nation. And I know of no more fitting place to have a patriotic celebration than in this great city, which witnessed the first consecration of liberty and of the Republic. As I stood on the great reviewing stand, witnessing the soldiers and sailors passing by, my heart was filled only with gratitude to the God of battles, who has so favored us, and gratitude to the brave soldiers and sailors who had won such signal victories on land and on sea, and had given a new meaning to American valor.

"It has been especially gratifying to me to participate not only with the people of Philadelphia, but with the people of the great West, where I have recently visited, in doing honor to the American army and the American navy. No nobler soldiers or sailors ever assembled under any flag. You had with you to-day the leaders of Santiago, Porto Rico and Guantanamo. We unfortunately had none of the heroes of Manila with us. But I am sure that our hearts go out to them to-night and to the brave Dewey and Otis and Merritt, and all the other gallant men that are now sustaining the flag in the harbor city of Manila."

(A voice, "How about Hobson?")

"The American people are always ready for any emergency, and if the Merrimac is to be sunk there is an American officer to do it. He succeeded in doing what our foe has been unable to do, sink an American ship. (Applause.)

"I ask you, gentlemen of the Clover Club, to unite with me in toasting the

Army and Navy of the United States, without whose valor and sacrifice we could not celebrate the victory we have been celebrating to-day. Not only the men at the front, not only the men on the battleships and in the battle line, but the men at home with ambition to go to fight the battles of American civilization, should be the recipients of the gratitude of the American people."

Hobson and his men were a great feature of the parade in the four-in-hand. Hobson, during this visit to Philadelphia was caught, surrounded and captured at his hotel and was forced to make a speech, of which there is this report:

"The young officer was plainly embarrassed. His red face suggested it, his trembling voice told it. In a low tone and frequently pausing, as if from a loss of a word, he said:

" 'Your reception has been so very kind that it seems almost as if I had lost the power to say anything.'

"Someone called out: 'Never mind, you had nerve enough to go into Santiago Harbor,' and then the crowd gave three cheers for Hobson.

"He began again. 'The incident you have referred to is one you unduly magnify. Believe me, it was really nothing more than a little bit of work, which came to my men and to me to do in the ordinary course of strategy in warfare. That was all it was, a little bit of work, and it is sheer exaggeration to say anything else.'

" 'Can't agree with you! Can't agree with you!' was the shouted answer from the crowd."

At the Clover Club jubilee dinner, Captain "Fighting Bob" Evans gave a wonderfully interesting account of the destruction of Cervera's fleet, closing with a grim picture of war the celebration of peace. He had been speaking of the blockade of Cuba, and insistently called upon to tell about Santiago, said:

"Of our little scrap, it was the prettiest mix-up that was ever seen. I want to say that no fleet ever met a braver enemy than we did at Santiago. Those Spaniards stood up and got killed in the best possible shape. Six hundred of them died in less than thirty minutes, so you can see that there was very little flinching on Cervera's ships.

"During the fight there were two very interesting moments, the first when the four big cruisers of the enemy came outside of the harbor, firing away with mechanical regularity and presenting a most magnificent spectacle. They were not hitting anything, but that made little difference at that time, they tried hard enough. As we closed in, there came a moment when the fleeing Spanish ships had an almost perfect chance to use their rams on our vessels. I submit now that not a single one changed his course a single inch. They came out of that harbor and ran away, and that was all they attempted to do, fighting as they went.

"The second point was when 'Dick' Wainwright misread a signal. I know he won't admit that he did misread it; however, I'll tell you the incident. In the Gloucester Wainwright was just off the harbor mouth when the two Spanish torpedo boat destroyers were noticed making straight at him. The Indiana signaled 'The enemy's torpedo boats are coming out.' Wainwright read it 'Close in and attack enemy's torpedo boats,' and you know the rest of the story.

"There was a dramatic picture which I want to call your attention to. It was after the Vizcaya had run ashore, and I had to stop the Iowa, some 400 yards away. I saw the survivors on a sand bar, which was merely a narrow strip of about 200 yards from shore, on either side of a small inlet. On one side a school of hungry sharks were making fierce rushes toward the men, and on the other, the Cubans were shooting away, utterly regardless of the fact that they were fighting a helpless foe. Out in front we were not supposed to be very friendly.

"Finally, I saw Captain Eulate, of the destroyed ship, coming toward my vessel in a small boat. Now Eulate is what you call a black Spaniard, one of those fellows that would cry as though his heart would break every few minutes when in trouble. He sat in the stern of a small boat that had belonged to his vessel. She was partly stove in and had about a foot of water, or I should say blood and water, in her bottom.

"As I looked down in the gangway I think it was the most horrible sight that I ever witnessed. In the bottom of the boat lay two dead Spaniards, one with his head completely shot away. The Spanish Captain was wounded in three places, and each of the four men who rowed his boat was more or less cut up. We slung a chair over the side and carefully hauled him on board.

"As he came up to the starboard gangway the marine guard saluted and he was received with all the honors of his rank. As he stepped toward me he burst into tears, threw his hands up in the air, and then, with a gesture of utter despair, but with all the grace of the pretty gentleman, loosed his sword belt and pressing a fervent kiss on the hilt of the weapon he extended it toward me. Every man on that ship knew that that Spaniard was giving up something of value equal to his life. I am not very good-natured, but I could not take that sword."

This met with loud cries of "You did right, Bob," and one lusty-lunged individual announced that there was not a man in the country that would take it. Captain Evans, who recognized the speaker, a friend from the rural districts, answered: "Oh, you don't know what some of those up-country Pennsylvanians would do. It was a pretty good sword."

Continuing, Captain Evans said: "I didn't know exactly what to do with the Spanish Captain to get him into our sick bay. As I was about to ask him of his wound he stepped toward the gangway and looked shoreward. About a quarter of a mile off lay the once magnificent vessel in which he had boasted he would tow the Brooklyn back to Spain.

"She was burning fore and aft, terrific columns of flame shooting up around her, and suddenly, with a burst of tears, Captain Eulate kissed his hand and bade fond farewell to the burning hulk and said with impassioned voice, 'Adios Viscaya.' As he did this the very same instant there came a tremendous roar and the Vizcaya's magazine blew her superstructure hundreds of feet into the air. Had the incident occurred that way on the stage anybody would have said it was too well timed.

"He turned back and we got him into the ship's hospital, where the surgeons placed him on his stomach to shave the hair around a small cut on the back of his head. I stood alongside of him, and rolling his eyes into the starboard corner he said to me, with a rather comical expression, 'I think I have heard of you before.' I told him I did not know how that could have been, and he asked: 'Did you not command the Indiana?' 'Yes,' I said; then he said, shaking his head as well as circumstances would permit, 'Yes, I have heard of you. You are "Bob" Evans.'

"I have often wondered just what he referred to. I have a notion that it would fit certain remarks regarding certain language that I was credited with having used in reference to an attack on Havana; language, by the way, which I never used. As I said before, the battle before Santiago was the prettiest imaginable kind of effect. Why, two torpedo boat destroyers came out, and inside of ten minutes we had them sounding. One sounded in 200 fathoms of water and sunk to rest there. The other preferred a berth with her nose on the beach.

"The Maria Teresa and Admiral Oquendo were on fire inside of five minutes after the fight had started. They made beautiful sweeps toward the shore, and were regular Fourth of July processions as they swept in on the beach. We helped them along a bit by landing a few shells in the stern. It was a pretty fight, but it should never be forgotten that the Spaniards fought their ships as hard and with as much valor as any men in any ships ever fought."

After the first cabinet meeting succeeding the peace jubilee, the President issued his annual Thanksgiving proclamation:

"BY THE PRESIDENT OF THE UNITED STATES.
A PROCLAMATION.

"The approaching November brings to mind the custom of our ancestors, hallowed by time and rooted in our most sacred traditions, of giving thanks to Almighty God for all the blessings he has vouchsafed to us during the past year.

"Few years in our history have afforded such cause for thanksgiving as this. We have been blessed by abundant harvests, our trade and commerce have been wonderfully increased, our public credit has been improved and strengthened, all sections of our common country have been brought together and knitted into closer bonds of national purpose and unity.

"The skies have been for a time darkened by the cloud of war; but as we were compelled to take up the sword in the cause of humanity, we are permitted to rejoice that the conflict has been of brief duration and the losses we have had to mourn, though grievous and important, have been so few, considering the great results accomplished, as to inspire us with gratitude and praise to the Lord of Hosts. We may laud and magnify His holy name that the cessation of hostilities came so soon as to spare both sides the countless sorrows and disasters that attend protracted war.

"I do, therefore, invite all my fellow citizens, as well those at home as those who may be at sea or sojourning in foreign lands, to set apart and observe Thursday, the twenty-fourth day of November, as a day of national thanksgiving, to come together in their several places of worship, for a service of praise and thanks to Almighty God for all the blessings of the year, for the mildness of seasons and the fruitfulness of the soil, for the continued prosperity of the people, for the devotion and valor of our countrymen, for the glory of our victory and the hope of a righteous peace, and to pray that the Divine guidance, which has brought us heretofore to safety and honor, may be graciously continued in the years to come.

"In witness whereof, etc.
  (Signed)   "WILLIAM M'KINLEY.
"By the President:
  "JOHN HAY, Secretary of State."

CHAPTER XVII.

EARLY HISTORY OF THE PHILIPPINES.

The Abolishment of the 31st of December, 1844, in Manila—The Mystery of the Meridian 180 Degrees West—What Is East and West?—Gaining and Losing Days—The Tribes of Native Filipinos—They Had an Alphabet and Songs of Their Own—The Massacre of Magellan—His Fate Like That of Captain Cook—Stories of Long Ago Wars—An Account by a Devoted Spanish Writer of the Beneficent Rule of Spain in the Philippines—Aguinaldo a Man Not of a Nation, But of a Tribe—Typhoons and Earthquakes—The Degeneracy of the Government of the Philippines After It Was Taken from Mexico—"New Spain"—The Perquisites of Captain-Generals—The Splendor of Manila a Century Ago.

The 31st of December was abolished in Manila in 1844. Up to that time it had been retained as the discoverers fixed it by pure piety and patriotism. Pope Alexander VI had issued a bull on the 4th of May, 1493, dividing the world into two hemispheres, which was quite correct, though it did not correspond to the secular lines of more modern days. The gracious object of His Holiness was to keep the peace of the world by dividing the lands taken from the heathen between the Spaniards and Portuguese. The East was to belong to Portugal. The line was drawn to include Brazil. The west was the hunting ground for heathen of Spain. The claim of Spain for the Philippines was that they were west. That was the way Magellenas (Magellan), the Portuguese navigator sailed through the straits named for him, and westward found the alleged Oriental islands, in which we, the people of the United States, are now so much interested. When sailing into the sunset seas he picked up a day, and never discovered his error for he did not get home, and the Captain who navigated his ship did not know he was out of time with the European world until he got as far around as the Cape Verd Islands. An added day was held in Manila, as a kind of affirmation of clear title, or trade mark of true righteousness, on the part of Spain. It is one of the enduring puzzles in going around the world that a day is gained or lost, and it is not always a sure thing whether there is a loss or gain. The perplexing problem is increased in its persistence if one sails westward over the 180 Meridian west from Greenwich, and goes beyond that line (which is not the one drawn by Alexander VI)—say to the Philippines, and turns back, as is done in the voyage from San Francisco to Manila, and vice versa.

In this case, the mystery of the meridian becomes something dreadful. One loses a day going west and gains one coming east, and it is a difficulty for a clear mind not to become cloudy over the account of loss and gain—or perhaps we may say profit and loss, when the account is closed. "The historian of the Philippine Expedition" lost a Wednesday going out, jumping from Tuesday to Thursday, and found an extra Thursday on the return—celebrated his birthday on another day than that on which he was born, and had to correct the ship account of his board bill, by adding a day. The Captain's clerk had forgotten it because it was not in the Almanac. Ship time begins a day at noon (and ends another), so when we crossed the meridian 180 degrees west at 2 p. m. by the sun, and the day was Thursday and to-morrow was Thursday also, the forenoon was yesterday by the ship. Therefore, Thursday was yesterday, to-day and to-morrow on the same day. The forenoon was yesterday—from 12 to 2 p. m. was to-day—and from 2 p. m. to midnight was to-morrow! It is no wonder "the historian," whose birthday was September the 2nd, found as he was on the west side of the meridian with the mystery that the folks at home in the states had celebrated it for him two days ago—one day he had lost, and the other they had gained. Jagor, the historian of the Philippines, before the days when Admiral Dewey grasped the reins of a thousand islands, and a thousand to spare, says in his "Philippine Islands," that "when the clock strikes 12 in Madrid, it is 8 hours 18 minutes and 41 seconds past 8 in the evening at Manila. The latter city lies 124 degrees 40 min. 15 sec. east of the former, 7 h. 54 min. 35 sec. from Paris. But it depends upon whether you measure time by moving with the sun or the other way. If westward the course of empire takes its way, Manila is a third of a day catching up with Madrid time. If we face the morning and go to meet it Manila is ahead. The absence of the right day for Sunday has long been gravely considered by the missionaries who have gone to heathen lands beyond the mysterious meridian that spoils all the holidays. One might establish a bank on that line and play between days, but there is only one little speck of land on the 180 degree meridian from pole to pole.

It may be very well worth considering whether the United States should not reestablish the 31st of December in Manila, and assert that we hold title to the Philippines not only by the victories of the fleet and armies of the United States, but by the favor of Alexander VI, whose bull the Spaniards disregarded after it had grown venerable with three centuries of usage. We quote a Spanish historian who colors his chapters to make a favorable show for his country on this subject, as follows: "From the Spaniards having traveled westwards to the Philippines, there was an error of a day in their dates and almanacs. This was corrected in 1844, when, by order of the Captain-General and the Archbishop, the 31st of December, 1844, was suppressed, and the dates of Manila made to agree with those of the rest of the world. A similar correction was made at the same time at Macao, where the Portuguese who had traveled eastward had an error of a day in an opposite direction." It will be noticed that the authority of the Archbishop was carefully obtained and quoted, but it was beyond his prerogative.

The early history of the Philippines bears few traces of the traditions and romances of the natives, but they were in possession of an alphabet when "discovered," and were then, as now, fond of music, singing their own melodies. The Hawaiians were enabled to get their old stories into print because they suddenly fell into the hands of masterful men who had a written language. The Icelanders were too literary for their own good, for they spoiled their history by writing it in poetry and mixing it with fiction, losing in that way the credit that belongs to them of being the true discoverers of America. The Filipinos were spared this shape of misfortune, not that they lacked imagination within a narrow range of vision, but they were wanting in expression, save in unwritten music. Their lyrical poetry was not materialized. The study of the natives must be studied as geology is. Geology and native history have been neglected in the Tagala country. The rocks of the Philippines have not been opened to be read like books. More is known of the botany of the islands than of the formation of the mountains and their foundations. The original inhabitants were Nigritos—a dwarfish race, very dark and tameless, still in existence, but driven to the parts of the country most inaccessible. They are of the class of dark savages, who smoke cigars holding the fiery ends between their teeth! The islands were invaded and extensively harassed by Malay tribes—the most numerous and active being the Tagala. Of this tribe is General Aguinaldo, and it is as a man with a tribe not a nation that he has become conspicuous. The other tribes of Malays will not sustain him if he should be wild enough to want to make war upon the United States. The Tagalas are cock fighters and live on the lowlands. They eat rice chiefly, but are fond of ducks and chickens, and they have an incredibly acute sense of smell, not a bad taste in food, and do not hanker to get drunk.

The Visayas are also a tribe. The Igolatas are next to the Tagala in numbers and energy. They show traces of Chinese and Japanese blood. There are no Africans in the Philippines, no sign of their blood. This may be attributed to Phillip's prohibition of negro slavery. General Greene, of New York, took with him to Manila a full-blooded black manservant, and he was a great curiosity to the Fili-

A RAILROAD STATION NORTH OF MANILA, SPANIARDS AIRING THEMSELVES.

THE BATTLE OF MANILA BAY—IN THE HEAT OF THE RAGING FIGHT.

pinos. When the English conquered Manila in 1762 they had Sepoy regiments, and held the city eighteen months. A good deal of Sepoy blood is still in evidence. The Chinese have been growing in importance in the Philippines. Their men marry the women of the islands and have large families, the boys of this class being wonderfully thrifty. The children of Englishmen by the native women are often handsome, and of strong organization. The females are especially comely.

The early history of the islands consists of accounts of contests with frontier rebels, attacks by pirates, and reprisals by the Spaniards, great storms and destructive earthquakes. It is remarkable that Magellan was, like Captain Cook, a victim of savages, whose existence he made known to civilized people, falling in a sea-side contest. Magellan had converted a captive chief to Christianity and baptised him as King Charles. More than two thousand of his subjects were converted in a day, and the great navigator set forth to conquer islands for the dominion of the Christian King, who lived on the isle of Zebu. The Christian monarch was entertained and received many presents, making return in bags of gold dust, fruit, oil and wine. His Queen was presented with a looking glass, and then she insisted upon baptism, and so great was the revival that Magellan set out to capture more people for the newly made Christian couple—invaded the island of Matau, and with forty-two men landed where the water was shallow, his allies remaining afloat by invitation of Magellan, to see how the Spaniards disposed of enemies. The Spanish landed at night, and on the morning found a great multitude of savages opposed to them, and fought for life, but were overwhelmed by thousands of warriors. The Admiral was in white armor, and fighting desperately, was at last wounded in his sword arm, and then in the face, and leg. He was deserted by his men, who sought to save themselves in the water, and killed many of his enemies, but his helmet and skull were crushed at one blow by a frantic savage with a huge club. There were thirty-two Spaniards killed, and one of the squadron of three ships was burned as there were not men enough to sail all the vessels. There is in Manila, in the walled city, where it is seen every day by thousands of American soldiers, a stately monument to the navigator who found the Philippines, and whose adventurous discoveries insured him immortality. His first landing on the Philippines was March 12th, 1521. less than thirty years after Columbus appeared in the West Indies, believing that he was in the midst of the ancient East Indies, and judging from the latitude in the neighborhood of the island empire of the Great Kahn.*

---

*This account of Magellan is from Antonio de Marga's rare volume published in Mexico.

"After the death of Magellan, Duarte Barbosa took the command and he and twenty of his men were treacherously killed by the Christian King, with whom they had allied themselves, one Juan Serrano was left alive amongst the natives. Magellan's 'Victory' was the first ship that circumnavigated the globe.

"Magellanes passed over to the service of the King of Castile, from causes which moved him thereto; and he set forth to the Emperor Charles V., our sovereign, that the Islands of Maluco fell within the demarcation of his crown of Castile, and that the conquest of them pertained to him conformably to the concession of Pope Alexander; he also offered to make an expedition and a voyage to them in the emperor's name, laying his course through that part of the delimitation which belonged to Castile, and availing himself of a famous astrologer and cosmographer named Ruyfarelo, whom he kept in his service.

"The Emperor (from the importance of the business) confided this voyage and discovery of Magellanes, with the ships and provisions which were requisite for it, with which he set sail and discovered the straits to which he gave his name. Through these he passed to the South Sea, and navigated to the islands of Tendaya and Sebu, where he was killed by the natives of Matan, which is one of them. His ships went on to Maluco, where their crews had disputes and differences with the Portuguese who were in the island of Terrenate; and at last, not being able to maintain themselves there, they left Maluco in a ship named the Victory, which had remained to the Castilians out of their fleet, and they took as Chief and Captain Juan Sebastian del Cano, who performed the voyage to Castile, by the way of India, where he arrived with very few of his men, and he gave an account to His Majesty of the discovery of the islands of the great archipelago, and of his voyage."

The work of De Morga has value as a novelty, as it is more than a defense—a laudation of the Spanish rule in the Philippines in the sixteenth century. The title page is a fair promise of a remarkable performance, and it is here presented:

THE
PHILIPPINE ISLANDS,
MOLUCCAS, SIAM, CAMBODIA,
JAPAN AND CHINA,
at the close of the Sixteenth Century
By ANTONIO DE MORGA.
Translated from the Spanish, with Notes and a Preface, and a Letter from Luis Vaez De Torres, Describing His Voyage Through the Torres Straits, by the
HON. HENRY E. J. STANLEY.

EARLY HISTORY OF THE PHILIPPINES. 205

The original work of De Morga was printed in Mexico in 1609, and has become extremely rare; there is no copy of it in the Bibliotheque Imperiale of Paris. This translation is from a transcription made for the Hakluyt Society from the copy in the Grenville Library of the British Museum; the catalogue of which states that "this book, printed at Mexico, is for that reason probably unknown to Bibliographers, though a book of great rarity."

The translator gives a new view to Americans of the part that Spaniards have played in the Philippines. He plunges deep into his subject, saying:

" The great point in which Manila has been a success, is the fact that the original inhabitants have not disappeared before the Europeans, and that they have been civilized, and brought into a closer union with the dominant race than is to be found elsewhere in similar circumstances. The inhabitants of the Philippines previous to the Spanish settlement were not like the inhabitants of the great Indian peninsula, people with a civilization as old as that of their conquerors. Excepting that they possessed the art of writing, and an alphabet of their own, they do not appear to have differed in any way from the Dayaks of Borneo as described by Mr. Boyle in his recent book of adventures amongst that people. Indeed, there is almost a coincidence of verbal expressions in the descriptions he and De Morga give of the social customs, habits, and superstitions of the two peoples they are describing; though many of these coincidences are such as are incidental to life in similar circumstances, they are enough to lead one to suppose a community of origin of the inhabitants of Borneo and Luzon." Mr. Consul Farren, Manila, March 13th, 1845, wrote and is quoted in support of this view as follows:

"The most efficient agents of public order throughout the islands are the local clergy, many of whom are also of the country. There are considerable parts of these possessions in which the original races, as at Ceylon, retain their independence, and are neither taxed nor interfered with; and throughout the islands the power of the government is founded much more on moral than on physical influence. The laws are mild, and peculiarly favorable to the natives. The people are indolent, temperate and superstitious. The government is conciliatory and respectable in its character and appearance, and prudent, but decisive in the exercise of its powers over the people; and united with the clergy, who are shrewd, and tolerant, and sincere, and respectable in general conduct, studiously observant of their ecclesiastical duties, and managing with great tact the native character."

March 29, 1851, Mr. Consul Farren wrote: "Without any governing power whatever, the greatest moral influence in these possessions is that which the priests possess, and divide among the monastic orders of Augustines, Recoletos, Dominicans, and Franciscans (who are all Spaniards), and the assistant native clergy. A population exceeding 3,800,000 souls is ranged into 677 pueblos or parishes, without reckoning the unsubdued tribes. In 577 of those pueblos there are churches, with convents or clerical residences attached, and about 500 of them are in the personal incumbency of those Spanish monks. The whole ecclesiastical subdivisions being embraced in the archbishopric of Manila and three bishoprics."

"The Philippines were converted to Christianity and maintained in it by the monastic orders, energetically protected by them (and at no very past period) against the oppressions of the provincial authorities, and are still a check on them in the interests of the people. The clergy are receivers in their districts of the capitation tax paid by the natives, and impose it; they are the most economical agency of the government."

The Archbishop of Manila is substantially of this judgment. De Morga opens his address to the reader:

"The monarchy of Kings of Spain has been aggrandized by the zeal and care with which they have defended within their own hereditary kingdoms, the Holy Catholic Faith, which the Roman Church teaches, against whatsoever adversaries oppose it, or seek to obscure the truth by various errors, which faith they have disseminated throughout the world. Thus by the mercy of God they preserve their realms and subjects in the purity of the Christian religion, deserving thereby the glorious title and renown which they possess of Defenders of the Faith. Moreover, by the valor of their indomitable hearts, and at the expense of their revenues and property, with Spanish fleets and men, they have furrowed the seas, and discovered and conquered vast kingdoms in the most remote and unknown parts of the world, leading their inhabitants to a knowledge of the true God, and to the fold of the Christian Church, in which they now live, governed in civil and political matters with peace and justice, under the shelter and protection of the royal arm and power which was wanting to them. This boast is true of Manila, and of Manila alone amongst all the colonies of Spain or the other European states. If the natives of Manila have been more fortunate than those of Cuba, Peru, Jamaica, and Mexico, it has been owing to the absence of gold, which in other places attracted adventurers so lawless that neither the Church nor Courts of justice could restrain them."

It is against the orders named as worthy exalted praise that the insurgents are most inflamed, and whose expulsion from the islands is certain in case of Philippine jurisdiction. The truth appears to be that the Spanish Colonial system was slower

A SUBURB OF MANILA, SHOWING A BUFFALO MARKET CART.

THE CATHEDRAL AT MANILA.

in the East Indies than in the West Indies and South America in producing the revolutionary rebellion that was its logical consequence, and the friars more and more became responsible for official oppression and gradually became odious.

It was New Spain—Mexico—that ruled the Philippines, until Mexican independence restricted her sovereignty. When a Commander-in-Chief died in the Philippines, it was sufficient to find amongst his papers a sealed dispatch, as Morga records, "From the high court of Mexico, which carried on the government when the fleet left New Spain, naming (in case the Commander-in-Chief died) a successor to the governorship." It was in virtue of such an appointment that Guido de Labazarris, a royal officer, entered upon those duties, and was obeyed. He, with much prudence, valor, and tact, continued the conversion and pacification of the islands, and governed them, and Morga states that in his time there came the corsair Limahon from China, with seventy large ships and many men-at-arms, against Manila. He entered the city, and having killed the master of the camp Martin de Goiti, in his house, along with other Spaniards who were in it, he went against the fortress in which the Spaniards, who were few in number, had taken refuge, with the object of taking the country and making himself master of it. The Spaniards, with the succor which Captain Joan de Salzado brought them from Vigan, of the men whom he had with him (for he had seen this corsair pass by the coast, and had followed him to Manila), defended themselves so valiantly, that after killing many of the people they forced him to re-embark, and to leave the bay in flight, and take shelter in the river of Pangasinam, whither the Spaniards followed him. There they burned his fleet, and for many days surrounded this corsair on land, who in secret made some small boats with which he fled and put to sea, and abandoned the islands.

The change of the name of the islands from Lazarus, which Magellan called them, to the Philippines and the capture of the native town of Manila and its conversion into a Spanish city is related by Morga in these words:

"One of the ships which sailed from the port of Navidad in company with the fleet, under the command of Don Alonso de Arellano, carried as pilot one Lope Martin, a mulatto and a good sailor, although a restless man; when this ship came near the islands it left the fleet and went forward amongst the islands, and, having procured some provisions, without waiting for the chief of the expedition, turned back to New Spain by a northerly course; either from the little inclination which he had for making the voyage to the isles, or to gain the reward for having discovered the course for returning. He arrived speedily, and gave news of having seen the islands, and discovered the return voyage, and said a few things with respect to his coming, without any message from the chief, nor any advices as to what happened to him. Don Alonzo de Arellano was well received by the High Court of Justice, which governed at that time, and was taking into consideration the granting of a reward to him and to his pilot; and this would have been done, had not the flagship of the Commander-in-Chief arrived during this time, after performing the same voyage, and bringing a true narrative of events, and of the actual condition of affairs, and of the settlement of Sebu; also giving an account of how Don Alonzo de Arellano with his ship, without receiving orders and without any necessity for it, had gone on before the fleet on entering among the isles, and had never appeared since. It was also stated that, besides these islands, which had peacefully submitted to His Majesty, there were many others, large and rich, well provided with inhabitants, victuals and gold, which they hoped to reduce to subjection and peace with the assistance which was requested; and that the Commander-in-Chief had given to all these isles the name of Philippines, in memory of His Majesty. The succor was sent to him immediately, and has been continually sent every year conformably to the necessities which have presented themselves; so that the land was won and maintained.

"The Commander-in-Chief having heard of other islands around Sebu with abundance of provisions, he sent thither a few Spaniards to bring some of the natives over in a friendly manner, and rice for the camp, with which he maintained himself as well as he could, until, having passed over to the island of Panay, he sent thence Martin de Goiti, his master of the camp, and other captains, with the men that seemed to him sufficient, to the side of Luzon, to endeavor to pacify it and bring it under submission to His Majesty; a native of that island, of importance, named Maomat was to guide them.

"Having arrived at the Bay of Manila, they found its town on the sea beach close to a large river, in the possession of, and fortified by a chief whom they called Rajamora; and in front across the river, there was another large town named Tondo; this was also held by another chief, named Rajamatanda. These places were fortified with palms, and thick arigues filled in with earth, and a great quantity of bronze cannon, and other large pieces with chambers. Martin de Goiti having began to treat with the chiefs and their people of the peace and submission which he claimed for them, it became necessary for him to break with them; and the Spaniards entered the town by force of arms, and took it, with the forts and artillery, on the day of Sta. Potenciana, the 19th of May, the year 1571; upon which the natives and their chiefs gave in, and made submission, and many others of the same island of Luzon did the same.

EARLY HISTORY OF THE PHILIPPINES.

"When the Commander-in-Chief, Legazpi, received news in Panay of the taking of Manila, and the establishment of the Spaniards there he left the affairs of Sebu, and of the other islands which had been subdued, set in order; and he entrusted the natives to the most trustworthy soldiers, and gave such orders as seemed fitting for the government of those provinces, which are commonly called the Visayas de los Pintados, because the natives there have their whole bodies marked with fire. He then came to Manila with the remainder of his people, and was very well received there: and established afresh with the natives and their chiefs the peace, friendship and submission to His Majesty which they had already offered. The Commander-in-Chief founded and established a town on the very site of Manila (of which Rajamora made a donation to the Spaniards for that purpose), on account of its being strong and in a well provisioned district, and in the midst of all the isles (leaving it its name of Manila, which it held from the natives). He took what land was sufficient for the city, in which the governor established his seat and residence; he fortified it with care, holding this object more especially in view, in order to make it the seat of government of this new settlement, rather than considering the temperature or width of the site, which is hot and narrow, from having the river on one side of the city, and the bay on the other, and at the back large swamps and marshes, which make it very strong.

"From this post he pursued the work of pacification of the other provinces of this great island of Luzon and of the surrounding districts; some submitting themselves willingly, others being conquered by force of arms, or by the industry of the monks who sowed the Holy Gospel, in which each and all labored valiantly, both in the time and governorship of the adelantado Miguel Lopez de Legazpi, and in that of other governors who succeeded him. The land was entrusted to those who had pacified it and settled in it, and heads named, on behalf of the crown, of the provinces, ports, towns, and cities, which were founded, together with other special commissions for necessities which might arise, and for the expenses of the royal exchequer. The affairs of the government, and conversion of the natives, were treated as was fit and necessary. Ships were provided each year to make the voyage to New Sapin, and to return with the usual supplies; so that the condition of the Philippine Islands, in spiritual and temporal matters, flourishes at the present day, as all know.

"The Commander-in-Chief, Miguel Lopez de Legazpi, as has been said, discovered the islands, and made a settlement in them, and gave a good beginning to their subjection and pacification. He founded the city of the Most Holy Name of Jesus in the provinces of the Pintados, and after that the city of Manila in the island of Luzon. He conquered there the province of Ylocos; and in its town and port, called Vigan, he founded a Spanish town, to which he gave the name of Villa Fernandina. So also he pacified the province of Pangasinan and the island of Mindoro. He fixed the rate of tribute which the natives had to pay in all the islands, and ordered many other matters relating to their government and conversion, until he died, in the year of 1574, at Manila, where his body lies buried in the monastery of St. Augustine.

"During the government of this Guido de Labazarris, trade and commerce were established between great China and Manila, ships coming each year with merchandise, and the governor giving them a good reception; so that every year the trade has gone on increasing."

The Encyclopaedia Britannica says that the Island Samai was called Filipina by Vellalohos, who sailed from Mexico in February, 1543. The capital was fixed at Manila in 1571, a distinction enjoyed three hundred and twenty-seven years. It was in a letter of Lagozpis in 1567 that the name Ilas Filipinos appeared for the first time.

The Dutch became very enterprising and venturesome in the Asiatic archipelagoes and gave the Philippines much attention, having many fights with the Spaniards. The Ladrones became well known as a resting place between the islands of Philip and New Spain—Mexico. The Chinese Pirates were troublesome, and the Spaniards, between the natives, the pirates and the Dutchmen, kept busy, and had a great deal of naval and military instruction. There were other varieties of life of an exciting character, in terrible storms and earthquakes. The storm season is the same in the Philippines as in the West Indies, and the tempests have like features. October is the cyclone and monsoon month. The most destructive storm in the island of Luzon of record was October 31st, 1876. Floods rolled from the mountains, and there was a general destruction of roads and bridges, and it is reported six thousand persons were killed.

So extensive and exposed is the Bay of Manila, it is one hundred and twenty knots in circumference—that it is not properly a harbor, but a stormy sheet of water. Admiral Dewey's fleet has had low steam in the boilers all the while to quickly apply the power of the engines for safety in case of a visitation from the dreaded typhoon, which comes on suddenly as a squall and rages with tornado intensity.

There are many volcanoes in the islands, and they exist from the North of Luzon to the Sulus in the extreme South, a distance as great as from Scotland to Sicily. There is one on Luzon that bears a close resemblance both in appearance

EARLY HISTORY OF THE PHILIPPINES. 271

and phenomena to Vesuvius. The likeness in eruptions is startling. The city of Manila has repeatedly suffered from destroying shocks, and slight agitations are frequent. Within historic times a mountain in Luzon collapsed, and a river was filled up while the earth played fountains of sand. The great volcano Taal, 45 miles south of Manila, is only 850 feet high, and on a small island in a lake believed to be a volcanic abyss, having an area of 100 square miles. Monte Cagua, 2,910 feet high, discharges smoke continually. In 1814 12,000 persons lost their lives on Luzon, the earth being disordered and rent in an appalling way. There were awful eruptions July 20 and October 24, 1867, forests of great trees buried in discharges of volcanoes. June 3, 1863, at 31 minutes after 7 in the evening, after a day of excessive heat, there was a shock at Manila lasting 30 seconds, in which 400 people were killed, 2,000 wounded, and 26 public and 570 private houses seriously damaged. The greater structures made heaps of fragments. That these calamities have taught the people lessons in building is apparent in every house, but one wonders that they have not taken even greater precautions. The forgetfulness of earthquake experiences in countries where they are familiar, always amazes those unaccustomed to the awful agitations and troubled with the anticipations of imagination. However, there never has been in the Philippines structural changes of the earth as great as in the center of the United States in the huge fissures opened and remaining lakes in the New Madrid convulsions.

In a surprising extent the Spanish government in the Philippines has been in the hands of the priests, especially the orders of the church. In the early centuries there was less cruel oppression than in Mexico and Peru. And yet there is in the old records a free-handed way of referring to killing people that shows a somewhat sanguinary state of society even including good citizens.

Blas Ruys de Herman Gonzales wrote to Dr. Morga from one of his expeditions, addressing his friend:

"To Dr. Antonio de Morga, Lieutenant of the Governor of the Filipine isles of Luzon, in the city of Manila, whom may our Lord preserve. From Camboia." This was in Cochin China, one of the Kings being in trouble, called upon Gonzales, who sympathized with him and wrote of the ceremony in which he assisted: "I came at his bidding, and he related to me how those people wished to kill him and deprive him of the kingdom, that I might give him a remedy. The Mambaray was the person who governed the kingdom, and as the king was a youth and yielded to wine, he made little account of him and thought to be king himself. At last I and the Spaniards killed him, and after that they caught his sons and killed them.

After that the capture of the Malay Cancona was undertaken, and he was killed, and there was security from this danger by means of the Spaniards. We then returned to the war, and I learned that another grandee, who was head of a province, wished to rise up, and go over to the side of Chupinanon; I seized him and killed him; putting him on his trial. With all this the King and kingdom loved us very much, and that province was pacified, and returned to the King. At this time a vessel arrived from Siam, which was going with an embassy to Manila, and put in here. There came in it Padre Fray Pedro Custodio. The King was much delighted at the arrival of the priest, and wished to set up a church for him."

Unquestionably there was degeneracy that began to have mastery in high places, and this can be distinctly made out early in this century, becoming more obvious in depravity, when Spain fell into disorder during the later years of the Napoleonic disturbances, and the authority and influence of Mexico were eliminated from Spain. I may offer the suggestion and allow it to vindicate its own importance, that if we have any Philippine Islands to spare, we should turn them over to the Republic of Mexico, taking in exchange Lower California and Sonora, and presenting those provinces to California to be incorporated in that State as counties. It was under Mexican rule that the Philippines were most peaceable and flourishing.

The late Government of the islands as revealed to the American officers who came into possession of Manila, was fearfully corrupt. It was proven by documents and personal testimony not impeachable, that a Captain-General's launch had been used to smuggle Mexican dollars, that the annual military expedition to the southern islands was a stated speculation of the Captain-General amounting to $200,000, in one case raised to $400,000, that the same high official made an excursion to all the custom houses on the islands ordered the money and books aboard his ship and never returned either, that one way of bribery was for presents to be made to the wives of officials of great power and distinction; one lady is named to whom business men when presenting a splendid bracelet, waited on her with two that she might choose the one most pleasing, and as she had two white arms, she kept both.

The frequent changes in Spanish rulers of the islands are accounted for by the demand for lucrative places, from the many favorites to whom it was agreeable and exemplary to offer opportunities to make fortunes. It goes hard with the deposed Spaniards that they had no chance to harvest perquisites, and must go home poor. This is as a fountain of little tears.

The city of Manila is not lofty in buildings, because it has been twice damaged to the verge of ruin by earthquakes and many times searched and shaken by tremendous gales, and is situated on the lands so low that it is not uplifted to the gaze of mankind—is not a city upon a hill, and yet it is "no mean city." Antonio de Morga says:

"The entrance of the Spaniards into the Philippines since the year 1564, and the subjection and conversion which has been effected in them, and their mode of government, and that which during these years His Majesty has provided and ordered for their good, has been the cause of innovation in many things, such as are usual to kingdoms and provinces which charge their faith and sovereign. The first has been that, besides the name of Philippines, which they took and received from the beginning of their conquest, all the islands are now a new kingdom and sovereignty, to which His Majesty Philip the Second, our sovereign, gave the name of New Kingdom of Castile, of which by his royal privilege, he made the city of Manila the capital, giving to it, as a special favor among others, a coat of arms with a crown, chosen and appointed by his royal person, which is a scutcheon divided across, and in the upper part a castle on the red field, and in the lower part a lion of gold, crowned and rampant, with a naked sword in the dexter hand, and half the body in the shape of a dolphin upon the waters of the sea, signifying that the Spaniards passed over them with arms to conquer this kingdom for the crown of Castile.

"The Commander-in-Chief, Miguel Lopez de Legazpi, first governor of the Philippines, founded the city of Manila, in the isle of Luzon, in the same site in which Rajamora had his town and fort (as has been said more at length), at the mouth of the river which pours out into the bay, on a point which is formed between the river and the sea. He occupied the whole of it with this town and divided it among the Spaniards in equal building plots, with streets and blocks of houses regularly laid out, straight and level leaving a great place, tolerably square, where he erected the cathedral church and municipal buildings; and another place of arms, in which stood the fort and there also the royal buildings; he gave sites to the monasteries and hospital and chapels, which would be built, as this was a city which would grow and increase every day, as has already happened; because in the course of time which passed by, it has become as illustrious as the best cities of all those parts.

"The whole city is surrounded by a wall of hewn stone of more than two and a half yards in width, and in parts more than three, with small towers and traverses at intervals; it has a fortress of hewn stone at the point, which guards the bar and the river, with a ravelin close to the water, which contains a few heavy pieces of artillery which command the sea and the river, and other guns on the higher part of the fort for the defense of the bar, besides other middling-sized field guns and swivel guns, with vaults for supplies and munitions, and a powder magazine, with its inner space well protected, and an abundant well of fresh water; also quarters for soldiers and artillerymen and a house for the Commandant. It is newly fortified on the land side, in the place of arms, where the entrance is through a good wall, and two salient towers furnished with artillery which command the wall and gate. This fortress named Santiago, has a detachment of thirty soldiers, with their officers, and eight artillerymen, who guard the gate and entrance in watches, under the command of an alcalde who lives within, and has the guard and custody of it.

"There is another fortress, also of stone, in the same wall, at the ditance of the range of a culverin, at the end of the wall which runs along the shore of the bay; this is named Nuestra Senora de Guia; it is a very large round block, with its courtyard, water and quarters, and magazines and other workshops within; it has an outwork jutting out towards the beach, in which there are a dozen of large and middle-sized guns, which command the bay, and sweep the walls which run from it to the port and fort of Santiago. On the further side it has a large salient tower with four heavy pieces, which command the beach further on, towards the chapel of Nuestra Senora de Guia. The gate and entrance of this is within the city, it is guarded by a detachment of twenty soldiers, with their officers, and six artillerymen, a commandant, and his lieutenant, who dwell within.

"On the land side, where the wall extends, there is a bastion called Sant Andres, with six pieces of artillery, which can fire in all directions, and a few swivel guns; and further on another outwork called San Gabriel, opposite the parian of the Sangleys, with the same number of cannon, and both these works have some soldiers and an ordinary guard.

"The wall is sufficiently high, with battlements and turrets for its defense in the modern fashions; they have a circuit of a league, which may be traversed on the top of the walls, with many stairs on the inside at intervals, of the same stonework, and three principal city gates, and many other posterns to the river and beach for the service of the city in convenient places. All of these gates are shut before nightfall by the ordinary patrol, and the keys are carried to the guard-room of the royal buildings; and in the morning, when it is day, the patrol returns with them and opens the city.

"The royal magazines are in the parade; in them are deposited and kept all the munitions and supplies, cordage, iron, copper, lead, artillery, arquebuses, and other things belonging to the royal treasury, with their special officials and workmen, who are under the command of the royal officers.

AN INSURGENT OUTLOOK NEAR MANILA.

DISPLAY IN MANILA PHOTOGRAPH GALLERY. INSURGENT LEADERS.

GROUP OF FILIPINOS WHO WANT INDEPENDENCE.

"Close to these magazines is the powder magazine, with its master, officials, and convicts, in which, on ordinary occasions, thirty mortars grind powder, and that which is damaged is refined.

"In another part of the city, in a convenient situation, is the cannon foundry, with its moulds, furnaces, and instrument founders, and workmen, who carry on the works.

"The royal buildings are very handsome, with a good view, and very roomy, with many windows opening seaward and to the parade; they are all of hewn stone, with two courts and high and low corridors with thick pillars."

The city of to-day verifies the descriptive talent and accuracy of this writer.

CHAPTER XVIII.

THE SOUTHERN PHILIPPINES.

Important Facts About the Lesser Islands of the Philippine Archipelago—Location, Size and Population—Capitals and Principal Cities—Rivers and Harbors—Surface and Soil—People and Products—Leading Industries—Their Commerce and Business Affairs—The Monsoons and Typhoons—The Terrors of the Tempests and How to Avoid Them.

The island and province of Mindoro lies in the strait of its name and south of Luzon. It has in the center an elevated plain, we quote from the military notes issued by the War Department, from which many sierras extend in different directions to the coast, making the latter rugged and dangerous. The island is of an oval form, with a prolongation of the northern portion toward the west. Though an easy day's sail from Manila, it is one of the least populous islands of the archipelago, being extremely mountainous, covered with dense forests, and in the more level parts near the coast full of marshes, and very unhealthful. The inhabitants of the coast are Tagals, but in the interior there is a low tribe of the Malayan race, probably the indigenes of the island, and called Manguianos, speaking a peculiar language and living in a very miserable manner on the products of a rude agriculture. There are also said to be some Negritos, but of these very little is known. There are many short streams. The island is 110 miles long and has an area of 3,087 square miles. The population is 106,170. There is little known of the mountains of the interior, as the inhabitants dwell mainly on the coasts. Mindoro constitutes one of the provinces of the Philippines under an alcalde.

The capital is Calapan, with a population of 5,585. It is situated to the north, on the harbor of its name, defended by a fort of regular construction; it has about 500 houses, among the notable stone ones being the parish, court house and jail, and casa real. It is the rsidence of the alcalde mayor and several public functionaries. The city is situated 96 miles from Manila.

Mount Kalavite is a long-backed promontory, the western slope of which forms Cape Kalavite, and the northern slope Point del Monte; the summit, about 2,000 feet high, appears dome-shaped when seen from the west, but from the north or south it shows a long ridge fairly level; the western end of this ridge is the highest part.

The capital of the province, Calapan, is a coast town. The inhabitants are occupied in hunting, fishing, and ordinary weaving. The commerce is insignificant. Sand banks extend in front of the town to a distance of one-half mile. To clear these, the northern Silonai islet should not be shut out by Point Calapan. On this line, near the north edge of the banks, the soundings are 36 to 46 fathoms.

The Semirara Islands form a group of eight islands, all surrounded by reefs.

Semirara, the largest of the group, is hilly, about 512 feet high at the highest part. The west coast includes several little bays almost entirely obstructed by reefs, on the edge of which are depths of 4¾ to 13 fathoms; and off the town of Semirara, which stands on the top of the hill facing the largest bay, the anchorage is very bad, even for coasters. The east coast is bordered by a reef, which extends about a mile from the northeast part of the island; on coming from the north this coast of the island must not be approached within three miles until the town of Semirara bears full west. There is anchorage at the south of the island in 5 to 8 fathoms, sand, during the northeast monsoon. Good coal for steaming purposes was found on the island by Captain Villavicencio, of the Spanish navy.

Tablas Island is mountainous, and on its northern extremity is the peak Cabezo de Tablas, 2,405 feet high; generally the coasts are clear and steep-to. Off the north end are two rocky islets, distant one cable from the coast; the larger one is clear and steep, the smaller one has rocks around it.

The west coast of Mindoro Island has no soundings off it excepting in the bays, or within one or two miles of the shore in some places. In the interior double and treble chains of mountains extend through the island, and some low points of land project from them into the sea.

Paluan Bay affords excellent shelter in the northeast monsoon, and is also a convenient place for vessels to obtain supplies when passing through Mindoro Strait. The bay is five miles wide at the entrance, of a semi-circular form, running back three miles in a northerly direction. There are no dangers in it.

A small river disembogues where good water can be obtained with facility; and on the beach there is plenty of driftwood. The coral projects one-half mile from the entrance of the river, and has 10 and 12 fathoms close to its edge.

Care must be taken when working into Paluan Bay, for the squalls come violently off the high land, and very sudden, and at night do not give the least warning.

The Calamianes are a group of high islands lying between the northeast end of Palawan and Mindoro, and extending between the parallels of 11 degrees 39 minutes and 12 degrees 20 minutes N., and the meridians of 119 degrees 47 minutes and 120 degrees 23 minutes E. Busuanga, the largest island of the group, is about 34 miles in extent NW. by W. and SE. by E., and 18 miles broad. It is very irregular in form, being indented with numerous deep bays. The islands and reefs which front its northeast side form the western side of Northumberland Strait.

These islands form, with the northern part of Palawan and the Cuyos Islands, a province, the capital of which is at Port Tai Tai. The climate of these islands is in general hot and unhealthful. Intermittent fevers and cutaneous diseases prevail, attributable, in all probability, to the great moisture and the insalubrious quality of the drinking water. All these islands are, generally speaking, hilly and broken. The industry of the locality is in collecting Salanganes (edible birds' nests), honey, and wax; but cultivation is not practiced to any great extent. The forests produce good timber for building or cabinet work.

Tara Island, when seen from the northward, shows a triple summit to its northwest end; while its southern part looks like a separate island, saddle-shaped. The island does not appear to be permanently inhabited; in March, 1885, it was occupied by parties from Busuanga, burning the grass and digging cassava.

Lagat is a small island 334 feet high, surrounded by a reef with a narrow passage between it and the reef off the south of Tara.

Botak Island, 800 feet high, is fairly well cultivated. Off its northern end there is a queer pin-shaped rock, and off its southern end are same sharp-pointed rocks. The vicinity has not been sounded.

The space included between the Sulu Archipelago to the south and Mindoro to the north, and having the Philippine Islands on the east and Palawan on the west, is distinguished by the name of the Sulu Sea. Although of great depth, 2,550 fathoms, this sea, which is in connection with the China and Celebes seas, and also with the Pacific by San Bernardino and Surigao straits, has a minimum deep-sea temperature of 50.5 degrees, reached invariably at 400 fathoms. As this temperature in the China Sea is at the depth of 200 fathoms, and in the Celebes Sea at 180 fathoms, and in the Pacific at 230 fathoms, it may be inferred that the Sulu Sea is prevented from freely interchanging its waters with those seas by ridges which do not exceed those depths.

In the Sulu Sea easterly winds with fine weather prevail in October, and the northeast monsoon is not established until November. In January and February it blows hardest, but not with the force of the China seas, and it is felt strongest before the openings between Panay and Negros, and Negros and Mindanao. At the end of May southwest winds begin to blow, and in a month become established, to terminate in October, bringing with them a season made up of rain squalls and tem-

THE PRINCIPAL GATE TO THE WALLED CITY.

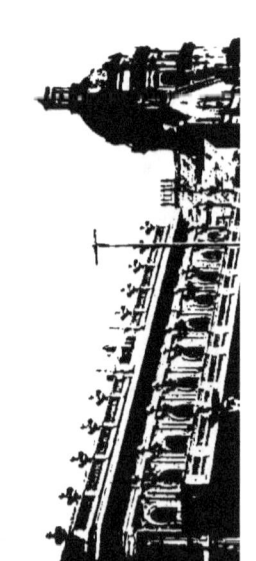

THE SOUTHERN PHILIPPINES.

posts, which take place principally in July and August. In September a heavy mist hangs about the coast of Mindanao.

The island and province of Paragua is the most western of the Philippine Archipelago, and is situated to the north of Borneo. It is long and narrow, following a northeast direction, and nearly closes on the southwest the Sea of Mindanao, which enters from the China Sea by Balabac Strait on the south and between Mindoro and Paragua on the north. A chain of high mountains, some 6,560 feet high, runs lengthwise of the narrow belt formed by the island, whose length is 266 miles. The northwest and northeast slopes are narrow. The island has extensive and well protected harbors and bays. The area is 2,315 square miles and the population 45,000.

The capital is Puerto Princesa, with a population of 1,589.

Panay is divided into three provinces, viz: Capiz to the north, Iloilo to the southeast, and Antique to the southwest. In general it is wild, with very high coasts, except in the northeastern part, where the latter are somewhat marshy. A mountain chain crosses the island from Point Juraojurao on the south as far as Point Potol on the north, following a direction almost parallel to the western coast. Large groups of sierras branch out to the right and left of the central chain; on the eastern slope begins another chain, running northeast to the extreme northeasterly point of the island. Owing to its cragginess, it has a great number of streams running in different directions. The area is 4,540 square miles.

The town of Iloilo stands on a low sandy flat on the right bank of a river; at the end of this flat is a spit on which a fort is built, and close to which there is deep water. Vessels of moderate draft (15 feet) can ascend the river a short distance and lie alongside wharves which communicate with the merchant houses, but large vessels must anchor outside near the spit. It is a town of great commercial importance, and a brisk coasting trade is carried on from it. The better class of houses in Iloilo are built on strong wooden posts, 2 or 3 feet in diameter, that reach to the roof; stone walls to the first floor, with wooden windows above, and an iron roof. The poorer class of dwellings are flimsy erections of nipa, built on four strong posts. The roads and bridges are in a deplorable condition and almost impassable in the rainy season.

The chief imports are Australian coal, and general merchandise from Europe, but most sailing ships arrive in ballast.

The exports are sugar, tobacco, rice, coffee, hides, and hemp; it is also the principal place of manufacture of piña, jusc, and sinamoya, a tissue greatly in use among the Philippines. In 1883, 93,750 tons of sugar were exported, principally to America.

Typhoons do not occur regularly, but in most years the tail of one passes over the place, which suffers also from the visitations of locusts.

Provisions of all kinds can be obtained, but the prices are higher than at Manila. In 1886 beef was 12½ cents per pound, bread 11 cents, vegetables 11 cents, fowls $2 per dozen. Water is scarce and is brought across from Guimaras in tank boats; it is supplied to the shipping at the rate of $1 per ton; the Europeans depend mainly upon rain water.

There are generally about 500 tons of coal in store, chiefly Australian; it is kept for the supply of local steamers that take in what they require alongside the wharves. Vessels in the roads can have it brought off in bulk in lighters or schooners at a cost of 50 cents a ton. Coolies can be hired at 75 cents per ton, but they will not coal vessels if they can get other work. Notice is required the day before coaling, as men are not kept in readiness. The price of coal in 1886 was $11.00 per ton.

There is regular weekly communication with Manila, which is 250 miles distant.

The Province of Capiz is bounded on the north by the Archipelago Sea, on the east by the District of Concepcion, on the south by the ridge separating it from Iloilo, and on the southwest by the mountains, separating it from the Province of Antique. Its very high mountains are covered with luxuriant vegetation, and give rise to many rivers which water the valleys of the province. There are gold and copper mines, and much tobacco, sugar, rice, and abaca is raised. During the year three fairs are held, in which articles of the country are bartered. The province is divided into two parts, called Ilaya and Aclan, which are irrigated by the rivers Panay and Adan, respectively. The area is 1,543 square miles and the population 189,171, distributed among 36 pueblos and 287 barrios.

The capital is Capiz, with a population of 13,676. It is situated 290 miles from Manila. It has a harbor for vessels of ordinary draft, and highroads to Iloilo, Antique, and the District of Concepcion. There is a steamer kept by the state, stopping at the harbor every 28 days and keeping up communication with Manila, Romblon, Iloilo, and Cebu.

The Province of Iloilo is to the southeast of the Province of Capiz and west of Antique. The ground is generally level, and, being irrigated by numerous rivers, is fertile, so that tobacco, cacao, sugar cane, abaca, rice, and maize are grown; besides, there is good pasturage for raising herds of cattle and horses, and gold and other mines are known. The principal industry is the manufacture of fabrics of sinamay, pina, jusi, etc., requiring over 30,000 looms. The dimensions are 99 miles in length by 27 miles in width, and the population is 472,728.

The capital is Iloilo, with a population of 10,380. It is situated 355 miles from Manila, and is the residence of the governor, captain of port, and a number of treasury, justice, and fomento officials. It has a pretty cathedral, a seminary, casa real, and court house. It is one of the most mercantile towns of the Visaya group, and has some industries, among which are a machine shop and foundry, a carriage factory, and a hat factory.

The Province of Bohol is bounded on the north by the sea between Cebu and Leyte, on the east by the Surigao Sea, on the south by the Sea of Mindanao, and on the west by the channel separating it from Cebu. The province is composed of the islands of Bohol and Dauis. They are somewhat mountainous and well wooded, and coffee, abaca, sugar cane, and tobacco are raised. In the mountains of Bohol game is plenty, and many coal and phosphate of iron mines are supposed to exist. Manufactures consist in fabrics of sinamay and other materials. The area is 1,617 square miles and the population 247,745.

The capital is Tagbilaran, with a population of 8,638. It is situated 365 miles from Manila.

The island and province of Cebu are the most important of the Visayas, on account of the central position, nature of the soil, and the industry of its numerous inhabitants. It is bounded on the north by the sea separating it from Masbate and Leyte, on the east by the sea separating it from Leyte and Bohol, on the south by the Mindanao Sea, and on the west by the Tanon Channel and the island of Negros. The area is 2,092 square miles and the population 504,076. Great mountain chains cross the island; the chief of these starts at the extreme north between Point Marab on the west and Baluarte on the east, and, continuing south between the two coasts, ends almost in the center of the island. Two other chains run along the coast, and one starts near Carcas, to the southwest of the city of Cebu, terminating on the south in Tanon Point. The coasts are high and the rivers of little importance.

The capital is Cebu, with a population of 35,243. It is the mercantile center of the islands, and is situated 460 miles from Manila. It is an Episcopal see, and has a good cathedral, Episcopal palace, casa real, court house, and private edifices, simple but tasty; there is also a postoffice and telegraph station. On the south, and at the entrance of the channel, is the castle of Point Cauit, and north of this the tower of Mandaui; both these fortifications communicate with the capital by means of a wagon road, the city being midway between them. At the capital reside the politico-military governor, a secretary, judge and attorney-general, a number of public functionaries, a captain of engineers, and the captain of the port.

THE SOUTHERN PHILIPPINES.

Maktan Island consists of an old coral reef, raised a few feet (8 or 10 at most) above the present sea level. At the northern part of the island, where a convent stands, a low cliff fringes the shore, being an upper stratum of the upheaved reef. The raised reef is here preserved, but over the portion of the island immediately fronting Cebu it has been removed by denudation, with the exception of a few pillar-like blocks which remain, and which are conspicuous from the anchorage. The surface is scooped out into irregular basins and sharp projecting pinnacles and covered in all directions with mud, resulting from the denudation. Nearly all the island is covered by mangroves, but on the part left dry there are plantations of cocoanuts.

The only town on the island is Opon, on the west coast, SW. of Mandaui Point in Cebu. It was here that Magellan was killed in 1521, after making the first passage across the Pacific.

The town of Cebu is the most ancient in the Philippines; it is the seat of government of the Visayan Islands, which include Cebu, Bohol, Panay, Negros, and Leyte, and it is the residence of a bishop. It is built on a large plain at the foot of the chain of hills that traverse the island throughout its length, and is a well-constructed, thriving place; the merchants' quarter is situated along the port, and includes some well-built stone houses, though many are of old construction. The huts of the Malays, for the most part fishermen, are on the beach, and form the west part of the city. The fort is a triangular edifice of stone, painted red, with an open square in front.

The island of Leyte is bounded on the north by the canal separating it from Samar, on the east by the Pacific Ocean, on the west by the sea separating it from Bohol and Cebu, and on the south by the one separating it from Mindanao. It is extensive and irregular, having an area of 3,087 square miles and a population of 210,491. A high and abrupt mountain chain crosses the island nearly parallel to the west coast; the coasts are high, with good natural harbors. In the northern part and on the western slopes of the great sierras, streams of potable water and also many lagoons abound. This is different from the eastern part, where the latter are scarce. The principal product of the island is abaca, but rice is also raised and cocoanut oil is extracted. There are unworked mines of gold, magnetite, and sulphur.

The capital is Tacloban, with a population of 5,226. It is situated 338 miles from Manila. Among the important towns are Baru, population 12,222; Borauen. 21,290; Cauyaia, 13,732; Dagami, 25,000; Hilongos, 13,713; Jaio, 12,475; Massin. 18,199; Palo, 17,736; Tauauau, 18,509.

The island of Negros is mountainous and wild; its coasts are difficult of access. and the breakers strong. except on the west coast from Point Bulucabo on the north of Palompon on the west, where it is marshy. A high mountain chain crosses it from Point Doong on the north to the harbor and point Bombonon on the south; from the last third extend several ramifications of high mountains, terminating on the coast at the extreme south and in the Sierra Dumaguete. Its streams are not important, being short and of little value. The ground is uneven but fertile. The natives irrigate their estates, and produce tobacco, coffee, sugar cane, and wheat. Manufactures consist in fabrics of abaca and canonegro, of which boat cables are made. The interior of the island, covered with thick forests, is almost unexplored, being inhabited by a few savages.

The Province of Western Negros is situated on Negros Island, it is bounded on the north by the Visayas Sea, on the west by the Paragua Sea, and on the south and east by the Province of Eastern Negros. The area is 1,929 square miles, and the population 226,995.

The capital is Bacolod, with a population of 6,268. It is the residence of the politico-military governor, the secretary, judge, attorney-general, and several public functionaries.

It is situated 379 miles from Manila.

The Province of Negros has a population of 94,782—the capital, Dumaguete, 13,613.

The Province of Romblon consists of the following six islands: Romblon (the principal one), Tablas, Sibuyan, Banton, Simara, and Maestre Campo. It is bounded on the north by the Tayabas Sea, on the south by the Visayas Sea, on the east by the Sea of Masbate, and on the west by the Sea of Mindoro. The area is 813 square miles, and the population 38,633, distributed among 13 barrios and 3 rancherias of infieles.

The capital is Romblon, with a population of 6,764. It is situated on the harbor of the same name at the north of the island, 204 miles from Manila, and is the residence of the politico-military commander.

The Island and Province of Samar is situated to the southeast of Luzon, it is bounded on the north by the Strait of San Bernardino, on the south by the Jahanetes Canal, separating it from Leyte Island, on the east by the Pacific Ocean, and on the west by the Visayas Sea. It is very mountainous, with high, steep coasts. A number of sierras and mountains extend in various directions, forming valleys and glens fertilized by numerous rivers, which, however, have little current and volume. The length of the island is 155 miles. The chief products are abaca, rice, and cocoanuts, oil being extracted from the latter. Among the medicinal plants the most highly valued is the catbalonga seed. Commerce is quite active in spite of the few means of communication and the dangerous coasts. The island is visited yearly by tornadoes which devastate crops and cause much damage to agriculture. The high mountains and thick forests of the interior are inhabited by a great number of savages who have sought refuge here. The area is 4,699 square miles, and the population 200,753, distributed among 43 pueblos, 208 visitas, and 3 rancherias of subdued infieles.

The capital is Catbalogan, population of 6,459, situated on the harbor and bay of like name on the west of the island 338 miles from Manila, and is the residence of the politico-military governor.

The Jolo Archipelago, formed of some 160 islands, is situated southwest of Mindanao and south of Basilan. It is bounded on the south by the Jolo Sea, on the northeast by Mindanao and on the west and southwest by Borneo. The small islands are covered with mangroves, while the large ones have thick forests of good timber, and the natives raise rice, maize, and various alimentary roots, ambergris being found on the coasts. The principal island, called Sulu, or Jolo (ch. 47, 48, 49, 50, p. 285), is occupied in a military way by the Spanish forces, whose chief, or governor, resides in the old capital, which has well-constructed and armed forts, a pier, etc. By royal decree of November 13, 1877, the sultanship was transformed into a civico-military government. The population consists of 500 aborigines, 612 Chinese traders, and 16,000 negroes.

Next to Luzon, the island of Mindanao is the most extensive and important of the Philippines.

By decree of July 30, 1860, the territorial division of this island was definitely established, and a civico-military government, under the denomination of Mindanao and adjacent islands, was created. It is divided into eight districts. The island is situated between Visayas on the north and Borneo on the south; it is bounded on the east by the Pacific Ocean, and on the west by the island of Paragua, the Strait of Balabac, and Borneo. The area is 16,595 square miles, and the population 611,300, of which 211,000 are Christians and the rest Mohammedans and Pagans. It is very extensive and irregular in form, possessing high and extended mountain chains, which have not been entirely explored, and which are grown over with very rich woods. It is inhabited almost throughout the interior by savages. Its rivers, some of great volume, are as follows: On the north coast and Butuan Bay, the Jabonga and Butuan; on the Macajalar coast, the Cagayan; in Eligan Bay, the Malanao and others of minor importance; in the cove of Dapitan, the Palaven.

In Port Kakule the greatest rise of tide is seven feet. In Surigao Strait the flood tide sets to the west, and the ebb to the east. The velocity of the stream in the strait reaches six knots at springs. There is a difference of about two hours between the time of high water at Surigao and in Surigao Strait. Fishermen roughly estimate that when the moon rises the ebb tide commences to run in Surigao Strait. From January to June there is but one high water during the twenty-four hours, in Surigao Strait, which occurs during the night. From July to December the same phenomenon takes place, but the time of high water is by day.

From observations made by the Spanish surveyors, it appears that the highest tide on the west coasts of the islands of the strait takes place at the same hour as the lowest tide on the east coasts.

The Mindanao river disembogues five miles to the south of Palak Harbor by two wide arms, on the northernmost of which is the town of Kota-batu, about $5\frac{1}{4}$ miles from the mouth. The river is navigable for 60 miles by vessels of $3\frac{1}{2}$ feet draught: it flows through a beautiful valley 30 miles in width, which scarcely shows any change of level; the valley is capable of producing tobacco, cacao, sugar, maize, and cotton; but this is only known at present by specimens produced. The course of the river lies SE. for 45 miles from its mouth to the lake Liguanasan, out of which it is seen to flow; from the other side of the lake the direction of the river is NNE. to its source in the Sugut Mountains. At 21 miles from the northern mouth the river divides into two arms, which enter the sea $4\frac{1}{2}$ miles apart.

In the northern part of Mindanao is the province of Surigao, bordered on the north by the Surigao Sea, on the east by the Pacific, on the south by the District of Davao, and on the west by the territory of the inficles. It is mountainous, but the Christian population resides on the coasts and in the northern point of the territory. The population is 95,775, distributed among 45 pueblos, 10 barrios, and 30 rancherias of subdued inficles. Abaca and palay are raised, and in the gold washings considerable gold of good quality is found.

Military notes on the Philippines affirm that the islands are, in many respects, Spain's best possessions. due to the abundance and variety of products, numerous and good ports, character of inhabitants, and on account of the vicinity of certain countries of eastern Asia, which are now entering upon a stage of civilization and commerce. The group is composed of some 2,000 islands. In 1762 Manila was taken and held by the English for a ransom of 1,000,000 pounds sterling. This, however, was never paid, and the islands were finally returned to Spain.

The archipelago extends from 5 degrees 32 minutes to 19 degrees 38 minutes, north latitude, and from 117 degrees to 126 degrees, east longitude. It thus covers about 1,000 miles north and south and 600 east and west.

The whole surface of the Philippines is essentially mountainous, the only plains that occur being alluvial districts at the river mouths and the spaces left by the intersection of the ranges. The principal ranges have a tendency to run north and south, with a certain amount of deflection east and west, as the case may be, so that the orographic diagram of the archipelago, as a whole, has a similarity to a fan, with northern Luzon as its center of radiation.

While none of the mountain peaks greatly exceed 8,000 feet in height, Apo, in Mindanao, is over 9,000 feet; Halson, in Mindoro, is over 8,900 feet; and Mayon, in Luzon, over 8,200. The latter is an active volcano, which has been the scene of several eruptions during the present century. Extinct or active craters are relatively as numerous in the Philippines as in the eastern archipelago, and as a consequence of these subterranean forces earthquakes are frequent and violent.

In 1627 one of the most elevated mountains of Cagayan disappeared, and on the island of Mindanao, in 1675, a passage was opened to the sea and a vast plain emerged. The more recent of the convulsions occurred in 1863 and in 1880. The destruction of property was great, especially in Manila.

The general belief is that the Philippines once formed a part of an enormous continent from which it was separated by some cataclysm. This continent probably extended from Celebes to the farthest Polinesian islands on the east, to New Zealand on the south, and the Mariana and Sandwich islands on the north.

These islands, according to Ramon Jordana, are divided into two volcanic regions, the eastern and the western. The principal point is the volcano Taal, located in the northeastern portion of the province of Batangas. It is situated on a small island in the center of the Bombon laguna, and has an altitude of 550 feet above sea level. Its form is conical, and the rock is composed of basalt feldspar with a small quantity of augite. The crater is supposed to be 232 feet deep. Its sides are almost vertical, and there are two steaming lagunas at its bottom.

In the regions embracing the provinces of Manila, Bulacan, Pampanga, Tarlac, and Pangasinan the soil is mostly composed of clay containing remnants of sea shells, a circumstance which gives rise to the belief that the coast of Manila has risen from the sea in not so remote an epoch. Smooth, dark gray tophus predominates; it forms the bed of the Rio Pasig, and rising forms hillocks in the vicinity of the city of Binangonan. Farther on, trachyte and banks of conchiferous sand predominate.

The vast plain of Panpanga extends to the north of Manila Bay, to the south of which is situated Mount Arayat, of doleritic nature.

The disposition of the mountain ranges in parallel chains affords space for the development of streams both in Luzon and Mindanao. The larger islands contain inland seas, into which pour countless small streams from the inland hills. Many of them open out into broad estuaries, and in numerous instances coasting vessels of light draft can sail to the very foot of the mountains. Rivers and inland lakes swarm with varieties of fish and shellfish. By reason of Spanish restrictions, but little can be said as to the character of the stream banks and beds. Four of the rivers are navigable, and, by the statements of those who have spent some little time on the islands, most are fordable. Drinking water is obtained by many of the towns from the rivers at points just above tide limits, and the water is said to be good. Bridges are few and crude, but are generally built to withstand heavy strain.

The island of Luzon abounds in rivers and streams. The following are the principal water courses:

Rio Grande de Cagayan, the source of which is in the northern slope of the Caraballo Norte. It has numerous affluents, among others the Magat and Bangag, and, after a course of about 200 miles, falls into the China Sea in the vicinity of Aparri.

Agno Grande starts in the north, in the neighborhood of the ranch of Loo, receives the affluents Tarlag and Camiling, as well as many others, has a course of about 112 miles, and falls into the Gulf of Lingayen.

Abra has its origin on the opposite slope to that where Agno Grande takes its rise; runs for about 87 miles, and, after receiving the affluent Suyoc, divides into three arms and falls into the China Sea over the sand bars of Butao, Nioig, and Dile.

Rio Grande de la Pampanga is called Rio Chico up to the lake of Canasen, near Arayat, where it changes its name after its junction with Rio Gapan. Its course is a little over 38 miles; it receives the Rio de San Jose and divides into a multitude of arms as it falls into the sea to the north of Manila Bay.

Rio Pasig has its source in the Bay Lagoon, and falls after a course of 19 miles into Manila Bay.

The military notes on the climate of the Philippines, the official record of the temperature and the gales and typhoons, and directions regarding the handling of ships in the peculiar tempests that prevail at certain seasons around the islands, are of absorbing popular interest, and of striking special usefulness.

Climate.—In the region of Manila the hottest season is from March to June, the greatest heat being felt in May before the rains set in, when the maximum temperature ranges from 80 degrees to 100 degrees in the shade. The coolest weather occurs in December and January, when the temperature falls at night to 60 or 65 degrees, and seldom rises in the day above 75 degrees. From November to February the sky is bright, the atmosphere cool and dry, and the weather in every way delightful. Observations made at the Observatortio Meteorologico de Manila have been compiled by the United States Weather Bureau, covering a record of from seventeen to thirty-two years, from which the following is an extract:

Temperature, degrees F.:
    Mean annual.. 80 degrees
    Warmest month... 82 degrees
    Coolest month.. 79 degrees
    Highest..100 degrees
    Lowest... 60 degrees

Humidity:
    Relative per cent....................................... 78
    Absolute grains per cubic foot........................... 8.75

Wind movements in miles:
    Daily mean... 134
    Greatest daily... 204
    Least daily.. 95

Prevailing wind direction—NE., November to April; SW., May to October.
    Cloudiness, annual per cent............................. 53
    Days with rain... 135

Rainfall in inches:
    Mean annual... 75.43
    Greatest monthly...................................... 120.98
    Least monthly... 55.65

The following is the mean temperature for the three seasons, at points specified:

	Cold.	Hot.	Wet.
Manila	72 degrees	87 degrees	84 degrees
Cebu	75 degrees	86 degrees	75 degrees
Davao	86 degrees	88 degrees	87 degrees
Sulu	81 degrees	82 degrees	83 degrees

Seasons vary with the prevailing winds (monsoons or trade winds) and are classed as "wet" and "dry." There is no abrupt change from one to the other, and between periods there are intervals of variable weather.

The Spanish description of seasons is as follows:

Seis meses de lodo—six months of mud.

Seis meses de polvo—six months of dust.

Seis meses de todo—six months of everything.

The northern islands lie in the track of the typhoons which, developing in the

Pacific, sweep over the China Sea from NE. to SW. during the southwest monsoon. They may be looked for at any time between May and November, but it is during the months of July, August, and September that they are most frequent. Early in the season the northern region feels the greatest force, but as the season advances the typhoon gradually works southward and the dangerous time at Manila is about the end of October and the beginning of November. Typhoons rarely, if ever, pass south of 9 degrees N. latitude. Sometimes the typhoon is of large diameter and travels slowly, so far as progressive movement is concerned; at others it is of smaller dimensions, and both the circular and progressive motions are more rapid. However they are always storms of terrific energy and frequently cause terrible destruction of crops and property on shore and of shipping at sea. Thunderstorms, often of great violence, are frequent in May and June, before the commencement of the rainy season. During July, August, September, and October the rains are very heavy. The rivers and lakes are swollen and frequently overflow, flooding large tracts of low country.

At Manila the average rainfall is stated to be from 75 to 120 inches per annum, and there the difference between the longest and shortest day is only 1 hour 47 minutes and 12 seconds. This rainfall, immense though it be, is small as compared with that of other parts of the archipelago; e. g., in Liano, NE. of Mindanao, the average yearly downpour is 142 inches.

Gales.—The gales of the Philippines may be divided into three classes, known by the local names of Colla, Nortada, and Baguio. The Colla is a gale in which the wind blows constantly from one quarter, but with varying force and with alternations of violent squalls, calms, and heavy rains, usually lasting at least three days; these gales occur during the southwest monsoon and their direction is from the southwest quarter. The Nortada is distinguished from the Collo, in that the direction is constant and the force steady, without the alternations of passing squalls and calms. The Nortada is generally indicative that a typhoon is passing not very far off. These gales occur chiefly in the northern islands, and their direction, as the name implies, is from the northward. Baguio is the local name for the revolving storm known as the typhoon, which, being the more familiar term, will be used in these notes

Typhoons.—These storms have their origin to the east or to the southeast of the Philippines, whence their course is westward, with a slight divergence to the north or south, the average direction appearing to be west by north. They occur in all months of the year, but the greater number take place about the time of the equinoxes. The most violent ones occur at the autumnal equinox, and on an average, two or three occur every year, and sometimes one follows another at a very short interval. It is believed that when one of these typhoons passes a high latitude in September there will be another in October of that year, and one may be looked for in November in a lower latitude. These tempests are not encountered in latitudes below 9 degrees N. The rate of progress of these storms is about 13 miles an hour; in none of those observed has it exceeded 14 miles nor fallen below 11 miles. The diameter of the exterior revolving circle of the storm varies from 40 to 130 miles, and the diameter of the inner circle or calm region, may be estimated at from 8 to 15 miles. The duration of the true typhoon at any one place is never longer than ten hours and generally much less. These storms are always accompanied by abundant rain, with low, dense clouds, which at times limit the horizon to a few yards distance, and are generally accompanied by electrical discharges. The barometer falls slowly for some days before the typhoon, then falls rapidly on its near approach, and reaches its lowest when the vortex is but a little way off. It then rises rapidly as the vortex passes away, and then slowly when it has gained some distance. Near the vortex there are usually marked oscillations. The typhoon generally begins with a northerly wind, light drizzling rain, weather squally and threatening, a falling barometer and the wind veering to the eastward, when the observer is to the northward of the path of the storm, and backing to the westward when he is to the southward of it; the wind and rain increase as the wind shifts, and the storm generally ends with a southerly wind after abating gradually.

The following warnings of the approach of a typhoon, and directions for avoiding the most dangerous part of it, are taken from the China Sea Directory: The earliest signs of a typhoon are clouds of a cirrus type, looking like fine hair, feathers or small white tufts of wool, traveling from east or north, a slight rise in the barometer, clear and dry weather, and light winds. These signs are followed by the usual ugly and threatening appearance of the weather which forebodes most storms, and the increasing number and severity of the gusts with the rising of the wind. In some cases one of the earliest signs is a long heavy swell and confused sea, which comes from the direction in which the storm is approaching, and travels more rapidly than the storm's center. The best and surest of all warnings, however, will be found in the barometer. In every case there is great barometric disturbance. Accordingly, if the barometer falls rapidly, or even if the regularity of its diurnal variation be interrupted, danger may be apprehended. No positive rule can be given as to the amount of depression to be expected, but at the center of some of the storms the barometer is said to stand fully 2 inches lower than outside the storm field. The average barometric gradient, near the vortex of the most violent of these storms, is said to be rather more than 1 inch in 50 nautical miles. As the center of the storm is approached the more rapid become the changes of wind, until at length, instead of its direction altering gradually, as is the case on first entering the storm field, the wind flies around at once to the opposite point, the sea meanwhile breaking into mountainous and confused heaps. There are many instances on record of the wind suddenly falling in the vortex and the clouds dispersing for a short interval, though the wind soon blows again with renewed fury.

In the northern hemisphere when the falling barometer and other signs create suspicion that a typhoon is approaching, facing the wind and taking 10 or 12 points to the right of it, will give the approximate bearing of its center. Thus, with the wind NE., the center will probably be from S. to SSE. of the observer's position. However, it is difficult to estimate the center of the vortex from any given point. This partly arises from the uncertainty as to the relation between the bearing of the center and the direction of the wind, and greatly from there being no means of knowing whether the storm be of large or small dimensions. If the barometer falls slowly, and the weather grows worse only gradually, it is reasonable to suppose that the storm center is distant; and conversely, with a rapidly falling barometer and increasing bad weather the center may be supposed to be approaching dangerously near.

Practical Rules.—When in the region and in the season of revolving storms, be on the watch for premonitory signs. Constantly observe and carefully record the barometer.

When on sea and there are indications of a typhoon being near, heave to and carefully observe and record the changes of the barometer and wind, so as to find the bearing of the center, and ascertain by the shift of the wind in which semicircle the vessel is situated. Much will often depend upon heaving to in time. When, after careful observation, there is reason to believe that the center of the typhoon is approaching, the following rules should be followed in determining whether to remain hove to or not, and the tack on which to remain hove to:

In the northern hemisphere, if the right-hand semicircle, heave to on the starboard tack. If in the left-hand semicircle, run, keeping the wind if possible, on the starboard quarter, and when the barometer rises, if necessary to keep the ship from going too far from the proper course, heave to on the port tack. When the vessel lies in the direct line of advance of the storm—which position is, as previously observed, the most dangerous of all—run with the wind on the starboard quarter. In all cases increase as soon as possible the distance from the center, bearing in mind that the whole storm field is advancing.

In receding from the center of a typhoon the barometer will rise and the wind and sea subside. It should be remarked that in some cases a vessel may, if the storm be traveling slowly, sail from the dangerous semicircle across the front of the storm, and thus out of its influence. But as the rate at which the storm is traveling is quite uncertain, this is a hazardous proceeding, and before attempting to cross the seaman should hesitate and carefully consider all the circumstances of the case, observing particularly the rate at which the barometer is falling.

Northward of the Equator the current is divided into north and south equatorial currents by the equatorial countercurrent, a stream flowing from west to east throughout the Pacific Ocean. The currents in the western part of the Pacific, to the northward of the Equator, are affected by the monsoons, and to the southward of the Equator they are deflected by the coast of Australia.

The trade drift, which flows to the westward between the parallels of 9 degrees and 20 degrees N., on reaching the eastern shores of the Philippine Islands again turns to the northward, forming near the northern limit of that group the commencement of the Japan stream. The main body of the current then flows along the east coast of Formosa, and from that island pursues a northeasterly course through the chain of islands lying between Formosa and Japan; and sweeping along the southeastern coast of Japan in the same general direction, it is known to reach the parallel of 50 degrees N. The limits and velocity of the Japan stream are considerably influenced by the monsoons in the China Sea, and by the prevailing winds in the corresponding seasons in the Yellow and Japan seas; also by the various drift currents which these periodic winds produce.

Admiral Dewey has forwarded to the navy department a memorandum on mineral resources of the Philippines prepared at the admiral's request by Professor George W. Becker of the United States geological survey. Only about a score of the several hundred islands, he says, are known to contain deposits of valuable minerals. He includes a table showing the mineral bearing islands and their resources. This table follows:

"Luzon, coal, gold, copper, lead, iron, sulphur, marble, kaolin; Sataanduanes, Sibuyan, Bohol and Panaoan, gold only; Marimduque, lead and silver; Mindoro, coal, gold and copper; Carraray, Batan, Rapu Rapu, Semarara, Negros, coal only; Masbete, coal and copper; Romblon, marble; Samar, coal and gold; Panay, coal, oil, gas, gold, copper, iron and perhaps mercury; Biliram, sulphur only; Leyte, coal, oil and perhaps mercury; Cebu, coal, oil, gas, gold, lead, silver and iron; Mindanao coal, gold, copper and platinum; Sulu archipelago, pearls."

The coal, Mr. Becker says, is analogous to the Japanese coal and that of Washington, but not to that of the Welsh or Pennsylvania coals. It might better be characterized as a highly carbonized lignite, likely to contain much sulphur as iron pyrites, rendering them apt to spontaneous combustion and injurious to boiler plates. Nevertheless, he says, when pyrites seams are avoided and the lignite is properly handled, it forms a valuable fuel, especially for local consumption.

Not least among the promising resources of the Philippines is a curious natural product. Several vegetable growths appear to possess the faculty of secreting mineral concretions, in all respects resembling certain familiar precious stones. The famous James Smithson was the first to give any real attention to these curious plant gems, but, though there can be no doubt of their authenticity, neither scientist nor merchant has followed this lead. One of the jewels, the bamboo opal, rivals the best stones in its delicate tints of red and green, but it is among the rarest, and 1,000 stems may be cut up before a single specimen be found.

CHAPTER XIX.

SPECIFICATIONS OF GRIEVANCES OF THE FILIPINOS.

An Official Copy of the Manifesto of the Junta Showing the Bad Faith of Spain in the Making and Evasion of a Treaty—The Declaration of the Renewal of the War of Rebellion—Complaints Against the Priests Defined—The Most Important Document the Filipinos Have Issued—Official Reports of Cases of Persecution of Men and Women in Manila by the Spanish Authorities—Memoranda of the Proceedings in Several Cases in the Court of Inquiry of the United States Officers.

The pages following, showing a cynical disregard of a solemn treaty by the Spaniards, a complete exposure of the reasons the Filipinos had for renewing the war, and the particulars of cases of individual wrongs suffered, as they were made known in the course of legal investigation, have been received direct from Manila, and enable us to complete the story of the Philippines with the testimony that the depravity of bad faith in regard to treaties, and incidents of personal cruelties in Spanish colonial governments, have illustrations in the Philippines as in Cuba, and demand of the American Nation in the hour of victory that Spain shall lose now and forever all her possessions in the East and West Indies, and be restricted to the peninsula and islands—the Canary and Balearic groups—that is, in two words to home rule. The circumstances of the treaty between the Philippine Junta—the treaty of Biyak—and the Spanish authorities, are of great notoriety, but the Philippine story has not until now reached the English speaking peoples. We give it from the official paper:

"On signing the Treaty of Biyak na bato, we, the natives of the Philippines and the government of Spain, agreed that between our armies be established an armistice which was to last three years from the date of the mentioned treaty.

"The natives were to lay down their arms and turn them over to the Spanish authorities with all their depot (maestranza, a manufactory of ammunition, for repairs of rifles, etc., etc.) their ammunitions and forts.

"The Spanish authorities, on the other hand, bound themselves to consent to the reforms (of public opinion amongst) the natives of the country claim; reforms which, according to the text of the decree of 9th August, 1897, the Captain and Guberno General assured us were granted and the execution of which was suspended on account of the insurrection.

A BIT OF SCENERY IN MINDANAO, SHOWING TROPICAL VEGETATION.

"The reforms asked for and granted were the following:

1. Expulsion or at least exclaustration of the religious orders.
2. Representation of the Philippines in the Spanish Cortes.
3. Application of real justice in the Philippines, equal for the Indian and for the Peninsular. Unity of laws between Spain and the Philippines. Participation of the Indians in the chief offices of the Civil Administration.
4. Adjustment of the property of the Parishes (church property) and of contributions in favor of the Indians.
5. Proclamation of the individual rights of the Indians, as also of the liberty of the press and of association.

"The same Spanish government agreed to pay the liberating government a war indemnity, reduced to the limited sum of 600,000 pesos, in payment of the arms, ammunitions, depots and forts which were surrendered, and in order to indemnify those who were to be obliged to live abroad during the term of the armistice, as an assistance to stay out of the Philippines while they were trying to establish themselves and looking for legitimate and decorous means of existence.

"It was agreed in like manner that General Don Fernando Primo de Rivera, Goberno General of the islands, should remain in his post during the time of the armistice, as a guarantee that the reforms be established.

"And, finally, said authority promised that he would propose and there would be conceded a very ample amnesty.

"Contrary to what was stipulated, the mentioned General was removed from his post shortly after the agreement was signed; and although the liberating government had fulfilled the laying down and delivery of the arms, ammunitions, depot and forts of its general encampment, the reforms were not established, only part of the offered indemnity has been paid and the amnesty remains a project only, some pardons being given.

"The government of Madrid, deriding the natives, and with contempt of what had signed as a gentleman the General Commander of their army in the field, tried, instead of carrying out the expulsion or exclaustration of the Priests, to elevate them more, nominating at once for the two bishoprics, vacant in the colonies, two Priests of those same religious orders that oppressed the country and were the first cause of the insurrection, the disorder and the general dissatisfaction in the islands; thus ridiculing the virtue, knowledge and worth of the numerous secular Spanish clergy, and especially of that of the Philippines.

"Not contented with this, they have raised and rewarded those Peninsulars who in the Philippines, as in Madrid, more cowardly and miserable still, because they abused their position and the protection of those same authorities who signed the treaty, insulted at banquets, assemblies and through the press, with epithets and jokes offensive and vulgar, the patient natives; as happened with the Peninsular Rafael Comenge, the protege and farcical table companion of the Priest, who amongst us performs the duties of the Archbishopric of Manila; the Minister of War has just conceded the said Comenge the grand cross of military merit, for shouting against us and imputing to us every kind of baseness and vices, knowing that he was lying, and for exacting from the gamblers of the Casino Espanol of Manila, as their president, the contribution of 30,000 pesos, to present General Primo de Rivera with a golden statute of that value, and, a curious coincident, this brave was one of the first who escaped from Manila, full of fear when the news arrived there that an American squadron would attack that port and that the risk he would run was real.

"You have seen before now, how that insect Wencestao Retana was rewarded with a cooked up deputyship to the Cortes, that salaried reptile of the Philippine convents, who, with the aid of that tyrant General Weyler, his worthy godfather, the despotic incendiary of the town of Calamba, of ominous memory amongst us, does nothing but vomit rabid foam, insulting us by day and night with calumnies and shrieks, in that paper whose expenses the Procurators of the Manila convents pay.

"Prepare yourselves also for seeing that a titled nobility be given to the well known 'Quioguiap' (fecer y Temprado), writer in the 'El Liberat,' of Madrid, who, to be in unison with the priests, does not cease to call us inferior race, troglodytes, without human nature or understanding, big boy; the same who, in order to deprive the rich 'Abellas' (father and son) of Carnarines, of the position they had conquered by their industry, economy and intelligence as almost exclusive purchasers of the Abaco (Manila hemp) of that region, tried and succeeded villainously in having them accused and shot in the camp of Bagumbayan; the same who afterwards sought in vain the reward of his criminal attempts, although conscious of his perverseness, to deliver to himself the produce of their harvest and their labor.

"Peace was hardly made, when General Primo de Rivera denied the existence of the agreement and shot day after day those same persons whom he had promised to protect, believing foolishly that, the nucleus of the revolution once destroyed, the insurgents would need thirty or forty years in order to reunite themselves; but he accepted freely the pension of the grand cross of San Fernando, which, as a reward for the peace, he was given.

"The same happened with bloodthirsty Monet, the author of the hecatomb of

SPECIFICATIONS OF GRIEVANCES OF THE FILIPINOS. 297

Zambales, who was promoted to the rank of a general and honored by a grand cross; also with his competitor in brutal deeds, General Tejeirs, the assassin of the Bisayos, and with the Vice Admiral Montojo, so severely punished later on, by whose orders the city of Cebu was destroyed and demolished, to revenge the death of an impure Recoleto Priest.

"In eloquent contrast with what the natives had to expect, there has not been one single concession or reward for the credulous Pedro A. Paterno, a Filipino, the only real agent of the miracle of the Peace, to whom they have denied even the modest historical title 'Maguinong' (Don).

"Add to all these infamies and indignities the removal of General Primo de Rivera, who, we repeat, was bound to remain in Manila during the three years of the armistice, and the nomination in his stead of another governor, General Augusti, who, completely without knowledge of the country, brought with him as his counsellor the unworthy Colonel Olive, the same who had proceeded with the utmost haste and greatest partiality and passion against the pretended chieftains, authors, protectors and followers of the sacred movement begun in August, 1896; who had, as military prosecutor for the 'Captain General,' exacted with insolent cynicism, and with the knowledge and consent of his superior officers, considerable sums of money from those who wished to be absolved, in order to imprison them again when they did not comply with all his extortions; the same who, with shameless partiality worked and used his influence all he could towards the shooting of the immortal Tagalo martyr, Dr. Jose Rizal; the same finally, who, during the command of weak General Blanco and of bloodthirsty and base General Polariyi demanded continually the imprisoning of the so-called 'Sons of the Country,' the descendants of the Europeans, that is, who had amongst us any importance by their learning, their industry, their fortunes or their lineage, and who were not willing to bribe him so as to be left in liberty.

"In view of this series of acts of faithlessness, of contempt, of insults, of crimes, and before all, the forgetting of the treaty, so recently as well as solemnly entered upon, those same who signed the treaty of Biyak na bato, have considered themselves free of the obligation to remain abroad and of keeping any longer the promised armistice.

"And, taking advantage of the Providential coming to the Philippines of the revenging squadron of the Great Republic of the United States of North America, they come back to their native soil proud and contented, to reconquer their liberty and their rights, counting on the aid and protection of the brave, decided, and noble

SPECIFICATIONS OF GRIEVANCES OF THE FILIPINOS.

Admiral Dewey, of the Anglo-Saxon squadron which has succeeded in beating and destroying the forces of the tyrants who have been annihilating the personality and energy of our industrious people, model of noble and glorious qualities.

"The moment has come, therefore, for the Filipinos to count themselves and to enter into rank and file in order to defend with zeal and resolution and with a virility of strong men, the soil that saw their birth as well as the honor of their name, making publicly and universally known their competence, ability and their civic, political and social virtues.

"Let us all fight united; seconding the revenging and humanitarian action of the North American Republic; and let us learn from her, accepting her counsels and her system, the way of living in order, peace and liberty, copying her institutions, which are the only adequate ones for the nations who wish to reconquer their personality in history, in the period we are passing.

"On going to battle, let us inscribe on our flag with clearness and accuracy the sacred legend of our aspirations.

"We want a stable government, elected by the people themselves; the laws of which are to be voted for by those same who have to keep them faithfully, conserving or modifying their present institutions in the natural times in the life of nations, but modeling them and taking us their own, the democratic ones of the United States of North America.

"We want the country to vote its taxes; those necessary for public services and to satisfy (pay in full) the assistance North America and the corporations, organizations and individuals who help us to rise out of our lethargic state, are rendering us; taking care at the same time to abolish all those which have for basis a social vice or an immoral action, like the lottery, the tax on gambling dens, on galleras (arenas for fights of game)cocks) and the farming out of the sale of opium. But before all, may there nevermore appear again that repugnant tax levied on Pederasty, which, to get two thousand pesos offended the universal conscience and the chaste name of 'Chinese Comedies.'

"We want plainest liberty in all its bearings, including that of ideas, association and the press, without arriving at lawlessness and disorder; just as it is established in that great, so well regulated Republic.

"We want to see the religion of the natives and of those that come to this country rigorously respected by the public powers and by the individuals in particular.

"We want Christianism, the basis of present civilization, to be the emblem and solid foundation of our religious institutions, without force or compulsion; that the native clergy of the country be that which direct and teach the natives in all the degrees of the ecclesiastical hierarchy.

"We want the maintenance of this clergy to be effected as the different regional governments may see fit, or, as the city councils or popular elective institutions established in every locality may determine.

"We want personal property to be absolutely and unconditionally respected; and, as a consequence, the recognition to the land holder of the property he cultivates and has improved by his labor, of the so-called Haciendas of the religious orders, who have usurped them and robbed them by the perverse acts of the confessionary, beguiling the fanaticism of ignorant women and or more than timid aged man, afraid of the vengeance the priests in their innate wickedness might meditate against their families, who extorted from them dues at the last moments of their existence denying them spiritual aid and divine rewards without the cession of their material interests before departing from this earth.

"We want the possessions of these land holders to be respected without their being obliged to pay any canon, lease or tax whatsoever of religious character, depressive or unjust, ceasing thus their detainment, anti-juridicial and anti-social, on the part of monarchial orders, rapacious orders whom, on the strength of their being a 'necessary evil,' the ignorant functionaries of Spanish administration, like themselves insatiable extortioners, have been aiding, in disdain of right, reason and equity.

"We want in order to consolidate the property, the ominous 'Inspection de Montes,' to disappear and cease in its actual functions, as a disorganizing and fiscalizing center of the titles of property of the natives, which on pretense of investigating and discovering the detainment of State lands, had the custom of declaring the property of the State or of others, such as was already cultivated and producing by the improvements made by the poor peasant, awarding such to their friends or to those who bribe them if the legitimate proprietor refused to give them, in shameless auction, what they asked for as a remuneration for what they called 'shutting their eyes,' as has happened lately, amongst other scandalous cases, in Mindoro, when staking out the limits of the new Hacienda adjudged there to the Recoleto Priests.

"We want public administration to be founded and to act on a basis of morality, economy and competence, in the charge of natives of the country or of such others who by their experience and learning can serve us as guides and teach us the basis and the system of those countries who have their economical, political and administrative offices and proceedings simplified and well organized.

SPECIFICATIONS OF GRIEVANCES OF THE FILIPINOS.

"We want the recognition of all the substantive rights of the human personality; guaranteed by judicial power, cemented in the principles in force in all the cultured nations; that the judicial authorities, when applying the laws, be penetrated by and identified with the spirit and the necessities of the locality; that the administration of justice be developed by simple, economical and decisive proceedings; and that judges and magistrates have their attributions limited by the functions of a jury and by verbal and public judgment, making thus disappear the actual state of affairs, of which prevarication and crooked dealings are the natural and necessary mark.

"We want sensible codes, adapted to our manner of being without differentiation of races and without odious privileges contrary to the principle of equality before the law.

"We want the increase and protection of our industries by means of subventions and of local and transient privileges without putting barriers to the general exchange of produce and of mercantile transactions with all the nations of the globe without exception.

"We want liberty of banking business, liberty of mercantile and industrial societies and companies, commercial liberty, and that the Philippines cease to be shut up amongst the walls of its convents, to become again the universal market, like that of Hongkong, that of Singapore, that of the Straits, that of Borneo, that of the Moluccas, and that of some of the autonomous colonies of Australia, countries which surround us; and that capital may with confidence develop all the elements of wealth of this privileged soil, without more duties or charges on import and export than those the circumstances of each epoch may require for determined purposes.

"We want roads, canals and ports, the dredging of our rivers and other waterways, railroads, tramways and all the means of locomotion and transport, on water and earth, with such help and assistance as may be needed to carry them out within a certain time and develop them conveniently.

"We want the suppression of the so-called 'Guardia Civil,' this pretorian and odious institution in whose malignment and inhuman meshes so many Philippine martyrs have suffered and expired; that center of tortures and iniquities, those contemptible flatterers of small tyrants and of the concupiscense of the priests, those insatiable extortioners of the poor native; those hardened criminals animated constantly in their perverseness by the impunity with which their accomplices, the representatives of despotism and official immorality, covered them.

SPECIFICATIONS OF GRIEVANCES OF THE FILIPINOS. 301

"In their stead we want a judicial and gubernatorial police, which is to watch over and oblige the fulfillment of existing laws and regulations without tortures and abuses.

"We want a local army, composed of native volunteers, strictly limited to what order and natural defense demands.

"We want a public instruction less levitical and more extensive in what refers to natural and positive sciences; so that it may be fitted to industrate woman as well as man in the establishment and development of the industries and wealth of the country, marine and terrestrial mining, forestal and industrial of all kinds, an instruction which is to be free of expenses in all its degrees and obligatory in its primary portion, leaving and applying to this object all such property as is destined to-day to supply the sustainment of the same; taking charge of the administration of such property a Council of Public Instruction, not leaving for one moment longer in the hands of religious institutions, since these teach only prejudice and fanaticism, proclaiming, as did not long since a rector of the university of Manila, that 'medicine and physical sciences are materialistic and impious studies,' and another, that 'political economy was the science of the devil.'

"We want to develop this public instruction, to have primary schools, normal schools, institutes of second degree, professional schools, universities, museums, public libraries, meteorological observatories, agricultural schools, geological and botanical gardens and a general practical and theoretical system of teaching agriculture, arts and handicraft and commerce. All this exists already in the country, but badly organized and dispersed, costing the contributors a good deal without practical results, which might have been expected, by the incompetency of the teachers and the favoritism employed in their nominations and remunerations.

"We want laws for hunting and fishing, and teaching and regular vigilance for the faithful carrying on of pisciculture, well-known already to the natives, for the advantageous disposing of their marine products, such as conch shell, mother of pearl, pearls, bichi de mer, ray skins, fish lime, etc., and for the raising of all kinds of animals useful for agricultural and industrial purposes and as victuals for the natives and for export.

"We want liberty of immigration and assistance for foreign settlers and capitalists, with such restrictions only, when there be an opportunity, as limit actually Chinese immigration, similar to legislature on this point in North America and Australia.

"We want, finally, anything that be just, equitable and orderly: all that may be basis for development, prosperity and well being; all that may be a propelling element of morality, virtue and respect to the mutual rights of all the inhabitants, in their minor relations and in those with the foreigner.

"Do not believe that the American nation is unbelieving or fanatically protestant, that it take to the scaffold or to the fire those who do not believe determined principles and practice special religious creeds; within that admirable organization, masterly and living model of perfection for the old nations of Europe and Asia, lives and prospers the Roman Catholic Church.

"There are some seven million inhabitants who profess that religion directed by natural clergy with their proper ministers, taken from that fold of Christ.

"Then there are bishops, archbishops, cardinals of the Roman Church, American subjects, beloved faithful of the Pope Leo XIII.

"There then is a Temporal Apostolical Delegate representative of the legitimate successor of St. Peter; there are parsons, canons, dignitaries and provisors, who live and teach in order peace and prosperity, respected by one and all, as you yourselves will be the day the American flag will influence in the spiritual direction of the Philippine people.

"Then there are cathedrals, parish churches, temples and chapels, sumptuous and admired, where they adore the same God of the Sinai and Golgotha, where severs and ostensive cult is rendered to Immaculate Virgin Mary and to the Saints you have on your altars and none dare to destroy, attack or prostitute them.

"There then are seminaries, convents, missions, fraternities, schools, everything Catholic, richly furnished, well kept up and perfectly managed to the glory of the religion.

"There resides His Eminence Cardinal Gibbons, a wise Roman Catholic prelate, American citizen, who recently and on occasion of the present war, has ordered, with consent of His Sanctity, that all the catholic clergy of the American nation raise daily prayers to the Most High to obtain the triumph of the arms of their country, for the good of religion and humanity, which cause, in the present conflict legitimately and unquestionably represents that government.

"And just as Christ, to be Messiah, had to be according to the prophecies, Jew and of the Tribe of Judah, that is: By right of his political fatherland, as by that of his native soil, of the chosen people, thus amongst you who ever wants to be a clergyman or merit being canon, dignitary, provisor, bishop, archbishop and cardinal, must as an indispensable condition, have been born on your proper soil, as is occurring absolutely in all the civilized nations of the old and new world, with the only exception of the Philippines.

"There may be priests, religious congregations, nuns and convents, but submissive to the laws of the country and obliged to admit in their bosom as formerly happened in these isles, as estimable and superior members of such institutions, those feel a vocation for a conventual life, as the noble and generous people of North America will demand, and will, do not doubt it, recognize these your legitimate rights.

FILIPINOS AND COUNTRYMEN.

"The protection of the great American Republic will make you respected and considered before the cultured powers, legitimately constituted; and your personality will be proclaimed and sanctioned everywhere.

"We have the duty to exact the rights we have just proclaimed and the 'natives' in all the isles and in all their different races, as well as the 'Mestizo Sangley,' as the 'Mestizo Espanol,' and the 'Son of the Country,' we all have the honorable duty of defending ourselves against the whip and the contempt of the Spaniards, accepting the protection and direction of the humane North American nation.

VIVA FILIPINOS

Hurrah for liberty and right.
Hurrah for the Grand Republic of the United States of North America.
Hurrah for President McKinley and Rear Admiral Dewey.

THE JUNTA PATRIOTICA.

"Hongkong, April, 1898."

Under the authority of the United States there have been inquiries by a court into the causes of the imprisonment of the inmates of the penitentiary and common jail at Manila, and others who have suffered from the enmities of the members of the government that ceased when the Spanish flag was taken down and the American flag raised. The memoranda following were made in the court proceedings, and state the facts as judicially established.

FULGENCIA TUAZON.

This lady was confined in Bilibid seven years ago (though the record shows July 11, 1898,) by order of the Governor-General, on a charge of selling counterfeit stamps. She was tried, and sentenced to six years' confinement; but the Judge accepted a bribe of $900 and released her about a week after her trial. A year afterwards she was again arrested by a new judge on the same charge, and $3,000 was demanded as the price of her liberty. This was refused, and imprisonment followed. She claims to have bought the stamps (which were telegraph stamps), from the Government.

DOROTEA ARTEAGA.

This young lady, who was a school teacher in her native province, Montinlupa, Manila province, was confined in Bilibid, August 8th, 1895, charged with "sacrilege and robbery," and insurrection. She came to Malate to see about her license as a school teacher, and was arrested by the civil guard on the above charge. She claims her arrest was instigated by a priest who had made overtures to her to have carnal intercourse with him, and had attempted the same, and had been repulsed and refused. To cover up his ill-doing he caused her arrest on the charge of having stolen part of the vessels used in the communion service of the Roman Catholic church. She has never been married and the Alcalde says, "Her conduct in prison has been very good."

SENORA MAXIMA GUERRERA.

This woman was born in Santa Cruz, in 1838, and has been confined in Bilibid since 1890, though the record shows that she was imprisoned July 11, 1898, by order of the Governor-General. This date, however, is admitted to be an error by the Alcalde, without any explanation of the error. The record shows that she was imprisoned because she objected to the Government taking wood off her property without paying for it. She claims that since her imprisonment, the Government has confiscated $40,000 worth of her property.

FELIPE REMENTINA.

This prisoner was confined in the year 1889, when only 12 years old. At that time a revolution was in progress in the province in which he resided, and he was "captured" by the Spanish forces and sent to Bilibid Carcel. He did not know with what he was charged, and while he was tried, he never received any sentence.

JOSE DAVID.

"I was put in here June 13th, 1898. Am a civilian and a 'Katipunan.' Was tried, but never sentenced." The foregoing is the testimony of the prisoner Jose David, and is quoted here as an example of the testimony of some hundreds of others, which is almost identical. Large numbers of the natives seem to be members of the "Katipunan" society, which appears to be a revolutionary brotherhood of some kind. They have been imprisoned for terms varying from one or two months to several years (in some cases ten or twelve years), upon the charge of belonging to this society; in very many cases without trial, and in the majority with no sentence whatever, and, very largely, simply "on susupicion."

AGAPITO CALIBUGAR.

This man was arrested by the Civil Guard, in July, 1889, in his own house, and was tried but not sentenced, or rather did not know what his sentence was. He was told that his sentence was served out, but he could not be returned to his own province of Negros because the Governor had no ships available for that purpose. He had no idea why he was arrested and tried. There are several other cases similar to this one, in which the charge is "resisting armed forces"—most of which were tried by court martial, and never sentenced.

GREGORIO DOMINGO.

This prisoner was confined in Bilibid Carcel on the 25th of November, 1896, the entry on the prison record against his name being "no se espresa"—"no charge expressed." He was, of course, neither tried nor sentenced, but had been in prison almost two years, with absolutely no reason attempted to be made for his confinement. This case is also cited as an example of many similar ones.

JOSE TRABADO.

This is the case of a man who was a member of the Katipunan society, but who was tried and sentenced. He was imprisoned in Bilibid Carcel, May 5th, 1898. his sentence being confinement "cardena perpetua"—"in chains forever." He was one of five men who received the same sentence for a like offence. He, with the others, was set free August 31st, 1898.

SILVINO DE CASTRO.

In this case the prisoner, who was formerly employed as a clerk in a grocery store, was imprisoned in Bilibid Carcel on the 25th of December, 1897, charged with having stolen $4.50 (Spanish, which represents about $2.25 American). His story was that he was sent out to collect a bill, but lost the said bill, and was therefore accused by his employer of stealing the money, and was imprisoned. He was tried, but never received any sentence.

DON FERNANDO SIERRA.

The prisoner above named is a full-blooded Spaniard, thirty-eight years of age, married, and has one child, three months old. He was confined in Bilibid, May 28, 1893, for "insulting" a civil guard, while drunk, and was tried and sentenced to six years and six months imprisonment. He had already served over five years of this sentence, when he was released September 2nd, 1898.

CRISTAN DEL CARMEN.

This man was confined in the Carcel De Bilibid, the "common prison," May 4th, 1898, and his offense was that he was "suspected of being an American!" For this heinous crime he was neither tried nor sentenced.

JULIAN SORIANO.

In this case the prisoner was confined in Bilibid, March 25th, 1895, after having been in prison one year in his province on suspicion of being implicated in the killing of a civil guard at a place colled Balauga. He was tried by a sergeant of the civil guard, who caused him to be tortured in order to wring a confession from him. This torture was inflicted by means of a thin rope or cord, tied very tightly around the muscles of the arm above the elbow (cutting into the flesh deeply), and left there in some instances for thirty days. In some cases the men were also hung up, the weight of the body being sustained by the cords around the arms. Several of the prisoners have deep scars on their arms caused by the torture. This man was never sentenced.

LEON BUENO.

The charge against this man was that he had stolen a pig, and he was confined in Bilibid, March 21st, 1893, after being tried and sentenced to eight years' imprisonment. He had already served over five years when released Sept. 3, 1898. —

JOSE CASTILLO.

This man was confined in Bilibid Carcel, December 15th, 1894, charged with "insulting the armed forces of Spain." His version of the reason for his imprisonment is as follows: His cousin and a lieutenant in the guardia civile were very close friends, and the said cousin, wishing to present a cow to the lieutenant, applied to the prisoner for one, which was given to him. Later on the cousin thought he would like to present his friend with another cow, so applied to the prisoner for cow No. 2, and was this time refused. In order to take vengeance on the prisoner, the cousin denounced him to the civil guard lieutenant as a "bandit," and he was arrested and imprisoned as above. The prisoner was sixty years of age.

ANASTACIO DE MESA.

The story of this prisoner seems to be particularly sad. He was a chorister or sacristan in a Roman Catholic church, with several others. and was arrested, with his companions, by the civil guard, charged with "sacrilege." The truth of the matter, however, seems to be as follows: The prisoner had a sweetheart with whom a lieutenant of the civil guard, named de Vega, appears to have been infatuated. After imprisoning Anastacio de Mesa and his companions upon the above charge, which seems to be without foundation entirely, de Vega took the girl, and compelled her by force and against her will to live with him as his mistress. The girl soon died, her end, no doubt, being hastened by the brutal cruelty of de Vega. These young men, hardly more than boys, were imprisoned on August 3, 1895. after having been tried by court martial, but not sentenced. They have now been liberated. It should be stated that de Vega himself constituted the "court martial" before which these boys were tried.

Note.—There are several cases of arrests for "insulting and resisting the armed forces of Spain." In the case of Pedro Javier, the accused was over seventy years old, and in that of Miguel de la Gruz, he was seventy-five years old; while in one or two other cases boys of ten or twelve years of age were arrested on the same charge.

CHAPTER XX.

HAWAII AS ANNEXED.

The Star Spangled Banner Up Again in Hawaii, and to Stay—Dimensions of the Islands—What the Missionaries Have Done—Religious Belief by Nationality—Trade Statistics—Latest Census—Sugar Plantation Laborers—Coinage of Silver—Schools—Coffee Growing.

The star spangled banner should have been waving in peaceful triumph over our central possessions in the Pacific for five years. Now Old Glory has ascended the famous flag-staff, from which it was mistakenly withdrawn, and is at home. Its lustrous folds are welcomed by a city that is strangely American, in the sense that it is what the world largely calls "Yankee," and does not mean bad manners by the most expressive word that has so vast a distinction. The shops of Honolulu are Americanized. There is a splendid blossoming of the flag of the country. The British parties of opposition have faded out. There is the wisdom in English statesmanship to be glad to see us with material interest in the Pacific Ocean. In this connection there is something better than a treaty.

Do not mispronounce the name of the capital city of the Hawaiian Islands. Call it Hoo-noo-luu-luu and let it sing itself. Remember that this city is not on the larger of the islands, but the third in size. The area of Hawaii, the greater island, is 4,210 square miles. Oahu, the Honolulu island, has 600 square miles, with a population of 40,205, and Hawaii has 33,285 people. The area of the islands, told in acres is, Hawaii, 2,000,000; Nani, 400,000; Oahu, 260,000; Kauai, 350,000; Malokai, 200,000; Lauai, 100,000; Nichan, 70,000; Kahloolawe, 30,000. The dimensions of the tremendous volcanoes that are our property now are startling:

DIMENSIONS OF KILAUEA, ISLAND OF HAWAII.

(The largest active Volcano in the World.)

Area, 4.14 square miles, or 2,650 acres.
Circumference, 41,500 feet, or 7.85 miles
Extreme width, 10,300 feet, or 1.95 miles.
Extreme length, 15,500 feet, or 2.93 miles.
Elevation, Volcano House, 1,040 feet.

DIMENSIONS OF MOKUAWEOWEO.

(The Summit Crater of Mauna Loa, Island of Hawaii.)

Area, 3.70 square miles, or 2,370 acres.
Circumference, 50,000 feet, or 9.47 miles.
Length, 19,500 feet, or 3.7 miles.
Width, 9,200 feet, or 1.74 miles.
Elevation, 13,675 feet.

DIMENSIONS OF HALEAKALA.

(The great Crater of Maui, the Largest in the World.)

Area, 19 square miles, or 12,160 acres.
Circumference, 105,600 feet, or 20 miles.
Extreme length, 39,500 feet, or 7.48 miles.
Extreme width, 12,500 feet, or 2.37 miles.
Elevation of summit, 10,032 feet.
Elevation of principal cones in crater, 8,032 and 7,572 feet.
Elevation of cave in floor of crater, 7,380 feet.

DIMENSIONS OF IAO VALLEY, MAUI.

Length (from Wailuku) about 5 miles.
Width of valley, 2 miles.
Depth, near head, 4,000 feet.
Elevation of Puu Kukui, above head of valley, 5,788 feet.
Elevation of Crater of Eke, above Waihee Valley, 4,500 feet.

Honolulu's importance comes from the harbor, and the favor of the missionaries. As to the general judgment of the work of the missionaries, there is nothing better to do than to quote Mr. Richard H. Dana's "Two Years Before the Mast." He said in that classic:

"It is no small thing to say of the missionaries of the American Board, that in less than forty years they have taught this whole people to read and write, to cipher and to sew. They have given them an alphabet, grammar and distionary; preserved their language from extinction; given it a literature and translated into it the Bible, and works of devotion, science and entertainment, etc. They have established schools, reared up native teachers, and so pressed their work that now the proportion of inhabitants who can read and write is greater than in New England. And, whereas, they found these islanders a nation of half-naked savages, living in the surf and on the sand, eating raw fish, fighting among themselves, tyrannized over by feudal chiefs and abandoned to sensuality, they now see them decently clothed, recognizing the law of marriage, knowing something of accounts, going to school and public worship more regularly than the people do at home, and the more elevated of them taking part in conducting the affairs of the constitutional monarchy under which they live, holding seats on the judicial bench and in the legislative chambers, and filling posts in the local magistracies."

Take away the tropical vegetation and the gigantic scenery and we have here, in our new Pacific possessions, a new Connecticut. The stamp of New England is upon this lofty land, especially in Honolulu, where the spires of the churches testify. There is much that is of the deepest and broadest interest in the possible missionary work here, on account of the remarkable race questions presented. Here are the nations and the people of mixed blood—the Chinese, Japanese and Portuguese—a population immensely representative of Oriental Asia. The measure of success of the missionaries under our flag in dealing with these people can hardly fail to be accepted by the world as a test of the practical results of the labor with the Asiatica. In this connection, the figures following, from the Hawaiian Annual of 1898, furnish a basis of solid information for study:

TABLE OF RELIGIOUS BELIEF, BY NATIONALITY.

(So Far as Reported in Census Returns, 1896.)

Nationalities.	Protestants.	Roman Catholics.	Mormons.
Hawaiians...	12,842	8,427	4,368
Part Hawaiians...	3,242	2,633	396
Hawaiian born foreigners...	1,801	6,622	15
Americans...	1,404	212	34
British...	1,184	180	7
Germans...	592	83	2
French...	6	57	....
Norwegians...	154	8	....
Portuguese...	146	7,812	1
Japanese...	711	49	4
Chinese...	837	67	49
South Sea Islanders...	178	42	3
Other nationalities...	176	171	7
Totals...	23,273	26,363	4,886

NOTE.—This table shows but 54,522 of the population (just about one-half) to have made returns of their religious belief. With 21,535 Japanese and 18,429

SPANIARDS READY TO EXECUTE INSURGENT PRISONERS.

AFTER AN EXECUTION—PROSTRATE FORMS ARE MEN SHOT.

A GROUP OF THE UNCONQUERABLE MOHAMMEDANS.

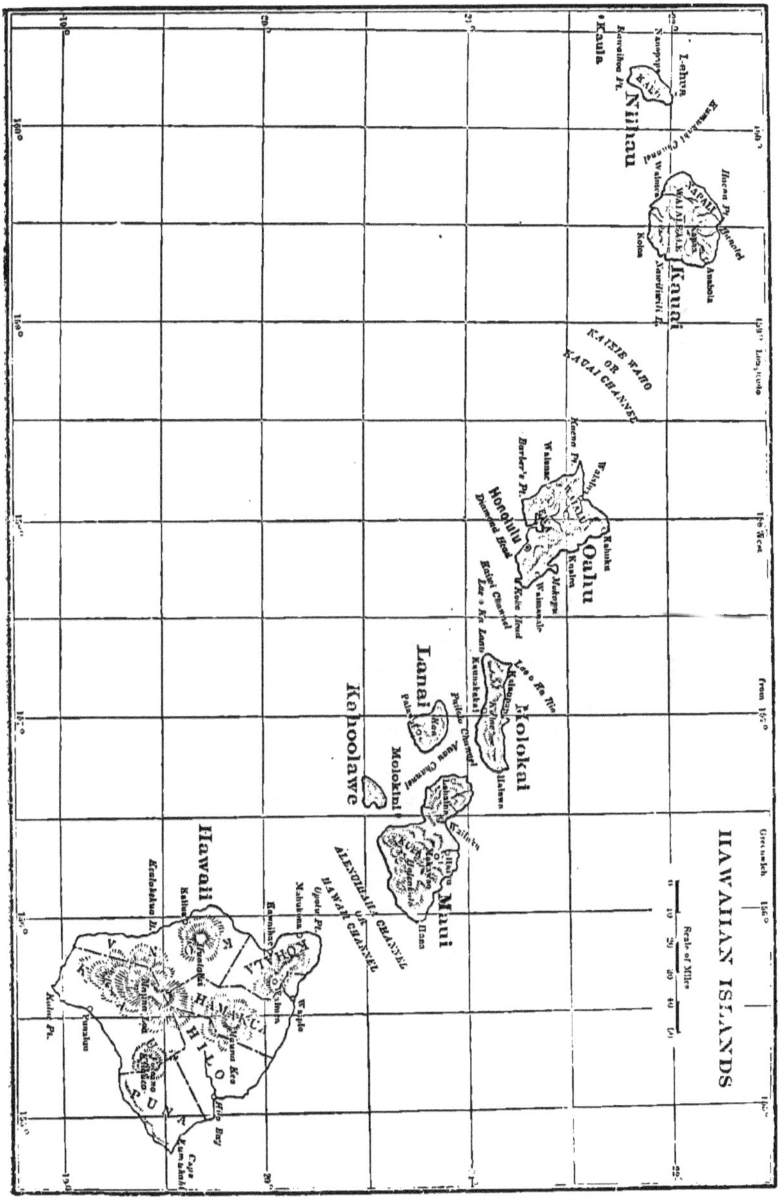

Chinese (probably Buddhists and Confucians) unreported because not provided for in the schedules, the great difference is largely accounted for.

The latest census returns show that of the whole population, 109,020, there are: Males, 72,517; females, 36,503. The latest information of labor, under contract for sugar-making, make the number of males on the island more than double that of the females. There has been an increase of population of more than 50,000 in the eighteen years from 1878 to 1896. The census of the several islands, taken September 27, 1896, shows:

	POPULATION			DWELLINGS			
	Male.	Female.	Total.	Inhabited.	Uninhabited.	Building.	Total.
Oahu	26,164	14,041	40,205	6,685	1,065	60	7,010
Hawaii	22,632	10,653	33,285	5,033	955	35	6,027
Molokai	1,335	972	2,307	651	92	3	746
Lanai	51	54	105	23	13	..	36
Maui	11,435	6,291	17,726	3,156	650	18	3,824
Niihau	76	88	164	31	3	..	34
Kauai	10,824	4,404	15,228	2,320	299	8	2,627
Totals	72,517	36,503	109,020	17,099	3,081	124	21,104

Hawaii's annual trade balance since 1879 is a notable record:

Year.	Imports.	Exports.	Excess Export Values.	Custom House Receipts.
1880	$3,673,268.41	$4,968,444.87	$1,295,176.46	$402,181.63
1881	4,547,978.64	6,885,436.56	2,337,457.92	423,192.01
1882	4,974,510.01	8,299,016.70	3,324,506.69	505,390.98
1883	5,624,240.09	8,133.343.88	2,509.103.79	577,332.87
1884	4,637,514.22	8,184,922.63	3,547,408.41	551,739.59
1885	3,830,544.58	9,158,818.01	5.328.273.43	502,337.38
1886	4,877,738.73	10,565,885.58	5,688.146.85	580,444.04
1887	4,943,840.72	9,707,047.33	4,763.206.61	595,002.64
1888	4,540,887.46	11,903,398.76	7,362,511.30	546,142.63
1889	5,438.790.63	14,039,941.40	8.601,150.77	550,010.16
1890	6,962,201.13	13,142,829.48	6,180,628.35	695,956.91
1891	7,438,582.65	10,395,788.27	2,957,205.62	732,594,93
1892	4,028.295.31	8,181.687.21	4,153,391.90	494,385.10
1893	4,363,177.58	10,962,598.09	5,599,420.51	545,754.16
1894	5,104,481.43	9,678,794.56	4,574,313.13	524,767.37
1895	5,714,017.54	8,474.138.15	2,760,120.61	547.149.40
1896	7,164,561.40	15,515,230.13	8,350,668.73	656,895.82

The percentage of imports from the United States in 1896 was 76.27; Great Britain, 10.54; Germany, 2.06; France, .25; China, 4.17; Japan, 3.86. In 1895 the export of sugar was 294,784,819 pounds; value, $7,975,500.41.

NATIONALITY OF VESSELS EMPLOYED IN FOREIGN CARRYING TRADE, 1889-1896.

NATIONS.	1889. No.	Tons.	1890. No.	Tons.	1891. No.	Tons.	1892. No.	Tons.
American	185	125,196	224	153,098	233	169,472	212	160,042
Hawaiian	44	56,670	35	43,641	21	26,869	11	4,340
British	22	21,108	16	22,912	33	52,866	30	55,317
German	5	3,337	9	7,070	9	9,005	5	5,978
Japanese	..	......	...	......	5	8,239	3	4,701
All others	9	12,268	9	9,980	10	8,401	11	8,201
Total	269	218,579	293	236,701	311	274,852	722	242,579

BONDED DEBT, ETC., HAWAIIAN ISLANDS, JUNE 30, 1897.

	Per Cent.	
Under Loan Act of 1876	7	$ 1,500.00
" " " 1882	6	67,400.00
" " " 1886	6	2,000,000.00
" " " 1888	6	190,000.00
" " " 1890	5 and 6	124,100.00
" " " 1892	5 and 6	82,100.00
" " " 1893	6	650,000.00
" " " 1896	5	222,000.00
		3,337,100.00
Due Postal Savings Bank Depositors		782,074.25
Total		$4,119,174.25

NUMBER AND NATIONALITY OF SUGAR PLANTATION LABORERS.

(Compiled from latest Report of Secretary Bureau of Immigration, December 31, 1897.)

Islands.	Hawaiians.	Portuguese.	Japanese.	Chinese.	S. S. Isl'ders.	All Others.	Total.
Hawaii	594	980	6,245	2,511	24	232	10,586
Mauai	580	526	2,010	1,114	45	110	4,385
Oahu	197	211	1,331	973	16	55	2,783
Kauai	244	551	3,307	1,691	30	203	6,026
Total, 1896	1,615	2,268	12,893	6,289	115	600	23,780
Total, 1895	1,584	2,497	11,584	3,847	133	473	20,120
Increase, 1896	31	....	1,309	2,442	....	127	3,660
Decrease, 1899	....	231	.....	....	18	....	.....

The number of day laborers, 11,917, or a little over one-half of the total force engaged. The Japanese and South Sea Islanders are about evenly divided in their numbers as to term and day service, while Hawaiians and Portuguese show each but a small proportion of their numbers under contract. Minors are reducing in number. Women laborers, numbering 1,024 in all, show a gain of 89 over 1875. Only thirty Hawaiian females are engaged among all the plantations, and confined to one plantation each in Oahu, Kauai and Maui.

The Hwaiian Annual of 1898 makes this annotation:

During the year various changes have occurred in the labor population of the country, and under the working of the present law, requiring a proportion of other than Asiatic of all immigrant labor introduced, there has already arrived one company of Germans, comprisingg 115 men, 25 women and 47 children, all of whom found ready engagements with various plantations.

Chinese arirvals in 1897 to take the place of Japanese whose terms were expiring, will alter the proportions of these nationalitis of plantation labor, and by the new law Asiatic laborers must return to their country at the expiration of their term of service, or re-engage; they cannot drift around the country, nor engage in competition with artizans or merchants.

The islands comprising the Hawaiian territory are Hawaii, Mauai, Oahu, Kauai, Molokai, Lauai, Niihau, Kahaalawe, Lehua and Molokini, "The Leper Prison," and, in addition, Nihoa, or Bird Island, was taken possession of in 1822; an expedition for that purpose having been fitted out by direction of Kaahumanu, and sent thither under the charge of Captain William Sumner.

Laysan Island became Hawaiian territory May 1st, 1857, and on the 10th of the same month Lysiansky Island was added to Kamehameha's realm by Captain John Paty.

Palmyra Island was taken possession of by Captain Zenas Bent, April 15th, 1862, and proclaimed Hawaiian territory in the reign of Kamehameha IV., as per "By Authority" notice in the "Polynesian" of June 21st, 1862.

Ocean Island was acquired September 20th, 1886, as per proclamation of Colonel J. H. Boyd, empowered for such service during the reign of Kalakaua.

Necker Island was taken possession of May 27th, 1894, by Captain James A. King, on behalf of the Hawaiian Government.

French Frigate Shoal was the latest acquisition, also by Captain King, and proclaimed Hawaiian territory July 13th, 1895.

Gardener Island, Mara or Moro Reef, Pearl and Hermes Reef, Gambia Bank, and Johnston or Cornwallis Island are also claimed as Hawaiian possessions, but there is some obscurity as to the dates of acquisition, and it is of record in the Foreign Office articles of convention between Hon. Charles St. Julien, the Commissioner and Political and Commercial Agent of His Majesty the King of the Hawaiian

HAWAII AS ANNEXED.

Islands, and John Webster, Esq., the Sovereign Chief and Proprietor of the group of islands known as Stewart's Islands (situated near the Solomon Group), whereby is ceded to the Hawaiian Government—subject to ratification by the King—the islands of Ihikaiana, Te Parena, Taore, Matua Awi and Matua Ivoto, comprising said group of Stewart's Islands. But the formalities do not seem to have been perfected, so that we are not certain that the Stewart's Islands are our possessions. The latest thorough census of the Hawaiian Islands was taken in September, 1896, but the population was closely estimated July 1st, 1897.

	Natives.	Chinese.	Japanese.	Portuguese.	All Other Foreigners.	Total
Population as per Census, September, 1896.....	39,504	21,616	24,407	15,191	8,302	109,020
Passengers—Arrivals—Excess over departures, 4th quarter, 1896.....	......	1,377	1,673	......	339	3,389
Excess over departures, 6 mos. to July 1, 1897.	......	2,908	396	58	207	3,569
Total	39,504	25,901	26,476	15,249	8,848	115,978

The following denominations of Hawaiian silver were coined during the reign of Kalakaua, at the San Francisco mint, and imported for the circulating medium of the islands in 1883 and 1884. They are of the same intrinsic value as the United States silver coins and were first introduced into circulation January 14th, at the opening of the bank of Claus Spreckles & Co. in Honolulu. The amount coined was $1,000,000, divided as follows:

```
Hawaiian Dollars.......  ............................$  500,000
    "    Half Dollars..............................     350,000
    "    Quarter Dollars...........................     125,000
    "    Dimes..................................          25,000
                                                      ----------
    Total...........  .............................$1,000,000
```

SCHOOLS, TEACHERS AND PUPILS FOR THE YEAR 1896.

		—Teachers.—			—Pupils.—	
	Schools.	Male.	Female.	Total.	Male.	Female.
Government	132	111	169	280	5,754	4,435
Independent	63	72	130	202	1,994	1,840
	195	183	299	482	7,748	6,275

HAWAII AS ANNEXED.

NATIONALITY OF PUPILS ATTENDING SCHOOLS FOR THE
YEAR 1896.

Nationality.	Male.	Female.
Hawaiian	3,048	2,432
Part-Hawaiian	1,152	1,296
American	219	198
British	105	151
German	152	136
Portuguese	2,066	1,534
Scandinavian	51	47
Japanese	242	155
Chinese	641	280
South Sea Islanders	15	13
Other foreigners	57	33
	7,748	6,275

Of the Japanese, 8.5 per cent. were born on the islands; of the Chinese, percentage born here, 10.3. Of a total of 41,711 Japanese and Chinese, 36,121 are males and 5,590 females. The figures show that the Asiatics are not at home.

The sugar industry in our new possessions has had great prominence agriculturally. The sugar interest of these islands has had a formidable influence in the United States. Recent events and the ascertained certainties of the future show that the people of the United States will soon raise their sugar supply on their own territory. The annexation of these sugar islands was antagonized because there was involved the labor contract system. As a matter of course, the United States will not change the labor laws of the nation to suit the sugar planters of Hawaii, who have been obtaining cheap labor through a system of Asiatic servitude. There is but one solution—labor will be better compensated in Hawaii than it has been, and yet white men will not be largely employed in the cultivation of sugar cane in our tropical islands. The beet sugar industry is another matter. There will be an end of the peculiar institution that has had strength in our new possessions, that brings, under contract, to Hawaii a mass of forty thousand Chinese and Japanese men, and turns over the majority of them to the plantations, whose profits have displayed an unwholesome aggrandizement. Once it was said cotton could not be grown in the cotton belt of our country without slave labor, but the latter trouble is, the cotton producers claim, there is too much of their product raised. A ten-million bale crop depresses the market. Already experiments have been tried successfully to pay labor in the sugar fields by the tons of cane delivered at the mills for grinding. This is an incident full of auspicious significance. A general feeling is expressed in the current saying that coffee raising is "the coming industry." The confidence that there is prosperity in coffee amounts to enthusiasm. Here are some of the statistics of coffee growers, showing number of trees and area, trees newly planted and trees in bearing:

NO. OF TREES OR AREA.

	Newly Planted.	1 to 3 year old.	Trees in Bearing.
J. C. Lenhart, Kaupo	2,000 trs.	4,000 trs.	....
Mokulau Coffee Co., Kaupo	2,000 trs.	10,000 trs.	2 acres.
E. E. Paxton, Kaupo	5,000 trs.	7,000 trs.	....
Native Patches throughout Kaupo	10 acres.	....	....
Lahaina Coffee and Fruit Co., Ltd., Lahaina	10,000 trs.	100,000 trs.	30,000 trs.
H. P. Baldwin, Honokahua	35,947 trs.	4,669 trs.	2,641 trs.
Waianae Coffee Plantation Co., Waianae	7,500 trs.	23,000 trs.	36,000 trs.
C. A. Wideman, Waianae	10,000 trs.	8,500 trs.	....
Makaha Coffee Co., Ltd., Waianae	112 acres.	....	....
Lanihau Plantation, Kailua	20,700 trs.	25,000 trs.	10,000 trs.
Kona Coffee Co., Ltd., Kailua	....	....	35 acres.
Geo. McDougal & Sons, Kailua	....	176 acres.	105 acres.
H. C. Achi, Holualoa	....	....	10,000 trs.
E. W. Barnard, Laupahoehoe	....	....	30,000 trs.
J. M. Barnard, Laupahoehoe	....	5,000 trs.	....
John Gaspar, Napoopoo	....	33,000 trs.	16,000 trs.
Manuel Sebastian, Kealakekua	....	....	8,000 trs.
J. G. Henriques, Kealakekua	....	....	3,000 trs.
C. Hooper, Kauleoli	....	2 acres.	12 acres.
J. Keanu, Keei	5 acres.	10 acres.	16 acres.
A. S. Cleghorn	3 acres.	....	100 acres.
Mrs. E. C. Greenwell	....	8 acres.	25 acres.
J. M. Monsarrat, Kolo	....	38 acres.	40 acres.
Queen Emma Plantation	....	....	25,000 trs.
L. M. Staples Plantation	....	25,000 trs.	12,000 trs.
Olaa Coffee Co., Ltd	50 acres.	90 acres.	....
Grossman Bros	100 acres.	30 acres.	....
B. H. Brown	2,260 trs.	2,000 trs.	3,225 trs.
Herman Eldart	40,000 trs.	20,000 trs.	7,000 trs.

The list of coffee growers is very long. That which is of greater interest is the showing made of the immense number of new trees. The coffee movement steadily gains force and the pace of progress is accelerated.

Everybody has not been pleased with annexation. The Japanese are not in a good humor about it. The minister of Japan got his orders evidently to leave for Japan when the news arrived that the question had been settled in Washington, and he left for Yokohama by the boat that brought the intelligence. Japanese journals of importance raise the question as to the propriety of our establishing a coal station here. There is some dissatisfaction among the Hawaiians, who are bewildered,

They are children who believe stories in proportion as they are queer. Many of them feel that they have a grievance. The young princess who is the representative of the extinguished monarchy is affable and respected. If the question as to giving her substantial recognition were left to the Americans here, they would vote for her by a large majority. It would not be bad policy for the government to be generous toward her. She is not in the same boat with the ex-Queen. The Americans who have been steadfast in upholding the policy that at last has prevailed are happy, but not wildly so, just happy. Now that they have gained their cause, their unity will be shaken by discussions on public questions and personal preferments.

There should be no delay in understanding that in this Archipelago the race questions forbid mankind suffrage, and that our new possessions are not to become states at once, or hurriedly; that it will take generations of assimilation to prepare the Hawaiian Islands for statehood.

The objection to the climate of the marvelous islands of which we have become possessed is its almost changeless character. There is no serious variation in the temperature. There is a little more rain in "winter" than in "summer." There is neither spring nor fall. The trade winds afford a slight variety, and this seems to be manipulated by the mountains, that break up the otherwise unsparing monotony of serene loveliness. The elevations of the craters, and the jagged peaks are from one thousand to thirteen thousand feet. If you want a change of climate, climb for cold, and escape the mosquitos, the pests of this paradise. There are a score of kinds of palms; the royal, the date, the cocoanut, are of them. The bread fruit and banana are in competition. The vegetation is voluptuous and the scenery stupendous. There is a constellation of islands, and they differ like the stars in their glories and like human beings in their difficulties.

CHAPTER XXI.

EARLY HISTORY OF THE SANDWICH ISLANDS.

Captain James Cook's Great Discoveries and His Martyrdom—Character and Traditions of the Hawaiian Islands—Charges Against the Famous Navigator, and effort to Array the Christian World Against Him—The True Story of His Life and Death—How Charges Against Cook Came to Be Made—Testimony of Vancouver, King and Dixon, and Last Words of Cook's Journal—Light Turned on History That Has Become Obscure—Savagery of the Natives—Their Written Language Took Up Their High Colored Traditions, and Preserved Phantoms—Scenes in Aboriginal Theatricals—Problem of Government in an Archipelago Where Race Questions Are Predominant—Now Americans Should Remember Captain Cook as an Illustrious Pioneer.

Regarding the islands in the Pacific that we have for a long time largely occupied and recently wholly possessed, the Hawaiian cluster that are the stepping stone, the resting place and the coal station for the golden group more than a thousand leagues beyond, we should remember Captain Cook as one of our own Western pioneers, rejoice to read his true story, and in doing so to form a correct estimate of the people who have drifted into the area of our Protection, or territory that is inalienably our own, to be thoroughly Americanized, that they may some day be worthy to become our fellow-citizens.

Sunday, January 18th, 1778, Captain Cook, after seeing birds every day, and turtles, saw two islands, and the next day a third one, and canoes put off from the shore of the second island, the people speaking the language of Otaheite. As the Englishmen proceeded, other canoes appeared, bringing with them roasted pigs and very fine potatoes. The Captain says: "Several small pigs were purchased for a six-penny nail, so that we again found ourselves in a land of plenty. The natives were gentle and polite, asking whether they might sit down, whether they might spit on the deck, and the like. An order restricting the men going ashore was issued that I might do everything in my power to prevent the importation of a fatal disease into the island, which I knew some of our men now labored under." Female visitors were ordered to be excluded from the ships. Captain Cook's journal is very explicit, and he states the particulars of the failure of his precautions. This is a subject that has been much discussed, and there is still animosity in the controversy. The discovery of the islands that he called the Sandwich, after his patron the Earl of Sandwich, happened in the midst of our Revolutionary war. After

Cook's explorations for the time, he sailed in search of the supposed Northwest passage, and that enterprise appearing hopeless, returned to the summer islands, and met his fate in the following December. Captain George Vancouver, a friend and follower of Cook, says, in his "Voyage of Discovery and Around the World." from 1790 to 1795:

"It should seem that the reign of George the Third had been reserved by the Great Disposer of all things for the glorious task of establishing the grand keystone to that expansive arch over which the arts and sciences should pass to the furthermost corners of the earth, for the instruction and happiness of the most lowly children of nature. Advantages so highly beneficial to the untutored parts of the human race, and so extremely important to that large proportion of the subjects of this empire who are brought up to the sea service deserve to be justly appreciated; and it becomes of very little importance to the bulk of our society, whose enlightened humanity teaches them to entertain a lively regard for the welfare and interest of those who engage in such adventurous undertakings for the advancement of science, or for the extension of commerce, what may be the animadversions or sarcasms of those few unenlightened minds that may peevishly demand, "what beneficial consequences, if any, have followed, or are likely to follow to the discoverers, or to the discovered, to the common interests of humanity, or to the increase of useful knowledge, from all our boasted attempts to explore the distant recesses of the globe?" The learned editor (Dr. Douglas, now Bishop of Salisbury) who has so justly anticipated this injudicious remark, has, in his very comprehensive introduction to Captain Cook's last voyage, from whence the above quotation is extracted, given to the public not only a complete and satisfactory answer to that question, but has treated every other part of the subject of discovery so ably as to render any further observations on former voyages of this description wholly unnecessary, for the purpose of bringing the reader acquainted with what had been accomplished, previously to my being honored with His Majesty's commands to follow up the labors of that illustrious navigator Captain James Cook; to whose steady, uniform, indefatigable and undiverted attention to the several objects on which the success of his enterprises ultimately depended, the world is indebted for such eminent and important benefits."

Captain George Vancouver pays, in the introduction of his reports, a remarkable tribute to Captain Cook, that should become familiar to the American people. for it is one of the features of prevalent Hawaiian literature that the great navigator is much disparaged, and denounced. One of the favorite theories of the missionaries has been that Cook's death at the hands of the savages was substantially the punishment inflicted by God, because the Captain allowed himself to be celebrated and worshipped as a god by the heathen, consenting to their idolatry when he should have preached to them, as was done with so much efficiency nearly half a century later. The fact is the natives had a great deal of "religion" of their own, and defended their superstitions with skill and persistence before yielding to the great simplicities of the Christian faith. Captain Cook, it must be admitted, did not attempt to preach the gospel. The gentleness of the natives turned out to contain a great deal that was most horrible.

The closing years of the last century were those of rapid progress in the art of navigation, and Captain Vancouver gives this striking summary of testimony:

"By the introduction of nautical astronomy into marine education, we are taught to sail on the hypothenuse, instead of traversing two sides of a triangle, which was the usage in earlier times; by this means the circuitous course of all voyages from place to place is considerably shortened; and it is now become evident that sea officers of the most common rate abilities who will take the trouble of making themselves acquainted with the principles of this science, will, on all suitable occasinos, with proper and correct instruments, be enabled to acquire a knowledge of their situation in the Atlantic, Indian or Pacific Oceans, with a degree of accuracy sufficient to steer on a meridianal or diagonal line, to any known spot, provided it be sufficiently conspicuous to be visible at any distance from five to ten leagues.

"This great improvement, by which the most remote parts of the terrestrial globe are brought so sasily within our reach, would nevertheless have been of comparatively little utility had not those happy means been discovered for preserving the lives and health of the officers and seamen engaged in such distant and perilous undertakings; which were so peacefully practiced by Captain Cook, the first great discoverer of this salutary system, in all his latter voyages around the globe. But in none have the effect of his wise regulations, regimen and discipline been more manifest than in the course of the expedition of which the following pages are designed to treat. To an unremitting attention, not only to food, cleanliness, ventilation, and an early administration of antiseptic provisions and medicines, but also to prevent as much as possible the chance of indisposition, by prohibiting individuals from carelessly exposing themselves to the influence of climate, or unhealthy indulgences in times of relaxation, and by relieving them from fatigue and the inclemency of the weather the moment the nature of their duty would permit them to retire, is to be ascribed the preservation of the health and lives of sea-faring people on long voyages."

"Those benefits did not long remain unnoticed by the commercial part of the British nation. Remote and distant voyages being now no longer objects of terror, enterprises were projected and carried into execution, for the purpose of establishing new and lucrative branches of commerce between Northwest America and China; and parts of the coast of the former that had not been minutely examined by Captain Cook became now the general resort of the persons thus engaged."

The special zeal and consistency with which Cook is defended by the English navigators who knew him and were competent to judge of the scope of his achievements is due in part to the venom of his assailants. The historian of the Sandwich Islands, Sheldon Dibble, says: "An impression of wonder and dread having been made, Captain Cook and his men found little difficulty in having such intercourse with the people as they chose. In regard to that intercourse, it was marked, as the world would say, with kindness and humanity. But it cannot be concealed that here and there at this time, in the form of loathsome disease, was dug the grave of the Hawaiian nation; and from so deep an odium it is to be regretted that faithful history cannot exempt even the fair name of Captain Cook himself, since it was evident that he gave countenance to the evil. The native female first presented to him was a person of some rank; her name was Lelemahoalani. Sin and death were the first commodities imported to the Sandwich Islands."

We have already quoted Captain Cook's first words on this subject. He had much more to say giving in detail difficulties rather too searching to be fully stated. As for the charge that Cook personally engaged in debauchery, it rests upon the tradition of savages, who had no more idea than wild animals of the restraint of human passion. It was debated among the islanders whether the white men should be assailed by the warriors, and it was on the advice of a native queen that the women were sent to make friends with the strangers; and this was the policy pursued. As for the decline of the natives in numbers, and the "digging the grave of the nation," the horror of the islands was the destruction of female infants, and also the habit of putting aged and helpless men and women to death. The general indictment against Captain Cook is that this amiable race was just about prepared for Christianity when he thrust himself forward as a god, and with his despotic licentiousness destroyed immediate possibilities of progress. In Sandwich Island notes by "a Haole" (that is to say, a white person) we see what may be said on the other side of the picture: "It becomes an interesting duty to examine their social, political and religious condition. The first feature that calls the attention to the past is their social condition, and a darker picture can hardly be presented to the contemplation of man. They had their frequent boxing matches on a public arena, and it was nothing uncommon to see thirty or forty left dead on the field of contest.

"As gamblers they were inveterate. The game was indulged in by every person, from the king of each island to the meanest of his subjects. The wager accompanied every scene of public amusement. They gambled away their property to the last vestige of all they possessed. They staked every article of food, their growing crops, the clothes they wore, their lands, wives, daughters, and even the very bones of their arms and legs—to be made into fishhooks after they were dead. These steps led to the most absolute and crushing poverty.

"They had their dances, which were of such a character as not to be conceived by a civilized mind, and were accompanied by scenes which would have disgraced even Nero's revels. Nearly every night, with the gathering darkness, crowds would retire to some favorite spot, where, amid every species of sensual indulgence they would revel until the morning twilight. At such times the chiefs would lay aside their authority, and mingle with the lowest courtesan in every degree of debauchery.

"Thefts, robberies, murders, infanticide, licentiousness of the most debased and debasing character, burying their infirm and aged parents alive, desertion of the sick, revolting cruelties to the unfortunate maniac, cannibalism and drunkenness, form a list of some of the traits in social life among the Hawaiians in past days.

"Their drunkenness was intense. They could prepare a drink, deadly intoxicating in its nature, from a mountain plant called the awa (Piper methysticum). A bowl of this disgusting liquid was always prepared and served out just as a party of chiefs were sitting down to their meals. It would sometimes send the victim into a slumber from which he never awoke. The confirmed awa drinker could be immediately recognized by his leprous appearance.

"By far the darkest feature in their social condition was seen in the family relation. Society, however, is only a word of mere accommodation, designed to express domestic relations as they then existed. 'Society' was, indeed, such a sea of pollution as cannot be well described. Marriage was unknown, and all the sacred feelings which are suggested to our minds on mention of the various social relations, such as husband and wife, parent and child, brother and sister, were to them, indeed, as though they had no existence. There was, indeed, in this respect, a dreary blank —a dark chasm from which the soul instinctively recoils. There were, perhaps, some customs which imposed some little restraint upon the intercourse of the sexes, but those customs were easily dispensed with, and had nothing of the force of established rules. It was common for a husband to have many wives, and for a wife also to have many husbands. The nearest ties of consanguinity were but little regarded, and among the chiefs, especially, the connection of brother with sister, and parent with child, were very common. For husbands to interchange wives, and for wives to interchange husbands, was a common act of friendship, and persons who would not do this were not considered on good terms of sociability. For a man or woman to refuse a solicitation was considered an act of meanness; and this sentiment was thoroughly wrought into their minds, that, they seemed not to rid themselves of the feeling of meanness in a refusal, to feel, notwithstanding their better knowledge, that to comply was generous, liberal, and social, and to refuse reproachful and niggardly. It would be impossible to enumerate or specify the crimes which emanated from this state of affairs. Their political condition was the very genius of despotism, systematically and deliberately conducted. Kings and chiefs were extremely jealous of their succession, and the more noble their blood, the more they were venerated by the common people."

Mr. Sheldon Dibble is a historian whose work was published in 1843. He complains most bitterly that the natives bothered the missionaries by trying to give them the benefit of native thought. They wanted to do some of the talking, and said very childish things, and were so intent on their own thoughts that they would not listen to the preachers. But it ought not to have been held to be an offense for a procession of heathen to march to a missionary's house and tell him their thoughts. That was an honest manifestation of profound interest—the slow ripening of a harvest field. Mr. Dibble's book is printed by the Mission Seminary, and Mr. Dibble says, page 21: "We know that all the inhabitants of the earth descended from Noah," therefore, the Hawaiians "must once have known the great Jehova and the principles of true religion." But the historian says on the next page that the Hawaiians were heathen from time immemorial, for, "Go back to the very first reputed progenitor of the Hawaiian race, and you find that the ingredients of their character are lust, anger, strife, malice, sensuality, revenge and the worship of idols." This is the elevation upon which Mr. Dibble places himself to fire upon the memory of the English navigator Captain James Cook. The first paragraph of the assault on Cook is this:

"How unbounded the influence of foreign visitors upon the ignorant inhabitants of the Pacific! If the thousands of our countrymen who visit this ocean were actuated by the pure principles of the religion of Jesus, how immense the good they might accomplish! But, alas! how few visitors to the Western hemisphere are actuated by such principles."

This is preparatory to the condemnation of Cook in these terms: "Captain Cook allowed himself to be worshipped as a god. The people of Kealakeakua declined trading with him, and loaded his ship freely with the best productions of the island. The priests approached him in a crouching attitude, uttering prayers, and exhibiting all the formalities of worship. After approaching him with prostration the priests cast their red kapas over his shoulders and then receding a little, they presented hogs and a variety of other offerings, with long addresses rapidly enunciated, which were a repetition of their prayers and religious homage.

"When he went on shore most of the people fled for fear of him, and others bowed down before him, with solemn reverence. He was conducted to the house of the gods, and into the sacred enclosure, and received there the highest homage. In view of this fact, and of the death of Captain Cook, which speedily ensued, who can fail being admonished to give to God at all times, and even among barbarous tribes, the glory which is his due? Captain Cook might have directed the rude and ignorant natives to the great Jehovah, instead of receiving divine homage himself.

"Kalaniopuu, the king, arrived from Maui on the 24th of January, and immediately laid a tabu on the canoes, which prevented the women from visiting the ship, and consequently the men came on shore in great numbers, gratifying their infamous purposes in exchange for pieces of iron and small looking-glasses. Some of the women washed the coating from the back of the glasses much to their regret, when they found that the reflecting property was thus destroyed.

"The king, on his arrival, as well as the people, treated Captain Cook with much kindness, gave him feather cloaks and fly brushes and paid him divine honors. This adoration, it is painful to relate, was received without remonstrance. I shall speak here somewhat minutely of the death of Captain Cook, as it develops some traits of the heathen character, and the influence under which the heathen suffer from foreign intercourse."

After setting forth the horrible character of the natives, Captain Cook is condemned and denounced because he did not refuse the homage of the ferocious savages, paid him as a superior creature. One of Cook's troubles was the frantic passion the islanders had to steal iron. The common people were the property of the chiefs, and they had no other sense of possession. They gave away what they had, but took what they wanted.

Mr. Dibble shows his animus when he charges that Cook did not give the natives the real value of their hogs and fruit, and also that he had no right to stop pilferers in canoes by declaring and enforcing a blockade. This is a trifling technicality much insisted upon. Dibble's account of the death of Cook is this:

"A canoe came from an adjoining district, bound within the bay. In the canoe were two chiefs of some rank, Kekuhaupio and Kalimu. The canoe was fired upon from one of the boats and Kalimu was killed. Kekuhaupio made the greatest speed till he reached the place of the king, where Captain Cook also was, and communicated the intelligence of the death of the chief. The attendants of the king were enraged and showed signs of hostility, but were restrained by the thought that Captain Cook was a god. At that instant a warrior, with a spear in his hand, approached Captain Cook and was heard to say that the boats in the harbor had killed his brother, and he would be revenged. Captain Cook, from his enraged appearance and that of the multitude, was suspicious of him, and fired upon him with his pistol. Then followed a scene of confusion, and in the midst Captain Cook being hit with a stone, and perceiving the man who threw it, shot him dead. He also struck a certain chief with his sword, whose name was Kalaimanokahoowaha. The chief instantly seized Captain Cook with a strong hand, designing merely to hold him and not to take his life; for he supposed him to be a god and that he could not die. Captain Cook struggled to free himself from the grasp, and as he was about to fall uttered a groan. The people immediately exclaimed, "He groans—he is not a god," and instantly slew him. Such was the melancholy death of Captain Cook.

"Immediately the men in the boat commenced a deliberate fire upon the crowd. They had refrained in a measure before, for fear of killing their Captain. Many of the natives were killed."

"Historian Dibble does not notice the evidence that Cook lost his life by turning to his men in the boats, ordering them not to fire. It was at that moment he was stabbed in the back. Dibble represents the facts as if to justify the massacre of the great navigator, because he allowed the heathen to think he was one of their gang of gods. But this presumption ought not to have been allowed to excuse prevarication about testimony. The importance of Dibble's history is that it is representative. He concludes with this eloquent passage: "From one heathen nation we may learn in a measure the wants of all. And we ought not to restrict our view, but, look at the wide world. To do then for all nations what I have urged in behalf of the Sandwich Islands, how great and extensive a work! How vast the number of men and how immense the amount of means which seem necessary to elevate all nations, and gain over the whole earth to the permanent dominion of the Lord Jesus Christ! Can 300,000,000 of pagan children and youth be trained and instructed by a few hands? Can the means of instructing them be furnished by the mere farthings and pence of the church? Will it not be some time yet before ministers and church members will need to be idle a moment for the want of work? Is there any danger of our being cut off from the blessed privilege either of giving or of going? There is a great work yet to be done—a noble work—a various and a

RIDING BUFFALOES THROUGH GROVES OF DATE PALMS.

A NATIVE HOUSE.

GREAT BRIDGE AT MANILA.

NATIVES FISHING FROM A CANAL BOAT.

difficult work—a work worthy of God's power, God's resources, and God's wisdom. What christendom has as yet done is scarcely worthy of being called a commencement. When God shall bring such energies into action as shall be commensurate with the greatness of the work—when he shall cause every redeemed sinner, by the abundant influence of His Holy Spirit, to lay himself out wholly in the great enterprise. then there will be a sight of moral sublimity that shall rivet the gaze of angels."

We quote this writer as to what became of the remains of Cook: "The body of Captain Cook was carried into the interior of the island, the bones secured according to their custom, and the flesh burned in the fire. The heart, liver, etc., of Captain Cook, were stolen and eaten by some hungry children, who mistook them in the night for the inwards of a dog. The names of the children were Kupa, Mohoole and Kaiwikokoole. These men are now all dead. The last of the number died two years since at the station of Lahaina. Some of the bones of Captain Cook were sent on board his ship, in compliance with the urgent demands of the officers; and some were kept by the priests as objects of worship." The "heart, liver, etc.," were of course given to the children to eat! The bones are still hidden, and presumably not much worshiped. The first of the remains of Captain Cook given up was a mass of his bloody flesh, cut as if from a slaughtered ox. After some time there were other fragments, including one of his hands which had a well known scar, and perfectly identified it. Along with this came the story of burning flesh, and denials of cannibalism. Mr. Dibble speaks of Cook's "consummate folly and outrageous tyranny of placing a blockade upon a heathen bay, which the natives could not possibly be supposed either to understand or appreciate." That blockade, like others, was understood when enforced. The historian labors to work out a case to justify the murder of Cook because he received worship. As to the acknowledgment of Cook as the incarnation of Lono, in the Hawaiian Pantheon, Captain King says:

"Before I proceed to relate the adoration that was paid to Captain Cook, and the peculiar ceremonies with which he was received on this fatal island, it will be necessary to describe the Morai, situated, as I have already mentioned, at the south side of the beach at Kakooa (Kealakeakua). It was a square solid pile of stones, about forty yards long, twenty broad, and fourteen in height. The top was flat and well paved, and surrounded by a wooden rail, on which were fixed the skulls of the captives sacrificed on the death of their chiefs. In the center of the area stood a ruinous old building of wood, connected with the rail on each side by a stone wall, which next divided the whole space into two parts. On the side next the country were five poles, upward of twenty feet high, supporting an irregular kind of scaffold;

on the opposite side toward the sea, stood two small houses with a covered communication.

"We were conducted by Koah to the top of this pile by an easy ascent leading from the beach to the northwest corner of the area. At the entrance we saw two large wooden images, with features violently distorted, and a long piece of carved wood of a conical form inverted, rising from the top of their heads; the rest was without form and wrapped round with red cloth. We were here met by a tall young man with a long beard, who presented Captain Cook to the images, and after chanting a kind of hymn, in which he was joined by Koah, they led us to that end of the Morai where the five poles were fixed. At the foot of them were twelve images ranged in a semicircular form, and before the middle figure stood a high stand or table, exactly resembling the Whatta of Othaheiti, on which lay a putrid hog, and under it pieces of sugar cane, cocoanuts, bread fruit, plantains and sweet potatoes. Koah having placed the Captain under the stand, took down the hog and held it toward him; and after having a second time addressed him in a long speech, pronounced with much vehemence and rapidity, he let it fall on the ground and led him to the scaffolding, which they began to climb together, not without great risk of falling. At this time we saw coming in solemn procession, at the entrance of the top of the Morai, ten men carrying a live hog and a large piece of red cloth. Being advanced a few paces, they stopped and prostrated themselves; and Kaireekeea, the young man above mentioned, went to them, and receiving the cloth carried it to Koah, who wrapped it around the Captain, and afterwards offered him the hog, which was brought by Kaireekeea with the same ceremony.

"Whilst Captain Cook was aloft in this awkward situation, swathed round with red cloth, and with difficulty keeping his hold amongst the pieces of rotten scaffolding, Kaireekeea and Koah began their office, chanting sometimes in concert and sometimes alternately. This lasted a considerable time; at length Koah let the hog drop, when he and the Captain descended together. He then led him to the images before mentioned, and, having said something to each in a sneering tone, snapping his fingers at them as he passed, he brought him to that in the center, which, from its being covered with red cloth, appeared to be in greater estimation than the rest. Before this figure he prostrated himself and kissed it, desiring Captain Cook to do the same, who suffered himself to be directed by Koah throughout the whole of this ceremony.

"We were now led back to the other division of the Morai, where there was a space ten or twelve feet square, sunk about three feet below the level of the area. Into this we descended, and Captain Cook was seated between two wooden idols,

Koah supporting one of his arms, whilst I was desired to support the other. At this time arrived a second procession of natives, carrying a baked hog and a pudding, some bread fruit, cocoanuts and other vegetables. When they approached us Kaireekeea put himself at their head, and presenting the pig to Captain Cook in the usual manner, began the same kind of chant as before, his companions making regular responses. We observed that after every response their parts became gradually shorter, till, toward the close, Kaireekeea's consisted of only two or three words, while the rest answered by the word Orono.

"When this offering was concluded, which lasted a quarter of an hour, the natives sat down fronting us, and began to cut up the baked hog, to peel the vegetables and break the cocoanuts; whilst others employed themselves in brewing the awa, which is done by chewing it in the same manner as at the Friendly Islands. Kaireekeea then took part of the kernel of a cocoanut, which he chewed, and wrapping it in a piece of cloth, rubbed with it the Captain's face, head, hands, arms and shoulders. The awa was then handed around, and after we had tasted it Koah and Pareea began to pull the flesh of the hog in pieces and put it into our mouths. I had no great objection to being fed by Pareea, who was very cleanly in his person, but Captain Cook, who was served by Koah, recollecting the putrid hog, could not swallow a morsel; and his reluctance, as may be supposed, was not diminished when the old man, according to his own mode of civility had chewed it for him.

"When this ceremony was finished, which Captain Cook put an end to as soon as he decently could, we quitted the Morai."

Evidently the whole purpose of Captain Cook in permitting this performance, was to flatter and gratify the natives and make himself strong to command them. The Captain himself was sickened, and got away as quickly as he could without giving offense. This was not the only case in which the native priests presented the navigator as a superior being. Perhaps the view the old sailor took of the style of ceremony was as there were so many gods, one more or less did not matter. Cook never attached importance to the freaks of superstition, except so far as it might be made useful in keeping the bloody and beastly savages in check. Bearing upon this point we quote W. D. Alexander's "Brief History of the Hawaiian People," pages 33-34:

"Infanticide was fearfully prevalent, and there were few of the older women at the date of the abolition of idolatry who had not been guilty of it. It was the opinion of those best informed that two-thirds of all the children born were destroyed in infancy by their parents. They were generally buried alive, in many cases in the very houses occupied by their unnatural parents. On all the islands the number of males was much greater than that of females, in consequence of the girls being more frequently destroyed than the boys. The principal reason given for it was laziness—unwillingness to take the trouble of rearing children. It was a very common practice for parents to give away their children to any persons who were willing to adopt them.

"No regular parental discipline was maintained, and the children were too often left to follow their own inclinations and to become familiar with the lowest vices.

"Neglect of the helpless. Among the common people old age was despised. The sick and those who had become helpless from age were sometimes abandoned to die or put to death. Insane people were also sometimes stoned to death."

Again we quote Alexander's History, page 49:

"Several kinds of food were forbidden to the women on pain of death, viz., pork, bananas, cocoanuts, turtles, and certain kinds of fish, as the ulua, the humu, the shark, the hihimanu or sting-ray, etc. The men of the poorer class often formed a sort of eating club apart from their wives. These laws were rigorously enforced. At Honaunau, Hawaii, two young girls of the highest rank, Kapiolani and Keoua, having been detected in the act of eating a banana, their kahu, or tutor, was held responsible, and put to death by drowning. Shortly before the abolition of the tabus, a little child had one of her eyes scooped out for the same offense. About the same time a woman was put to death for entering the eating house of her husband, although she was tipsy at the time."

Captain Cook seems to have committed the unpardonable sin in not beginning the stated work of preaching the gospel a long generation before the missionaries arrived, and the only sound reason for this is found in Dibble's History, in his statement that the islanders steadily degenerated until the missions were organized.

Writers of good repute, A. Fornander, chief of them, are severe with Captain Cook on account of his alleged greed, not paying enough for the red feathers woven into fanciful forms. Perhaps that is a common fault in the transactions of civilized men with barbarians. William Penn is the only man with a great reputation for dealing fairly with American Red Men, and he was not impoverished by it. Cook gave nails for hogs, and that is mentioned in phrases that are malicious. Iron was to the islanders the precious metal, and they were not cheated. A long drawn out effort has been made to impress the world that Cook thought himself almost a god, and was a monster. The natives gave to the wonderful people who came to them in ships, liberally of their plenty, and received in return presents that pleased them, articles of utility. Beads came along at a later day. The natives believed Cook one of the heroes of the imagination that they called gods. He sought to propitiate them and paid for fruit and meat in iron and showy trifles. His policy of progress was to introduce domestic animals.

Note the temper of Mr. Abraham Fornander, a man who has meant honesty of statement, but whose information was perverted:

"And how did Captain Cook requite this boundless hospitality, that never once made default during his long stay of seventeen days in Kealakeakua, these magnificent presents of immense value, this delicate and spontaneous attention to every want, this friendship of the chiefs and priests, this friendliness of the common people? By imposing on their good nature to the utmost limit of its ability to respond to the greedy and constant calls of their new friends; by shooting at one of the king's officers for endeavoring to enforce a law of the land, an edict of his sovereign that happened to be unpalatable to the new comers, and caused them some temporary inconvenience, after a week's profusion and unbridled license; by a liberal exhibition of his force and the meanest display of his bounty; by giving the king a linen shirt and a cutlass in return for feather cloaks and helmets, which, irrespective of their value as insignia of the highest nobility in the land, were worth singly at least from five to ten thousand dollars, at present price of the feathers, not counting the cost of manufacturing; by a reckless disregard of the proprieties of ordinary intercourse, even between civilized and savage man, and a wanton insult to what he reasonably may have supposed to have been the religious sentiments of his hosts." This is up to the mark of a criminal lawyer retained to prove by native testimony that Captain James Cook was not murdered, but executed for cause. The great crime of Cook is up to this point that of playing that he was one of the Polynesian gods. Fornander says: "When the sailors carried off, not only the railing of the temple, but also the idols of the gods within it, even the large-hearted patience of Kaoo gave up, and he meekly requested that the central idol at least might be restored. Captain King failed to perceive that the concession of the priests was that of a devotee to his saint. The priests would not sell their religious emblems and belongings for "thirty pieces of silver," or any remuneration, but they were willing to offer up the entire Heiau, and themselves on the top of it, as a holocaust to Lono, if he had requested it. So long as Cook was regarded as a god in their eyes they could not refuse him. And though they exhibited no resentment at the request, the want of delicacy and consideration on the part of Captain Cook is none the less glaring. After his death, and when the illusion of godship had subsided, his spoliation of the very Heiau in which he had been deified was not one of the least of the grievances which native annalists laid up against him."

Contrast this flagrancy in advocacy of the cause of the barbarous natives with the last words Cook wrote in his journal. We quote from "A Voyage to the Pacific Ocean," by Captain James Cook, F. R. S., (Vol. II., pages 251-252):

"As it was of the last importance to procure a supply of provisions at these islands; and experience having taught me that I could have no chance to succeed in this, if a free trade with the natives were to be allowed; that is, if it were left to every man's discretion to trade for what he pleased, and in what manner he pleased; for this substantial reason, I now published an order prohibiting all persons from trading, except such as should be appointed by me and Captain Clarke; and even these were enjoined to trade only for provisions and refreshments. Women were also forobidden to be admitted into the ships, except under certain restrictions. But the evil I intended to prevent, by this regulation, I soon found had already got amongst them.

"I stood in again the next morning till within three or four miles of the land, where we were met with a number of canoes laden with provisions. We brought to, and continued trading with the people in them till four in the afternoon, when, having got a pretty good supply, we made sail and stretched off to the northward.

"I had never met with a behavior so free from reserve and suspicion in my intercourse with any tribe of savages as we experienced in the people of this island. It was very common for them to send up into the ship the several articles they brought for barter; afterward, they would come in themselves and make their bargains on the quarter-deck.

"We spent the night as usual, standing off and on. It happened that four men and ten women who had come on board the preceding day still remained with us. As I did not like the company of the latter, I stood in shore toward noon, principally with a view to get them out of the ship; and, some canoes coming off, I took that opportunity of sending away our guests.

"In the evening Mr. Bligh returned and reported that he had found a bay in which was good anchorage, and fresh water in a situation tolerably easy to be come at. Into this bay I resolved to carry the ships, there to refit and supply ourselves with every refreshment that the place could afford. As night approached the greater part of our visitors retired to the shore, but numbers of them requested our permission to sleep on board. Curiosity was not the only motive, at least with some, for the next morning several things were missing, which determined me **not** to entertain so many another night.

"At eleven o'clock in the forenoon we anchored in the bay, which is called by the natives Karakaooa, (Kealakeakua), in thirteen fathoms water, over a sandy bottom, and about a quarter of a mile from the northeast shore. In this situation the south point of the bay bore south by west, and the north point west half north. We moored with the stream-anchor and cable, to the northward, unbent the sails and struck yards and topmasts. The ships continued to be much crowded with natives, and were surrounded by a multitude of canoes. I had nowhere, in the course of my voyages, seen so numerous a body of people assembled in one place. For, besides those who had come off to us in canoes, all the shore of the bay was covered with spectators, and many hundreds were swimming around the ships like shoals of fish. We could not but be struck with the singularity of this scene, and perhaps there were few on board who lamented our having failed in our endeavors to find a northern passage homeward last summer. To this disappointment we owed our having it in our power to revisit the Sandwich Islands, and to enrich our voyage with a discovery which, though the last, seemed in many respects to be the most important that had hitherto been made by Europeans, throughout the extent of the Pacific Ocean."

This is the end of Cook's writing. His murder followed immediately. He fell by the hands of people for whom his good will was shown in his last words. The concluding pages of the journal answer all the scandals his enemies have so busily circulated.

There is a gleam of humor that shows like a thread of gold in the midst of the somber tragedies of the Sandwich Islands, and we must not omit to extract it from "The Voyage of Discovery Around the World" by Captain George Vancouver, when he spent some time in Hawaii, and gives two bright pictures—one of a theatrical performance, and the other the happy settlement of the disordered domestic relations of a monarch.

A GIFTED NATIVE ACTRESS AND SOME ROYAL DRAMATISTS.

"There was a performance by a single young woman of the name of Puckoo, whose person and manners were both very agreeable. Her dress, notwithstanding the heat of the weather, consisted of an immense quantity of cloth, which was wreaths of black, red and yellow feathers; but, excepting these, she wore no dress a manner as to give a pretty effect to the variegated pattern of the cloth; and was otherways disposed with great taste. Her head and neck were decorated with wreaths of black, red and yellow feathers; but, excepting these, she wore no dress from the waist upwards. Her ankles, and nearly half way up her legs, were decorated with several folds of cloth, widening upwards, so that the upper parts extended from the leg at least four inches all round; this was encompassed by a piece of net work, wrought very close, from the meshes of which were hung the small teeth of dogs, giving this part of her dress the appearance of an ornamented funnel. On her wrists she wore bracelets made of the tusks of the largest hogs. These were highly polished and fixed close together in a ring, the concave sides of the tusks being outwards; and their ends reduced to a uniform length, curving naturally away from the center, were by no means destitute of ornamental effect. Thus equipped, her appearance on the stage, before she uttered a single word, excited considerable applause.

"These amusements had hitherto been confined to such limited performances; but this afternoon was to be dedicated to one of a more splendid nature, in which some ladies of consequence, attendants on the court of Tamaahmaah, were to perform the principal parts. Great pains had been taken, and they had gone through many private rehearsals, in order that the exhibition this evening might be worthy of the public attention; on the conclusion of which, I purposed by a display of fireworks, to make a return for the entertainment they had afforded us.

"About four o'clock we were informed it was time to attend the royal dames; their theatre, or rather place of exhibition, was about a mile to the southward of our tents, in a small square, surrounded by houses, and sheltered by trees, a situation as well chosen for the performance, as for the accommodation of the spectators; who, on a moderate computation, could not be estimated at less than four thousand, of all ranks and descriptions of persons.

"The dress of the actresses was something like that worn by Puckoo, though made of superior materials, and disposed with more taste and elegance. A very considerable quantity of their finest cloth was prepared for the occasion; of this their lower garment was formed, which extended from their waist half down their legs, and was so plaited as to appear very much like a hoop petticoat. This seemed the most difficult part of their dress to adjust, for Tamaahmaah, who was considered to be a profound critic, was frequently appealed to by the women, and his directions were implicitly followed in many little alterations. Instead of the ornaments of cloth and net-work, decorated with dogs' teeth, these ladies had each a green wreath made of a kind of bind weed, twisted together in different parts like a rope, which was wound round from the ankle, nearly to the lower part of the petticoat. On their wrists they wore no bracelets nor other ornaments, but across their necks and shoulders were green sashes, very nicely made, with the broad leaves of the tee, a plant that produces a very luscious sweet root, the size of a yam. This part of their dress was put on the last by each of the actresses; and the party being now fully attired, the king and queen, who had been present the whole time of their dressing, were obliged to withdraw, greatly to the mortification of the latter, who would gladly have taken her part as a performer, in which she was reputed to excel very highly. But the royal pair were compelled to retire, even from the exhibition, as they are prohibited by law from attending such amusements, excepting on the festival of the new year. Indeed, the performance of this day was contrary to the established rules of the island, but being intended as a compliment to us, the innovation was permitted.

"As their majesties withdrew, the ladies of rank and the principal chiefs began to make their appearance. The reception of the former by the multitude was marked by a degree of respect that I had not before seen amongst any inhabitants of the countries in the Pacific Ocean. The audience assembled at this time were standing in rows, from fifteen to twenty feet deep, so close as to touch each other; but these ladies no sooner approached in their rear, in any accidental direction, than a passage was instantly made for them and their attendants to pass through in the most commodious manner to their respective stations, where they seated themselves on the ground, which was covered with mats, in the most advantageous situation for seeing and hearing the performers. Most of these ladies were of a corpulent form, which, assisted by their stately gait, the dignity with which they moved, and the number of their pages, who followed with fans to court the refreshing breeze, or with fly-flaps to disperse the offending insects, announced their consequence as the wives, daughters, sisters, or other near relations of the principal chiefs, who, however, experienced no such marks of respect or attention themselves; being obliged to make their way through the spectators in the best manner they were able.

"The time devoted to the decoration of the actresses extended beyond the limits of the quiet patience of the audience, who exclaimed two or three times, from all quarters, "Hoorah, hoorah, poaliealee," signifying that it would be dark and black night before the performance would begin. But the audience here, like similar ones in other countries, attending with a pre-disposition to be pleased, was in good humor, and was easily appeased, by the address of our faithful and devoted friend Trywhookee, who was the conductor of the ceremonies, and sole manager on this occasion. He came forward and apologized by a speech that produced a general laugh, and, causing the music to begin, we heard no further murmurs.

"The band consisted of five men, all standing up, each with a highly polished wooden spear in the left, and a small piece of the same material, equally well finished, in the right hand; with this they beat on the spear, as an accompaniment to their own voices in songs, that varied both as to time and measure, especially the latter; yet their voices, and the sounds produced from the rude instruments, which differed according to the place on which the tapering spear was struck, appeared to accord very well. Having engaged us a short time in this vocal performance, the court ladies made their appearance, and were received with shouts of the greatest applause. The musicians retired a few paces, and the actresses took their station before them.

"The heroine of the piece, which consisted of four or five acts, had once shared the affections and embraces of Tamaahmaah, but was now married to an inferior chief, whose occupation in the household was that of the charge of the king's apparel. This lady was distinguished by a green wreath round the crown of the head; next to her was the captive daughter of Titeeree; the third a younger sister to the queen, the wife of Crymamahoo, who, being of the most exalted rank, stood in the middle. On each side of these were two of inferior quality, making in all seven actresses. They drew themselves up in a line fronting that side of the square that was occupied by ladies of quality and the chiefs. These were completely detached from the populace, not by any partition, but, as it were, by the respectful consent of the lower orders of the assembly; not one of which trespassed or produced the least inaccommodation.

"This representation, like that before attempted to be described, was a compound of speaking and singing; the subject of which was enforced by gestures and actions. The piece was in honor of a captive princess, whose name was Crycowculleneaow; and on her name being pronounced, every one present, men as well as women, who wore any ornaments above their waists, were obliged to take them off, though the captive lady was at least sixty miles distant. This mark of respect was unobserved by the actresses whilst engaged in the performance; but the instant any one sat down, or at the close of the act, they were also obliged to comply with this mysterious ceremony.

"The variety of attitudes into which these women threw themselves, with the rapidity of their action, resembled no amusement in any other part of the world within my knowledge, by a comparison with which I might be enabled to convey some idea of the stage effect thus produced, particularly in the three first parts.

in which there appeared much correspondence and harmony between the tone of their voices and the display of their limbs. One or two of the performers being not quite so perfect as the rest, afforded us an opportunity of exercising our judgment by comparison; and it must be confessed, that the ladies who most excelled, exhibited a degree of graceful action, for the attainment of which it is difficult to account.

"In each of these first parts the songs, attitudes and actions appeared to me of greater variety than I had before noticed amongst the people of the great South Sea nation on any former occasion. The whole, though I am unequal to its description, was supported with a wonderful degree of spirit and vivacity; so much indeed that some of their exertions were made with such a degree of agitating violence as seemed to carry the performers beyond what their strength was able to sustain; and had the performance finished with the third act, we should have retired from their theatre with a much higher idea of the moral tendency of their drama, than was conveyed by the offensive, libidinous scene, exhibited by the ladies in the concluding part. The language of the song, no doubt, corresponded with the obscenity of their actions; which were carried to a degree of extravagance that were calculated to produce nothing but disgust, even to the most licentious."

From "A Voyage of Discovery," by Captain George Vancouver:

THE RECONCILIATION BY STRATEGY OF A KING WITH ONE OF HIS QUEENS.

"Tahowmotoo was amongst the most constant of our guests; but his daughter, the disgraced queen, seldom visited our side of the bay. I was not, however, ignorant of her anxious desire for a reconciliation with Tamaahmaah; nor was the same wish to be misunderstood in the conduct and behavior of the king, in whose good opinion and confidence I had now acquired such a predominancy that I became acquainted with his most secret inclinations and apprehensions.

"His unshaken attachment and unaltered affection for Tahowmannoo was confessed with a sort of internal self conviction of her innocence. He acknowledged with great candor that his own conduct had not been exactly such as warranted his having insisted upon a separation from his queen; that although it could not authorize, it in some measure pleaded in excuse for her infidelity: and for his own, he alleged, that his high rank and supreme authority was a sort of licence for such indulgences.

"An accommodation which I considered to be mutually wished by both parties was urged in the strongest terms by the queen's relations. To effect this desirable purpose, my interference was frequently solicited by them; and as it concurred with my own inclination, I resolved on embracing the first favorable opportunity to use my best endeavors for bringing a reconciliation about. For although, on our former visit, Tahowmannoo had been regarded with the most favorable impressions, yet, whether from her distresses, or because she had really improved in her personal accomplishments, I will not take upon me to determine, but certain it is that one or both of these circumstances united had so far prepossessed us all in her favor, and no one more so than myself, that it had long been the general wish to see her exalted again to her former dignities. This desire was probably not a little heightened by the regard we entertained for the happiness and repose of our noble and generous friend Tamaahmaah, who was likely to be materially affected not only in his domestic comforts, but in his political situation, by receiving again and reinstating his consort in her former rank and consequence.

"I was convinced beyond all doubt that there were two or three of the most considerable chiefs of the island whose ambitious views were inimical to the interests and authority of Tamaahmaah; and it was much to be apprehended that if the earnest solicitations of the queen's father (whose condition and importance was next in consequence to that of the king) should continue to be rejected, that there could be little doubt of his adding great strength and influence to the discontented and turbulent chiefs, which would operate highly to the prejudice, if not totally to the destruction, of Tamaahmaah's regal power; especially as the adverse party seemed to form a constant opposition, consisting of a minority by no means to be despised by the executive power, and which appeared to be a principal constituent part of the Owhyean politics.

"For these substantial reasons, whenever he was disposed to listen to such discourse, I did not cease to urge the importance and necessity of his adopting measures so highly essential to his happiness as a man, and to his power, interest and authority as the supreme chief of the island. All this he candidly acknowledged, but his pride threw impediments in the way of a reconciliation, which were hard to be removed. He would not himself become the immediate agent; and although he considered it important that the negotiation should be conducted by some one of the principal chiefs in his fullest confidence, yet, to solicit their good offices after having rejected their former overtures with disdain, was equally hard to reconcile to his feelings. I stood nearly in the same situation with his favorite friends; but being thoroughly convinced of the sincerity of his wishes, I spared him the mortification of soliciting the offices he had rejected, by again proffering my services. To this he instantly consented, and observed that no proposal could have met his mind so completely; since, by effecting a reconciliation through my friendship, no umbrage could be taken at his having declined the several offers of his countrymen by any of the individuals; whereas, had this object been accomplished by any one of the chiefs, it would probably have occasioned jealousy and discontent in the minds of the others.

"All, however, was not yet complete; the apprehension that some concession might be suggested, or expected, on his part, preponderated against every other consideration; and he would on no account consent, that it should appear that he had been privy to the business, or that it had been by his desire that a negotiation had been undertaken for this happy purpose, but that the whole should have the appearance of being purely the result of accident.

"To this end it was determined that I should invite the queen, with several of her relations and friends, on board the Discovery, for the purpose of presenting them with some trivial matters, as tokens of my friendship and regard; and that, whilst thus employed, our conversation should be directed to ascertain whether an accommodation was still an object to be desired. That on this appearing to be the general wish, Tamaahmaah would instantly repair on board in a hasty manner, as if he had something extraordinary to communicate; that I should appear to rejoice at this accidental meeting, and by instantly uniting their hands, bring the reconciliation to pass without the least discussion or explanation on either side. But from his extreme solicitude lest he should in any degree be suspected of being concerned in this previous arrangement, a difficulty arose how to make him acquainted with the result of the proposed conversation on board, which could not be permitted by a verbal message; at length, after some thought, he took up two pieces of paper, and of his own accord made certain marks with a pencil on each of them, and then delivered them to me. The difference of these marks he could well recollect; the one was to indicate that the result of my inquiries was agreeable to his wishes, and the other that it was contrary. In the event of my making use of the former, he proposed that it should not be sent on shore secretly, but in an open and declared manner, and by way of a joke, as a present to his Owhyhean majesty. The natural gaiety of disposition which generally prevails among these islanders, would render this supposed disappointment of the king a subject for mirth, would in some degree prepare the company for his visit, and completely do away with every idea of its being the effect of a preconcerted measure.

"This plan was accordingly carried into execution on the following Monday. Whilst the queen and her party, totally ignorant of the contrivance, were receiving the compliments I had intended them, their good humor and pleasantry were infinitely heightened by the jest I proposed to pass upon the king, in sending him a piece of paper only, carefully wrapped up in some cloth of their own manufacture, accompanied by a message; importing, that as I was then in the act of distributing favors to my Owhyhean friends, I had not been unmindful of his majesty.

"Tamaahmaah no sooner received the summons, than he hastened on board, and, with his usual vivacity, exclaimed before he made his appearance that he was come to thank me for the present I had sent him, and for my goodness in not having forgotten him on this occasion. This was heard by everyone in the cabin before he entered; and all seemed to enjoy the joke except the poor queen, who appeared to be much agitated at the idea of being again in his presence. The instant that he saw her his countenance expressed great surprise, he became immediately silent, and attempted to retire; but, having posted myself for the especial purpose of preventing his departure, I caught his hand and, joining it with the queen's, their reconciliation was instantly completed. This was fully demonstrated, not only by the tears that involuntarily stole down the cheeks of both as they embraced each other and mutually expressed the satisfaction they experienced; but by the behavior of every individual present, whose feelings on the occasion were not to be repressed; whilst their sensibility testified the happiness which this apparently fortuitous event had produced.

"A short pause, produced by an event so unexpected, was succeeded by the sort of good humor that such a happy circumstance would naturally inspire; the conversation soon became general, cheerful and lively, in which the artifice imagined to have been imposed upon the king bore no small share. A little refreshment from a few glasses of wine concluded the scene of this successful meeting.

"After the queen had acknowledged in the most grateful terms the weighty obligations which she felt for my services on this occasion, I was surprised by her saying, as we were all preparing to go on shore, that she had still a very great favor to request; which was, that I should obtain from Tamahmaah a solemn promise that on her return to his habitation he would not beat her. The great cordiality with which the reconciliation had taken place, and the happiness that each of them had continued to express in consequence of it, led me at first to consider this entreaty of the queen as a jest only; but in this I was mistaken, for, notwithstanding that Tamaahmaah readily complied with my solicitation, and assured me nothing of the kind should take place, yet Tahowmannoo would not be satisfied without my accompanying them home to the royal residence, where I had the pleasure of seeing her restored to all her former honors and privileges, highly to the satisfaction of all the king's friends, but to the utter mortification of those who by their scandalous reports and misrepresentations had been the cause of the unfortunate separtion.

"The domestic affairs of Tamaahmaah having thus taken so happy a turn, his mind was more at liberty for political considerations; and the cession of Owhyhee to his Britannic Majesty now became an object of his serious concern."

Captain Cook makes a strong plea in his journal that he was the very original discoverer of the Sandwich Islands. Referring to the wonderful extent of the surface of the earth in which the land is occupied by the Polynesial race, he exclaims:

"How shall we account for this nation's having spread itself, in so many detached islands, so widely disjoined from each other, in every quarter of the Pacific Ocean! We find it, from New Zealand in the South, as far as the Sandwich Islands, to the North! And, in another direction, from Easter Islands to the Hebrides! That is, over an extent of sixty degrees of latitude, or twelve hundred leagues, North and South! And eighty-three degrees of longitude, or sixteen hundred and sixty leagues, East and West! How much farther, in either direction, its colonies reach, is not known; but what we know already, in consequence of this and our former voyage, warrants our pronouncing it to be, though perhaps not the most numerous, certainly, by far, the most extensive, nation upon earth.

"Had the Sandwich Islands been discovered at an early period by the Spaniards, there is little doubt that they would have taken advantage of so excellent a situation, and have made use of Atooi, or some other of the islands, as a refreshing place to the ships, that sail annually from Acapulco for Manilla. They lie almost midway between the first place and Guam, one of the Ladrones, which is at present their only port in traversing this vast ocean; and it would not have been a week's sail out of their common route to have touched at them; which could have been done without running the least hazard of losing the passage, as they are sufficiently within the verge of the easterly trade wind. An acquaintance with the Sandwich Islands would have been equally favorable to our Buccaneers, who used sometimes to pass from the coast of America to the Ladrones, with a stock of food and water scarcely sufficient to preserve life. Here they might always have found plenty, and have been within a month's sure sail of the very part of California which the Manilla ship is obliged to make, or else have returned to the coast of America, thoroughly refitted, after an absence of two months. How happy would Lord Anson have been, and what hardships he would have avoided, if he had known that there was a group of islands half way between America and Tinian, where all his wants could have been effectually supplied; and in describing which the elegant historian of that voyage would have presented his reader with a more agreeable picture than I have been able to draw in this chapter."

And yet there seems to be reason for believing that there was a Spanish ship cast away on one of the Hawaiian group, and that their descendants are distinctly marked men yet: There was also a white man and woman saved from the sea at some unknown period, of course since Noah, and they multiplied and replenished, and the islanders picked up somewhere a knack for doing things in construction of boats and the weaving of mats that hint at a crude civilization surviving in a mass of barbarianism.

Captain George Dixon names the islands discovered by Captain Cook on his last voyage:

"Owhyhee (Hawaii), the principal, is the first to the southward and eastward, the rest run in a direction nearly northwest. The names of the principals are Mowee (Maui), Morotoy (Molokai), Ranai (Lanai), Whahoo (Oahu), Attooi (Kauai), and Oneehow (Niihau)."

This account Dixon gives of two curious and rather valuable words: "The moment a chief concludes a bargain, he repeats the word Coocoo thrice, with quickness, and is immediately answered by all the people in his canoe with the word Whoah, pronounced in a tone of exclamation, but with greater or less energy, in proportion as the bargain he has made is approved."

The great and celebrated Kamehameha, who consolidated the government of the islands, did it by an act of treachery and murder, thus told in Alexander's history:

"The Assassination of Keoua.—Toward the end of the year 1791 two of Kamehameha's chief counsellors, Kamanawa and Keaweaheulu, were sent on an embassy to Keoua at Kahuku in Kau. Keoua's chief warrior urged him to put them to death, which he indignantly refused to do.

"By smooth speeches and fair promises they persuaded him to go to Kawaihae, and have an interview with Kamehameha, in order to put an end to the war, which had lasted nine years. Accordingly he set out with his most intimate friends and

SOUTHERN ISLANDERS SHOWING COCOANUT PALM AND THE MONKEY TREE.

A REVIEW OF SPANISH FILIPINO VOLUNTEERS.

A SPANISH FESTIVAL IN MANILA.

twenty-four rowers in his own double canoe, accompanied by Keaweaheulu in another canoe, and followed by friends and retainers in other canoes.

"As they approached the landing at Kawaihae, Keeaumoku surrounded Keoua's canoe with a number of armed men. As Kamakau relates: 'Seeing Kamehameha on the beach, Keoua called out to him, "Here I am," to which he replied, "Rise up and come here, that we may know each other."'

"As Keoua was in the act of leaping ashore, Keeaumoku killed him with a spear. All the men in Keoua's canoe and in the canoes of his immediate company were slaughtered but one. But when the second division approached, Kamehameha gave orders to stop the massacre. The bodies of the slain were then laid upon the altar of Puukohola as an offering to the blood-thirsty divinity Kukailimoku. That of Keoua had been previously baked in an oven at the foot of the hill as a last indignity. This treacherous murder made Kamehameha master of the whole island of Hawaii, and was the first step toward the consolidation of the group under one government."

This is one of those gentle proceedings of an amiable race, whose massacre of Captain Cook has been so elaborately vindicated by alleged exponents of civilization.

There is found the keynote of the grevious native government in an incident of the date of 1841 by which "the foreign relations of the government became involved with the schemes of a private firm. The firm of Ladd & Co. had taken the lead in developing the agricultural resources of the islands by their sugar plantation at Koloa and in other ways, and had gained the entire confidence of the king and chiefs. On the 24th of November, 1841, a contract was secretly drawn up at Lahaina by Mr. Brinsmade, a member of the firm, and Mr. Richards, and duly signed by the king and premier, which had serious after-consequences. It granted to Ladd & Co. the privilege of "leasing any now unoccupied and unimproved localities" in the islands for one hundred years, at a low rental, each millsite to include fifteen acres, and the adjoining land for cultivation in each locality not to exceed two hundred acres, with privileges of wood, pasture, etc. These sites were to be selected within one year, which term was afterwards extended to four years from date."

Of course there are many safeguards, particularly in this case, but the points of the possession of land conceded, the time for the people to recover their rights never comes.

One of the difficulties in the clearing up of the foggy chapters of the history of the Hawaiian islands is that within the lifetime of men who were young at the close of the last century, the Hawaiian tongue became a written language, and made the traditions of savages highly colored stories, in various degrees according to ignorance, prejudice and sympathy, accepted as historical. The marvels accomplished by the missionaries influenced them to deal gently with those whose conversion was a recognized triumph of Christendom, and there was an effort to condemn Captain Cook, who had affected to nod as a God, as a warning to blasphemers. Still, the truth of history is precious as the foundations of faith to men of all races and traditions, and the Englishman who surpassed the French, Spaniards and Portuguese in discoveries of islands in the vast spaces of the Pacific Ocean, should have justice at the hands of Americans who have organized states and built cities by that sea, and possess the islands that have been named its paradise because endowed surpassingly with the ample treasures of volcanic soil and tropical climate. There the trade winds bestow the freshness of the calm and mighty waters, and there is added to the bounty of boundless wealth the charms of luxuriant beauty. All Americans should find it timely to be just to Captain Cook, and claim him as one of the pioneers of our conquering civilization.

CHAPTER XXII.

THE START FOR THE LAND OF CORN STALKS.

Spain Clings to the Ghost of Her Colonies—The Scene of War Interest Shifts from Manila—The Typhoon Season—General Merritt on the Way to Paris—German Target Practice by Permission of Dewey—Poultney Bigelow with Canoe, Typewriter and Kodak—Hongkong as a Bigger and Brighter Gibraltar.

When Spain gave up the ghosts of her American colonies, and the war situation was unfolded to signify that the fate of the Philippines was referred to a conference, and Aguinaldo announced the removal of his seat of government to Molones, one hour and a half from Manila, the scene of greatest interest was certainly not in the city and immediate surroundings. Then it was plain the American army must remain for some time, and would have only guard duty to perform. The Spaniards had succumbed and were submissive, having laid down their arms and surrendered all places and phases of authority. The insurgents' removal of their headquarters declared that they had abandoned all claim to sharing in the occupation of the conquered city, and their opposition to the United States, if continued in theory, was not to be that in a practical way. Between the American, Spanish and Philippine forces there was no probability of disputed facts or forms that could be productive of contention of a serious nature. There was but one question left in this quarter of the world that concerned the people of the United States, and that whether they would hold their grip, snatched by Dewey with his fleet, and confirmed by his government in sending an army, making our country possessors of the physical force to sustain our policy, whatever it might be, on the land as well as on the sea. Whether we should stay or go was not even to be argued in Manila, except in general and fruitless conversation. Then came the intelligence that General Merritt had been called to Paris and General Greene to Washington, and there was a deepened impression that the war was over. It was true that the army was in an attitude and having experiences that were such as travelers appreciate as enjoyable, and that no other body of soldiers had surroundings so curious and fascinating. The most agreeable time of the year was coming on, and the sanitary conditions of the city, under the American administration, would surely improve constantly, and so would the fare of the men, for the machinery in all departments was working smoothly. The boys were feeling pretty well, because they found their half dollars dollars—

the Mexican fifty-cent piece, bigger and with more silver in it than the American standard dollar, was a bird. A dollar goes further if it is gold in Manila than in an American city, and if our soldiers are not paid in actual gold they get its equivalent, and the only money question unsettled is whether the Mexican silver dollar is worth in American money fifty cents or less. One of the sources of anxieties and disappointment and depression of the American soldiers in Manila has been the irregularity and infrequency with which they get letters. If one got a letter or newspaper from home of a date not more than six weeks old he had reason to be congratulated. The transports trusted with the mails were slow, and communications through the old lines between Hongkong and San Francisco, Yohohama and Vancouver, were not reliably organized. There were painful cases of masses of mail on matter precious beyond all valuation waiting at Hongkong for a boat, and an issue whether the shorter road home was not by way of Europe. This is all in course of rapid reformation. There will be no more mystery as to routes or failures to connect. The soldiers, some of whom are ten thousand miles from home, should have shiploads of letters and papers. They need reading matter almost as much as they do tobacco, and the charming enthusiasm of the ladies who entertained the soldier boys when they were going away with feasting and flattery, praise and glorification, should take up the good work of sending them letters, papers, magazines and books. There is no reason why soldiers should be more subject to homesickness than sailors, except that they are not so well or ill accustomed to absence. The fact that the soldiers are fond of their homes and long for them can have ways of expression other than going home. A few days after the news of peace reached Manila, the transports were inspected for closing up the contracts with them under which they were detained, and soón they began to move. When the China was ordered to San Francisco, I improved the opportunity to return to the great republic. There was no chance to explore the many islands of the group of which Manila is the Spanish Capital. General Merritt changed the course of this fine ship and added to the variety of the voyage by taking her to Hongkong to sail thence by way of the China Sea, the Indian Ocean, the Arabian Gulf, the Red Sea, the Suez Canal and the Mediterranean, to Paris. Our route to San Francisco, by way of Hongkong, Nagasaki, Sunanaski, Kobe and the Yokohama light, was 6,905 knots, about seven thousand seven hundred statute miles, and gave us glimpses of the Asia shore, the west coast of Formosa and the great ports of Hongkong and Nagasaki. The first thing on the Sea of China, in the month of September, is whether we shall find ourselves in the wild embrace of a typhoon. It was the season for those terrible tempests and when we left Manila the information that one was about due was

THE START FOR THE LAND OF CORN STALKS.

not spared us. We heard later on that the transport ahead of us four days, the Zealandia, was twenty-eight hours in a cyclone and much damaged—wrung and hammered and shocked until she had to put into Nagasaki for extensive repairs. The rainfall was so heavy during the storm that one could not see a hundred yards from the ship, and she was wrung in so furious a style in a giddy waltz, that the Captain was for a time in grave doubt whether she would not founder. The rule is when one is in the grasp of the oriental whirl to run through it, judging from the way of the wind, the shortest way out. There is a comparatively quiet spot in the center, and if the beset navigator can find the correct line of flight, no matter which way as relates to the line of his journey, he does well to take it. Often in this sea, as in this case, there were uncertainties as to directions. The rain narrowed observation like a dense fog, and there was danger of running upon some of the islands and snags of rocks. The battered vessel pulled through a cripple, with her boats shattered, her deck cracked across by a roller, and her crew were happy to find a quiet place to be put in order. "To be or not to be" an American instead of a Spanish or Asiatic city was the parting thought as the China left Manila Bay, and the dark rocks of Corrigedor faded behind us, and the rugged rocks that confront the stormy sea loomed on our right, and the violet peaks of volcanic mountains bounded our eastern horizon. The last view we had of the historic bay, a big German warship was close to the sentinel rock, that the Spaniards thought they had fortified, until Dewey came and saw and conquered, swifter than Caesar, and the Germans, venturing some target practice, by permission of Dewey, who relaxes no vigilance of authority. Hongkong is 628 miles from Manila, and the waters so often stirred in monstrous wrath, welcomed us with a spread of dazzling silk. The clumsy junks that appeared to have come down from the days of Confucius, were languid on the gentle ripples. The outstanding Asian islands, small and grim, are singularly desolate, barren as if splintered by fire, gaunt and forbidding. Hongkong is an island that prospers under the paws of the British lion, and it is a city displayed on a mountain side, that by day is not much more imposing than the town of Gibraltar, which it resembles, but at night the lights glitter in a sweeping circle, the steep ascent of the streets revealed by many lamps, and here and there the illumination climbs to the tops of the mountains that are revealed with magical efforts of color and form. The harbor is entered by an ample, but crooked channel, and is land-locked, fenced with gigantic bumps that sketch the horizon, and with their heads and shoulders are familiar with the sky. Here General Merritt, with his personal staff, left us, and between those bound from this port east and west, we circumnavigated the earth.

THE START FOR THE LAND OF CORN STALKS.

Mr. Poultney Bigelow, of Harper's Weekly, who dropped in by the way just to make a few calls at Manila, and has a commission to explore the rivers and lagoons of China with his canoe, left us, in that surprising craft, plying his paddle in the fashion of the Esquimaux, pulling right and left, hand over hand, balancing to a nicety on the waves and going ashore dry and unruffled, with his fieldglass and portfolio, his haversack and typewriter machine that he folds in a small box as if it was a pocket comb, and his kodak, with which he is an expert. He has not only ransacked with his canoe the rivers of America, but has descended the Danube and the Volga. He puts out in his canoe and crosses arms of the sea, as a pastime, makes a tent of his boat if it rains, fighting the desperadoes of all climes with the superstition, for which he is indebted to their imagination for his safety in running phenomenal hazards, that he is a magician. Marco Polo was not so great a traveler or so rare an adventurer as Bigelow, and, having left Florida under a thunder cloud of the scowl of an angry army for untimely criticisms, he has invaded the celestial empire in his quaint canoe, and he can beat the Chinese boatmen on their own rivers, and sleep like a sea bird on the swells of green water, floating like a feather, and safe in his slumbers as a solon goose with his head under his wing. However, he has not a winged boat, a bird afloat sailing round the purple peaks remote, as Buchanan Reed put it in his "Drifting" picture of the Vesuvian bay, for Bigelow uses a paddle. There has been a good deal of curiosity as well as indignation about his papers on the handling of our Cuban expedition before it sailed, and it is possible he was guilty of the common fault of firing into the wrong people. He was in Washington in June, and he and I meeting on the Bridge of Spain over the Pesang in Manila in August, we had, between us, put a girdle about the earth. Some say such experiences are good to show how small the earth is, but I am more than ever persuaded that it is big enough to find mankind in occupation and subsistence until time shall be no more. In the dock at Hongkong was Admiral Dewey's flagship Olympia, and while she had the grass scratched from her bottom, the gallant crew were having a holiday with the zest that rewards those who for four months were steadily on shipboard with arduous cares and labors. H. B. M. S. Powerful, of 12,000 tons displacement, with four huge flues and two immense military masts, presided at Hongkong under orders to visit Manila. The mingling of the English and Chinese in Hongkong is a lively object lesson, showing the extent of the British capacity to utilize Asiatic labor, and get the profit of European capital and discipline, an accumulation that requires an established sense of safety—a justified confidence in permanency.

The contrast between the city of Hongkong and that of Manila is one that

THE START FOR THE LAND OF CORN STALKS.

Americans should study now, to be instructed in the respective colonial systems of England and Spain. Hongkong is clean and solid, with business blocks of the best style of construction, the pavements excellent in material and keeping, shops full of goods, all the appliances of modern times—a city up to date. There are English enough to manage and Chinese enough to toil. There are two British regiments, one of them from India, the rank and file recruited from the fighting tribes of northern mountaineers. There are dark, tall men, with turbans, embodiment of mystery, and Parsees who have a strange spirituality of their own, and in material matters maintain a lofty code of honor, while their pastime is that of striving while they march to push their heads into the clouds. There are no horses in Hongkong, the coolies carrying chairs on bamboo poles, or trotting with two-wheelers, an untiring substitute for quadrupeds, and locomotion on the streets or in the boats is swift and sure. I had an address to find in the city, on a tip at Manila of the presence of a literary treasure, and my chairmen carried me, in a few minutes, to a tall house on a tall terrace, and the works of a martyr to liberty in the Philippines were located. The penalty for the possession of these books in Manila was that of the author executed by shooting in the back in the presence of a crowd of spectators. The cost of the carriers was thirty cents in silver—fifteen cents in United States money—and the men were as keen-eyed as they were sure-footed, and the strength of their tawny limbs called for admiration. They were not burdened with clothes, and the play of the muscles of their legs was like a mechanism of steel, oiled, precise, easy and ample in force. The China took on a few hundred tons of coal, which was delivered aboard from heavy boats by the basketful, the men forming a line, and so expert were they at each delivery, the baskets were passed, each containing about half a bushel—perhaps there were sixty baskets to the ton—at the rate of thirty-five baskets in a minute. Make due allowances and one gang would deliver twenty tons of coal an hour. The China was anchored three-quarters of a mile from the landing, and a boat ride was ten cents, or fifteen if you were a tipster. The boats are, as a rule, managed by a man and his wife; and, as it is their own, they keep the children at home. The average families on the boats—and I made several counts—were nine, the seven children varying from one to twelve years of age. The vitality of the Chinese is not exhausted, or even impaired.

CHAPTER XXIII.

KODAK SNAPPED AT JAPAN.

Glimpses of China and Japan on the Way Home from the Philippines—Hongkong a Greater Gibraltar—Coaling the China—Gangs of Women Coaling the China —How the Japanese Make Gardens of the Mountains—Transition from the Tropics to the Northern Seas—A Breeze from Siberia—A Thousand Miles Nothing on the Pacific—Talk of Swimming Ashore.

Formosa was so far away eastward—a crinkled line drawn faintly with a fine blue pencil, showing as an artistic scrawl on the canvass of the low clouds—we could hardly claim when the sketch of the distant land faded from view, that we had seen Japan. When Hongkong, of sparkling memory, was lost to sight, the guardian walls that secluded her harbor, closing their gates as we turned away, and the headlands of the celestial empire grew dim, a rosy sunset promised that the next day should be pleasant, our thoughts turned with the prow of the China to Japan. We were bound for Nagasaki, to get a full supply of coal to drive us across the Pacific, having but twelve hundred tons aboard, and half of that wanted for ballast. It was at the mouth of the harbor of Nagasaki that there was a settlement of Dutch Christians for some hundreds of years. An indiscreet letter captured on the way to Holland by a Portuguese adventurer and maliciously sent to Japan, caused the tragic destruction of the Christian colony. The enmity of Christian nations anxious to add to their properties in the islands in remote seas was so strong that any one preferred that rather than his neighbors might aggrandize the heathen should prevail. The first as well as the last rocks of Japan to rise from and sink into the prodigous waters, through which we pursued our homeward way, bathing our eyes in the delicious glowing floods of eastern air, were scraggy with sharp pinnacles, and sheer precipices, grim survivals of the chaos that it was, before there was light. I have had but glimpses of the extreme east of Asia, yet the conceit will abide with me that this is in geology as in history the older world, as we classify our continents, that a thousand centuries look upon us from the terrible towers, lonesome save for the flutter of white wings, that witness the rising of the constellations from the greater ocean of the globe. But there are green hills as we approach Nagasaki, and on a hillside to the left are the white walls of a Christian church with a square tower, stained with traditions of triumphs and suffering and martyrdom long ago. Nagasaki is like Hongkong in its land-locked harbor, in clinging to a mountain side, in the circle of illumination at night and the unceasing paddling of boats from ship to ship and between the ships and landings. One is not long in discovering that here are a people more alert, ingenious, self-confident and progressive than the Chinese. As we approached the harbor there came to head us off, an official steam launch, with men in uniform, who hailed and commanded us to stop. Two officers with an intense expression of authority came aboard, and we had to give a full and particular account of ourselves. Why were we there? Coaling. Where were we from? Manila and Hongkong. Where were we going? San Francisco. Had we any sickness on board? No. We must produce the ship doctor, the list of passengers, and manifest of cargo. We had no cargo. There were a dozen passengers. It was difficult to find fault with us. No one was ill. We wanted coal. What was the matter? We had no trouble at Hongkong. We could buy all the coal we wanted there, but preferred this station. We had proposed to have our warships cleaned up at Nagasaki, but there were objections raised. So the job went to the docks at Hongkong, and good gold with it. Why was this? Oh yes; Japan wanted, in the war between the United States and Spain, to be not merely formally, but actually neutral! The fact is that the Japanese Empire is not pleased with us. They had, in imperial circles, a passion for Honolulu, and intimated their grief. Now they are annoyed because that little indemnity for refusing the right to land Japanse labor was paid by the Hawaiian Government before the absorption into the United States. As the Hawaiian diplomatic correspondence about this was conducted with more asperity than tact, if peace were the purpose, it was a good sore place for the Japanese statesmen to rub, and they resent in the newspapers the facile and cheap pacification resulting from the influence of the United States. In addition the Japanese inhabitants, though they have a larger meal than they can speedily digest in Formosa, are not touched with unqualified pleasurable feeling because we have the Philippines in our grasp. If Japan is to be the great power of the Pacific, it is inconvenient to her for us to hold the Hawaiian, the Aleutian and the Philippine groups of islands. The Philippines have more natural resources than all the islands of Japan, and our Aleutian Islands that are waiting for development would probably be found, if thoroughly investigated, one of our great and good bargains. The average American finds himself bothered to have to treat the Japanese seriously, but we must, for they take themselves so, and are rushing the work on new ships of war so that they will come out equal with ourselves in sea power. They have ready for war one hundred thousand men. If we did not hold any part of the Pacific Coast, this might be a matter of indifference, but we have three Pacific States, and there is no purpose to cede them to the Japanese. It would not be statesmanship to give up the archipelagoes we possess, even if we consider them as lands to hold for the hereafter. It is not deniable that the Japanese have good reason to stand off for strict examination the ships of other nations that call at their ports. The British and Chinese have had an experience of the bubonic plague at Hongkong, and the Japanese are using all the power of arms and the artifice of science they possess to keep aloof from the disastrous disease, which is most contagious. The China had called at Hongkong, and hence the sharp attentions at a coaling station where there are about seventy-five thousand inhabitants of the Japanese quarters, which are an exhibit of Old Japan, and most interesting. Nagasaki has, indeed, the true Japanese flavor. If there had been a sick man on our ship we should have been quarantined. Further on we were halted in the night off the city of Kobe, to the sound of the firing of a cannon, for we had dropped there a passenger, Mr. Tilden, the Hongkong agent of the Pacific Mail line, and if our ship had been infected with plague he might have passed it on to Japan! I had gone to bed, and was called up to confront the representative of the Imperial Government of the Japanese, and make clear to his eyes that I had not returned on account of the plague. Authorities of Japan treat people who are quarantined in a way that removes the stress of disagreeableness. All are taken ashore and to a hospital. There is furnished a robe of the country, clean and tidy in all respects. The common clothing is removed and fumigated. It is necessary for each quarantined person to submit to this and also to a bath, which is a real luxury, and after it comes a cup of tea and a light lunch. There was an actual case of plague on an American ship at this city of Kobe not long ago, at least. it was so reported with pretty strong corroborative evidence. The symptom in the case on the ship was that of a fever, probably pneumonia. The man was landed and examined. The plague fever resembles pneumonia at an early stage. The Japanese physicians found signs of plague and the end came soon. The sick man, taken ashore in the afternoon, at nine o'clock was dead, transferred at once to the crematory, in two hours reduced to ashes, and the officers of the ship informed that if they wanted to carry the "remains" to America they would be sealed in a jar and certified. The ship's officers did not want ashes, and the Japs hold the jar. They are so "advanced" that cremation is becoming a fad with them. It would not be surprising to find that the impending danger of the Japanese is excessive imitative progress, which is not certain to be exactly the right thing for them. They have reached a point where it is worth while to examine the claim of new things with much care before adopting them. We have very high authority to examine all things for goodness sake, before committing ourselves to hold them fast. We had to take aboard eighteen hundred tons of coal at Nagasaki. A fleet of arks with thirty tons of Japanese coal approached and gathered around the ship, which has sixteen places to throw coal into the bunkers. So the coal business was carried on by from twelve to fifteen gangs, each of about ten men and twenty women! The latter were sturdy creatures, modestly attired in rough jackets and skirts. There were not far from thirty bamboo baskets to the gang. One man stood at the porthole, and each second emptied a coal basket, using both hands, and throwing it back into the barge with one hand, the same swing of the arm used to catch the next basket hurled to him with a quick, quiet fling. There were three men of a gang next the ship, the third one standing in the barge, served with baskets by two strings of women. At the end of the string furthest from the ship the coal was shoveled into the baskets by four men, and there were two who lifted and whirled them to the women. The numbers and order of the laborers varied a little at times from this relation, yet very little, but frequently a lump of coal was passed without using a basket. The work of coaling was carried on all night, and about thirty-six hours of labor put in for a day. There was a great deal of talking among the laborers during the few moments of taking places, and some of it in tones of high excitement, but once the human machine started there was silence, and then the scratching of the shovels in the coal, and the crash of the coal thrown far into the ship were heard. It is, from the American contemplation, shocking for women to do such work, but they did their share with unflinching assiduity, and without visible distress. When the night work was going on they were evidently fatigued, and at each change that allowed a brief spell of waiting, they were stretched out on the planks of the boats, the greater number still, but some of the younger ones talking and laughing. There did not seem to be much flirtation, nothing like as much as when both sexes of Europeans are engaged in the same wheat or barley field harvesting. There were, it is needful to remark, neither lights nor shadows to invite the blanishments of courting. The coal handling women were from fifteen to fifty years of age, and all so busy the inevitable babies must have been left at home. I have never seen many American or European babies "good" as weary mothers use the word, as the commonest Japanese kids. They do not know how to cry, and a girl of ten years will relieve a mother of personal care by carrying a baby, tied up in a scarf, just its head sticking out (I wish they could be induced to use more soap and water on the coppery heads, from which pairs of intent eyes stare out with sharp inquiry, as wild animals on guard). The girl baby bearer, having tied the child so that it appears to be a bag, slings it over her shoulder, and it interferes but slightly with the movements of the nurse; does not discernibly embarrass her movements. The men colliers, it must be admitted, are a shade reckless in the scarcity of their drapery when they are handling baskets in the presence of ladies.

They do usually wear shirts with short tails behind, and very economical breech-cloths, but their shirts are sleeveless, and the buttons are missing on collar and bosom. The only clothing beneath the knees consists of straw sandals. The precipitation of perspiration takes care of itself. There are no pocket handkerchiefs.

Nagasaki has good hotels, a pleasant, airy European quarter, and shops stored with the goods of the country, including magnificent vases and other pottery that should meet the appreciation of housekeepers. There is no city in Japan more typically Japanese, few in which the line is so finely and firmly drawn between the old and the new, and that to the advantage of both.

It is hardly possible for those who do not visit Japan to realize what a bitter struggle the people have had with their native land, or how brilliant the victory they have won. The passage of the China through the inner sea and far along the coast gave opportunity to see, as birds might, a great deal of the country. The inner sea is a wonderfully attractive sheet of water, twice as long as Long Island Sound, and studded with islands, a panorama of the picturesque mountains everywhere, deep nooks, glittering shoals, fishing villages by the sea, boats rigged like Americans, flocks of white sails by day, and lights at night, that suggest strings of street lamps. The waters teem with life. Evidently the sea very largely affords industry and sustenance to the people, for there is no bottom or prairie land, as we call the level or slightly rolling fields in America. There was not a spot from first to last visible in Japan, as seen from the water, or in an excursion on the land, where there is room to turn around a horse and plow. The ground is necessarily turned up with spades and mellowed with hoes and rakes, all, of course, by human hands. This is easy compared with the labor in constructing terraces. The mountains have been conquered to a considerable extent in this way, and it is sensational to see how thousands of steep places have been cut and walled into gigantic stairways, covering slopes that could hardly answer for goat pasture, until the shelves with soil placed on them for cultivation have been wrought, and the terraces are like wonderful ladders bearing against the skies. So rugged is the ground, however, that many mountains are unconquerable, and there are few traces of the terraces, though here and there, viewed from a distance, the evidences that land is cultivated as stairways leaning against otherwise inaccessible declivities. I have never seen elsewhere anything that spoke so unequivocally of the endless toil of men, women and children to find footings upon which to sow the grain and fruit that sustain life. It is not to be questioned that the report, one-twelfth, only of the surface of Japan is under tillage, is accurate. The country is more mountainous than the Alleghenies, and some of it barren as the wildest of the Rockies on the borders of the bad lands, and it is volcanic, remarkably so, even more subject to earthquakes than the Philippines. The whole of Japan occupies about as much space as the two Dakotas or the Philippines, and the population is forty-two millions. With work as careful and extensive as that of the agricultural mountaineers of Japan, the Dakotas would support one hundred million persons. But they would have to prevent the washing away of the soil and the waste through improvident ignorance or careless profligacy of any fertilizer, or of any trickle of water needed for irrigation. One of the features of the terraces is that the rains are saved by the walls that sustain the soil, and the gutters that guide the water conserve it, because paved with pebbles and carried down by easy stages. irrigating one shelf after another of rice or vegetables, whatever is grown, until the whole slope not irreclaimable is made to blossom and the mountain torrents saved in their descent, not tearing away the made ground, out of which the means of living grows, but percolating through scores of narrow beds, gardens suspended like extended ribbons of verdure on volcanic steeps, refreshing the crops to be at last ripened by the sunshine. This is a lesson for the American farmer—to be studied more closely than imitated—to grow grass, especially clover, to stop devastation by creeks, with shrubbery gifted with long roots to save the banks of considerable streams, and, where there is stone, use it to save the land now going by every freshwater rivulet and rivers to the seas, to the irreparable loss of mankind. It is the duty of man who inherits the earth that it does not escape from him, that his inheritance is not swept away by freshets. We are growing rapidly, in America, in the understanding of this subject, beginning to comprehend the necessity of giving the land that bears crops the equivalent of that which is taken from it, that the vital capital of future generations may not be dissipated and the people grow ever poor and at last perish.

A ride in a jinrikisha, a two-wheeler, with a buggy top and poles for the biped horse to trot between, from Nagasaki to a fishing village over the mountains, five miles away, passing at the start through the Japanese quarter, long streets of shops, populous and busy, many diligent in light manufacturing work, and all scant in clothing—the journey continuing in sharp climbs alongside steep places and beside deep ravines, the slopes elaborately terraced, and again skirting the swift curves of a rapid brook from the mountains, that presently gathered and spread over pretty beds of gravel, providing abundant fresh water bathing, in which a school of boys, leaving a small guard for a light supply of clothing ashore—the ride ending in a village of fishermen that, by the count of the inhabitants, should be a town—permitted close observation of the Japanese in a city and a village, on their sky-scraping gardens and in the road, going to and coming from market, as well as in places of roadside entertainment; and at last a seaside resort, in whose shade a party of globe-trotters were lunching, some of them, I hear, trying to eat raw fish. There could hardly have been contrived a more instructive exhibit of Japan and the Japanese. The road was obstructed in several places by cows bearing bales of goods from the city to the country, and produce from the hanging gardens to the streets, an occasional horse mustered in, and also a few oxen. The beast of burden most frequently overtaken or encountered was the cow, and a majority of the laborers were women. There were even in teams of twos and fours, carrying heavy luggage, men and women, old, middle-aged and young, barefooted or shod with straw, not overloaded, as a rule, and some walking as if they had performed their tasks and were going home. On the road it was patent there was extraordinary freedom from care as to clothing, and no feeling of prejudice or dismay if portions of it esteemed absolutely essential in North America and Europe had been left behind or was awaiting return to the possessor. This applies to both sexes. The day was warm, even hot, and the sun shone fiercely on the turnpike—for that is what we would call it—making walking, with or without loads, a heating exercise. Even the bearing of baskets, and the majority of the women carried them, was justification under the customs of the country for baring the throat and chest to give ample scope for breathing, and there is no restriction in the maintenance of the drooping lines of demarkation, according to the most liberal fashionable allowances, in dispensing with all the misty suggestions of laces to the utmost extent artists could ask, for the study of figures. Beauty had the advantage of the fine curves of full inhalations of the air that circulated along the dusty paths between the sea and the mountains. It is a puzzle that the artists of Japan have not better improved the unparalleled privilege of field and wall sketching, that they enjoy to a degree not equalled within the permission of the conventional construction of that which is becoming in the absence of the daylight habilaments of any great and polite people. The art schools of Japan, out of doors, on the highway, even, cannot fail to produce atmospheric influences of which the world will have visions hereafter, and the Latin quarter of Paris will lose its reputation that attracts and adjusts nature to inspiration.

When we had succeeded, at Kobe, in convincing the authorities that none of the passengers on the China had picked up the plague at Hongkong, we put out into the big sea, and shaped our course for the fairer land so far away, not exactly a straight line, for the convexity of the earth that includes the water, for the ocean—particularly the Pacific—is rounded so that the straightest line over its surface is a curved line, if astronomically mentioned. We struck out on the great Northern circle, purposing to run as high as the forty-eighth parallel, almost to our Alutian Islands, and pursued our course in full view, the bald cliffs of Japan changing their color with the going down of the sun. When morning came the purple bulk of the bestirring little empire still reminded us of the lights and shadows of Asia and the missionary labors of Sir Edwin Arnold, which have a flavor of the classics and a remembrance of the Scriptures. "Yonder," said the Captain, "is the famous mountain of Japan, Fugeyana. "It is not very clearly seen, for it is distant. Oh, you are looking too low down and see only the foot-hills—that is it, away up in the sky!" It was there, a peak so lofty that it is solitary. We were to have seen it better later, but as the hours passed there was a dimness that the light of declining day did not disperse, and the mountain stayed with us in a ghostly way, and held its own in high communion.

As we were leaving Asian waters there came a demand for typhoons that the Captain satisfied completely, saying he was not hunting for them, but the worst one he ever caught was five hundred miles east of Yokohama. The tourists were rather troubled. The young man who had been in the wild waltz of the Zealandia did not care for a typhoon. We had been blessed with weather so balmy and healing, winds so soft and waves so low, that the ship had settled down steady as a river steamboat. We pushed on, but the best the China could do was fourteen knots and a half an hour, near 350 knots a day, with a consumption of 135 tons of coal in twenty-four hours. So much for not having been cleaned up so as to give the go of the fine lines. The China had been in the habit of making sixty miles a day more than on this trip, burning less than 100 tons of coal. As we climbed in the ladder of the parallels of latitude, we began to notice a crispness in the air, and it was lovely to the lungs. It was a pleasure, and a stimulant surpassing wine, to breathe the north temperate ozone again, and after a while to catch a frosty savor on the breeze. We had forgotten, for a few days, that we were not in a reeking state of perspiration. Ah! we were more than a thousand miles north of Manila, and that is as far as the coast of Maine to Cuba. The wind followed us, and at last gained a speed greater than our own; then it shifted and came down from the northwest. It was the wind that swept from Siberia, and Kamschatka's grim peninsula pointed us out. The smoke from our funnels blew black and dense away southeast, and did not change more than a point or two for a week. The Pacific began to look like the North Atlantic. There came a "chill out of a cloud" as in the poetic case of Annabel Lee. There had been, during our tropical experience, some outcries for the favor of a few chills, but now they were like the typhoons. When it was found that they might be had we did not want them. After all, warm weather was not so bad, and the chills that were in the wind that whistled from Siberia were rather objectionable. It was singular to call for one, two, three blankets, and then hunt up overcoats. White trousers disappeared two or three days after the white coats. Straw hats were called for by the wind. One white cap on an officer's head responded alone to the swarm of white caps on the water. The roll of the waves impeded our great northern circle. We could have made it, but we should have had to roll with the waves. We got no higher than 45 degrees. We had our two Thursdays, and thought of the fact that on the mystical meridian 180, where three days get mixed up in one! The Pacific Ocean, from pole to pole, so free on the line where the dispute as to the day it is, goes on forever, that only one small island is subject to the witchery of mathematics, and the proof in commonplace transactions unmixed with the skies that whatever may be the matter with the sun—the earth do move, is round, do roll over, and does not spill off the sea in doing so. At last came shrill head winds, and as we added fifteen miles an hour to this speed, the harp strings in the rigging were touched with weird music, and we filled our lungs consciously and conscientiously with American air, experiencing one of the old sensations, better than anything new.

It was figured out that we were within a thousand miles of the continent, and were getting home. When one has been to the Philippines, what's a thousand miles or two! "Hello, Captain Seabury! It is only about a thousand miles right ahead to the land. You know what land it is, don't you? Well, now, you may break the shaft or burst the boilers, fling the ship to the sperm whales, like the one that was the only living thing we saw since Japan entered into the American clouds of the West. We are only a thousand miles away from the solid, sugary sweet, redolent, ripe American soil, and if there is anything the matter we do not mind, why we will just take a boat and pull ashore." But we would have had a hard time if the Captain had taken us up in the flush of the hilarity that laughed at a thousand miles, when the breeze brought us the faint first hints that we were almost home, after a voyage of five thousand leagues. The wind shifted to the south and increased until it roared, and the waves were as iron tipped with blue and silver, hurling their salty crests over our towering ship; and we were in the grasp—

On the Pacific of the terrific
Storm King of the Equinox.

Mr. Longfellow mentioned the storm wind gigantic, that shook the Atlantic at the time of the equinox—the one that urges the boiling surges bearing seaweed from the rocks; and all those disappointed because they had not bounded on the billows of the briny enough for healthy exercises, were satisfied in the reception by the tremendous Pacific when nigh the shore, which was once the western boundary, but is so no more, of that blessed America, of which her sons grow fonder the farther

SPANIARDS REPELLING INSURGENT'S ATTACK ON A CONVENT.

BUSINESS CORNER IN MANILA

A NATIVE IN REGIMENTALS.

A COUNTRY PAIR.

PEASANT COSTUMES.

WOODMAN IN WORKING GARB.

they roam. God's country, as the boys and girls call it reverently, when they are sailing the seas, was veiled from us in a fog that blanketed the deep. For five thousand miles our ship had been in a remorseless solitude. No voice had come to us; no spark of intelligence from the universe touched us, save from the stars and the sun, but at the hour of the night, and the point of the compass, our navigator had foretold, we should hear the deep-throated horn on Reyes point—it came to us out of the gloomy abyss—and science had not failed. Across the trackless waste we had been guided aright, and there was music the angels might have envied in the hoarse notes of the fog-horn that welcomed the wanderers home.

CHAPTER XXIV.

OUR PICTURE GALLERY.

Annotations and Illustrations—Portraits of Heroes of the War in the Army and Navy, and of the Highest Public Responsibilities—Admirals and Generals, the President and Cabinet—Photographs of Scenes and Incidents—The Characteristics of the Filipinos—Their Homes, Dresses and Peculiarities in Sun Pictures—The Picturesque People of Our New Possessions.

The portrait of President McKinley is from the photograph that seems to his friends upon the whole the most striking of his likenesses. That of the Secretary of State, the Honorable John Hay, is certainly from the latest and best of his photos. The Postmaster General, the Honorable Charles Emory Smith, and Secretary Bliss, are presented in excellent form and the whole Cabinet with unusual faithfulness. Our naval and military heroes in the war that has introduced the American nation to the nations of the earth as a belligerent of the first class, cannot become too familiar to the people, for they are of the stuff that brightens with friction, and the more it is worn gives higher proof that it is of both the precious metals in war, gold and steel.

Admiral Dewey, as we have set forth in this volume, is not thus far fairly dealt with in the pictures that have been taken. He is a surprise to those who meet him face to face—so far has photography failed to adequately present him, but the portrait we give is the best that has been made of him.

Major-General Merritt retains the keen, clear cut face, and the figure and bearing of an ideal soldier that has characterized him since, as a youth just from West Point, he entered the army and won his way by his courage and courtesy, his brilliant conduct and excellent intelligence, his dashing charges and superb leadership, to a distinguished position and the affectionate regard of the army and the people. In the Indian wars, after the bloody struggle of the States was over, he outrode the Indians on the prairies and was at once their conqueror and pacificator. He ranks in chivalry with the knights, and his work at Manila was the perfection of campaigning that produced conclusive results with a comparatively small shedding of blood.

The likeness of the Archbishop of Manila was presented me by His Grace at the close of a personal interview, and represents him as he is. The chapter devoted to him is meant to do him simple justice as a man and priest. The fact that he bestowed upon me in the inscription with which he greatly increased the value of his portrait a military dignity to which I have no title is an expression only of his friendliness. He frankly stated his pleasure in meeting an American who would convey to the President of the United States the message he gave me about the American army, to which he was indebted for security and peace of mind.

General Aguinaldo gave me his photograph, and the flag of the Filipinos with him in the effort to establish an independent government, republican in form. One is not always sure of that which happens in the Philippines, even when one reads about it. I am prepared to believe that there is much truth in the dispatch saying a majority of the Congress of the insurgents at Molores favor annexation to the United States. The whole truth probably is that they would gladly have this country their Protector at large, supreme in the affairs international, they to legislate in respect to local affairs. They need to know, however, that their Congress must become a territorial legislature, and that the higher law for them is to be the laws of Congress. The Philippine flag is oriental in cut and color, having red and blue bars—a white obtuse angle—the base to the staff, and a yellow moon with fantastic decorations occupying the field. This flag is one that Admiral Dewey salutes with respect. General Aguinaldo is giving much of his strength to the production of proclamations, and his literary labors should be encouraged.

On a September morning two years ago, Dr. Jose Rizal was shot by a file of soldiers on the Manila Luneta, the favorite outing park, bordering on the bay. The scene was photographed at the moment the Doctor stood erect before the firing squad, and the signal from the officer in command was awaited for the discharge of the volley killing the most intellectual man of his race. Dr. Rizal is known as the Tagalo Martyr. The Tagalos are of the dominant tribe of Malays. General Aguinaldo is of this blood, as are the great majority of the insurgents. The Doctor is more than the martyr of a tribe. He is the most talented and accomplished man his people and country has produced. A history of Luzon from his pen is a bulky volume full of facts. I was not able to procure all of his books. Anyone in Manila found in possession of one of them during Spanish rule, would have been taken to the ground selected for human butchery in the appointed place of festivity, and shot as he was, making a holiday for the rulers of the islands. He wrote two novels, "Touch Us Not" and "The Filibusters," the latter a sequel of the former. These are books using the weapons put into the hand of genius to smite oppressors in command of the force of arms. The novels are said to be interesting as novels, —rather sensational in their disregard of the personal reputation of his foes, the friars, but all along between the lines there was argument, appeals for the freedom of the

Filipinos, for freedom of speech, conscience and country. There are pamphlets printed the size of an average playing card, from thirty to forty pages each, one "Don Rodriguez," and another "The Telephone." These I obtained in Hongkong from the hands of the niece—daughter of the sister of the Doctor,—and she presented me also his poem written when in the shadow of death, of which this volume gives a prose translation. The poem is the farewell of the author to his friends, his country and the world. It is given in prose because in that style the spirit of the poet, indeed the poetry itself, can be rendered with better results, than by striving to sustain the poetic form. The poem would be regarded as happy and affecting in the thought that is in it, the images in which the ideas gleam, the pathos of resignation, the ascendency of hope, if there were nothing in the attendant circumstances that marked it with the blood of historic tragedy. This poetry that it would have been high treason to own in Manila, for it would not have been safe in any drawer however secret, was treasured by the relatives of the martyr at Hongkong. The niece spoke excellent English, and there was at once surprise and gratification in the family that an American should be interested in the Doctor who sacrificed himself to the freedom of his pen, so much as to ascend the steep places of the city to seek his writings for the sake of the people for whose redemption he died. On the page showing the face of the Doctor and the scene of his execution, there are two men in black, the victim standing firm as a rock to be shot down, and the priest retiring after holding the crucifix to the lips of the dying; and the portrait of the beautiful woman to whom the poet was married a few hours before he was killed. It is said that Rizal wanted to go to Cuba, but Captain-General Weyler answered a request from him that he might live there, that he would be shot on sight if he set foot on Cuban soil. Rizal, hunted hard, attempted to escape in disguise on a Spanish troop ship carrying discharged soldiers to Spain, but was detected while on the Red Sea, returned to Manila and shot to death. I stood on the curbstone that borders the Luneta along the principal pleasure drive, between the whispering trees and the murmuring surf of the bay, just where the martyred poet and patriot waited and looked over the waters his eyes beheld, the last moment before the crash of the rifles that destroyed him, and in the distance there was streaming in the sunshine the flag of our country—the star spangled banner, and long, long may it wave, over a land of the free and home of the brave!

The picture of the cathedral shows a tower that was shattered from the foundation to the cross by the earthquake of 1863. Ambitious architecture must conform to the conditions imposed by such disasters, and the great edifice is greatly changed.

OUR PICTURE GALLERY.

In our gallery we treat Admirals Sampson and Schley as the President set the example. As there was glory for all at Santiago, there was advancement for both. We present them together. The wholesome, manly face of General Lee is in the gallery. His country knows him and thinks of him well.

The bombarded church of Cavite shows that shells spare nothing sacred in their flights and concussions. The Bridge of Spain is the one most crossed in passing between the old walled city and the newer town that was not walled, but was formidably intrenched where rice swamps were close to the bay. The public buildings are commodious and would be higher, but the earth is uncertain, and sky-scrapers are forbidden by common prudence. Our picture of the principal gate of the walled city is taken truly, but does not give the appearance of extreme antiquity, of the reality. The wall looks old as one that has stood in Europe a thousand years.

Naturally the gallery has many works of art representative of Manila. The shipping in the habor is an advertisement of a commerce once extensive. Each picture that shows a woman, a man, or tree; a wood-cutter, a fisherman, or a house, opens for the spectator a vista that may be interpreted by the intelligent. A veritable picture is a window that reveals a landscape. That which is most valuable in a gallery like this is the perfect truth not everywhere found, for the eyes that see a picture that is really representative, setting forth the colors, the light, and the substance of things find that which does not fade when the story is told.

There is one most hideous thing in our gallery—that of the head of a Spaniard, bleeding, just severed from the body—the weapon used, a naked dagger in a clenched hand—around the ghastly symbol a deep black border. This is one of the ways of the Katapuna society—the League of Blood—have of saying what they would have us understand are their awful purposes. There are terrible stories about this Blood League—that they bleed themselves in the course of their proceedings, and each member signs his name with his own blood—that they establish brotherhood by mingling their blood and tasting it. They are the sworn enemies of the Spaniards, and particularly of the priests. I inquired of Senor Agoncillo, the Philippine commissioner to Paris, whether those bloody stories were true. He scoffed at the notion that they might be so, and laughed and shouted "No, no!" as if he was having much fun. But Agoncillo is a lawyer and a diplomat, and I had heard so much of this horrid society I did not feel positive it was certain that its alleged blood rites were fictitious. Of one thing I am sure—that the dreadful picture is no joke, and was not meant for a burlesque, though it might possibly be expected to perform the office of a scarecrow. It cannot be doubted that there are oath-bound secret societies that are regarded by the Spaniards as fanatical, superstitious, murderous and deserving death.

There is a good deal of feeble-minded credulity among the Filipinos, that is exhibited in the stories told by Aguinaldo. He has many followers who believe that he has a mighty magic, a charm, that deflects bullets and is an antidote for poison. Intelligent people believe this imbecility is one of the great elements of his power— that his leadership would be lost if the supernaturalism attached to him should go the way of all phantoms. Aguinaldo is said not to have faith in the charm, for he takes very good care of himself.

We give several views of executions at Manila. As a rule, these pictures are not fine productions of art. They are taken under such conditions of light and background that they are somewhat shadowy. This sinister addition to our gallery seems to be the first time the photographs of executions have been reproduced. The photos were not furtively taken. There is no secrecy about the process, no attempts to hide it from the Spaniards. Executions in the Philippines were in the nature of dramatic entertainments. There were often many persons present, and ladies as conspicuous as at bull fights. There is no more objections offered to photographing an execution than a cock fight, which is the sport about which the Filipinos are crazily absorbed. It is the festal character to the Spaniard of the rebel shooting that permits the actualities to be reproduced, and hence these strange contributions to our gallery.

Many of our pictures are self-explanatory. They were selected to show things characteristic, and hence instructive, peasants' customs—women riding buffaloes through palm groves—native houses, quaint costumes. "The insurgent outlook" reveals a native house—a structure of grasses. This is a perfect picture. The southern islanders, and the group of Moors, the dressing of the girls, work in the fields, the wealth of vegetation, the dining room of the Governor-General prepared for company, General Merritt's palatial headquarters before he had taken the public property into his care and suited it to his convenience; the Spanish dude officer, showing a young man contented in his uniform, and a pony pretty in his harness.

We reproduce the war department map of the Philippine islands. It will be closely studied for each island has become a subject of American interest. The imprint of the war department is an assurance of the closest attainable accuracy. The map of the Hawaiian islands clearly gives them in their relative positions and proportions as they are scattered broadcast in the Pacific. The Philippine and Hawaiian groups as they thus appear will be found more extensive than the general fancy has painted them. The Philippine Archipelago has been held to resemble a fan, with Luzon for the handle. The shape is something fantastic. It is worth while to note that the distance between the north coast of Luzon and the Sulu Archipelago is equal to that from England to Southern Italy.

There are pictures in our gallery that could only be found at the end of a journey of ten thousand miles, and they go far to show the life of the people of a country that is in such relations with ourselves the whole world is interested. There is truth-telling that should be prized in photography, and our picture gallery is one of the most remarkable that has been assembled.

CHAPTER XXV.

CUBA AND PORTO RICO.

Conditions In and Around Havana—Fortifications and Water Supply of the Capital City—Other Sections of the Pearl of the Antilles—Porto Rico, Our New Possession, Described—Size and Population—Natural Resources and Products—Climatic Conditions—Towns and Cities—Railroads and Other Improvements—Future Possibilities.

There was the fortune of good judgment in attacking the Spaniards in Cuba at Santiago and Porto Rico, the points of Spanish possession in the West Indies farthest south and east, instead of striking at the west, landing at Pinar del Rio, the western province, and moving upon the fortifications of Havana, where the difficulties and dangers that proved so formidable at Santiago would have been quadrupled, and our losses in the field and hospital excessive. The unpreparedness of this country for war has not even up to this time been appreciated except by military experts and the most intelligent and intent students of current history. The military notes prepared in the War Department of the United States at the beginning of the war with Spain, contain the following of Santiago de Cuba:

This city was founded in 1514, and the famous Hernando was its first mayor. It is the most southern place of any note on the island, being on the twentieth degree of latitude, while Havana, the most northern point of note, is 23 degrees 9 minutes 26 seconds north latitude. The surrounding country is very mountainous, and the city is built upon a steep slope; the public square, or Campo de Marte, is 140 to 160 feet above the sea, and some of the houses are located 200 feet high. The character of the soil is reported to be more volcanic than calcareous; it has suffered repeatedly from earthquakes. It is the second city in the island with regard to population, slightly exceeding that of Matanzas and Puerto Principe. So far as American commerce is concerned, it ranks only ninth among the fifteen Cuban ports of entry. It is located on the extreme northern bank of the harbor of Santiago de Cuba, a harbor of the first class and one of the smallest; hence, as is believed, the great liability of its shipping to infection. According to the chart of the Madrid hydrographic bureau, 1863, this harbor is, from its sea entrance to its extreme northern limit, 5 miles long, the city being located 4 miles from its entrance, on the northeastern side of the harbor. The entrance is for some little distance very narrow—

not more than 220 yards wide—and may be considered about 2 miles long, with a width varying from one-eighth to five-eighths of a mile. For the remaining 3 miles the harbor gradually widens, until at its northern extremity it is about 2 miles wide. The city is so situated in a cove of the harbor that the opposite shore is only about one-half mile distant. At the wharves from 10 to 15 feet of water is found, and within 300 to 500 yards of the shore from 20 to 30 feet. This, therefore, is probably the anchorage ground. Three or more so-called rivers, besides other streams, empty into this harbor, and one of these, the Caney River, empties into the harbor at the northern limit of the city, so that its water flows from one island extremity through the whole harbor into the sea. The difference here, as elsewhere in Cuba, between low and high tide is about 2 feet. Population in 1877 was 40,835, and 5,100 houses. This city is one of the most noted yellow-fever districts in the island. The population in 1896 was 42,000.

The following has been reported:

Preparations for mounting new and heavy ordnance is now going on at the entrance of the bay (March 5, 1898).

New and heavier guns are also ordered for Punta Blanca, on the right of the bay near Santiago City.

Plans have been made for constructing two batteries in the city of Santiago, one about 25 yards in front of the American consulate and the other about two blocks in rear.

Cayo Rolones, or Rat Island, located near the middle of the bay, is the Government depository for powder, dynamite, and other explosives.

The elevation on the right of the entrance, where stands Castle Morro, is 40 yards above the sea level, while the hill on the left is 20 yards.

"La Bateria Nueva de la Estrella" is mounted with four revolving cannons.

The fortifications of Havana were carefully covered in the military notes, and thus enumerated:

There are fifteen fortifications in and about the city of Havana, more or less armed and garrisoned, besides a work partly constructed and not armed, called Las Animas, and the old bastions along the sea wall of the harbor. These works are as follows:

Nos. 1 and 2 are earthen redans on the sea coast, east of Havana.

Velazo Battery, just east of, and a part of, El Morro.

El Morro, a sea coast fort, with flanking barbette batteries, east of harbor entrance.

Twelve Apostles, a water battery lying at the foot of Morro, with a field across the harbor's mouth. It is a part of Morro.

Cabana, a stone-bastioned work with both land and water front, in rear of El Morro, and directly opposite the city of Havana.

San Diego, a stone-bastioned work with only land fronts, east of Cabana.

Atares, a stone-bastioned work on hill at southwestern extremity of Havana Bay, near the old shipyard called the arsenal.

San Salvador de la Punta, a stone-bastioned work west of harbor entrance, with small advanced and detached work, built on a rock near harbor mouth.

La Reina, a stone work, in shape the segment of a circle, placed on the seacoast, at western limits of city, on an inlet called San Lazardo.

Santa Clara, a small but powerful seacoast battery of stone and earth, placed about 1½ miles west of harbor.

El Principe, a stone-bastioned redoubt west of Havana.

Nos. 3 A, 3 B, and 4 are earthen redans on the seacoast west of Havana.

There are, in addition, several works built for defense, but now used for other purposes or abandoned. These are:

The Torreon de Vigia, a martello tower placed on the inlet of San Lazaro opposite Reina.

The old fort called La Fuerza, built three hundred and fifty years ago, near the Plaza de Armas, and now used for barracks and public offices.

The work called San Nazario, situated north of El Principe, but now used in connection with the present cartridge factory, abandoned for defensive purposes.

The partially constructed fort called Las Animas, southeast of Principe, lying on a low hill, partly built but useless and unarmed.

The old sea wall extending from near La Punta to the Plaza de Armas, unarmed, and useless except as a parapet for musketry.

The old arsenal, on the west of the inner bay, now used as repair works for ships, useless for defense.

The old artillery and engineer storehouses near La Punta, probably once used as strongholds, now mere storehouses for munitions of war.

There are, besides, in the vicinity of Havana, three old and now useless stone works—one at Chorrera, the mouth of the Almendarez River, about 4 miles from Havana harbor; another at Cojimar, on the coast, about 3 miles eastward of Cabana, and the third at the inlet called La Playa de Mariano, about 7 miles west of Havana.

Batteries Nos. 1 and 2 were equipped with, No. 1, four Hontoria 6-inch guns; two Nordenfeldt 6-pounders; No. 2, two Krupp 12-inch guns; four Hontoria 3-inch mortars. The 12-inch Krupps were to stand off battleships attempting to force the harbor, or to bombard the Morro. The Valago battery, a part of the Morro, an out-work on the edge of the cliff, mounting four 11-inch Krupp guns separated by earth traverses.

The Morro, commenced in 1589 and finished in 1597, is important for historical associations. It is a most picturesque structure, and is useful as a lighthouse and prison, and is mounted with twelve old 10-inch, eight old 8-inch, and fourteen old 4-inch guns.

Cabana, finished in 1774 at a cost of $14,000,000, lies some 500 yards southeast of El Morro, on the east side of Havana Bay. Toward the city it exposes a vertical stone wall of irregular trace, with salients at intervals. Toward the Morro is a bastioned face protected by a deep ditch, sally port, and drawbridge. Eastward and southward a beautifully constructed land front incloses the work. This front is protected by ditches 40 or more feet deep, well constructed glacis, stone scarp, and counterscarp. Cabana is a magnificent example of the permanent fortifications constructed a century ago. Probably 10,000 men could be quartered in it.

The entrance to Cabana is by the sally port that opens upon the bridge across the moat lying between Cabana and El Morro. Upon entering, the enormous extent of the work begins to be perceived, parapet within parapet, galleries, casemates, and terrepleins almost innumerable, all of stone and useless. There are no earth covers or traverses, and no protection against modern artillery.

Cabana is the prison for offenders against the State, and the scene of innumerable executions. From an exterior or salient corner of the secretary's office of the headquarters there leads a subterranean passage 326 meters long, 2.5 meters wide, and 1.86 high, excavated in the rock. It conducts to the sea, debouching at the mouth of a sewer, 87 meters from the Morro wharf. At exactly 132 meters along the road rising from the Morro pier or wharf to the Cabana, there will be found by excavating the rock on the left of the road, at a depth of 3 meters, a grating, on opening which passage will be made into a road 107 meters long, 1.6 high, and 1.42 wide, leading to the same exit as the Cabana secret way. These passages are most secret, as all believe that the grating of the sewer, seen from the sea, is a drain.

The battery of Santa Clara is the most interesting of the fortifications of Havana, and one of the most important. It lies about 100 yards from the shore of the gulf, at a point where the line of hills to the westward runs back (either naturally or artificially) into quarries, thus occupying a low salient backed by a hill. Here are three new Krupp 11-inch guns, designed to protect El Principe, the land side of Havana. It is 187 feet above sea level and completely dominates Havana, the bay, Morro, Cabana, the coast northward, Atares, and from east around to south, the approaches of the Marianao Road, Cristina, and the Western Railroad for about 3 kilometers, i. e., between Cristina and a cut at that distance from the station. Principe gives fire upon Tulipan, the Cerro, the Hill of the Jesuits, and the valley through which passes the Havana Railroad, sweeping completely with its guns the railroad as far as the cut at Cienaga, 2½ to 3 miles away. It dominates also the hills southward and westward toward Puentes Grandes and the Almendarez River, and country extending toward Marianao, also the Calzada leading to the cemetery and toward Chorrera; thence the entire sea line (the railroad to Chorrera is partly sheltered by the slope leading to Principe. This is by all means the strongest position about Havana which is occupied. Lying between it and the hill of the Cerro is the hill of the Catalan Club, right under the guns of the work and about one-half mile away. The Marianao Road is more sheltered than the Havana, as it runs near the trees and hill near the Cerro. The only points which dominate the hill of the Principe lie to the south and southeast in the direction of Jesus del Monte and beyond Regla. On its southern, southeastern, and southwestern faces the hill of Principe is a steep descent to the calzada and streets below. The slope is gradual westward and around by the north. From this hill is one of the best views of Havana and the valley south. El Principe lies about one-half mile from the north coast, from which hills rise in gradual slopes toward the work. It is Havana gossip that El Principe is always held by the Spanish regiment in which the Captain-General has most confidence. The military notes pronounce El Principe undoubtedly the strongest natural position about Havana now occupied by defensive works. Its guns sweep the heights of the Almendares, extending from the north coast southward by the hills of Puentes Grandes to the valley of Cienaga, thence eastward across the Hill of the Jesuits and the long line of trees and houses leading to the Cerro. The country beyond the Cerro is partly sheltered by trees and hills, but eastward El Principe commands in places the country and the bay shore, and gives fire across Havana seaward.

The most vulnerable spot in the defenses of Havana is the aqueduct of Isabella II, or the Vento. The water is from the Vento Springs, pure and inexhaustible, nine miles out of Havana.

All three of the water supplies to Havana, the Zanja and the two aqueducts of

Ferdinand VII and of the Vento, proceed from the Almendares and run their course near to each other, the farthest to the west being the Zanja and to the east the Vento.

At Vento Springs is constructed a large stone basin, open at the bottom, through which springs bubble. From this reservoir the new aqueduct leads. It is an elliptical tunnel of brick, placed under ground, and marked by turrets of brick and stone placed along its course.

From the Vento Reservoir the new aqueduct crosses the low valley south of Havana, following generally the Calzada de Vento, which becomes, near the Cerro, the Calzada de Palatino, to a point on the Western Railway marked 5 kilometers (about); hence the calzada and the aqueduct closely follows the railway for about a mile, terminating at a new reservoir.

The Vento water is the best thing Havana has, and indispensable. The old sources of supply are intolerable. The main water supply is the Zanja. Throughout the most of its course this river flows through unprotected mud banks; the fluids of many houses, especially in the Cerro ward which it skirts, drain into them; men, horses, and dogs bathe in it; dead bodies have been seen floating in it, and in the rainy season the water becomes very muddy. In fine, the Zanja in its course receives all which a little brook traversing a village and having houses and back yards on its banks would receive. The water can not be pure, and to those who know the facts the idea of drinking it is repulsive. This supply had long been insufficient to the growing city, and in 1835 the well-protected and excellent aqueduct of Ferdinand VII was completed. It taps the Almendares River a few hundred yards above filters mentioned, hence carried by arches to the east El Cerro, and for some distance nearly parallel to the Calzada del Cerro, but finally intersecting this. These works are succeeded by the Famous Vento. When Havana is fought for hereafter the fight will be at the Vento Springs. This remark is not made in the military notes, but the military men know it well. When General Miles expected to attack Havana he procured all the accessible surveys and detail of information, official and through special observation and personal knowledge obtainable of the water works. Life could not be sustained many days in the city of Havana without the water of the adorable Vento.

A special interest attaches to Havana, as it is to be a city under the control of the United States. The surface soil consists for the most part of a thin layer of red, yellow, or black earths. At varying depths beneath this, often not exceeding 1 or 2 feet, lie the solid rocks. These foundation rocks are, especially in the northern and more modern parts of the city toward the coast of the sea and not of the harbor, Quarternary, and especially Tertiary, formations, so permeable that liquids emptied into excavations are absorbed and disappear.

In other parts of the city the rocks are not permeable, and pools are formed. In proportion as the towns of Cuba are old, the streets are narrow. In Havana this peculiarity is so positive that pedestrians cannot pass on the sidewalks, nor vehicles on the streets. Less than one-third of the population live on paved streets, and these are as well paved and kept as clean, it is believed cleaner, than is usual in the United States. The remainder live on unpaved streets, which, for the most part, are very filthy. Many of these, even in old and densely populated parts of the city, are no better than rough country roads, full of rocks, crevices, mud holes, and other irregularities, so that vehicles traverse them with difficulty at all times, and in the rainy season they are sometimes impassable for two months. Rough, muddy, or both, these streets serve admirably as permanent receptacles for much decomposing animal and vegetable matter. Finally, not less, probably more, than one-half the population of Havana live on streets which are constantly in an extremely insanitary condition, but these streets, though so numerous, are not in the beaten track of the pleasure tourist.

In the old intramural city, in which live about 40,000 people, the streets vary in width, but generally they are 6.8 meters (about 22 feet wide, of which the sidewalks occupy about 7.5 feet. In many streets the sidewalk at each side is not even 18 inches wide. In the new, extramural town, the streets are generally 10 meters (32.8 feet) wide, with 3 meters (nearly 10 feet) for the sidewalks, and 7 meters (23 feet) for the wagonway. There are few sidewalks in any except in the first four of the nine city districts.

More than two-thirds of the population live in densely inhabited portions of the city, where the houses are crowded in contact with each other. The average house lot does not exceed 27 by 112 feet insize. There are 17,259 houses, of which 15,494 are one-story, 1,552 are two stories, 186 are three stories, and only 27 are four stories, with none higher. At least 12 in every 13 inhabitants live in one-story houses; and as the total civil, military, and transient population exceeds 200,000 there are more than 12 inhabitants to every house. Tenement houses may have many small rooms, but each room is occupied by a family. Generally the one-story houses have four or five rooms; but house rent, as also food and clothing, is rendered so expensive by taxation, by export as well as import duties, that it is rare for workmen, even when paid $50 to $100 a month, to enjoy the exclusive use of one of these mean little houses; reserving one or two rooms for his family, he rents the balance. This condition of affairs is readily understood when it is known that so great a necessity as flour cost in Havana $15.50 when its price in the United States was $6.50 per barrel.

In the densely populated portions of the city the houses generally have no back yard, properly so called, but a flagged court, or narrow vacant space into which sleeping rooms open at the side, and in close proximity with these, at the rear of this contracted court are located the kitchen, the privy, and often a stall for animals. In the houses of the poor, that is, of the vast majority of the population, there are no storerooms, pantries, closets, or other conveniences for household supplies. These are furnished from day to day, even from meal to meal, by the corner groceries; and it is rare, in large sections of Havana, to find any one of the four corners of a square without a grocery.

The walls of most of the houses in Havana are built of "mamposteria" or rubble masonry, a porous material which freely absorbs atmospheric as well as ground moisture. The mark of this can often be seen high on the walls, which varies from 2 to 7 feet in the houses generally. The roofs are excellent, usually flat, and constructed of brick tiles. The windows are, like the doors, unusually high, nearly reaching the ceiling, which, in the best houses only, is also unusually high. The windows are never glazed, but protected by strong iron bars on the outside and on the inside by solid wooden shutters, which are secured, like the doors, with heavy bars or bolts, and in inclement weather greatly interfere with proper ventilation. Fireplaces with chimneys are extremely rare, so that ventilation depends entirely on the doors and windows, which, it should be stated, are by no means unusually large in most of the sleeping rooms of the poor. Generally in Havana, less generally in other cities, the entrances and courtyards are flagged with stone, while the rooms are usually floored with tile or marble. With rare exceptions the lowest floor is in contact with the earth. Ventilation between the earth and floor is rarely seen in Cuba. In Havana the average height of the ground floor is from 7 to 11 inches above the pavement, but in Havana, and more frequently in other Cuban towns, one often encounters houses which are entered by stepping down from the sidewalk, and some floors are even below the level of the street. In Havana some of the floors, in Matanzas more, in Cardenas and Cienfuegos many are of the bare earth itself, or of planks raised only a few inches above the damp ground.

The narrow entrance about 400 yards in width and 1.200 in length, opens into the irregular harbor, which has three chief coves or indentations, termed "ensenadas." The extreme length of the harbor from its sea entrance to the limit of the most distant ensenada is 3 miles, and its extreme breadth $1\frac{1}{2}$ miles; but within the entrance the average length is only about 1, and the average breadth about two-thirds of a mile. However, because of the irregularly projecting points of land which form the ensenadas, there is no locality in the harbor where a vessel can possibly anchor farther than 500 yards from the shore. Its greatest depth is about 40 feet, but the anchorage ground for vessels drawing 18 feet of water is very contracted, not exceeding one-half the size of the harbor. The rise and fall of the tide does not exceed 2 feet.

The Cuban city next in celebrity to Havana is Matanzas, and it is one likely to become a favorite of Americans, as the country in the vicinity is distinguished by beauty as well as remarkable for fertility. Matanzas was first regularly settled in 1693. It is in the province of Matanzas, 54 miles west of Havana, by the most direct of the two railroads which unite these two cities, and is situated on the western inland extremity of the bay of Matanzas, a harbor of the first class. Matanzas is divided into three districts, viz, the central district of Matanzas, which, about half a mile in width across the center of population, lies between the two little rivers, San Juan to the south, and the Yumuri to the north; the Pueblo Nuevo district, south of the San Juan, and around the inland extremity of the harbor; and the district of Versalles, north of the Yumuri, nearest to the open sea, as also to the anchorage ground, and, sanitarily, the best situated district in the city. About two-thirds of the population are in the district of Matanzas, and the Pueblo Nuevo district has about double the population of Versalles. Pueblo Nuevo stands on ground originally a swamp, and is low, flat, and only 3 or 4 feet above the sea. The Matanzas district has many houses on equally low ground, on the harbor front, and on the banks of the two rivers which inclose this district; but from the front and between these rivers the ground ascends, so that its houses are from 2 to even 100 feet above the sea; however, the center of population, the public square, is only about 20 feet above sea level. Versalles is on a bluff of the harbor, and its houses are situated, for the most part, from 15 to 40 feet above the sea. The district of Matanzas has ill constructed and useless sewers in only two streets, and no houses connected therewith. So much of this district and of Versalles as is built on the hill slope is naturally well drained, but the Pueblo Nuevo district, and those parts of Matanzas built in immediate proximity to the banks of the river, are very ill drained.

Since 1872 Matanzas has had an aqueduct from the Bello spring, 7 miles distant. The supply is alleged to be both abundant and excellent. But of the 4,710 houses in the city 840 stand on the hills outside the zone supplied by the waterworks, while of the remaining 3,870 houses within this zone only about 2,000 get their water from the waterworks company. Hence more than half of the houses of Matanzas (2,710) do for the most part get their supply in kegs by purchase in the streets. There are a few public fountains, as also some dangerous wells. The streets are 30 feet wide, with 24 feet wagon way. Few of them are paved, some are very poor roads, but, for the most part, these roads are in good condition. In the Matanzas district some of the streets are of solid stone, and natural foundation rock of the place, for the superficial soil is so thin that the foundation rocks often crop out. Of this very porous rock most of the houses are built. The houses have wider fronts, larger air spaces in rear, are not so crowded, and are better ventilated than the houses of Havana. As is usual in Cuba, the ground floors are generally on a level with the sidewalk, and some are even below the level of the streets. A heavy rain floods many of the streets of Matanzas, the water running back into and beneath the houses. The porous limestone of which the houses are built greatly favors absorption.

The population of Matanzas and suburbs was about 50,000 at the beginning of the war.

Porto Rico is not quite as large as Connecticut, but larger than the States of Delaware and Rhode Island. The climate of the island is delightful, and its soil exceedingly rich. In natural resources it is of surpassing opulence. The length of the island is about one hundred miles, and its breadth thirty-five, the general figure of it being like the head of a sperm whale. The range of mountains is from east to west, and nearly central. The prevalent winds are from the northwest, and the rainfall is much heavier on the northern shores and mountain slopes than on the southern. The height of the ridge is on the average close to 1,500 feet, one bold peak, the Anvil being 3,600 feet high. The rainy north and the droughty south, with the lift of the land from the low shores to the central slopes and rugged elevations, under the tropical sun, with the influence of the great oceans east, south and north, and the multitude of western and southern islands, give unusual and charming variety in temperature. Porto Rico is, by the American people, even more than the Spaniards, associated with Cuba. But is is less than a tenth of Cuban proportions. Porto Rico has 3,600 square miles to Cuba's 42,000, but a much greater proportion of Porto Rico than of Cuba is cultivated. Less than one-sixteenth of the area of Cuba has been improved, and while her population is but 1,600,000, according to the latest census, and is not so much now. Porto Rico, with less than a tenth of the land of Cuba, has half the number of inhabitants. Largely Porto Rico is peopled by a better class than the mass of the Cubans. Cuba is wretchedly provided with roads, one of the reasons why the Spaniards were incapable of putting down insurrections. If they had expended a fair proportion of the revenues derived from the flourishing plantations and the monopolies of Spanish favoritisms that built up Barcelona and enriched Captain-Generals, and in less degree other public servants, the rebellions would have been put down. The Spanish armies in Cuba, however, were rather managed for official speculation and peculation, were more promenaders than in military enterprise and the stern business of war. With Weyler for an opponent, Gomez, as a guerilla, could have dragged on a series of skirmishes indefinitely. The story of the alleged war in Cuba between the Spaniards and the Cubans was on both sides falsified, and the American people deceived. Porto Rico does not seem to have appealed so strongly to the cupidity of the Spaniards as Cuba did, and to have been governed with less brutality. The consequence is there has not been a serious insurrection in the smaller island for seventy years, and it falls into our possession without the impoverishment and demoralization of the devastation of war—one of the fairest gems of the ocean.

It was October 18th that the American flag was raised over San Juan. The following dispatch is the official record:

"San Juan, Porto Rico, Oct. 18.—Secretary of War, Washington, D. C.: Flags have been raised on public buildings and forts in this city and saluted with national salutes. The occupation of the island is now complete.

"BROOKE, Chairman."

On the morning of the 18th, the 11th regular infantry with two batteries of the 5th artillery landed. The latter proceeded to the forts, while the infantry lined up on the docks. It was a holiday for San Juan and there were many people in the streets. Rear-Admiral Schley and General Gordon, accompanied by their staffs, proceeded to the palace in carriages. The 11th infantry regiment and band with Troop H, of the 6th United States cavalry then marched through the streets and formed in the square opposite the palace.

At 11:40 a. m., General Brooke, Admiral Schley and General Gordon, the United States evacuation commissioners, came out of the palace with many naval officers and formed on the right side of the square. The streets behind the soldiers were thronged with townspeoeple, who stood waiting in dead silence.

At last the city clock struck 12, and the crowds, almost breathless and with eyes fixed upon the flagpole, watched for developments. At the sound of the first gun from Fort Morro, Major Dean and Lieutenant Castle, of General Brooke's staff, hoisted the stars and stripes, while the band played "The Star Spangled Banner." All heads were bared and the crowds cheered. Fort Morro, Fort San Cristobal and the United States revenue cutter Manning, lying in the harbor, fired twenty-one guns each.

Senor Munoz Rivera, who was president of the recent autonomist council of secretaries, and other officials of the late insular government were present at the proceedings. Many American flags were displayed.

Acknowledgment has been made of the better condition of Porto Rico than of Cuba, but the trail of the serpent of colonial Spanish government appears. Mr. Alfred Somamon writes in the Independent:

"The internal administration of the island disposes of a budget of about $3,300,-000, and is a woeful example of corrupt officialism. Of this sum only about $650,000 is expended in the island, the remainder being applied to payment of interest on public debt, salaries of Spanish officials, army, navy, and other extra-insular expenditures. But the whole of the revenue is collected in the island."

An article of great value by Eugene Deland, appeared in the Chatauquan of September, on the characteristics of Porto Rico, and we present an extract, showing its admirable distinction of accurate information well set forth:

"The mountain slopes are covered with valuable timbers, cabinet and dye-woods, including mahogany, walnut, lignum vitae, ebony, and logwood, and various medicinal plants. Here, too, is the favorite zone of the coffee tree, which thrives best one thousand feet above sea level. The valleys and plains produce rich harvests of sugar-cane and tobacco. The amount of sugar yielded by a given area is said to be greater than in any other West Indian island. Rice, of the mountain variety and grown without flooding, flourishes almost any place and is a staple food of the laboring classes. In addition to these products cotton and maize are commonly cultivated, and yams, plantains, oranges, bananas, cocoanuts, pineapples, and almost every other tropical fruit are grown in abundance. Among indigenous plants are several noted for their beautiful blossoms. Among these are the coccoloba, which grows mainly along the coasts and is distinguished by its large, yard-long purple spikes, and a talauma, with magnificent, ororous, white flowers.

"Of wild animal life Porto Rico has little. No poisonous serpents are found, but pestiferous insects, such as tarantulas, centipedes, scorpions, ticks, fleas, and mosquitos, supply this deficiency in a measure. All sorts of domestic animals are raised, and the excellent pasture-lands support large herds of cattle for export and home consumption, and ponies, whose superiority is recognized throughout the West Indies.

"The mineral wealth of the island is undeveloped, but traces of gold, copper, iron, lead, and coal are found. Salt is procured in considerable quantities from the lakes.

"Porto Rico carries on an extensive commerce, chiefly with Spain, the United States, Cuba, Germany, Great Britain, and France. In 1895 the volume of its trade was one-half greater than that of the larger British colony—Jamaica. The United States ranks second in amount of trade with the island. During the four years from 1893-96 Spain's trade with the colony averaged $11,402,888 annually, and the United States, $5,028,544. The total value of Porto Rican exports for 1896 was $18,341,-430, and of imports, $18,282,690, making a total of $36,624,120, which was in excess over any previous year. The exports consist almost entirely of agricultural products. In 1895 coffee comprised about sixty per cent. and sugar about twenty-eight per cent. of their value; leaf tobacco, molasses, and honey came next. Maize, hides, fruits, nuts, and distilled spirits are also sent out in considerable quantities. Over one-half of the coffee exported goes to Spain and Cuba, as does most of the tobacco, which is said to be used in making the finest Havana cigars; the sugar and molasses are, for the most part, sent to the United States. Among imports, manufactured articles do not greatly exceed agricultural. Rice, fish, meat and lard, flour, and manufactured tobacco are the principal ones. Customs duties furnish about two-thirds of the Porto Rican revenue, which has for several years yielded greater returns to Spain than that of Cuba.

"The climate of Porto Rico is considered the healthiest in the Antilles. The heat is considerably less than at Santiago de Cuba, a degree and a half farther north. The thermometer seldom goes above 90 degrees. Pure water is readily obtained in most of the island. Yellow fever seldom occurs, and never away from the coast. The rainy season begins the first of June and ends the last of December, but the heavy downpours do not come on until about August 1st.

"In density of population also this island ranks first among the West Indies, having half as many inhabitants as Cuba, more than eleven times as large. Of its 807,000 people, 326,000 are colored and many of the others of mixed blood. They differ little from other Spanish-Americans, being fond of ease, courteous, and hospitable, and, as in other Spanish countries, the common people are illiterate, public education having been grievously neglected. The natives are the agriculturists of the country, and are a majority in the interior, while the Spaniards, who control business and commerce, are found mainly in the towns and cities.

"The numerous good harbors have naturally dotted the seaboard with cities and towns of greater or less commercial importance. San Juan, Ponce, Mayaguez, Aguadilla, Arecibo and Fajardo all carry on extensive trade. Intercourse between coast towns is readily had by water, but is to be facilitated by a railroad around the island, of which 137 miles have been built and 170 miles more projected. The public highways of the island are in better condition than one might expect. According to a recent report of United States Consul Stewart, of San Juan, there are about one hundred and fifty miles of good road. The best of this is the military highway connecting Ponce on the southern coast with San Juan on the northern. This is a macadamized road, so excellently built and so well kept up that a recent traveler in the island says a bicycle corps could go over it without dismounting. Whether it is solid enough to stand the transportation of artillery and heavy army trains we shall soon know. Of telegraph lines Porto Rico has four hundred and seventy miles, and two cables connect it with the outside world, one running from Ponce and the other from San Juan."

Mr. Alfred Solomon, already quoted as an instructive contributor to the Independent, writes:

"The population of Porto Rico, some 800,000, is essentially agricultural. A varied climate, sultry in the lowlands, refreshing and invigorating in the mountain ranges, makes possible the cultivation of almost every variety of known crop—sugar, tobacco, coffee, annatto, maze, cotton and ginger are extensively grown; but there are still thousands of acres of virgin lands awaiting the capitalist. Tropical fruits flourish in abundance, and the sugar-pine is well known in our market, where it brings a higher price than any other pine imported. Hardwood and fancy cabinet wood trees fill the forests, and await the woodman's ax. Among these are some specimens of unexampled beauty, notably a tree, the wood of which, when polished, resembles veined marble, and another, rivaling in beauty the feathers in a peacock's tail. Precious metals abound, although systematic effort has never been directed to the locating of paying veins. Rivers and rivulets are plenty, and water-power is abundant; and the regime should see the installation of power plants and electric lighting all over the island, within a short time after occupation. On the lowlands, large tracts of pasturage under guinea grass and malojilla feed thousands of sleek cattle, but, as an article of food, mutton is almost unknown. The native pony, small, wiry and untirable, has a world-wide reputation, and for long journeys is unequaled, possessing a gait, as they say in the island, like an arm-chair.

"Perhaps a third of the population of the island is of African descent; but, strangely enough, the colored people are only to be found on the coast, and are the fishermen, boatmen and laborers of the seaports. The cultivation of the crops is entirely in the hands of the jibaro, or peasant, who is seldom of direct Spanish descent, while the financiering and exportation is conducted almost entirely by peninsulares, or Spanish-born colonists, who monopolize every branch of commerce to the exclusion of the colonian-born subject.

"Coffee planting is largely engaged in, returning from ten to fifteen per cent. on capital. Improved transportation facilities, abolition of export dues and the consolidation of small estates would, doubtless, help toward better results. This crop is marketed in Europe—London, Havre and Barcelona—where better prices are obtainable than in New York. With the exception of a few plantations in strong hands, most of this property could be purchased at a fair valuation, and would prove to be a very profitable investment.

"Cocoa grows wild on the lowlands, but has not been cultivated to any appreciable extent. Small consignments sent to Europe have been pronounced superior to the Caracas bean. The tree takes a longer period than coffee to come to maturity and bear fruit; but once in bearing the current expenses are less and the yield far greater. The same remarks apply to the cultivation of rubber, which, although a most profitable staple with an ever-increasing market, has received no attention whatever.

"Corn is raised in quantities insufficient for home consumption. Of this cereal three crops can be obtained in two years; sometimes two a year. The demand is constant, and the price always remunerative.

"In Porto Rico, as in most other West Indian islands, sugar is king. In the treatment of this product the lack of capital has been sadly felt. Planters possess only the most primitive machinery, and in the extraction of the juice from the cane the proportion of saccharine matter has been exceedingly small. Great outlay is necessary for the installation of a complete modern crushing and centrifugal plant."

A flattering picture of our new possessions is drawn in McClure's Magazine, by Mr. George B. Waldron.

"Here, then, are Cuba and Porto Rico in the Atlantic, and the Hawaiian and Philippine groups in the Pacific, whose destiny has become intertwined with our own. Their combined area is 168,000 square miles, equaling New England, New York, Pennsylvania, and New Jersey. Their population is about 10,000,000, or perhaps one-half of that of these nine home States. The Philippines, with three-quarters of the entire population, and Porto Rico, with 800,000 people, alone approach our own Eastern States in density. Cuba, prior to the war, was about as well populated as Virginia, and the Hawaiian group is as well peopled as Kansas. What, then, can these islands do for us?

CUBA AND PORTO RICO.   381

"Americans use more sugar in proportion to population than any other nation of the world. The total consumption last year was not less than 2,500,000 tons. This is enough to make a pyramid that would overtop the tallest pyramid of Egyptian fame. Of this total, 2,200,000 tons came from foreign countries, the Spanish possessions and Hawaii sending about twenty-five per cent. Five years earlier, when our imports were less by half a million tons, these islands supplied double this quantity, or nearly two-thirds of the nation's entire sugar import. But that was before Cuba had been devastated by war and when she was exporting 1,100,000 tons of sugar to other countries. Restore Cuba to her former fertility, and the total sugar crop of these islands will reach 1,500,000 tons, or two-thirds our present foreign demand."

There is much more in Mr. Waldron's summary of the vast addition that has been made to our resources by the occupation and possession of the islands that have recently been gathered under our wings by the force of our arms. It is enough to know that with the tropical islands we have gained, we have in our hands the potentialities, the luxuries, the boundless resources including, as we may, and must, Alaska, of all the zones of the great globe that we inhabit in such ample measure.

The following notes were compiled for the information of the army, and embody all reliable information available.

The notes were intended to supplement the military map of Porto Rico. The following books and works were consulted and matter from them freely used in the preparation of the notes: Guia Geografico Militar de Espana y Provincias Ultramarinas, 1879; Espana, sus Monumentos y Artes, su Naturaleza e Historia, 1887; Compendio de Geografia Militar de Espana y Portugal, 1882; Anuario de Comercio de Espana, 1896; Anuario Militar de Espana, 1898; Reclus, Nouvelle Geographic Universelle, 1891; Advance Sheets American Consular Reports, 1898; An Account of the Present State of the Island of Porto Rico, 1834; The Statesman's Year Book, 1898.

Situation.—Porto Rico is situated in the Torrid Zone, in the easternmost part of the Antilles, between latitude 17 deg. 54 min. and 18 deg. 30 min. 40 sec. N. and longitude 61 deg. 54 min. 26 sec. and 63 deg. 32 min. 32 sec. W. of Madrid. It is bounded on the north by the Atlantic, on the east and south by the sea of the Antilles, and on the west by the Mona Channel.

Size.—The island of Porto Rico, the fourth in size of the Antilles, has, according to a recent report of the British consul (1897), an extent of about 3,668 square miles—35 miles broad and 95 miles long. It is of an oblong form, extending from east to west.

Population.—Porto Rico is the first among the Antilles in density of population and in prosperity. The Statesman's Year Book, 1898, gives the population (1887) at 813,937, of which over 300,000 are negroes, this being one of the few countries of tropical America where the number of whites exceeds that of other races. The whites and colored, however, are all striving in the same movement of civilization, and are gradually becoming more alike in ideas and manners. Among the white population the number of males exceeds the number of females, which is the contrary of all European countries.* This is partly explained by the fact that the immigrants are mostly males. On an average the births exceed the deaths by double. The eastern portion of the island is less populous than the western.

Soil.—The ground is very fertile, being suitable for the cultivation of cane, coffee, rice, and other products raised in Cuba, which island Porto Rico resembles in richness and fertility.

Climate.—The climate is hot and moist, the medium temperature reaching 104 degs. F. Constant rains and winds from the east cool the heavy atmosphere of the low regions. On the heights of the Central Cordillera the temperature is healthy and agreeable.

Iron rusts and becomes consumed, so that nothing can be constructed of this metal. Even bronze artillery has to be covered with a strong varnish to protect it from the damp winds.

Although one would suppose that all the large islands in the Tropics enjoyed the same climate, yet from the greater mortality observed in Jamaica, St. Domingo, and Cuba, as compared with Porto Rico, one is inclined to believe that this latter island is much more congenial than any of the former to the health of Europeans. The heat, the rains, and the seasons are, with very trifling variations, the same in all. But the number of mountains and running streams, which are everywhere in view in Porto Rico, and the general cultivation of the land, may powerfully contribute to purify the atmosphere and render it salubrious to man. The only difference of temperature to be observed throughout the island is due to altitude, a change which is common to every country under the influence of the Tropics.

In the mountains the inhabitants enjoy the coolness of spring, while the valleys would be uninhabitable were it not for the daily breeze which blows generally from the northeast and east. For example, in Ponce the noonday sun is felt in all its rigor, while at the village of Adjuntas, 4 leagues distant in the interior of the mountains, the traveler feels invigorated by the refreshing breezes of a temperate clime. At one place the thermometer is as high as 90 deg., while in another it is sometimes under 60 deg. Although the seasons are not so distinctly marked in this climate as they are in Europe (the trees being always green), yet there is a distinction to be made between them. The division into wet and dry seasons (winter and summer) does not give a proper idea of the seasons in this island; for on the north coast it sometimes rains almost the whole year, while sometimes for twelve or fourteen months not a drop of rain falls on the south coast. However, in the mountains at the south there are daily showers. Last year, for example, in the months of November, December, and January the north winds blew with violence, accompanied by heavy showers of rain, while this year (1832) in the same months, it has scarcely blown a whole day from that point of the compass, nor has it rained for a whole month. Therefore, the climate of the north and south coasts of this island, although under the same tropical influence, are essentially different.

As in all tropical countries, the year is divided into two seasons—the dry and the rainy. In general, the rainy season commences in August and ends the last of December, southerly and westerly winds prevailing during this period. The rainfall is excessive, often inundating fields and forming extensive lagoons. The exhalations from these lagoons give rise to a number of diseases, but, nevertheless, Porto Rico is one of the healthiest islands of the archipelago.

In the month of May the rains commence, not with the fury of a deluge, as in the months of August and September, but heavier than any rain experienced in Europe. Peals of thunder reverberating through the mountains give a warning of their approach, and the sun breaking through the clouds promotes the prolific vegetation of the fields with its vivifying heat. The heat at this season is equal to the summer of Europe, and the nights are cool and pleasant; but the dews are heavy and pernicious to health. The following meteorological observations, carefully made by Don Jose Ma. Vertez, a Captain of the Spanish navy, will exhibit the average range of temperature:

Degrees of heat observed in the capital of Porto Rico, taking a medium of five years.

DEGREES OF HEAT OBSERVED IN THE CAPITAL OF PORTO RICO, TAKING A MEDIUM OF FIVE YEARS.

Hours of the Day.	Jan.	Feb.	Mar.	Apr.	May.	June.	July.	Aug.	Sept.	Oct.	Nov.	Dec.
Seven in the morning	72	72½	74	78	78	82	85	86	80½	77	75	75
Noon	82	81	82	83	85	86	90	92	88	85	84	80
Five in the evening	78	74	78	80	81	84	87	90	83	82	80	79

The weather, after a fifteen or twenty days' rain, clears up and the sun, whose heat has been hitherto moderated by partial clouds and showers of rain, seems, as it were, set in a cloudless sky. The cattle in the pastures look for the shade of the trees, and a perfect calm pervades the whole face of nature from sunrise till between 10 and 11 o'clock in the morning, when the sea breeze sets in. The leaves of the trees seem as if afraid to move, and the sea, without a wave or ruffle on its vast expanse, appears like an immense mirror. Man partakes in the general languor as well as the vegetable and brute creation.

The nights, although warm, are delightfully clear and serene at this season. Objects may be clearly distinguished at the distance of several hundred yards, so that one may even shoot by moonlight. The months of June and July offer very little variation in the weather or temperature. In August a suffocating heat reigns throughout the day, and at night it is useless to seek for coolness; a faint zephyr is succeeded by a calm of several hours. The atmosphere is heavy and oppressive, and the body, weakened by perspiration, becomes languid; the appetite fails, and the mosquitos, buzzing about the ears by day and night, perplex and annoy by their stings, while the fevers of the tropics attack Europeans with sudden and irresistible violence. This is the most sickly season for the European. The thermometer frequently exceeds 90 deg. The clouds exhibit a menacing appearance, portending the approach of the heavy autumnal rains, which pour down like a deluge. About the middle of September it appears as if all the vapors of the ocean had accumulated in one point of the heavens. The rain comes down like an immense quantity of water poured through a sieve; it excludes from the view every surrounding object, and in half an hour the whole surface of the earth becomes an immense sheet of water. The rivers are swollen and overflow their banks, the low lands are completely inundated, and the smallest brooks become deep and rapid torrents.

In the month of October the weather becomes sensibly cooler than during the preceding months, and in November the north and northeast winds generally set in, diffusing an agreeable coolness through the surrounding atmosphere. The body becomes braced and active, and the convalescent feels its genial influence. The north wind is accompanied (with few exceptions) by heavy showers of rain on the north coast; and the sea rolls on that coast with tempestuous violence, while the south coast remains perfectly calm.

When the fury of the north wind abates, it is succeeded by fine weather and a clear sky. Nothing can exceed the climate of Porto Rico at this season; one can only compare it to the month of May in the delightful Province of Andalusia, where the cold of winter and the burning heat of summer are tempered by the cool freshness of spring. This is considered to be the healthiest season of the year, when a European may visit the tropics without fear.

The small islands, destitute of wood and high mountains, which have a powerful effect in attracting the clouds, suffer much from drought. It sometimes happens that in Curacao, St. Bartholomews, and other islands there are whole years without a drop of rain, and after exhausting their cisterns the inhabitants are compelled to import water from the rivers of other islands.

"The land breeze" is an advantage which the large islands derive from the inequality of their surface; for as soon as the sea breeze dies away, the hot air of the valleys being rarified, ascends toward the tops of the mountains, and is there condensed by cold, which makes it specifically heavier than it was before; it then descends back to the valleys on both sides of the ridge. Hence a night wind (blowing on all sides from the land toward the shore) is felt in all the mountainous countries under the torrid zone. On the north shore the wind comes from the south, and on the south shore from the north.

Storms.—The hurricanes which visit the island, and which obey the general laws of tropical cyclones, are one of the worst scourges of the country. For hours before the appearance of this terrible phenomenon the sea appears calm; the waves come from a long distance very gently until near the shore, when they suddenly rise as if impelled by a superior force, dashing against the land with extraordinary violence and fearful noise. Together with this sign, the air is noticed to be disturbed, the sun red, and the stars obscured by vapor which seems to magnify them. A strong odor is perceived in the sea, which is sulphureous in the waters of rivers, and there are sudden changes in the wind. These omens, together with the signs of uneasiness manifested by various animals, foretell the proximity of a hurricane.

This is a sort of whirlwind, accompanied by rain, thunder and lightning, sometimes by earthquake shocks, and always by the most terrible and devastating circumstances that can possibly combine to ruin a country in a few hours._ A clear, serene day is followed by the darkest night; the delightful view offered by woods and prairies is diverted into the deary waste of a cruel winter; the tallest and most robust cedar trees are uprooted, broken off bodily, and hurled into a heap; roofs, balconies, and windows of houses are carried through the air like dry leaves, and in all directions are seen houses and estates laid waste and thrown into confusion.

The fierce roar of the water and of the trees being destroyed by the winds, the cries and moans of persons, the bellowing of cattle and neighing of horses, which are being carried from place to place by the whirlwinds, the torrents of water inundating the fields, and a deluge of fire being let loose in flashes and streaks of lightning, seem to announce the last convulsions of the universe and the death agonies of nature itself.

Sometimes these hurricanes are felt only on the north coast, at others on the south coast, although generally their influence extends throughout the island.

In 1825 a hurricane destroyed the towns of Patillas, Maunabo, Yabucoa, Humacao, Gurabo, and Caguas, causing much damage in other towns in the east, north, and center of the island. The island was also visited by a terrible hurricane in 1772.

Earthquakes.—Earthquakes are somewhat frequent, but not violent or of great consequence. The natives foretell them by noticing clouds settle near the ground for some time in the open places among the mountains. The water of the springs emits a sulphurous odor or leaves a strange taste in the mouth; birds gather in large flocks and fly about uttering shriller cries than usual; cattle bellow and horses neigh, etc. A few hours beforehand the air becomes calm and dimmed by vapors which arise from the ground, and a few moments before there is a slight breeze, followed at intervals of two or three minutes by a deep rumbling noise, accompanied by a sudden gust of wind, which are the forerunners of the vibration, the latter following immediately. These shocks are sometimes violent and are usually repeated, but owing to the special construction of the houses, they cause no damage.

Tides.—For seven hours the tide runs rapidly in a northwest direction, returning in the opposite direction with equal rapidity for five hours.

Orography.—The general relief of Porto Rico is much inferior in altitude to that of the rest of the Great Antilles, and even some of the Lesser Antilles have mountain summits which rival it.

A great chain of mountains divides the islands into two parts, northern and southern, which are called by the natives Banda del Norte and Banda del Sur. This chain sends out long ramifications toward the coasts, the interstices of which form beautiful and fertile valleys, composed in the high parts of white and red earths, on the spurs of black and weaker earths, and near the coasts of sand.

To the northwest and following a direction almost parallel with the northern coast, the Sierra of Lares extends from Aguadilla to the town of Lares, where it divides into two branches, one going north nearly to the coast, near Arecibo harbor, and the other extending to the spurs of the Sierra Grande de Banos; this latter starting from Point Guaniquilla, crosses the island in its entire length, its last third forming the Sierra of Cayey.

The whole island may be said to form a continuous network of sierras, hills, and heights. Of these the Sierra del Loquillo is distinguished for its great altitude (the highest peak being Yunque, in the northeast corner of the island and visible from the sea, a distance of 120 kilometers), as is also Laivonito Mountain, near the south coast.

The following are the four highest mountains, with their heights above the sea level: Yunque, in Luquillo, 1,290 yards; Guilarte, in Adjuntas, 1,180 yards; La Somanta, in Aybonito, 1,077 yards; Las Tetas de Cerro Gordo, in San German, 860 yards. All are easily ascended on foot or horseback, and there are coffee plantations near all of them.

Approximate Height of Towns Above the Sea Level.—Aybonito, with its acclimatization station, 970 yards; Adjuntas, an almost exclusively Spanish town, 810 yards; Cayey, with a very agreeable climate, 750 yards; Lares, with a very agreeable climate, 540 yards; Utuado, with a very agreeable climate, 480 yards; Muricao, an exclusively Spanish town, 480 yards. To ascend to all these towns there are very good wagon roads. There are no fortifications of any kind in them, but they are surrounded on all sides by mountains.

Hydrography.—Few countries of the extent of Porto Rico are watered by so many streams. Seventeen rivers, taking their rise in the mountains, cross the valleys of the north coast and empty into the sea. Some of these are navigable 2 or 3 leagues from their mouths for schooners and small coasting vessels. Those of Manati, Loisa, Trabajo, and Arecibo are very deep and broad, and it is difficult to imagine how such large bodies of water can be collected in so short a course. Owing to the heavy surf which continually breaks on the north coast, these rivers have bars across their embouchures which do not allow large vessels to enter. The rivers of Bayamo and Rio Piedras flow into the harbor of the capital, and are also navigable for boats. At high water small brigs may enter the river of Arecibo with perfect safety and discharge their cargoes, notwithstanding the bar which crosses its mouth.

The rivers of the north coast have a decided advantage over those of the south coast, where the climate is drier and the rains less frequent. Nevertheless, the south, west, and east coasts are well supplied with water; and, although in some seasons it does not rain for ten, and sometimes twelve months on the south coast, the rivers are never entirely dried up.

From the Cabeza de San Juan, which is the northeast extremity of the island, to the cape of Mala Pascua, which lies to the southeast, 9 rivers fall into the sea.

From Cape Mala Pascua to Point Aguila, which forms the southwest angle of the island, 16 rivers discharge their waters on the south coast.

On the west coast 3 rivers, 5 rivulets, and several fresh-water lakes communicate with the sea. In the small extent of 330 leagues of area there are 46 rivers, besides a countless number of rivulets and branches of navigable water.

The rivers of the north coast are stocked with delicious fish, some of them large enough to weigh two quintals.

From the river of Arecibo to that of Manati, a distance of 5 leagues, a fresh-water lagoon, perfectly navigable for small vessels through the whole of its extent, runs parallel to the sea at about a mile from the shore.

In the fertile valley of Anasco, on the western coast, there is a canal formed by nature, deep and navigable. None of the rivers are of real military importance; for, though considering the shortness of their course, they attain quite a volume, still it is not sufficient for good-sized vessels.

The rivers emptying on the north coast are Loisa, Aguas Prietas, Arecibo, Bayamon, Camuy, Cedros, Grande, Guajataca de la Tuna, Lesayas, Loquillo, Manati, Rio Piedras, Sabana, San Martin, Sibuco, Toa, and Vega.

Those emptying on the east coast are Candelero, Dagua, Fajardo, Guayanes, Majogua, and Maonabo.

On the south coast: Aquamanil, Caballon, Cana, Coamo, Descalabrado, Guanica, Guayama, Guayanilla, Jacagua, Manglar, Penuela, Ponce and Vigia.

On the west coast: Aguada, Boqueron, Cajas, Culebrina, Chico, Guanajibo, Mayagüez, and Rincon.

The limits of the Loisa river are: On the east, the sierra of Luquillo (situated near the northeast corner of the island); on the south, the sierra of Cayey, and on the west, ramifications of the latter. It rises in the northern slopes of the sierra of Cayey, and, running in a northwest direction for the first half of its course and turning to northeast in the second half, it arrives at Loisa, a port on the northern coast, where it discharges its waters into the Atlantic. During the first part of its course it is known by the name of Cayagua.

The Sabana river has, to the east and south, the western and southern limits of the preceding river, and on the west the Sierra Grande, or De Barros, which is situated in the center of the general divide, or watershed. It rises in the sierra of Cayey, and, with the name of Pinones river, it flows northwest, passing through Aibonito, Toa Alta, Toa Baja, and Dorado, where it discharges into the Atlantic to the west of the preceding river.

The Manati river is bounded on the east and south by the Sierra Grande and on the west by the Siales ridge. It rises in the Sierra Grande, and parallel with the preceding river, it flow through Siales and Manati, to the north of which latter town it empties into the Atlantic.

The Arecibo river is bounded on the east by the Siales mountain ridge, on the south by the western extremity of the Sierra Grande, and on the west by the Lares ridge. It rises in the general divide, near Adjuntas, and flows north through the town of Arecibo to the Atlantic, shortly before emptying into which it receives the Tanama river from the left, which proceeds from the Lares Mountains.

The Culebrina river is bounded on the south and east by the Lares mountain ridge, and on the north by small hills of little interest. From the Lares Mountains it flows from east to west and empties on the west coast north of San Francisco de la Aguada, in the center of the bay formed between Point Penas Blancas and Point San Francisco.

The Anasco river is formed by the Lares mountain ridge. It rises in the eastern extremity of the mountains called Tetas de Cerro Gordo, flowing first northwest and then west, through the town of its name and thence to the sea.

The Guanajivo river has to its north the ramifications of the Lares ridge, to the east the Tetas de Cerro Gordo Mountains, and on the south Torre Hill. In the interior of its basin is the mountain called Cerro Montuoso, which separates its waters from those of tis affluent from the right, the Rosaria river. It rises in the general divide, flowing from east to west to Nuestra Senora de Montserrat, where it receives the affluent mentioned, the two together then emptying south of Port Mayaguez.

The Coamo river is bounded on the west and north by the Sierra Grande, and on the west by the Coamo ridge. It rises in the former of these sierras, and flowing from north to south it empties east of Coamo Point, after having watered the town of its name.

The Salinas river is bounded on the west by the Coamo ridge, on the north by the general divide, and on the east by the Cayey ridge. It rises in the southern slopes of the Sierra Grande and flowing from north to south through Salinas de Coamo, empties into the sea.

Coasts, Harbors, Bays, and Coves.—The northern coast extends in an almost straight line from east to west, and is high and rugged. The only harbors it has are the following: San Juan de Porto Rico, surrounded by mangrove swamps and protected by the Cabras and the Cabritas islands and some very dangerous banks; the anchoring ground of Arecibo, somewhat unprotected; and the coves of Cangrejos and Condado. During the months of November, December, and January, when the wind blows with violence from the east and northeast, the anchorage is dangerous in all the bays and harbors of this coast, except in the port of San Juan. Vessels are often obliged to put to sea on the menacing aspect of the heavens at this season, to avoid being driven on shore by the heavy squalls and the rolling waves of a boisterous sea, which propel them to destruction. During the remaining months the ports on this coast are safe and commodious, unless when visited by a hurricane, against whose fury no port can offer a shelter, nor any vessel be secure. The excellent port of San Juan is perfectly sheltered from the effects of the north wind. The hill, upon which the town of that name and the fortifications which defend it are built, protects the vessels anchored in the harbor. The entrance of this port is narrow, and requires a pilot; for the canal which leads to the anchorage, although deep enough for vessels of any dimensions, is very narrow, which exposes them to run aground. This port is several miles in extent, and has the advantage of having deep canals to the east, among a wood of mangrove trees, where vessels are perfectly secure during the hurricane months. Vessels of 250 tons can at present unload and take in their cargoes at the wharf. Harbor improvements have been recently made here.

On the northwest and west are the coves of Aguadilla, the town of this name being some 4 kilometers inland. There are the small coves of Rincon, Anasco, and Mayaguez, the latter being protected and of sufficient depth to anchor vessels of moderate draft; the harbor of Real de Cabo Rojo, nearly round, and entered by a narrow channel; and the cove of Boqueron. The spacious bay of Aguadilla is formed by Cape Borrigua and Cape San Francisco. When the north-northwest and southwest winds prevail it is not a safe anchorage for ships. A heavy surf rolling on the shore obliges vessels to seek safety by putting to sea on the appearance of a north wind. Mayaguez is also an open roadstead formed by two projecting capes. It has good anchorage for vessels of a large size and is well sheltered from the north winds. The port of Cabo Rojo has also good anchorage. It is situated S. one-fourth N. of the point of Guanajico, at a distance of $5\frac{1}{2}$ miles. Its shape is nearly circular, and it extends from east to west 3 to 4 miles. At the entrance it has 3 fathoms of water, and 16 feet in the middle of the harbor. The entrance is a narrow canal.

The south coast abounds in bays and harbors, but is covered with mangroves

CUBA AND PORTO RICO. 391

and reefs, the only harbor where vessels of regular draft can enter being Guanica and Ponce. The former of these is the westernmost harbor on the southern coast, being at the same time the best, though the least visited, owing to the swamps and low tracts difficult to cross leading from it to the interior. The nearest towns, San German, Sabana Grande, and Yauco, carry on a small trade through this port.

In the port of Guanica, vessels drawing 21 feet of water may enter with perfect safety. Its entrance is about 100 yards wide, and it forms a spacious basin, completely landlocked. The vessels may anchor close to the shore. It has, in the whole extent, from $6\frac{1}{2}$ to 3 fathoms, the latter depth being formed in the exterior of the port. The entrance is commanded by two small hills on either side, which if mounted with a few pieces of artillery would defy a squadron to force it. This port would be of immense advantage in time of war. The national vessels and coasters would thus have a secure retreat from an enemy's cruiser on the south coast. There are no wharves, but vessels could disembark troops by running alongside the land and running out a plank. Coamo Cove and Aguirre and Guayama are also harbors. The port of Jovos, near Guayama, is a haven of considerable importance. It is a large and healthy place, and the most Spanish of any city on the island after San Juan. There are good roads to the capital. Vessels of the largest kind may anchor and ride in safety from the winds, and the whole British navy would find room in its spacious bosom. It has 4 fathoms of water in the shallowest part of the entrance. However, it is difficult to enter this port from June to November, as the sea breaks with violence at the entrance, on account of the southerly winds which reign at that season. It has every convenience of situation and locality for forming docks for the repair of shipping. The large bay of Anasco, on the south coast, affords anchorage to vessels of all sizes. It is also safe from the north winds. Although on the eastern coast there are many places for vessels to anchor, yet none of them are exempt from danger during the north winds except Fajardo, where a safe anchorage is to be found to leeward of two little islands close to the bay, where vessels are completely sheltered.

The island of Vieques has also several commodious ports and harbors, where vessels of the largest size may ride at anchor.

On the east coast is Cape Cabeza de San Juan, Points Lima, Candeleros, and Naranjo, and Cape Mala Pascua; on the south coast, Point Viento, Tigueras, Corchones, Arenas, Fama or Maria, Cucharas, Guayanilla, Guanica, and Morillos de Cabo Rojo; on the west coast, points San Francisco, Cadena, Guanijito, Guaniquilla, and Palo Seco.

CUBA AND PORTO RICO.

Highways.—There are few roads or ways of communication which are worthy of mention, with the exception of the broad pike which starts from the capital and runs along the coast, passing through the following towns: Aguadilla, Bayamon, Cabo Rojo, Humacao, Juana Diaz, Mayaguez, Ponce, and San German. It has no bridges; is good in dry weather, but in the rainy season is impassible for wagons and even at times for horsemen.

For interior communication there are only a few local roads or paths. They are usually 2 yards in width, made by the various owners, and can not be well traveled in rainy weather. They are more properly horse and mule trails, and oblige people to go in single file. In late years much has been attempted to improve the highways connecting the principal cities, and more has been accomplished than in Spanish colonies. There is a good made road connecting Ponce on the southern coast with San Juan the capital. Other good roads also extend for a short distance along the north coast and along the south coast. The road from Guayama is also said to be a passably good one.

There are in the island about 150 miles of excellent road, and this is all that receives any attention, transportation being effected elsewhere on horse back. In the construction of a road level foundation is sought, and on this is put a heavy layer of crushed rock and brick, which, after having been well packed and rounded, is covered with a layer of earth. This is well packed also, and upon the whole is spread a layer of ground limestone, which is pressed and rolled until it forms almost a glossy surface. This makes an excellent road here where the climate is such that it does not affect it, and when there is no heavy traffic, but these conditions being changed, the road, it is thought, would not stand so well.

From Palo Seco, situated about a mile and a half from the capital, on the opposite side of the bay, a carriage road, perfectly level, has been constructed for a distance of 22 leagues to the town of Aguadilla on the west coast, passing through the towns of Vegabaja, Manati, Arecibo, Hatillo, Camuy, and Isabella. This road has been carried for several leagues over swampy lands, which are intersected by deep drains to carry off the water.

The road from Aguadilla to Mayaguez is in some parts very good, in other parts only fair. From Aguadilla to Aguada, a distance of a league, the road is excellent and level. From thence to Mayaguez, through the village of Rincon and the town of Anasco, the road is generally good, but on the seashore it is sometimes interrupted by shelving rocks. Across the valley of Anasco the road is carried through a boggy tract, with bridges over several deep creeks of fresh water. From thence to the large commercial town of Mayaguez the road is uneven and requires some improvement. But the roads from Mayaguez and Ponce to their respective ports on the seashore can not be surpassed by any in Europe. They are made in a most substantial manner, and their convex form is well adapted to preserve them from the destruction caused by the heavy rains of the climate. These roads have been made over tracts of swampy ground to the seacoast, but with little and timely repair they will last forever.

A road, which may be called a carriage road, has been made from Ponce to the village of Adjuntas, situated 5 leagues in the interior of the mountains. The road along the coast, from Ponce to Guayama, is fairly good; from thence to Patillas there is an excellent carriage road for a distance of 3 leagues; from the latter place to the coast is a high road well constructed. From Patillas to Fajardo, on the eastern coast, passing through the towns of Maimavo, Yubacao, Humacao, and Naguabo, the roads are not calculated for wheel vehicles, in consequence of being obliged to ascend and descend several steep hills. That which crosses the mountain of Mala Pascua, dividing the north and east coasts, is a good and solid road, upon which a person on horseback may travel with great ease and safety. The road crossing the valley of Yubacao, which consists of a soft and humid soil, requires more attention than that crossing the mountain of Mala Pascua, which has a fine, sandy soil.

From Fajardo to the capital, through the towns of Luquillo, Loisa, and Rio Piedras, the road is tolerably good for persons on horseback as far as Rio Piedras, and from thence to the city of San Juan, a distance of 2 leagues, is an excellent carriage road, made by the order and under the inspection of the Captain-General, part of it through a mangrove swamp. Over the river Loisa is a handsome wooden bridge, and on the road near Rio Piedras is a handsome stone one over a deep rivulet.

One of the best roads in the island extends from the town of Papino, situated in the mountains, to the town of Aguadilla on the coast, distant 5½ leagues, through the village of La Moca; in the distance of 3 leagues from the latter place, it is crossed by 10 deep mountain rivulets, formerly impassable, but over which solid bridges have now been built, with side railings. In the mountainous district within the circumference of a few leagues no less than 47 bridges have been built to facilitate the communication between one place and the other.

The following are the roads of 6 meters width, 4½ in center of pounded stone. They have iron bridges and are in good shape for travel all the year.

(1) *San Juan to the Shore near Ponce.*—From San Juan to Ponce the central

road is exactly 134 kilometers. Distances along the line are: Rio Piedras, 11; Caguas, 25; to Cayei, 24; Aybonito, 20; Coamo, 18; Juana Diaz, 20; to Ponce, 13; and to the shore, 3. Exact.

(2) San Juan to Bayamon.—By ferry fifteen minutes to Catano, and from there by road to Bayamon 10 kilometers. This passes alongside the railway.

(3) Rio Piedras to Mameyes, 36 kilometers; from Rio Piedras to Carolina, 12; to Rio Grande, 19; to Mameyes, 5.

(4) Cayei to Arroyo, 35 kilometers; from Cayei to Guayama, 25; to Arroyo, 8; from San Juan to Arroyo, via Cayei, is 95 kilometers.

(5 Ponce to Adjuntas, 32 kilometers.

(6) San German to Anasco, 33 kilometers; from San German to Mayaguez, 21 kilometers; Mayaguez to Anasco, 12; Mayaguez to Mormigueros, 11; Mayaguez to Cabo Rojo, 18; Mayaguez to Las Marias, 23; Mayaguez to Maricao, 35; Hormigueras to San German, 14. Near Mayaguez the roads are best. There are good roads in all directions.

(7) Aguadilla to San Sebastian, 18.

(8) Arecibo to Utuado, 33.

Highways of first class in the island, 335 kilometers.

Along these roads are, at a distance of 8 to 10 kilometers, a fort, stone, and brick barracks, or large buildings, where the Spanish troops stop and rest when on the march.

Railroads.—In 1878 a report was presented to the minister of the colonies on a study made by the engineer and head of public works of the island in view of constructing a railroad which should start from the capital and, passing through all the chief towns and through the whole island, return to the point of departure.

Of this railroad the following parts have been completed: San Juan, along the coast through Rio Piedras, Bayamon, Dorado, Arecibo, and Hatillo, to Camuy; Aguadilla, through Aguado, Rincon, Anasco, and Mayaguez, to Hornigueros. A branch of this railroad from Anasco, through San Sebastian, to Lares. Ponce, through Guayanilla, to Yauco. This latter railroad follows the southern coast line and is followed by a wagon road throughout its course. In one place the railroad and road run within a few hundred yards of the coast line. According to the Statesman's Year Book for 1898 there are in operation 137 miles of railroad, besides over 170 miles under construction.

All the railroads are single track, and the gauge is 1 meter 20 centimeters, or 3 feet 11¼ inches.

The following are the railways of 1-meter gauge:
(1) San Juan to Rio Piedras, 11 kilometers.
(2) Catano to Bayamon, 10 kilometers.
(3) Anasco to San Sebastian and Lares, 35 kilometers.
Total of three lines, 56 kilometers.

The lines are all in good shape; have plenty of engines and cars; speed, 20 kilometers per hour; use coal for fuel imported from the United States; supply usually large, may be small now; hard coal; fine stations; plenty of water, and everything in shape for business.

Telegraphs.—The capital communicates with the principal towns of the coast and interior by means of a well-connected telegraph system. There are in all some 470 miles of telegraph.

Telephones.—The British Consular Report says that the telephone system of San Juan, Ponce, and Mayaguez have recently been contracted for by local syndicates. In Ponce a United States company obtained the contract for the material. There are 100 stations already connected, and it is expected that 200 more will be in operation shortly.

Administration.—From an administrative standpoint, Porto Rico is not considered as a colony, but as a province of Spain, assimilated to the remaining provinces. The Governor-General, representing the monarchy, is at the same time Captain-General of the armed forces. In each chief town resides a military commander, and each town has its alcalde, or mayor, appointed by the central power. The provincial deputation is elected by popular suffrage under the same conditions as in Spain. The regular peace garrison is composed of about 3,000 men, and the annual budget amounts to some 20,000,000 pesos.

Education.—In 1887 only one-seventh of the population could read and write, but of late years progress in public instruction has been rapid.

Agriculture, Industry, and Commerce.—In 1878 there arrived in the harbors of the island 1,591 vessels of different nationalities and 1,534 departed. The value of products imported was 14,787,551 pesos, and that of articles exported was 13,070,020 pesos. The following are the relative percentages of values:

Flags.	Relation. Per Cent.
Spanish	49.91
American	13.47
English	21.43
Various Nations	15.19
Total	100.00

Navigation is very active, but the part the inhabitants take in the commercial fleet is small. The Porto Ricans are not seagoing people. The eastern part of the island offers less advantage to commerce than the western, being to the windward and affording less shelter to vessels.

Porto Rico has more than seventy towns and cities, of which Ponce is the most important. Ponce has 22,000 inhabitants, with a jurisdiction numbering 47,000. It is situated on the south coast of the island, on a plain, about 2 miles from the seaboard. It is the chief town of the judicial district of its name, and is 70 miles from San Juan. It is regularly built, the central part almost exclusively of brick houses, and the suburbs of wood. It is the residence of the military commander, and the seat of an official chamber of commerce. There is an appellate criminal court, besides other courts; 2 churches, one Protestant, said to be the only one in the Spanish West Indies; 2 hospitals besides the military hospital, a home of refuge for old and poor, 2 cemeteries, 3 asylums, several casinos, 3 theaters, a market, a municipal public library, 3 first-class hotels, 3 barracks, a park, gas works, a perfectly equipped fire department, a bank, thermal and natural baths, etc. Commercially, Ponce is the second city of importance on the island. A fine road leads to the port (Playa), where all the import and export trade is transacted. Playa has about 5,000 inhabitants, and here are situated the custom house, the office of the captain of the port, and all the consular offices. The port is spacious and will hold vessels of 25 feet draft. The climate, on account of the sea breezes during the day and land breezes at night, is not oppressive, but very hot and dry; and, as water for all purposes, including the fire department, is amply supplied by an aqueduct 4,442 yards long, it is said that the city of Ponce is perhaps the healthiest place in the whole island. There is a stage coach to San Juan, Mayaguez, Guayama, etc. There is a railroad to Yauco, a post office, and a telegraph station.

It is believed that Ponce was founded in 1600; it was given the title of villa in 1848, and in 1877 that of city. Of its 34 streets the best are Mayor, Salud, Villa, Vives, Marina, and Comercio. The best squares are Principal and Las Delicias, which are separated by the church of Nuestra Senora de Guadalupe. The church, as old as the town itself, began to be reconstructed in 1838 and was finished in 1847. It is 86 yards long by 43 broad, and has two steeples, rich altars, and fine ornaments.

The theater is called the Pearl, and it deserves this name, for it is the finest on the island. It has a sculptured porch, on the Byzantine order, with very graceful columns. It is mostly built of iron and marble and cost over 70,000 pesos. It is 52 yards deep by 29 wide. The inside is beautiful, the boxes and seats roomy and nicely decorated. It may, by a mechanical arrangement, be converted into a dancing hall.

About 1½ miles northeast of the town are the Quintana thermal baths, in a building surrounded by pretty gardens. They are visited by sufferers from rheumatism and various other diseases.

San Juan is a perfect specimen of a walled town, with portcullis, moat, gates, and battlements. The wall surrounding this town is defended by several batteries. Facing the harbor are those of San Fernando, Santa Catalina, and Santa Toribio. Looking toward the land side is Fort Abanico, and toward the ocean the batteries of San Antonio, San Jose, and Santa Teresa, and Fort Princesa. The land part has two ditches, or cuts, which are easy to inundate. The fort and bridge of San Antonio that of San Geronimo, and the Escambron battery situated on a tongue of land which enters the sea. Built over two hundred and fifty years ago, the city is still in good condition and repair. The walls are picturesque, and represent a stupendous work and cost in themselves. Inside the walls the city is laid off in regular squares, six parallel streets running in the direction of the length of the island and seven at right angles.

The peninsula on which San Juan is situated is connected with the mainland by three bridges. The oldest, that of San Antonio, carries the highway across the shallow San Antonio Channel. It is a stone-arched bridge about 350 yards long including the approaches. By the side of this bridge is one for the railroad and one for the tramway which follows the main military highway to Rio Piedras.

Among the buildings the following are notable: The palace of the Captain-General, the palace of the intendencia, the town hall, military hospital, jail. Ballaja barracks, theater, custom house, cathedral, Episcopal palace, and seminary. There is no university or provincial institute of second grade instruction, and only one college, which is under the direction of Jesuit priests. The houses are closely and compactly built of brick, usually of two stories, stuccoed on the outside and painted in a variety of colors. The upper floors are occupied by the more respectable people, while the ground floors, almost without exception, are given up to the negroes and the poorer class, who crowd one upon another in the most appalling manner.

The population within the walls is estimated at 20,000 and most of it lives on the ground floor. In one small room, with a flimsy partition, a whole family will reside. The ground floor of the whole town reeks with filth, and conditions are most unsanitary. In a tropical country, where disease readily prevails, the consequences of such herding may be easily inferred. There is no running water in the town. The entire population depend upon rain water, caught upon the flat roofs of the buildings and conducted to the cistern, which occupies the greater part of the inner court-yard that is an essential part of Spanish houses the world over, but that here, on account of the crowded conditions, is very small. There is no sewerage, except for surface water and sinks, while vaults are in every house and occupy whatever remaining space there may be in the patios not taken up by the cisterns. The risk of contaminating the water is very great, and in dry seasons the supply is entirely exhausted. Epidemics are frequent, and the town is alive with vermin, fleas, cockroaches, mosquitoes, and dogs.

The streets are wider than in the older part of Havana, and will admit two carriages abreast. The sidewalks are narrow, and in places will accommodate but one person. The pavements are of a composition manufactured in England from slag, pleasant and even, and durable when no heavy strain is brought to bear upon them, but easily broken, and unfit for heavy traffic. The streets are swept once a day by hand, and, strange to say, are kept very clean.

From its topographical situation the town should be healthy, but it is not. The soil under the city is clay mixed with lime, so hard as to be almost like rock. It is consequently impervious to water and furnishes a good natural drainage.

The trade wind blows strong and fresh, and through the harbor runs a stream of sea water at a speed of not less than three miles an hour. With these conditions no contagious diseases, if properly taken care of, could exist; without them the place would be a veritable plague spot.

Besides the town within the walls there are small portions just outside, called the Marina and Puerta de Tierra, containing two or three thousand inhabitants each. There are also two suburbs, one, San Turce, approached by the only road leading out of the city, and the other, Catano, across the bay, reached by ferry. The Marina and the two suburbs are situated on sandy points or spits, and the latter are surrounded by mangrove swamps.

The entire population of the city and suburbs, according to the census of 1887, was 27,000. It is now (1896) estimated at 30,000. One-half of the population consists of negroes and mixed races.

There is but little manufacturing, and it is of small importance. The Standard Oil Company has a small refinery across the bay, in which crude petroleum brought from the United States is refined. Matches are made, some brooms, a little soap, and a cheap class of trunks. There are also ice, gas, and electric light works.

CHAPTER XXVI.

THE LADRONES.

The Island of Guam a Coaling Station of the United States—Discovery, Size and Products of the Islands.

When the Philippine expedition on its way to Manila incidentally ran up the Stars and Stripes over the Island of Guam, there was perhaps no thought of the island becoming a permanent part of our domain. However, the fortunes of war are such that the island is likely to become ours permanently as a coaling station in the Pacific.

Magellan named these islands the Ladrones from the Latin word "latro," meaning a robber, because of the thievish propensities of the natives. According to Magellan's reports, the native people of these islands had reduced stealing to a science of such exactness that the utmost vigilance could not prevail against their operations. The group was named the Mariana Islands by the Jesuits, who settled in them in 1667.

The Ladrone group consists of twenty islands, of which five are inhabited. The group extends forty-five miles from north to south, and is located between 13 deg. and 21 deg. north latitude, and between 144 deg. and 146 deg. east longitude. The principal islands are Guam, Rota and Linian. They were discovered by Magellan in 1521, and have belonged to Spain ever since. Their population is 11,000. The soil is fertile and densely wooded. The climate is temperate.

Guam, the southernly and principal island, is 100 miles in circumference, and has a population of 8,100, of which 1,400 are Europeans. Its central part is mountainous, and it has a small volcano. The products are guacas, bananas, cocoa, oranges and limes. The natives are noted as builders of the most rapidly sailing canoes in the world.

With Guam as a part of the territory of the United States, we have a direct line of possessions across the Pacific, in the order of Hawaii, Guam and the Philippines; while in a northwesterly direction from our Pacific coast we have the islands forming a part of Alaska. By holding all these islands we will be prepared to control practically the commerce of the Pacific, the future great commercial highway of the world.

THE PHILIPPINE ISLANDS.

The Shaded Part of the Map Shows the Portion of the Archipelago under the Control of the United States.

CHAPTER XXVII.

THE OFFICIAL TITLE TO OUR NEW POSSESSIONS IN THE INDIES.

Full Text of the Treaty of Peace with Spain Handed the President of the United States as a Christmas Gift for the People, at the White House, 1898—The Gathered Fruit of a Glorious and Wonderful Victory.

On an August midnight the good ship Peru, Major-General Otis with his staff and General Hughes, and a thousand regular cavalry and "the historian of the Philippines" aboard, approached within a few miles, an immense mass of darkness. About where the mouth of Manila Bay should be there was, deep in the east and at a considerable elevation, a spark of white, and in a few seconds a red light, keener than stars, and in half a minute there were the sharp flashes again, and we knew that there were friends watching and waiting—that "our flag was still there," that Admiral Dewey and General Merritt of the Navy and Army of the United States had upheld the symbol of the sovereignty of the Great Republic of North America, that the lights glowed down from the massive rock of Corregidor, that through the shadows that fell on these darksome waters the American squadron had entered into immortality less than four months before, and that with the morning light we should look upon the famous scene of triumphant Americanism. We had been fifteen days out of the world, for there were only the southern constellations to tell us, the southern cross so high and the north star so low, and the dazzling scorpion with diamond claws touching the central blue dome, to say how far down into the tropics we were, while the clouds of flame rested on the serenities of the matchless sea; and what had the great deep in its mysterious resplendence been whispering along the enchanting shores of the islands of Asia—the true Indies, Oriental or Occidental as might be—what had the wild waves that beat against the volcanic coasts made known in the boats wafted by the welcoming winds? We knew of the bloody days on the hills of Santiago, and the fate of the fleet of Admiral Cervera, and there must be news of other victories! Our ship turned away from the looming rock that sent forth flashes as if to say all is well, in the universe that we in our vast adventure had almost abandoned. And when the day dawned and the green hills and blue mountains and the silvery waters were revealed we turned to the left, where Dewey led his squadron to the right, and there was the bay hundred and twenty knots in circumference. Yonder were the white walls of

Cavite, and further along domes and steeples, masts and heavy lines of buildings, a wide spread city crouching on a plain rising a few feet above the tides. It was Manila. Presently a boat swept near, and what was that, a dozen words repeated here and there—Merritt in possession of the city—of course, that was what he was there for,—but who said "there was a declaration of peace?" The strange statement was made. What—could it be that Spain had surrendered? Surely the President would not stop pushing things until he had gathered the fruits of victory? No, there was a protocol, and that was a treaty in fact! France had been the medium of negotiation. Spain had sued for peace, and terms were granted. Cuba was surrendered. Porto Rico was ceded to us. The Spaniards claimed that they had given up Manila after peace was settled, and they must repossess it. But Merritt was ashore was he not, and going to stay? Dewey had not given up anything, had he? Surely not! But there was to be a conference, a meeting of joint commissioners held at Paris to provide a treaty, that was to say the details—all the important points were fixed irrevocably except the fate of the Philippines! At this point the news of the morning gave out, all except the particulars of the seige, the high claims of the Spaniards, the dissatisfaction of the insurgents. It was some days before the realization of the situation was perfected. The full terms of the protocol were not made known at once. Spain gave up the West Indies and a Ladrone island, and the United States was to hold the city, bay and harbor of Manila pending the conclusion of a treaty of peace which should determine the control, disposition and government of the Philippines. Certainly this was the conclusive surrender of Spain! General Merritt was ordered to Paris, and there represented the army of the United States, and its faith and honor and glory. Our Peace Commissioners were Wm. R. Day, Cushman K. Davis, William P. Frye, George Gray and Whitelaw Reid, who started for Paris September 18. The Spanish Commissioners made a long struggle, and protracted their unhappy task for more than two months, using all arts of procrastination and persuasion, claiming that the United States should pay the Cuban debt, and striving for allowances of indemnity, yielding at last to the inevitable. The text of the treaty is in seventeen articles as follows:

Article I.—Spain renounces all right of sovereignty over Cuba. Whereas said isle when evacuated by Spain is to be occupied by the United States, the United States, while the occupation continues, shall take upon themselves and fulfill the obligations which, by the fact of occupation, international law imposes on them for the protection of life and property.

Article II.—Spain cedes to the United States the Island of Porto Rico and the other islands now under her sovereignty in the West Indies and the Isle of Guam in the archipelago of the Marianas or Ladrones.

Article III.—Spain cedes to the United States the archipelago known as the Philippine Islands, which comprise the islands situated between the following lines: A line which runs west to east near the twentieth parallel of north latitude across the center of the navigable canal of Bachi, from the 118th to the 127th degrees of longitude east of Greenwich, from here to the width of the 127th degree of longitude east to parallel 4 degrees 45 minutes of north latitude. From here following the parallel of north latitude 4 degrees 45 minutes to its intersection with the meridian of longitude 119 degrees 35 minutes east from Greenwich. From here following the meridian of 119 degrees 35 minutes east to the parallel of latitude 7 degrees 40 minutes north. From here following the parallel of 7 degrees 40 minutes north to its intersection with 116 degrees longitude east. From here along a straight line to the intersection of the tenth parallel of latitude north with the 118th meridian east, and from here following the 118th meridian to the point whence began this demarcation. The United States shall pay to Spain the sum of $20,000,000 within three months after the interchange of the ratifications of the present treaty.

Article IV.—The United States shall, during the term of ten years, counting from the interchange of the ratifications of the treaty, admit to the ports of the Philippine Islands Spanish ships and merchandise under the same conditions as the ships and merchandise of the United States.

Article V.—The United States, on the signing of the present treaty, shall transport to Spain at their cost the Spanish soldiers whom the American forces made prisoners of war when Manila was captured. The arms of these soldiers shall be returned to them. Spain, on the interchange of the ratifications of the present treaty, shall proceed to evacuate the Philippine Islands, as also Guam, on conditions similar to those agreed to by the commissions named to concert the evacuation of Porto Rico and the other islands in the Western Antilles according to the protocol of Aug. 12, 1898, which shall continue in force until its terms have been completely complied with. The term within which the evacuation of the Philippine Islands and Guam shall be completed shall be fixed by both Governments. Spain shall retain the flags and stands of colors of the warships not captured, small arms, cannon of all calibers, with their carriages and accessories, powders, munitions, cattle, material and effects of all kinds belonging to the armies of the sea and land of Spain in the Philippines and Guam. The pieces of heavy caliber which are not field artillery mounted in fortifications and on the coasts shall remain in their places for a period of six months from the interchange of the ratifications of the present treaty, and the United States may during that period buy from Spain said material if both Governments arrive at a satisfactory agreement thereon.

Article VI.—Spain, on signing the present treaty, shall place at liberty all prisoners of war and all those detained or imprisoned for political offences in consequence of the insurrections in Cuba and the Philippines and of the war with the United States. Reciprocally the United States shall place at liberty all prisoners of war made by the American forces, and shall negotiate for the liberty of all Spanish prisoners in the power of the insurgents in Cuba and the Philippines. The Government of the United States shall transport, at their cost, to Spain, and the Government of Spain shall transport, at its cost, to the United States, Cuba, Porto Rico and the Philippines, conformably to the situation of their respective dwellings, the prisoners placed or to be placed at liberty in virtue of this article.

Article VII.—Spain and the United States mutually renounce by the present treaty all claim to national or private indemnity, of whatever kind, of one Government against the other, or of their subjects or citizens against the other Government, which may have arisen from the beginning of the last insurrection in Cuba, anterior to the interchange of the ratifications of the present treaty, as also to all indemnity as regards costs occasioned by the war. The United States shall judge and settle the claims of its citizens against Spain which she renounces in this article.

Article VIII.—In fulfilment of Articles I., II. and III. of this treaty Spain renounces in Cuba and cedes in Porto Rico and the other West Indian isles, in Guam and the Philippine archipelago, all buildings, moles, barracks, fortresses, establishments, public roads and other real property which by custom or right are of the public domain, and as such belong to the crown of Spain. Nevertheless, it is declared that this renouncement or cession, as the case may be, referred to in the previous paragraph, in no way lessens the property or rights which belong by custom or law to the peaceful possessor of goods of all kinds in the provinces and cities, public or private establishments, civil or ecclesiastical corporations or whatever bodies have judicial personality to acquire and possess goods in the above-mentioned, renounced or ceded territories, and those of private individuals, whatever be their nationality.

The said renouncement or cession includes all those documents which exclusively refer to said renounced or ceded sovereignty which exist in the archives of the peninsula. When these documents existing in said archives only in part refer to said sovereignty, copies of said part shall be supplied, provided they be requested. Similar rules are to be reciprocally observed in favor of Spain with respect to the documents existing in the archives of the before-mentioned islands. In the above-mentioned renunciation or cession are comprised those rights of the crown of Spain and of its authorities over the archives and official registers, as well administrative as judicial, of said islands which refer to them and to the rights and properties of their inhabitants. Said archives and registers must be refully preserved, and all individuals, without exception, shall have the right to obtain, conformably to law, authorized copies of contracts, wills and other documents which form part of notarial protocols or which are kept in administrative and judicial archives, whether the same be in Spain or in the islands above mentioned.

Article IX.—Spanish subjects, natives of the peninsula, dwelling in the territory whose sovereignty Spain renounces or cedes in the present treaty, may remain in said territory or leave it, maintaining in one or the other case all their rights of property, including the right to sell and dispose of said property or its produces; and, moreover, they shall retain the right to exercise their industry, business or profession, submitting themselves in this respect to the laws which are applicable to other foreigners. In case they remain in the territory they may preserve their Spanish nationality by making in a registry office, within a year after the interchange of the ratifications of this treaty, a declaration of their intention to preserve said nationality. Failing this declaration they will be considered as having renounced said nationality and as having adopted that of the territory in which they may reside. The civil rights and political status of the native inhabitants of the territories hereby ceded to the United States shall be determined by Congress.

Article X.—The inhabitants of the territories whose sovereignty Spain renounces or cedes shall have assured to them the free exercise of their religion.

Article XI.—Spaniards residing in the territories whose sovereignty Spain cedes or renounces shall be subject in civil and criminal matters to the tribunals of the country in which they reside, conformably with the common laws which regulate their competence, being enabled to appear before them in the same manner and to employ the same proceedings as the citizens of the country to which the tribunal belongs must observe.

Article XII.—Judicial proceedings pending on the interchange of the ratifications of this treaty in the territories over which Spain renounces or cedes sovereignty shall be determined conformably with the following rules: First, sentences pronounced in civil cases between individuals or in criminal cases before the above-mentioned date, and against which there is no appeal or annulment conformably with the Spanish law, shall be considered as lasting, and shall be executed in due form by competent authority in the territory within which said sentences should be carried out. Second, civil actions between individuals which on the aforementioned date have not been decided shall continue their course before the tribunal in which the lawsuit is proceeding or before that which shall replace it. Third, criminal actions pending on the aforementioned date before the supreme tribunal of Spain against citizens of territory which, according to this treaty, will cease to be Spanish, shall continue under its jurisdiction until definite sentence is pronounced, but once sentence is decreed its execution shall be intrusted to competent authority of the place where the action arose.

Article XIII.—Literary, artistic and industrial rights of property acquired by Spaniards in Cuba, Porto Rico, the Philippines and other territories ceded on the interchange of ratifications of this treaty shall continue to be respected. Spanish scientific, literary and artistic works which shall not be dangerous to public order in said territories shall continue entering therein with freedom from all customs duties for a period of ten years dating from the interchange of the ratifications of this treaty.

Article XIV.—Spain may establish consular agents in the ports and places of the territories whose renunciation or cession are the object of this treaty.

Article XV.—The Government of either country shall concede for a term of ten years to the merchant ships of the other the same treatment as regards all port dues, including those of entry and departure, lighthouse and tonnage dues, as it concedes to its own merchant ships not employed in the coasting trade. This article may be repudiated at any time by either Government giving previous notice thereof six months beforehand.

Article XVI.—Be it understood that whatever obligation is accepted under this treaty by the United States with respect to Cuba is limited to the period their occupation of the island shall continue, but at the end of said occupation they will advise the Government that may be established in the island that it should accept the same obligations.

Article XVII.—The present treaty shall be ratified by the Queen Regent of Spain and the President of the United States, in agreement and with the approval of the Senate, and ratifications shall be exchanged in Washington within a period of six months from this date or earlier if possible.

The treaty of peace will be ratified by the Senate. It appears before ratification, as was the case of the protocol, through the favor of the French translations. The treaty fitly crowns the triumphs of the war. The payment of the small indemnity of twenty million dollars only covers at a reasonable estimate the public property of Spain, in territory ceded to us, that was beyond the lines of the areas that formally submitted to our arms.

www.ingramcontent.com/pod-product-compliance
Lightning Source LLC
Chambersburg PA
CBHW022147300426
44115CB00006B/376